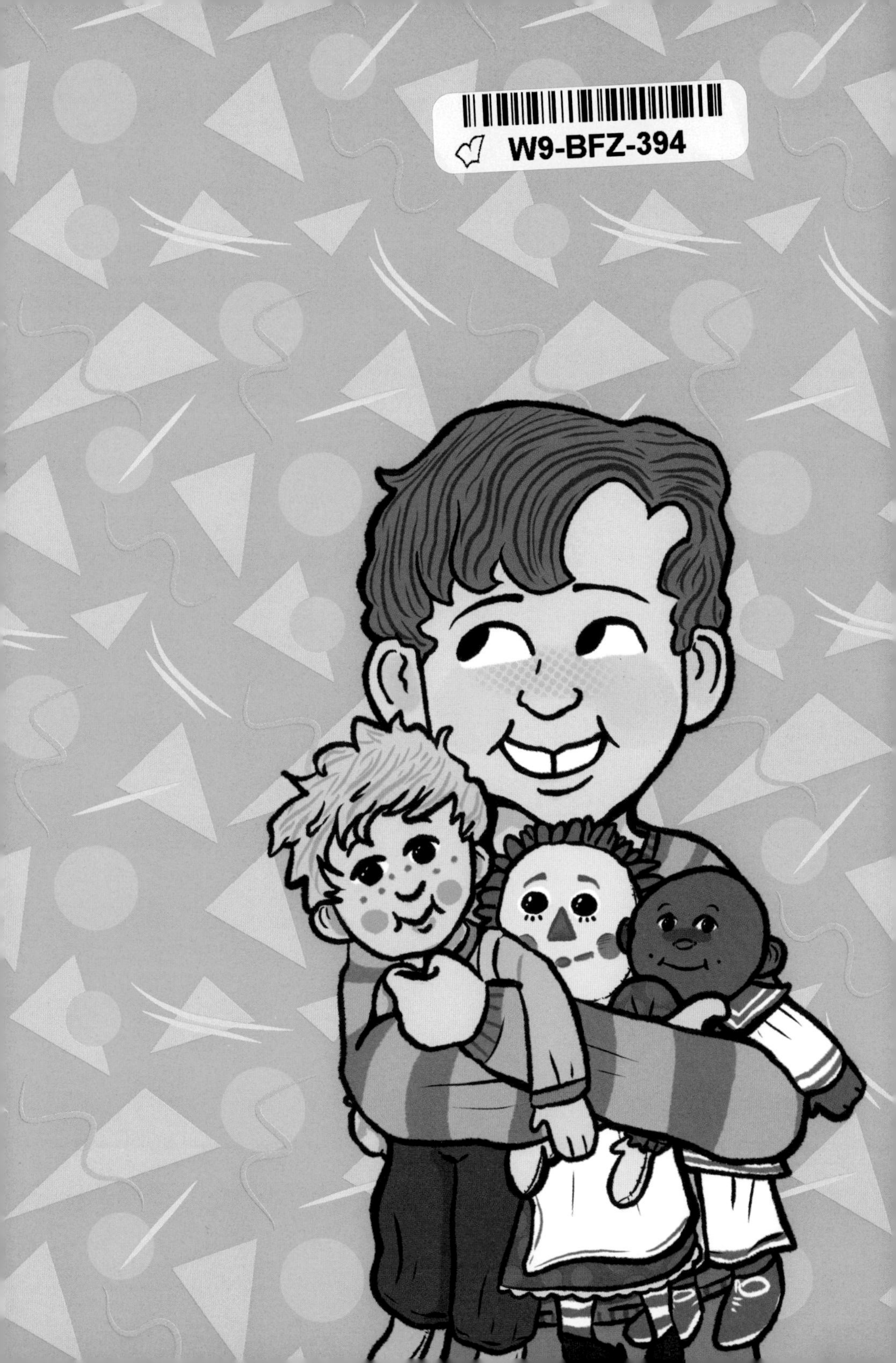

OTHER BOYS

DAMIAN ALEXANDER

:01
First Second
New York

First Second

Published by First Second
First Second is an imprint of Roaring Brook Press,
a division of Holtzbrinck Publishing Holdings Limited Partnership
120 Broadway, New York, NY 10271
firstsecondbooks.com
mackids.com

Library of Congress Control Number: 2021904463

Our books may be purchased in bulk for promotional, educational, or business use. Please contact
your local bookseller or the Macmillan Corporate and Premium Sales Department at (800) 221-7945
ext. 5442 or by email at MacmillanSpecialMarkets@macmillan.com.

First edition, 2021
Edited by Robyn Chapman and Steve Foxe
Cover design by Molly Johanson
Interior book design by Damian Alexander and Molly Johanson

Inked and colored digitally in Procreate.

Printed in China by RR Donnelley Asia Printing Solutions Ltd., Dongguan City, Guangdong Province

ISBN 978-1-250-22281-7 (paperback)
1 3 5 7 9 10 8 6 4 2

ISBN 978-1-250-22282-4 (hardcover)
1 3 5 7 9 10 8 6 4 2

Don't miss your next favorite book from First Second!
For the latest updates go to firstsecondnewsletter.com and sign up for our enewsletter.

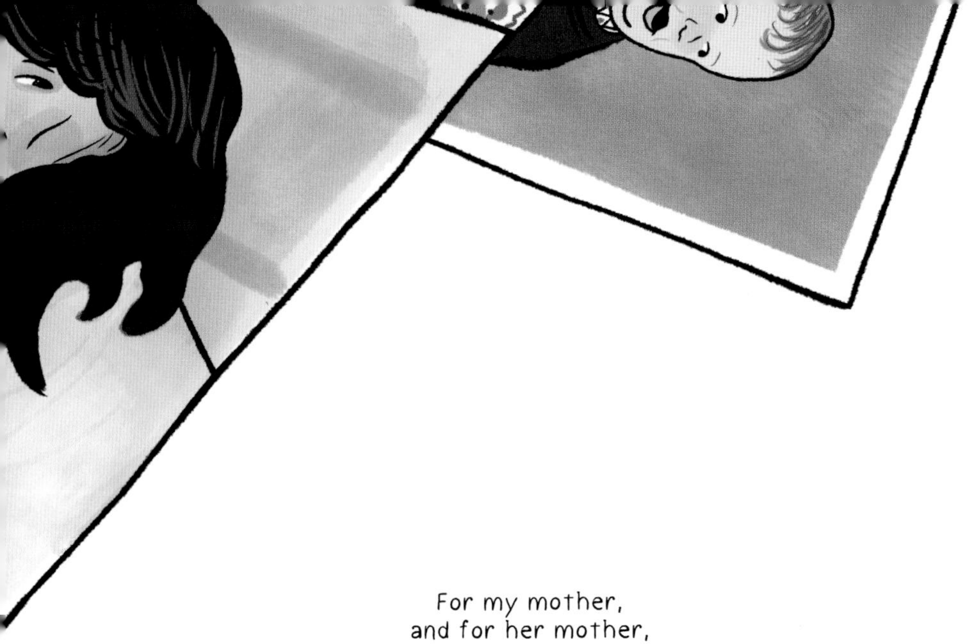

For my mother,
and for her mother,
who raised me

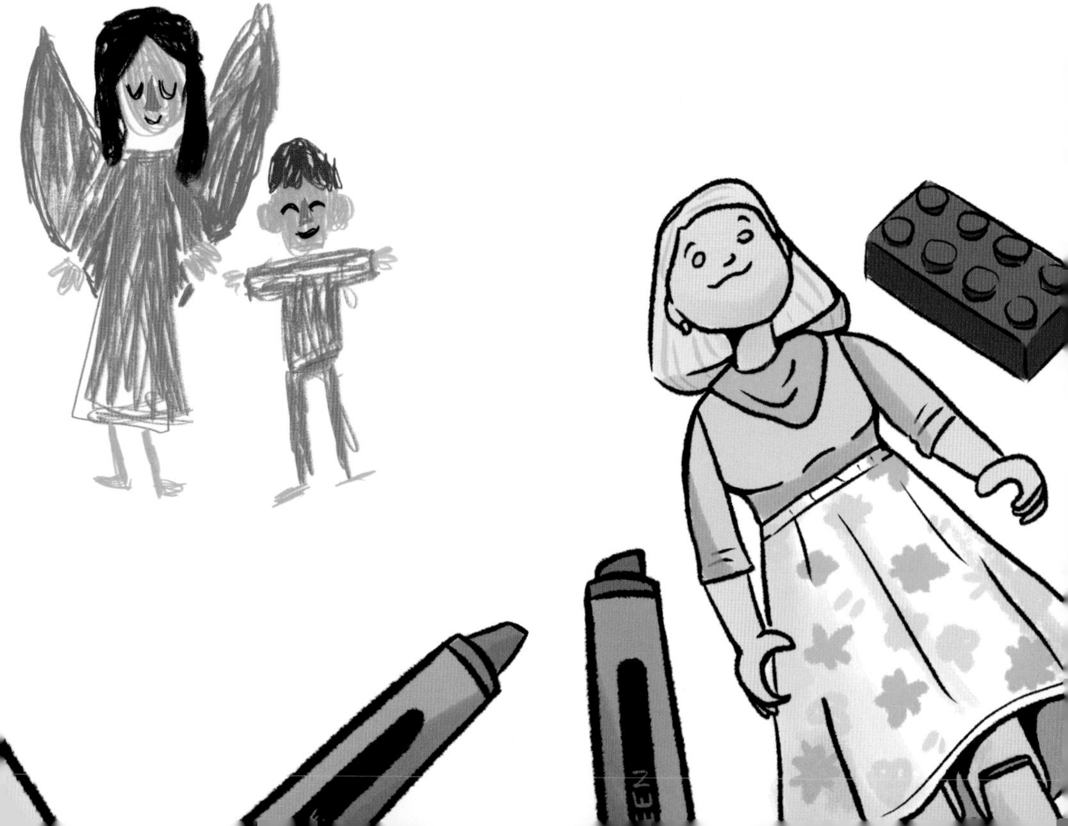

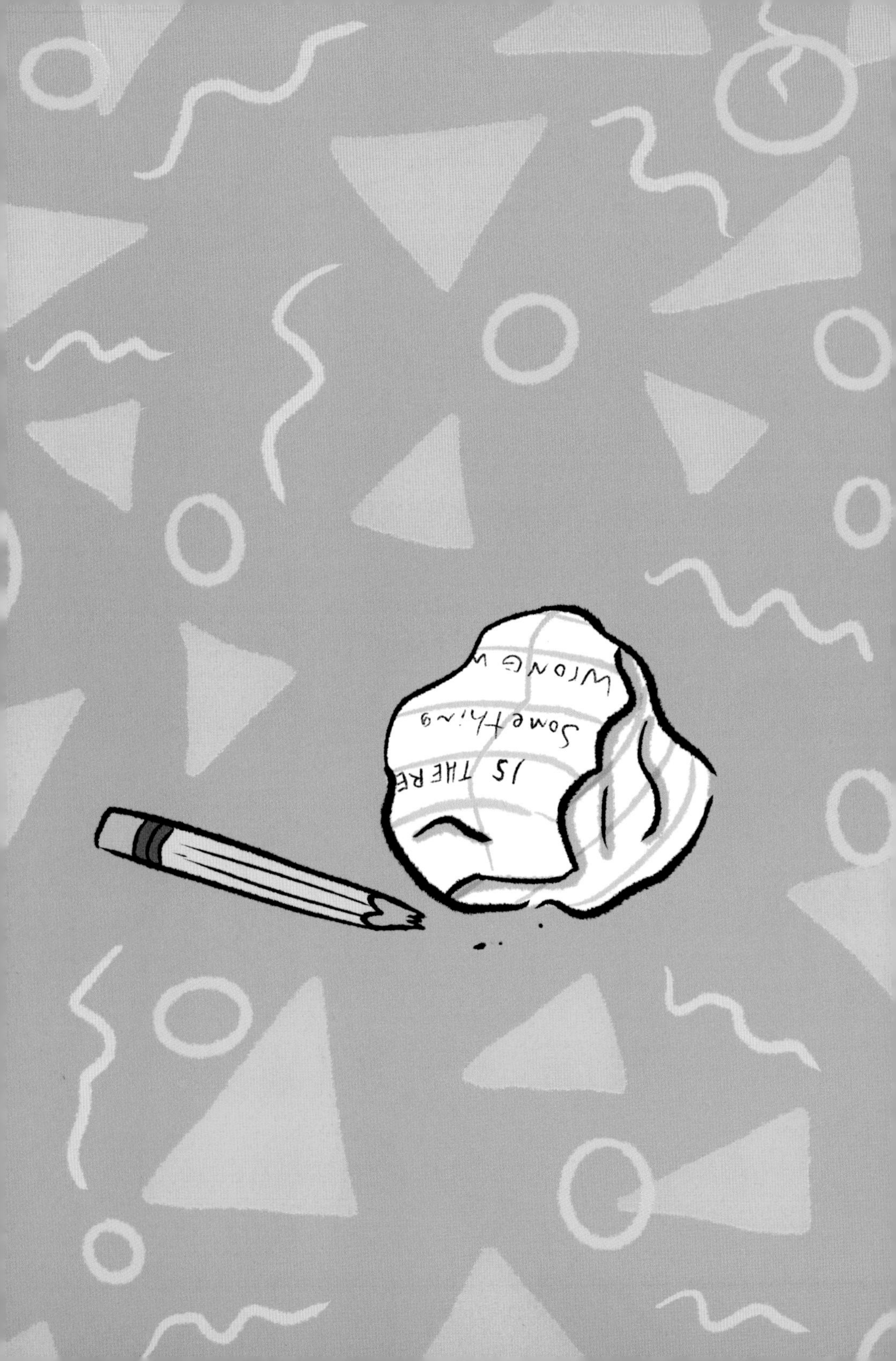
IS THERE
Something
WRONG

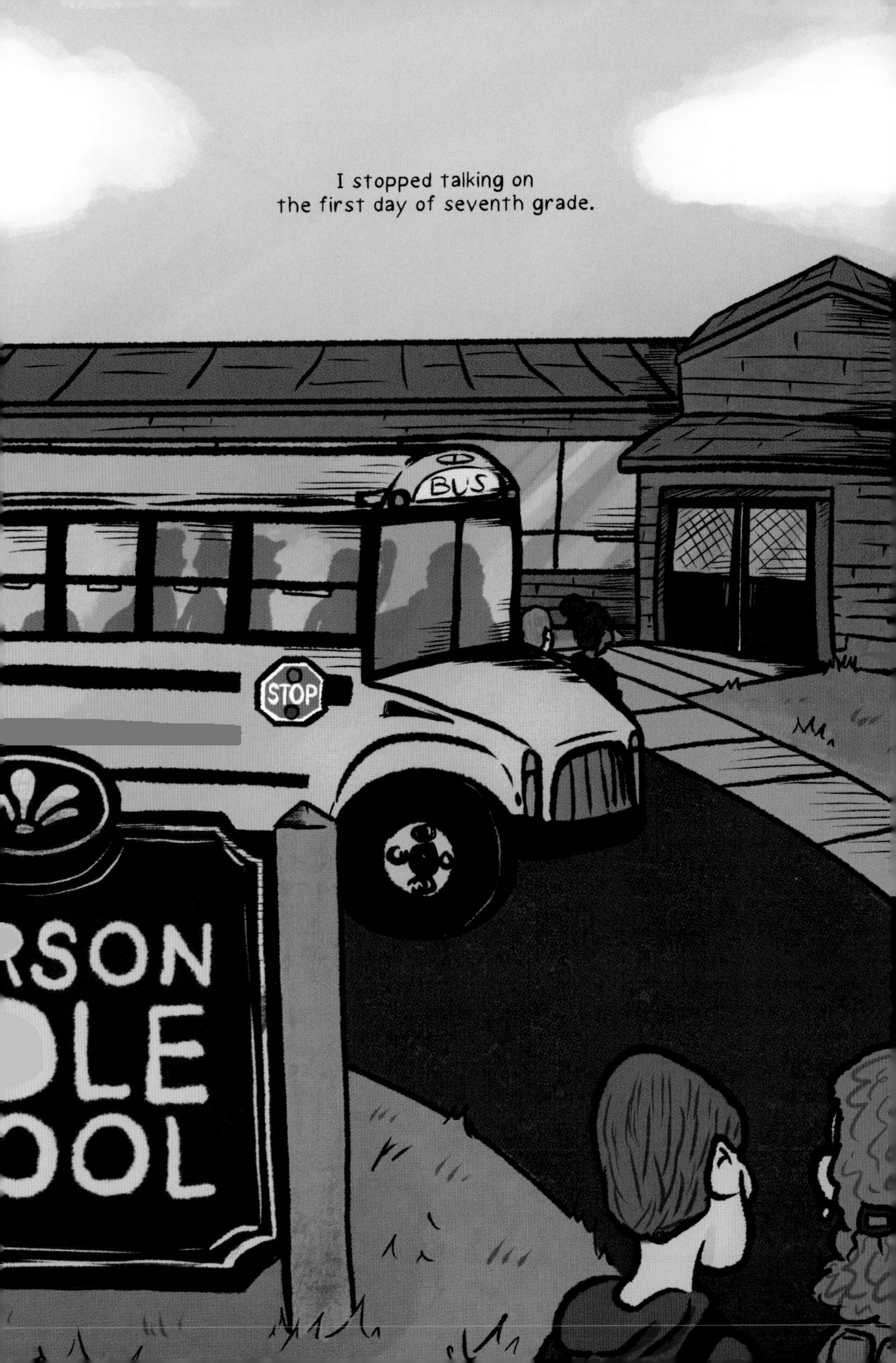
I stopped talking on
the first day of seventh grade.
BUS
STOP
RSON
OOL

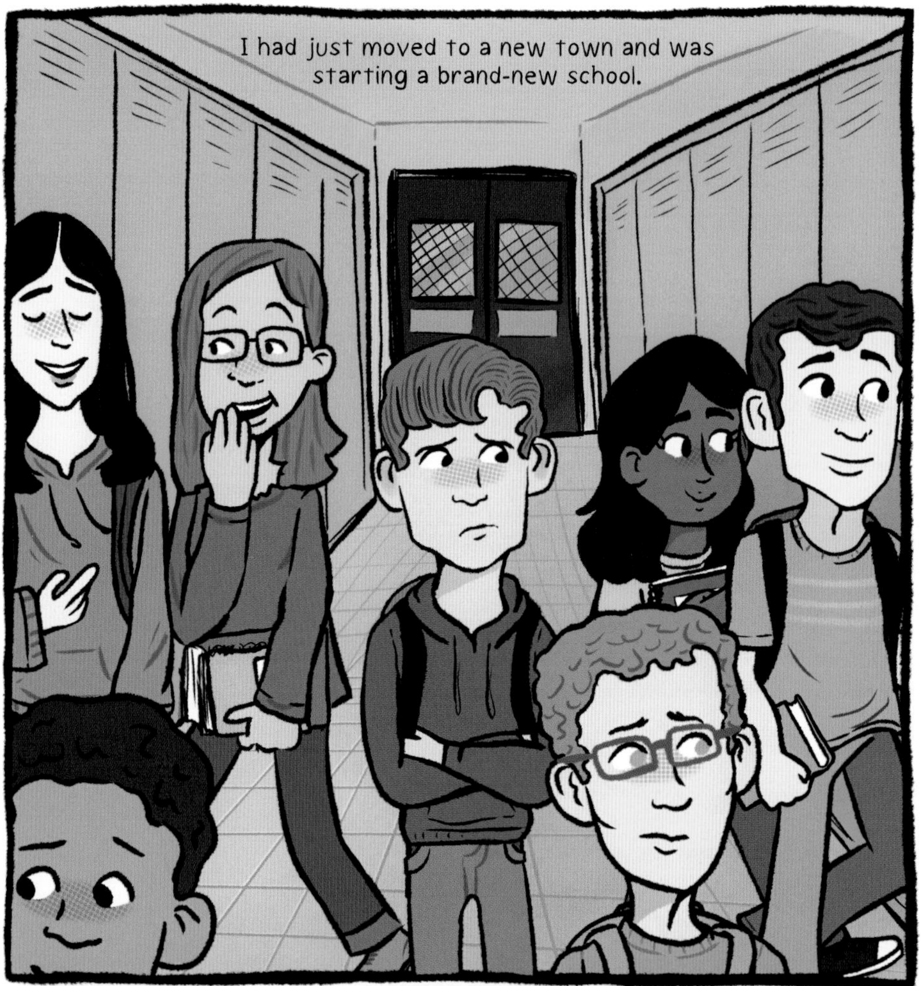
I had just moved to a new town and was starting a brand-new school.

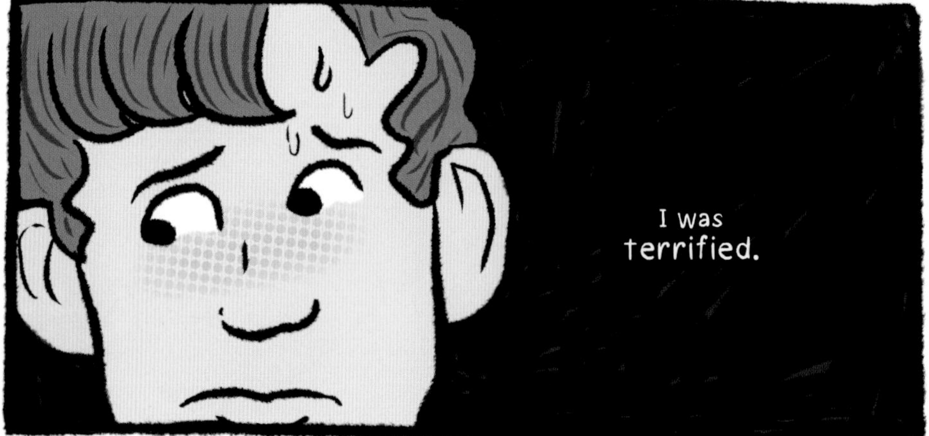
I was terrified.

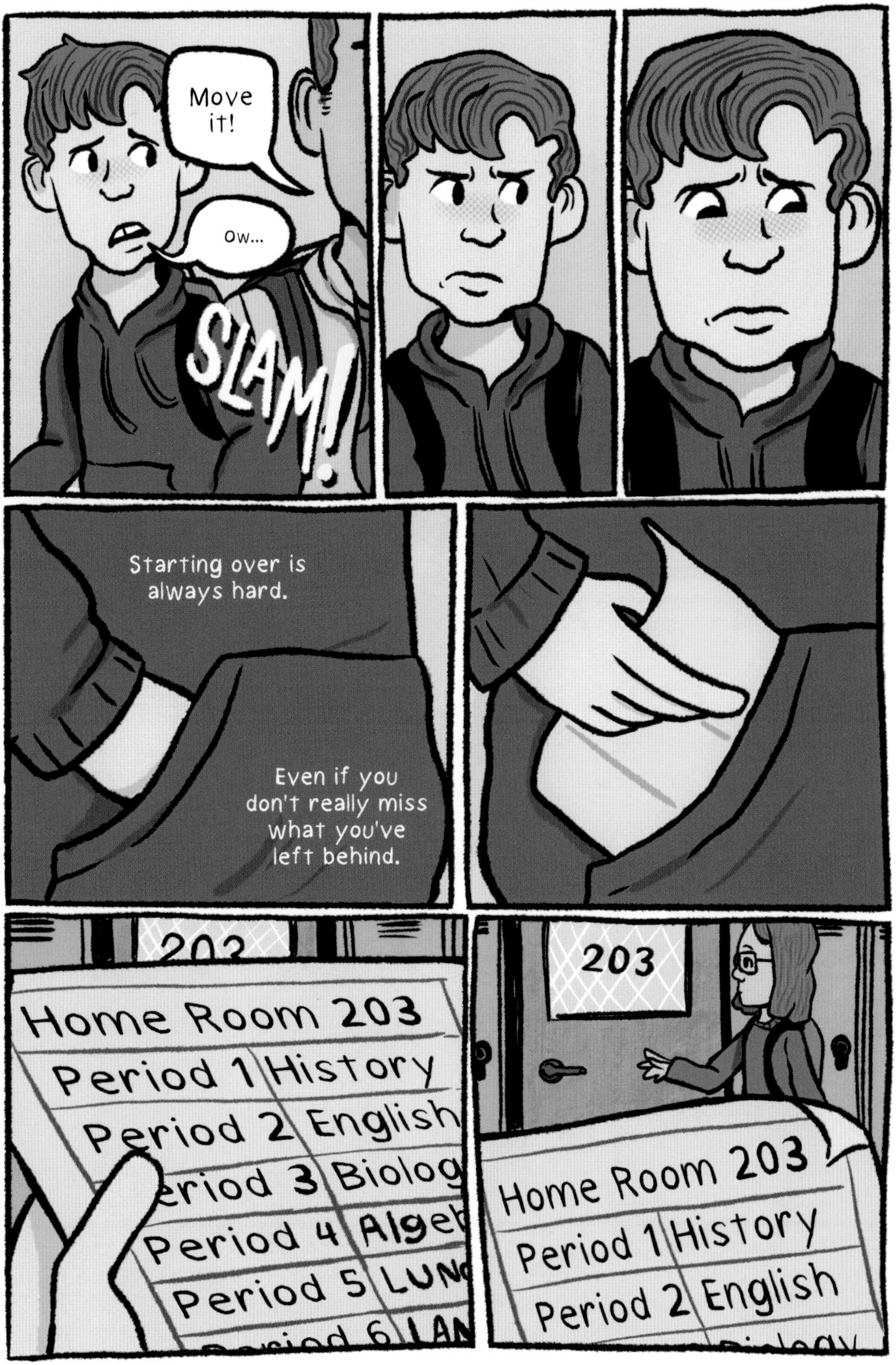

Move it!
Ow...
SLAM!
Starting over is always hard.
Even if you don't really miss what you've left behind.
Home Room 203
Period 1 History
Period 2 English
Period 4
Period 5
203
Home Room 203
Period 1 History
Period 2 English

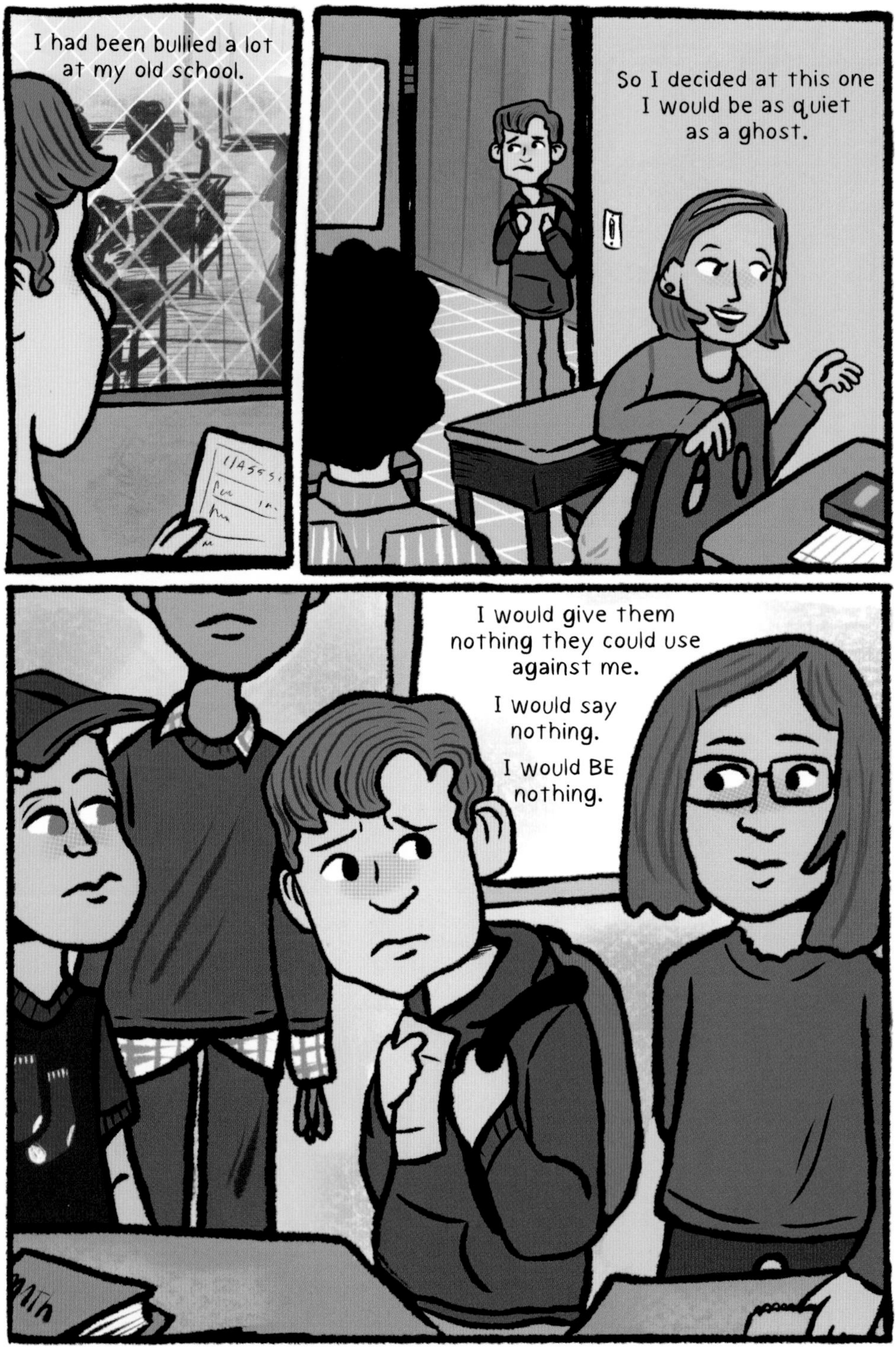
I had been bullied a lot at my old school.
So I decided at this one I would be as quiet as a ghost.
I would give them nothing they could use against me.
I would say nothing.
I would BE nothing.

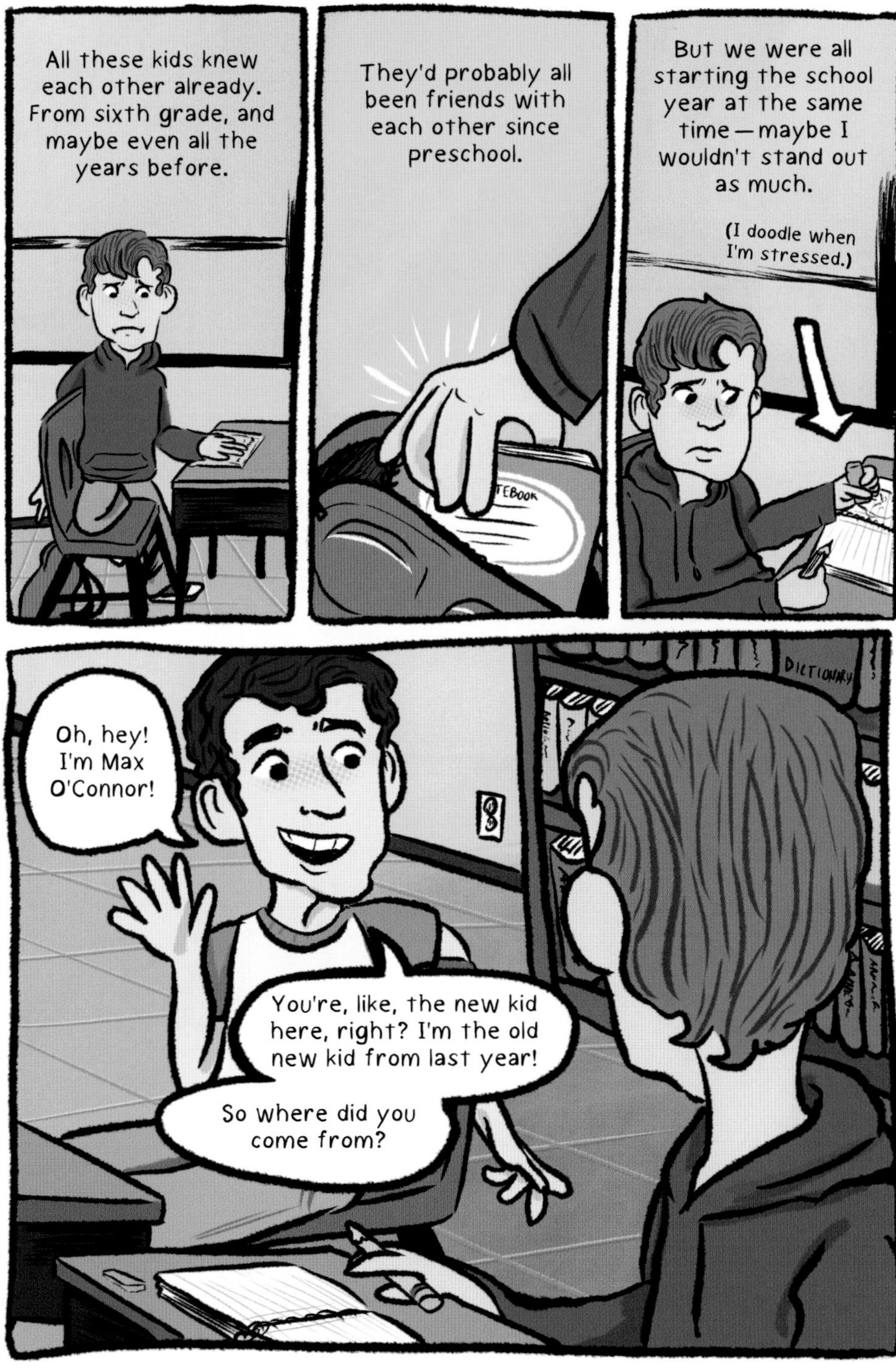
All these kids knew each other already. From sixth grade, and maybe even all the years before.
They'd probably all been friends with each other since preschool.
TEBOOK
But we were all starting the school year at the same time—maybe I wouldn't stand out as much.
(I doodle when I'm stressed.)
DICTIONARY
Oh, hey! I'm Max O'Connor!
You're, like, the new kid here, right? I'm the old new kid from last year!
So where did you come from?

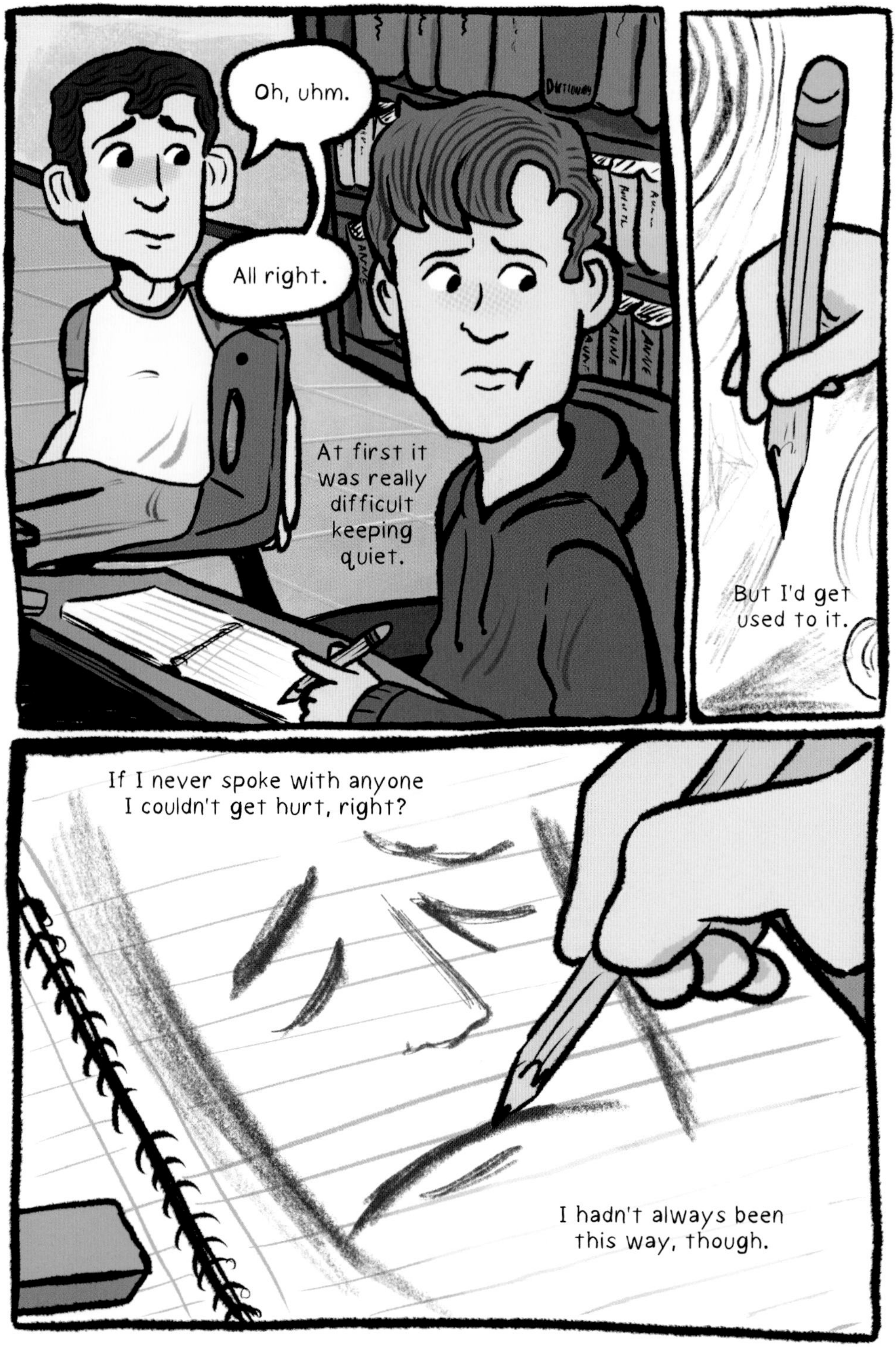
Oh, uhm.
All right.
At first it was really difficult keeping quiet.
But I'd get used to it.
If I never spoke with anyone I couldn't get hurt, right?
I hadn't always been this way, though.

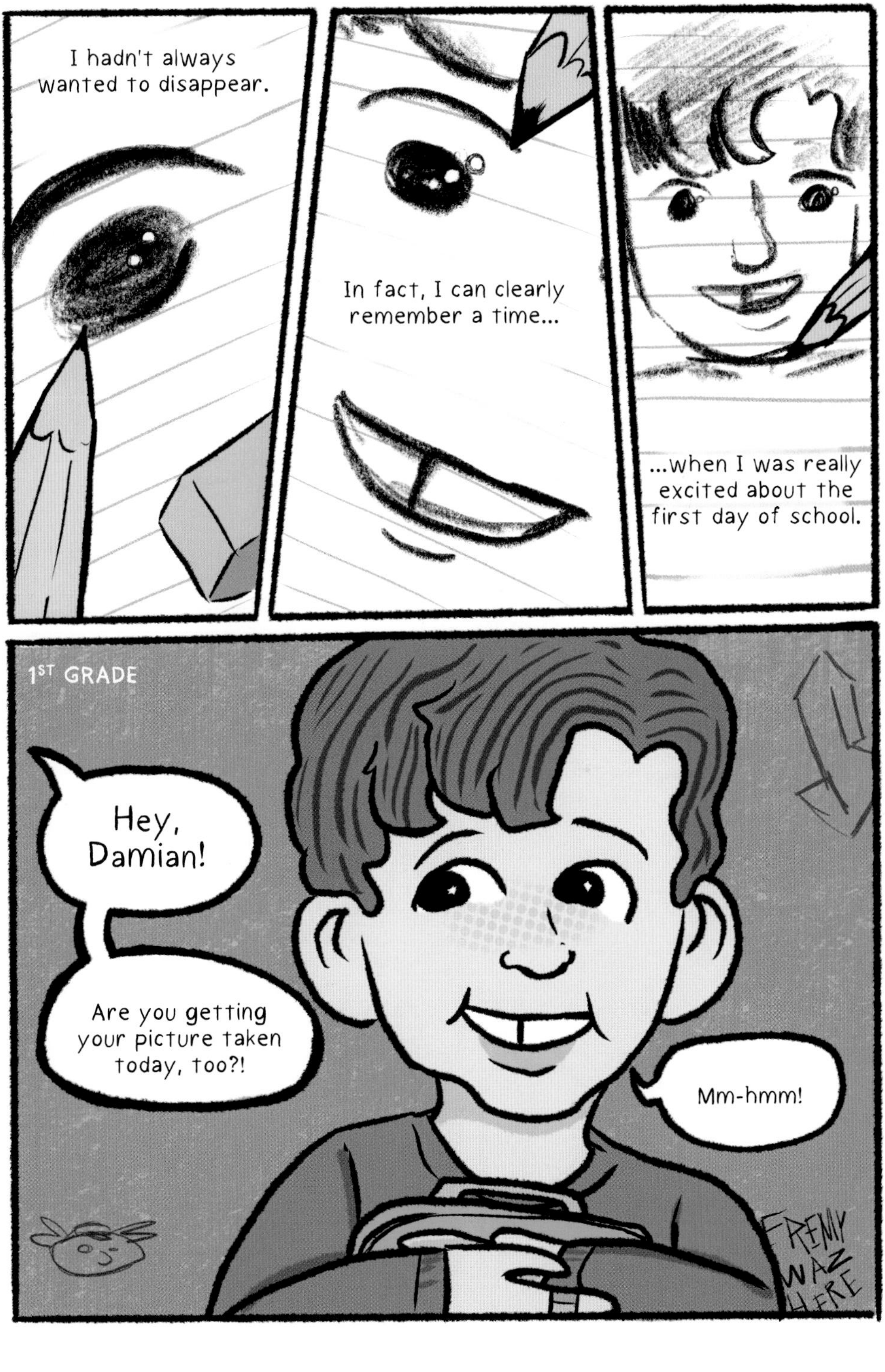
I hadn't always wanted to disappear.
In fact, I can clearly remember a time...
...when I was really excited about the first day of school.
1ST GRADE
Hey, Damian!
Are you getting your picture taken today, too?!
Mm-hmm!
FRENY WAZ HERE

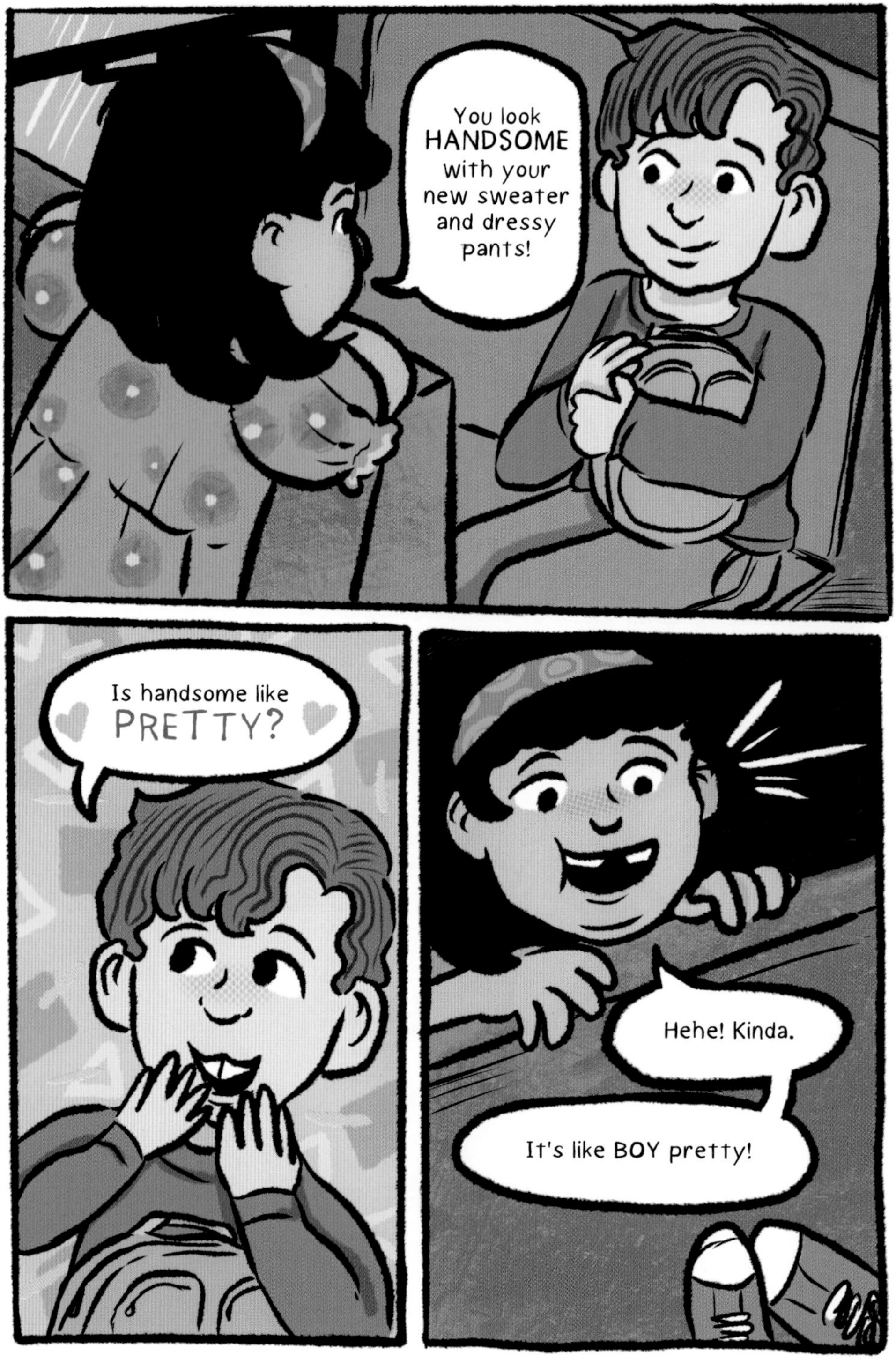
You look HANDSOME with your new sweater and dressy pants!
Is handsome like PRETTY?
Hehe! Kinda.
It's like BOY pretty!

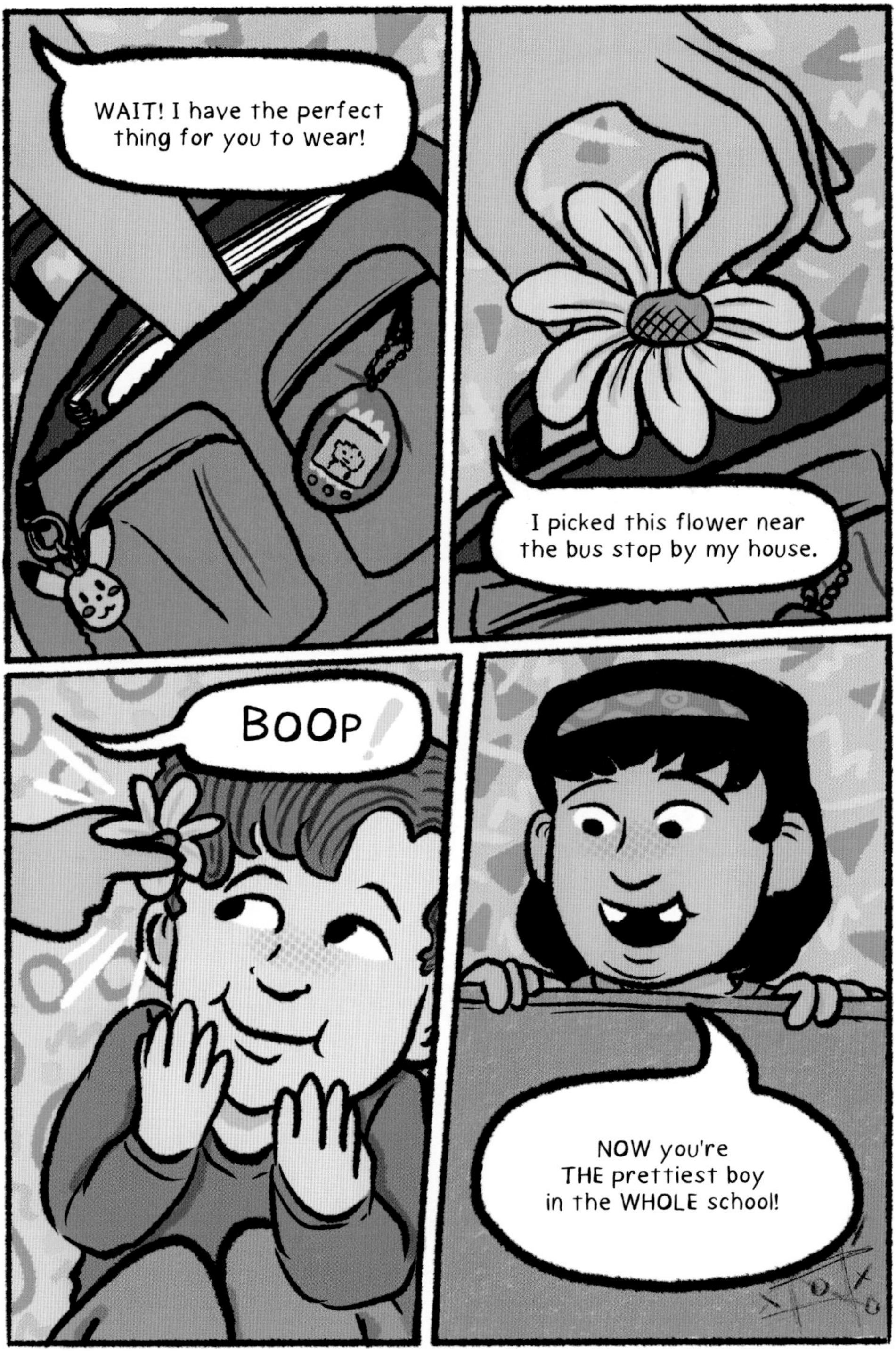
WAIT! I have the perfect thing for you to wear!
I picked this flower near the bus stop by my house.
BOOP!
NOW you're THE prettiest boy in the WHOLE school!

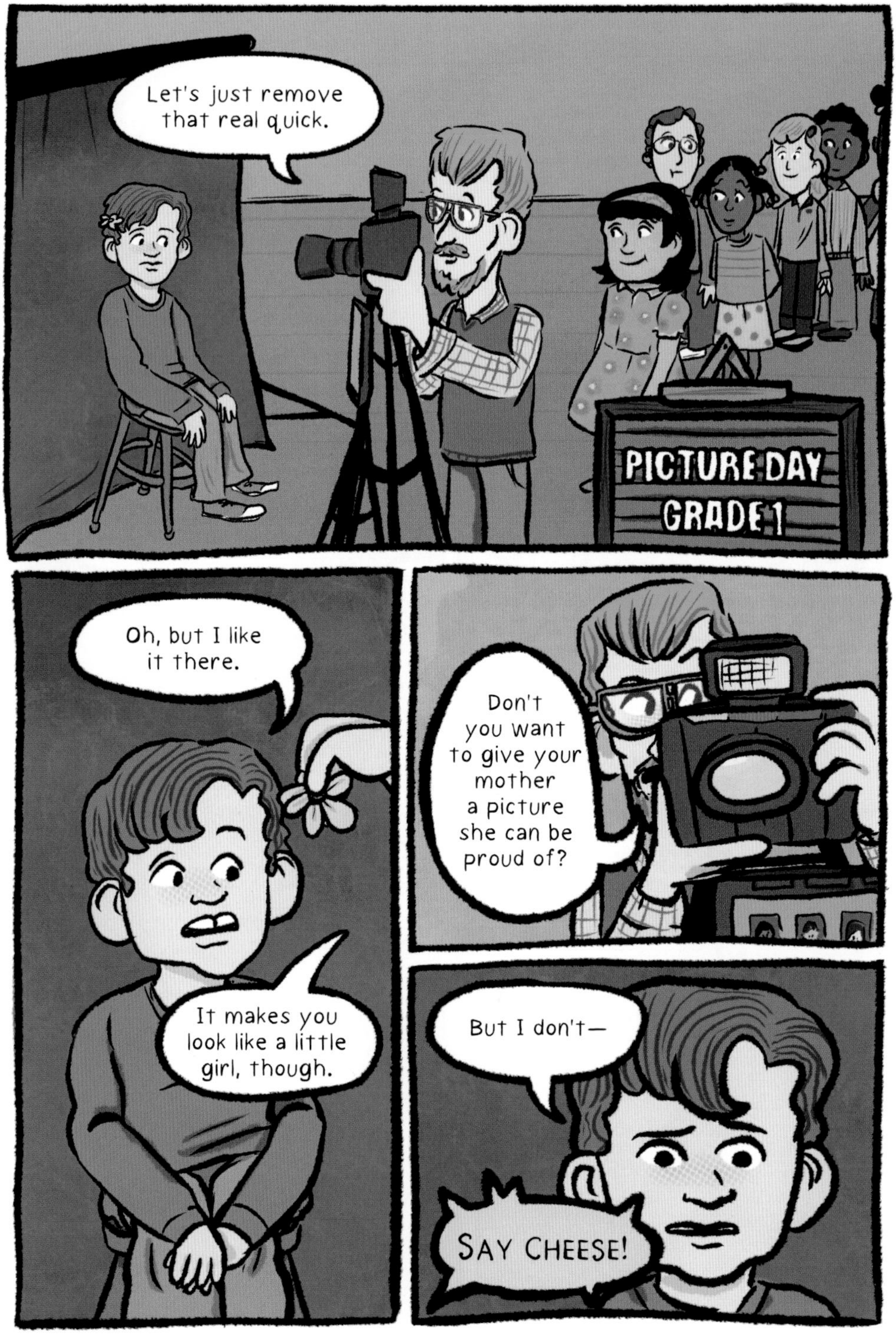
Let's just remove that real quick.
PICTURE DAY
GRADE 1
Oh, but I like it there.
It makes you look like a little girl, though.
Don't you want to give your mother a picture she can be proud of?
But I don't—
SAY CHEESE!

I look so ugly in this.

Mine's bad, too. My mom says school pictures are always goofy looking.

Yesterday she showed me some of her really ugly ones! Didn't your mom ever show you her old school pictures?

Oh, I don't have one of those.

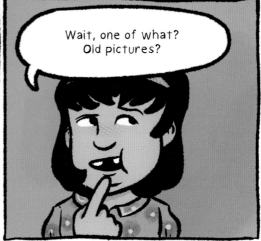

Wait, one of what? Old pictures?

13

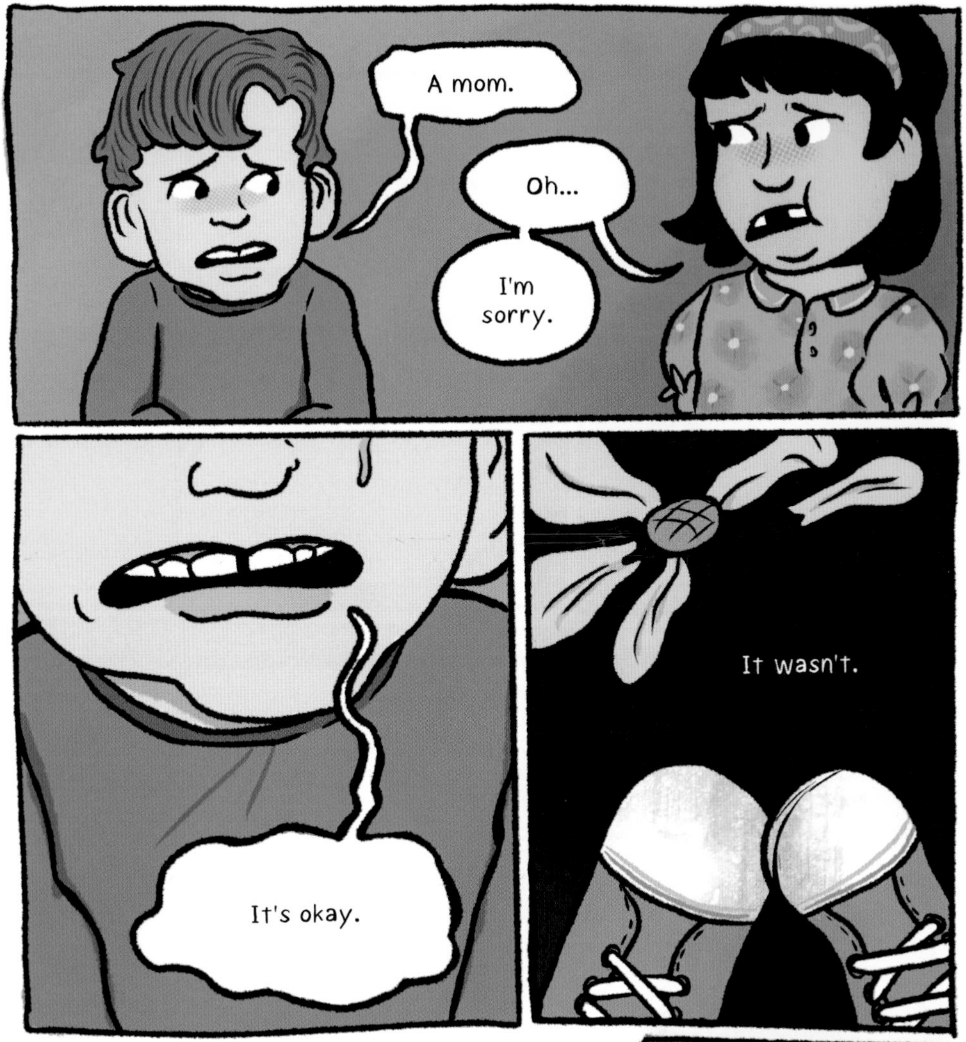
A mom.
Oh...
I'm sorry.
It's okay.
It wasn't.

People always feel so sorry for me
when I tell them I don't have a mom.
But I didn't want to make Sylvia
or anyone else feel sad.

I just didn't have a mother...

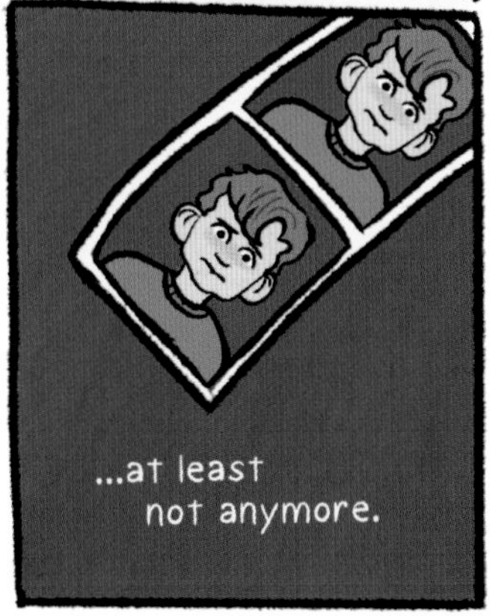
...at least
not anymore.

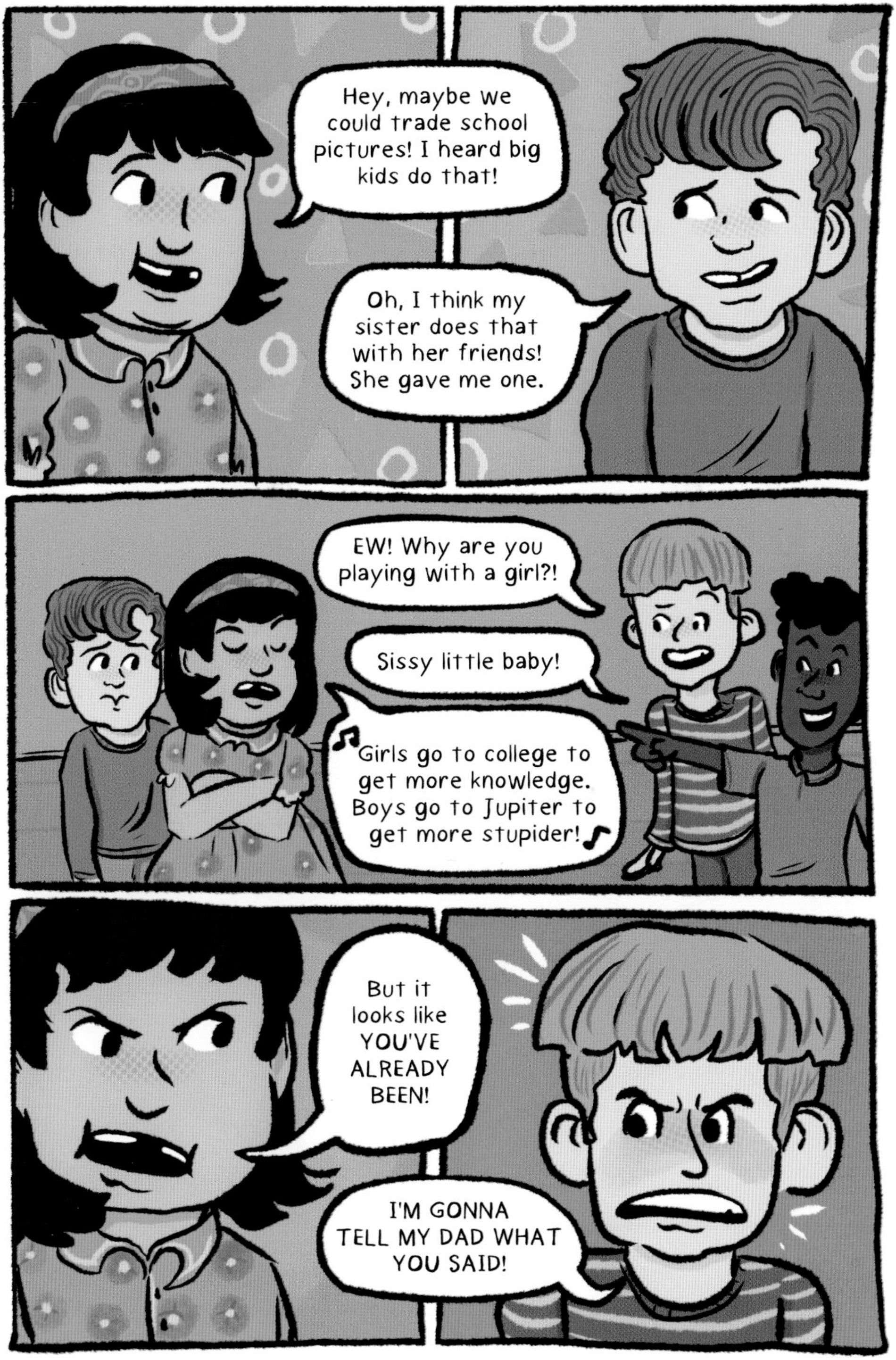
Hey, maybe we could trade school pictures! I heard big kids do that!
Oh, I think my sister does that with her friends! She gave me one.
EW! Why are you playing with a girl?!
Sissy little baby!
Girls go to college to get more knowledge. Boys go to Jupiter to get more stupider!
But it looks like YOU'VE ALREADY BEEN!
I'M GONNA TELL MY DAD WHAT YOU SAID!

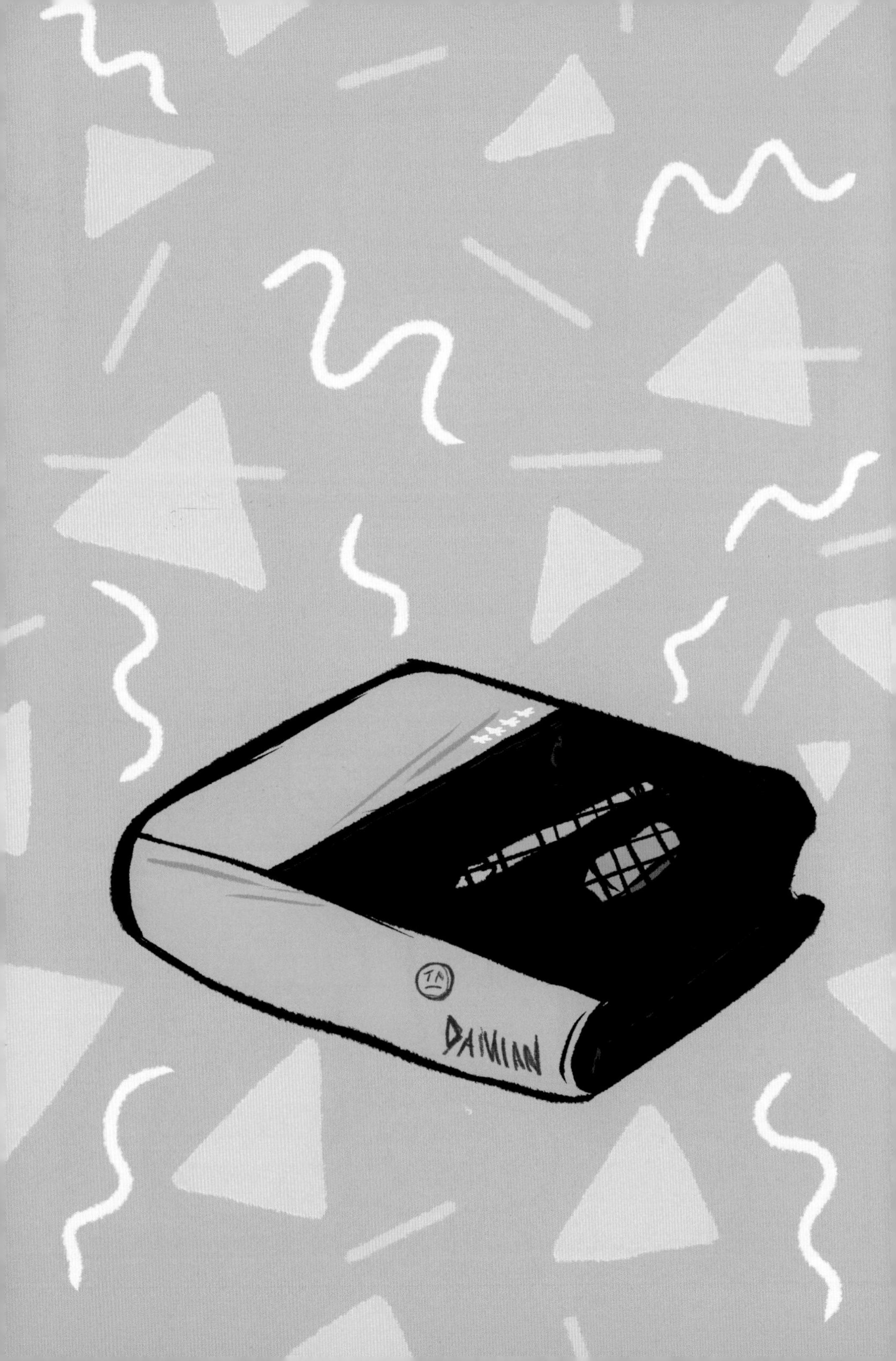
DAMIAN

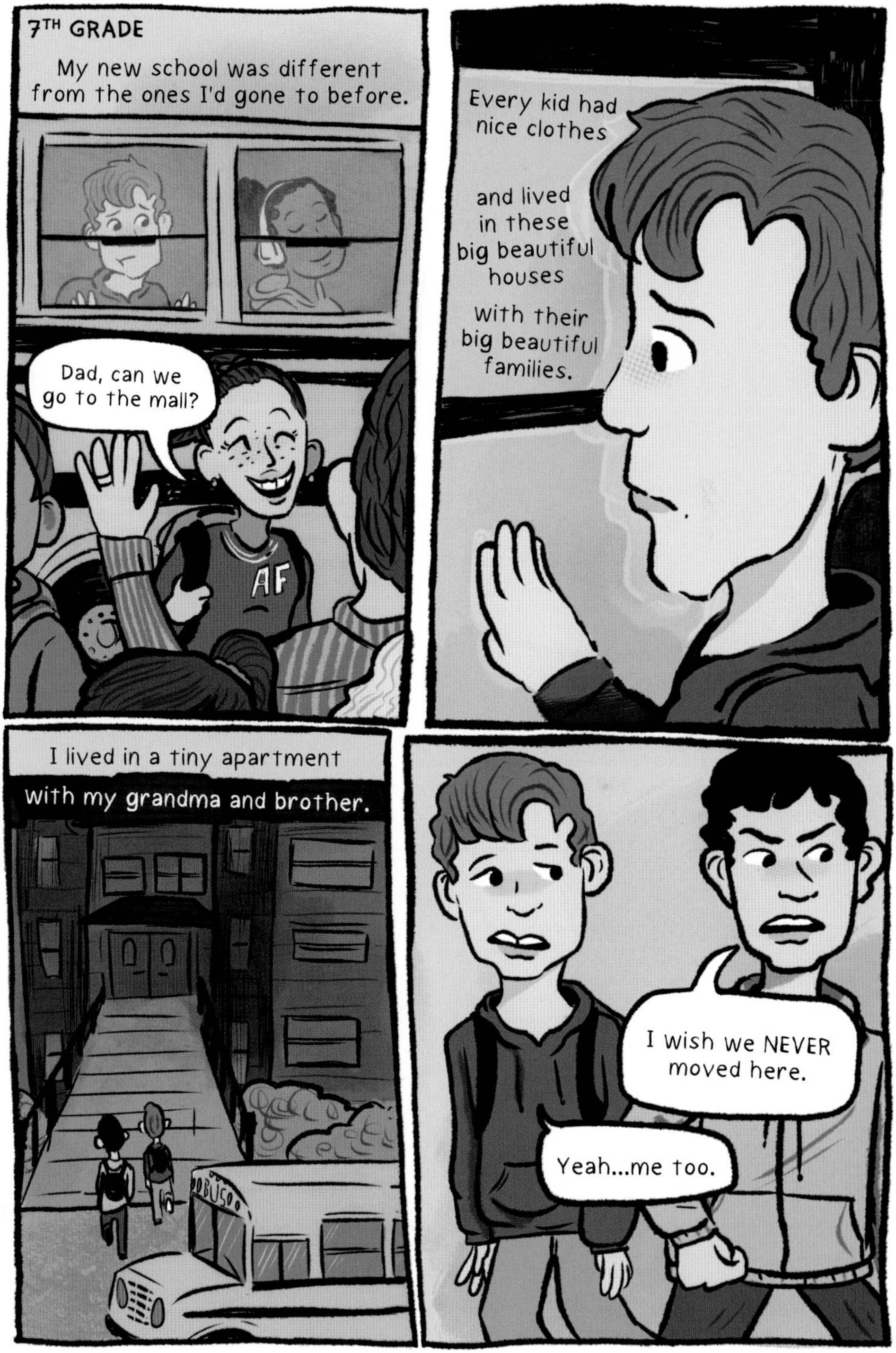
7TH GRADE
My new school was different from the ones I'd gone to before.
Dad, can we go to the mall?
AF
Every kid had nice clothes
and lived in these big beautiful houses
with their big beautiful families.
I lived in a tiny apartment
with my grandma and brother.
I wish we NEVER moved here.
Yeah...me too.

I always thought kids were extremely wealthy
if their families had the simplest things.

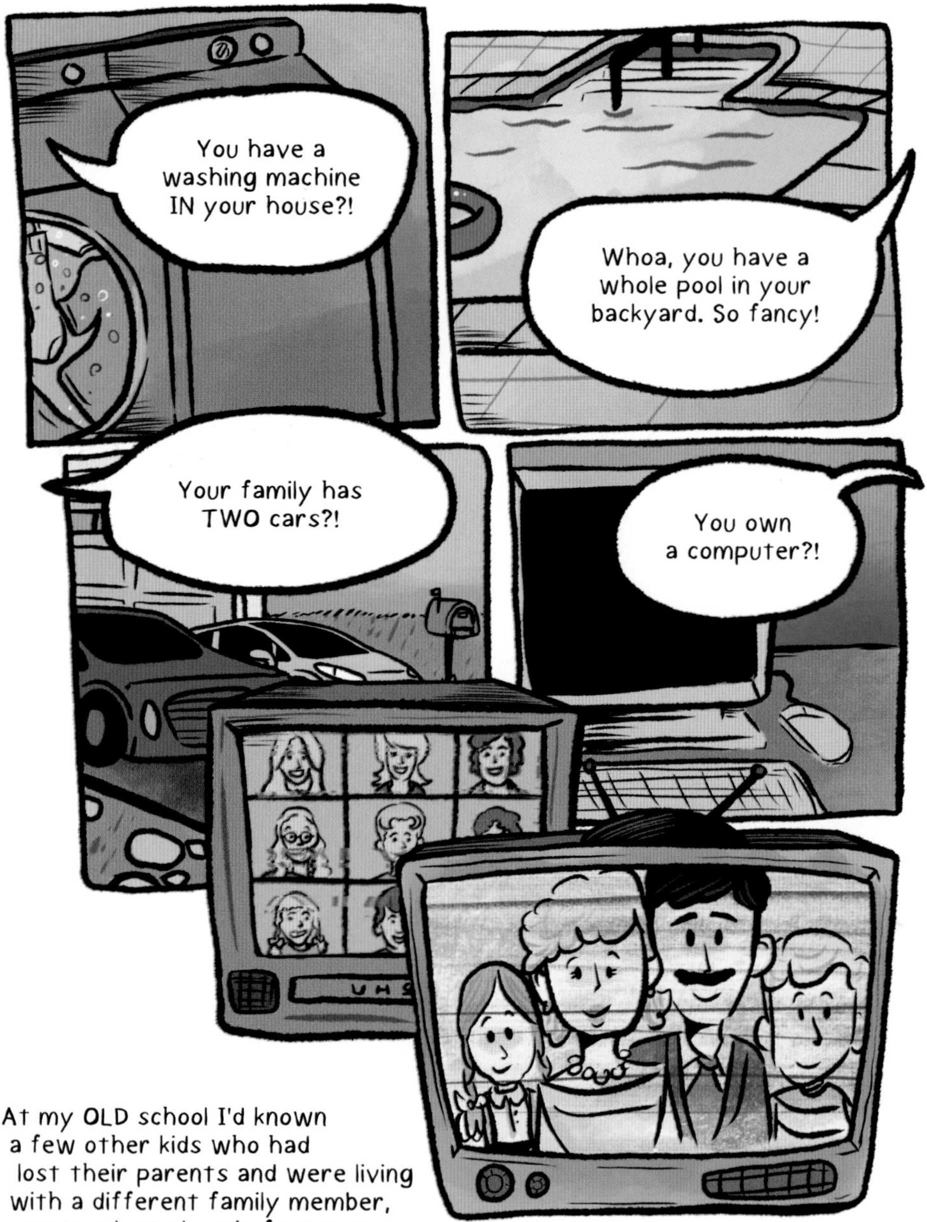
You have a washing machine IN your house?!
Whoa, you have a whole pool in your backyard. So fancy!
Your family has TWO cars?!
You own a computer?!

At my OLD school I'd known a few other kids who had lost their parents and were living with a different family member, were adopted, or in foster care.

But at my NEW school it seemed everyone was like the perfect families you see on old TV shows.

The kids at this school weren't so nice about it, either.

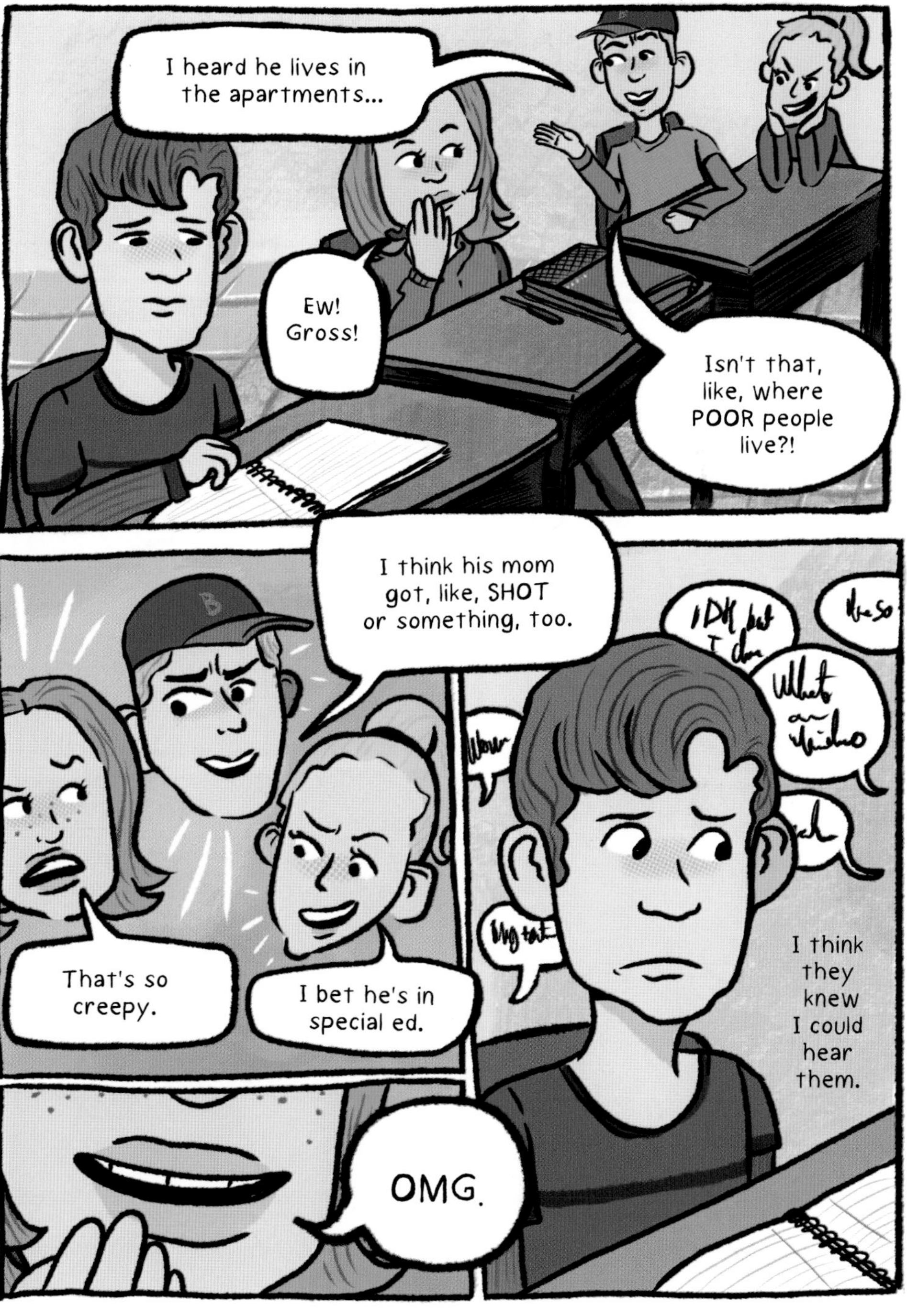
I heard he lives in the apartments...
Ew! Gross!
Isn't that, like, where POOR people live?!
I think his mom got, like, SHOT or something, too.
That's so creepy.
I bet he's in special ed.
OMG.
I think they knew I could hear them.

My classmates seemed to vaguely know things about my life that I hadn't told them.

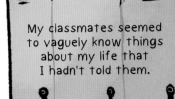

Eventually I caught on that my grandmother had let teachers know about my mother.

Some teachers had told my classmates, so they'd be "sensitive" around me.

(bracing myself)

Hey, it's that kid.

They weren't.

It was weird being with all these kids whose normal was so different from mine.

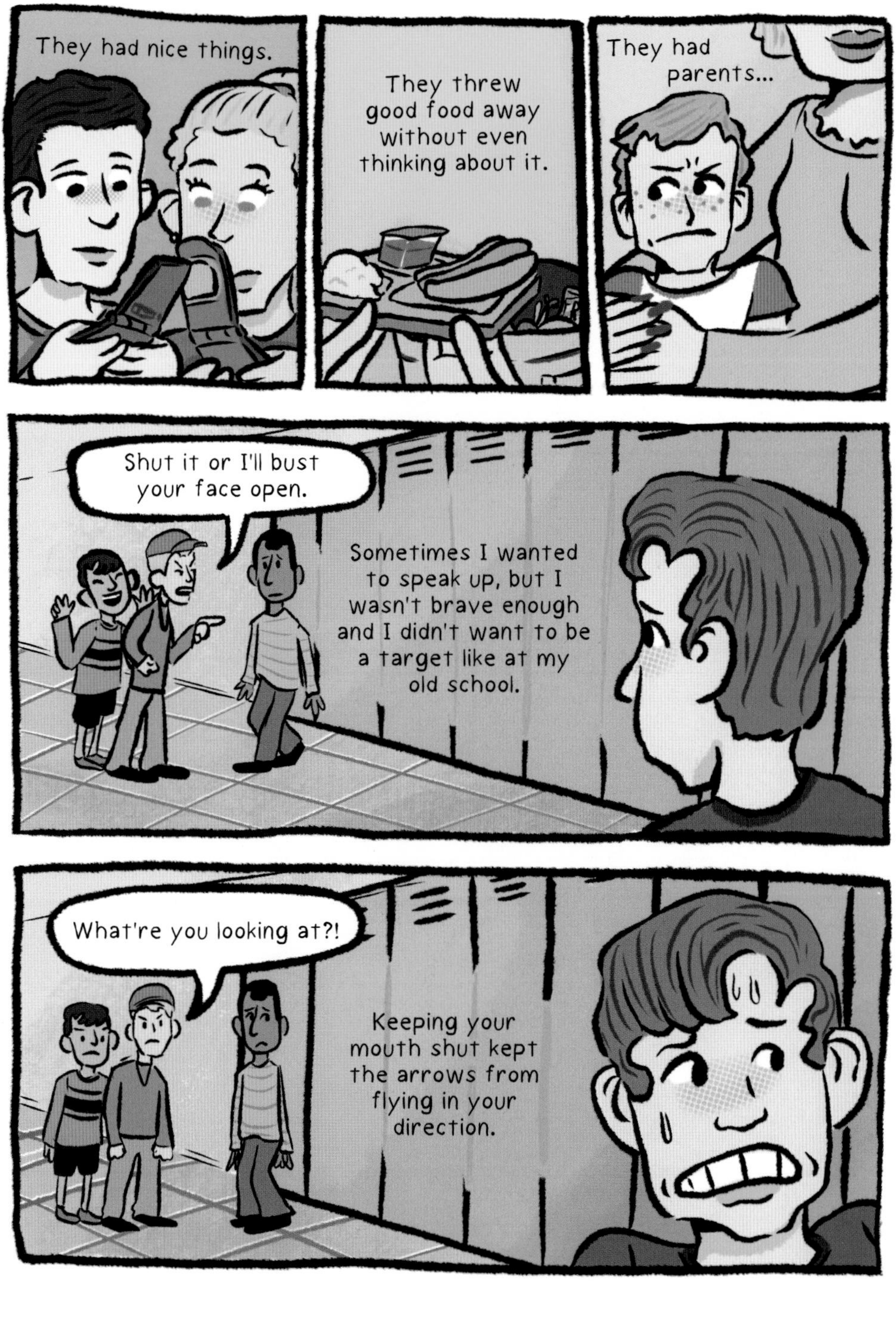
They had nice things.
They threw good food away without even thinking about it.
They had parents...
Shut it or I'll bust your face open.
Sometimes I wanted to speak up, but I wasn't brave enough and I didn't want to be a target like at my old school.
What're you looking at?!
Keeping your mouth shut kept the arrows from flying in your direction.

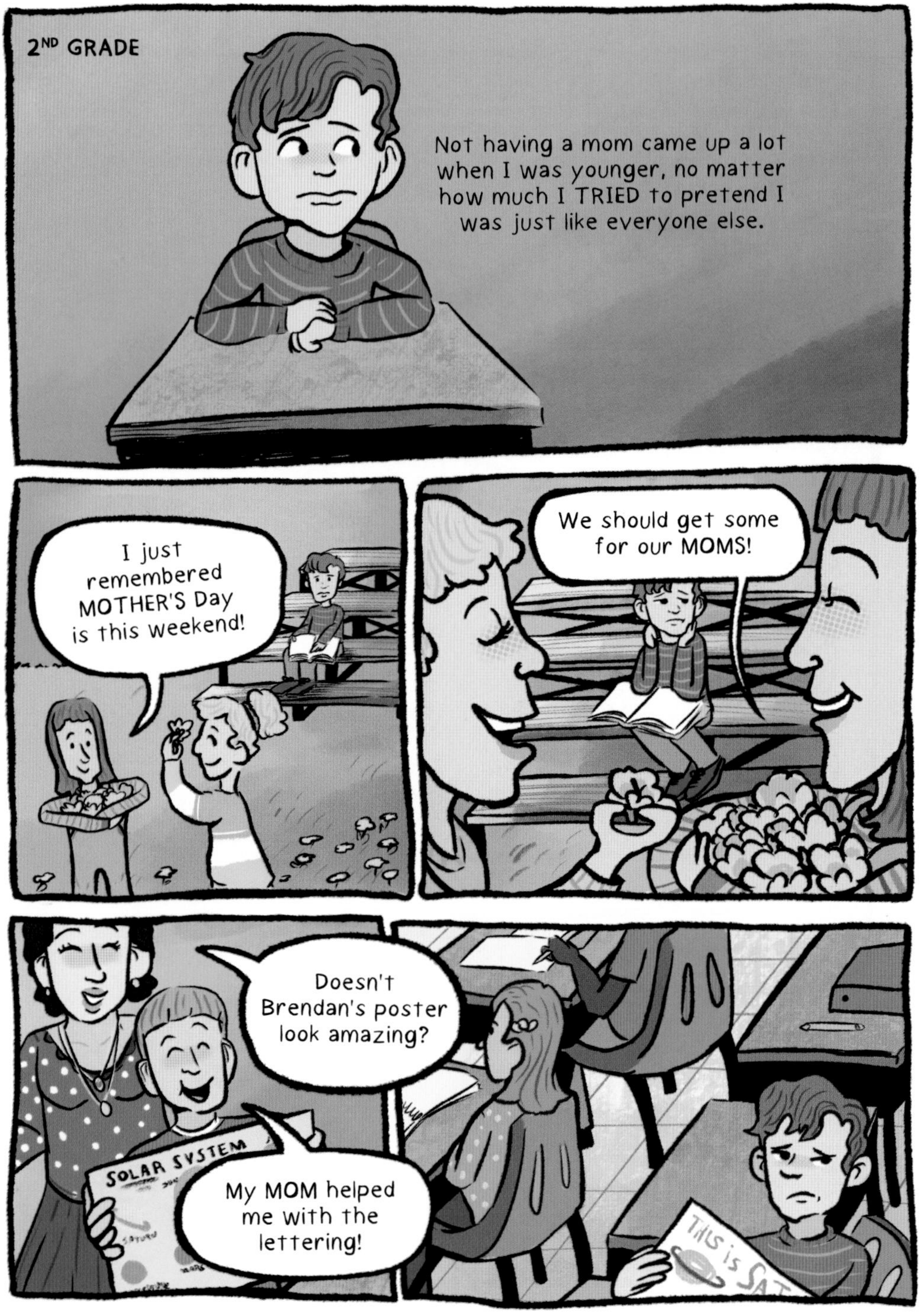
2ND GRADE
Not having a mom came up a lot when I was younger, no matter how much I TRIED to pretend I was just like everyone else.
I just remembered MOTHER'S Day is this weekend!
We should get some for our MOMS!
Doesn't Brendan's poster look amazing?
SOLAR SYSTEM
My MOM helped me with the lettering!
THIS is SAT

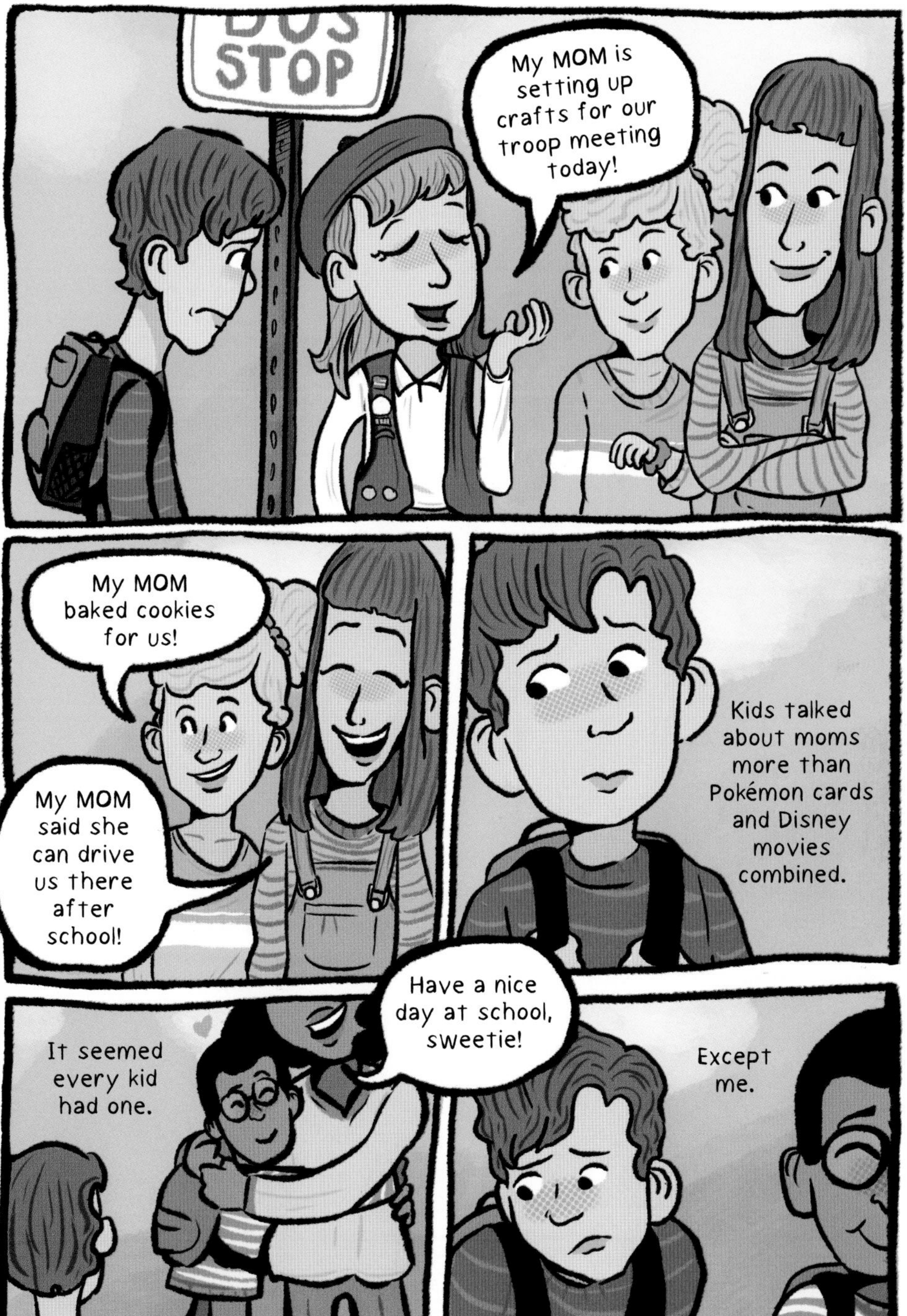
BUS STOP
My MOM is setting up crafts for our troop meeting today!
My MOM baked cookies for us!
My MOM said she can drive us there after school!
Kids talked about moms more than Pokémon cards and Disney movies combined.
It seemed every kid had one.
Have a nice day at school, sweetie!
Except me.

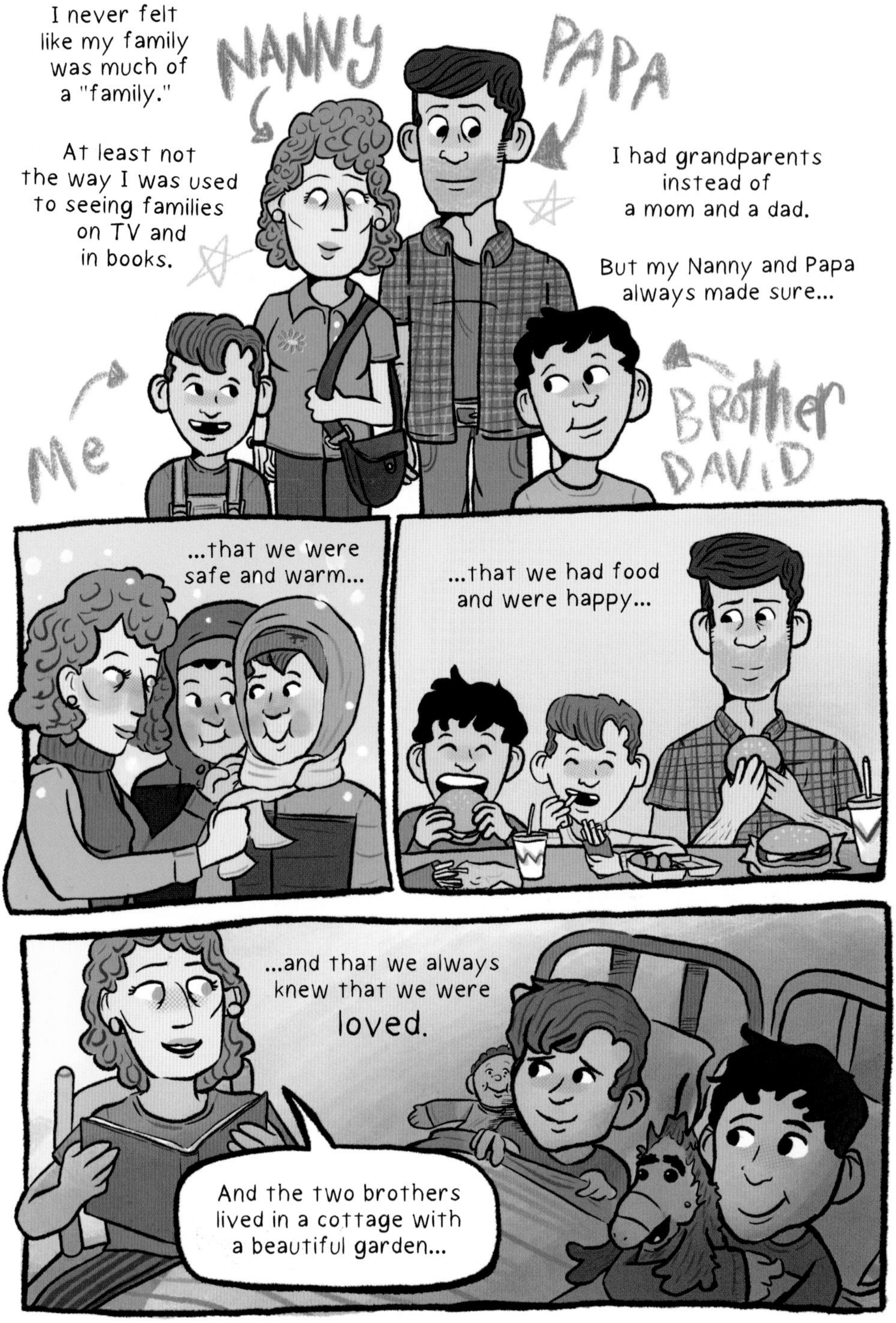
I never felt like my family was much of a "family."
At least not the way I was used to seeing families on TV and in books.
NANNY
PAPA
I had grandparents instead of a mom and a dad.
But my Nanny and Papa always made sure...
ME
BROTHER DAVID
...that we were safe and warm...
...that we had food and were happy...
...and that we always knew that we were loved.
And the two brothers lived in a cottage with a beautiful garden...

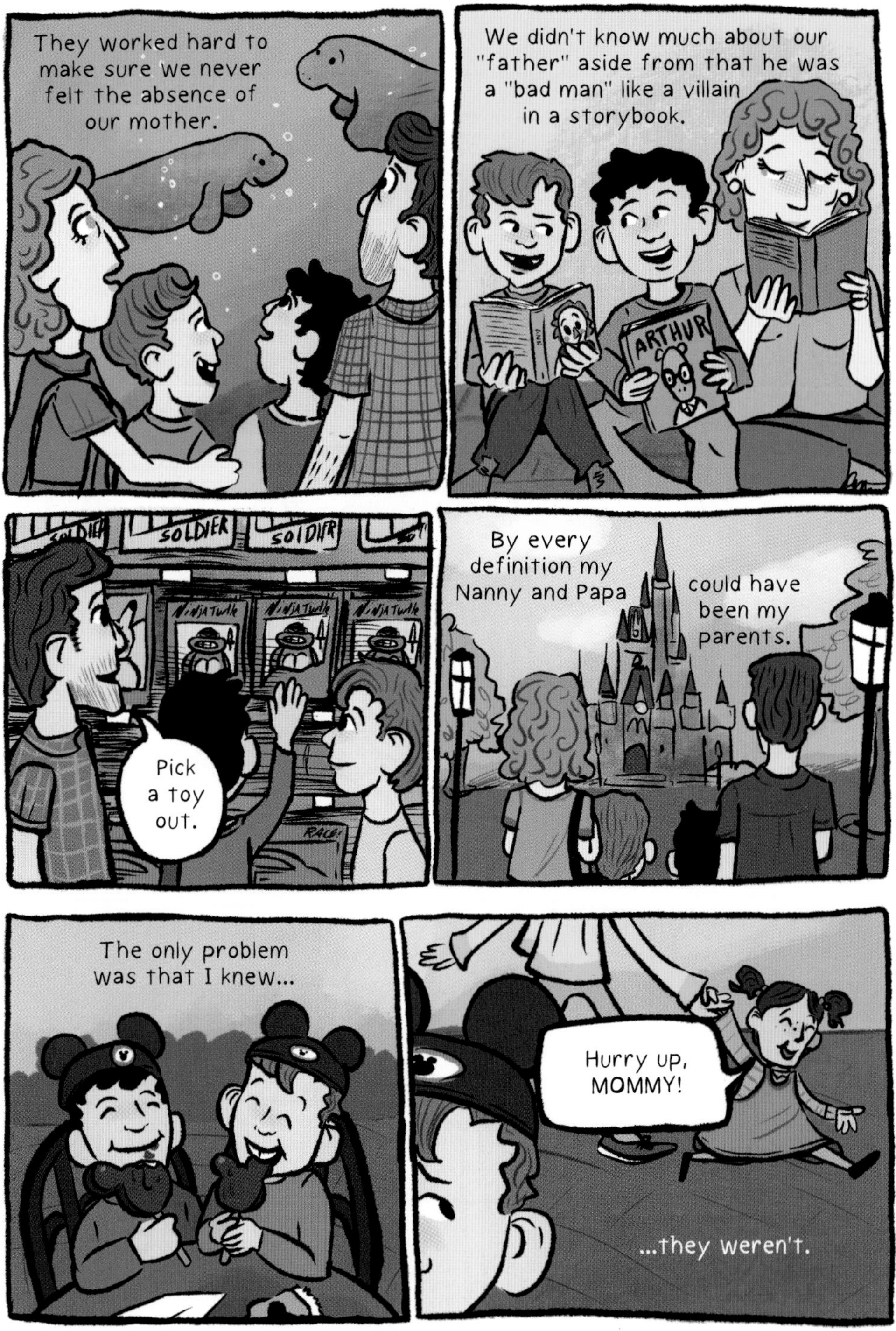
They worked hard to make sure we never felt the absence of our mother.
We didn't know much about our "father" aside from that he was a "bad man" like a villain in a storybook.
ARTHUR
SOLDIER
SOLDIER
Pick a toy out.
By every definition my Nanny and Papa
could have been my parents.
The only problem was that I knew...
Hurry up, MOMMY!
...they weren't.

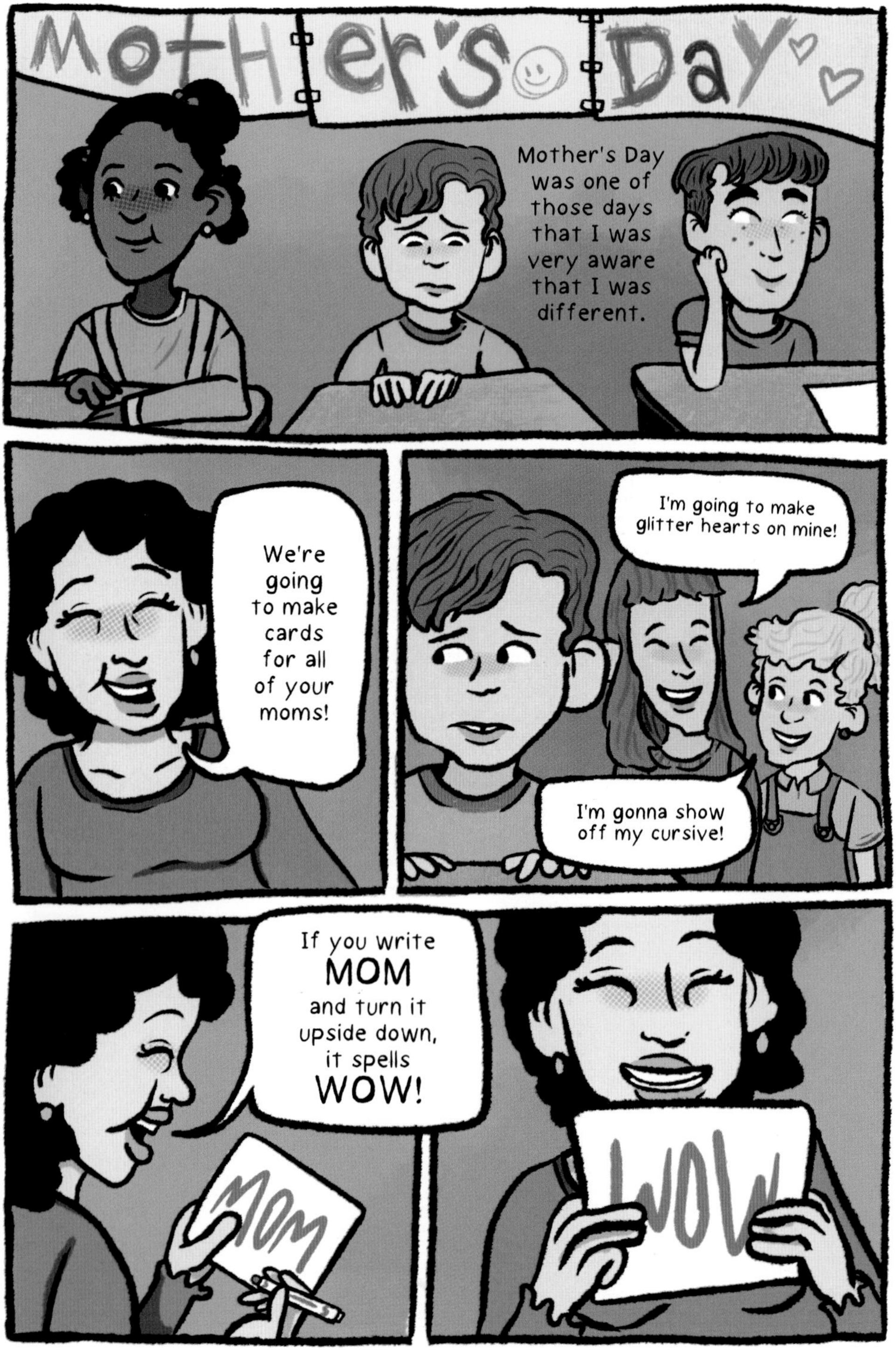
Mother's Day
Mother's Day was one of those days that I was very aware that I was different.
We're going to make cards for all of your moms!
I'm going to make glitter hearts on mine!
I'm gonna show off my cursive!
If you write MOM and turn it upside down, it spells WOW!
MOM
WOW

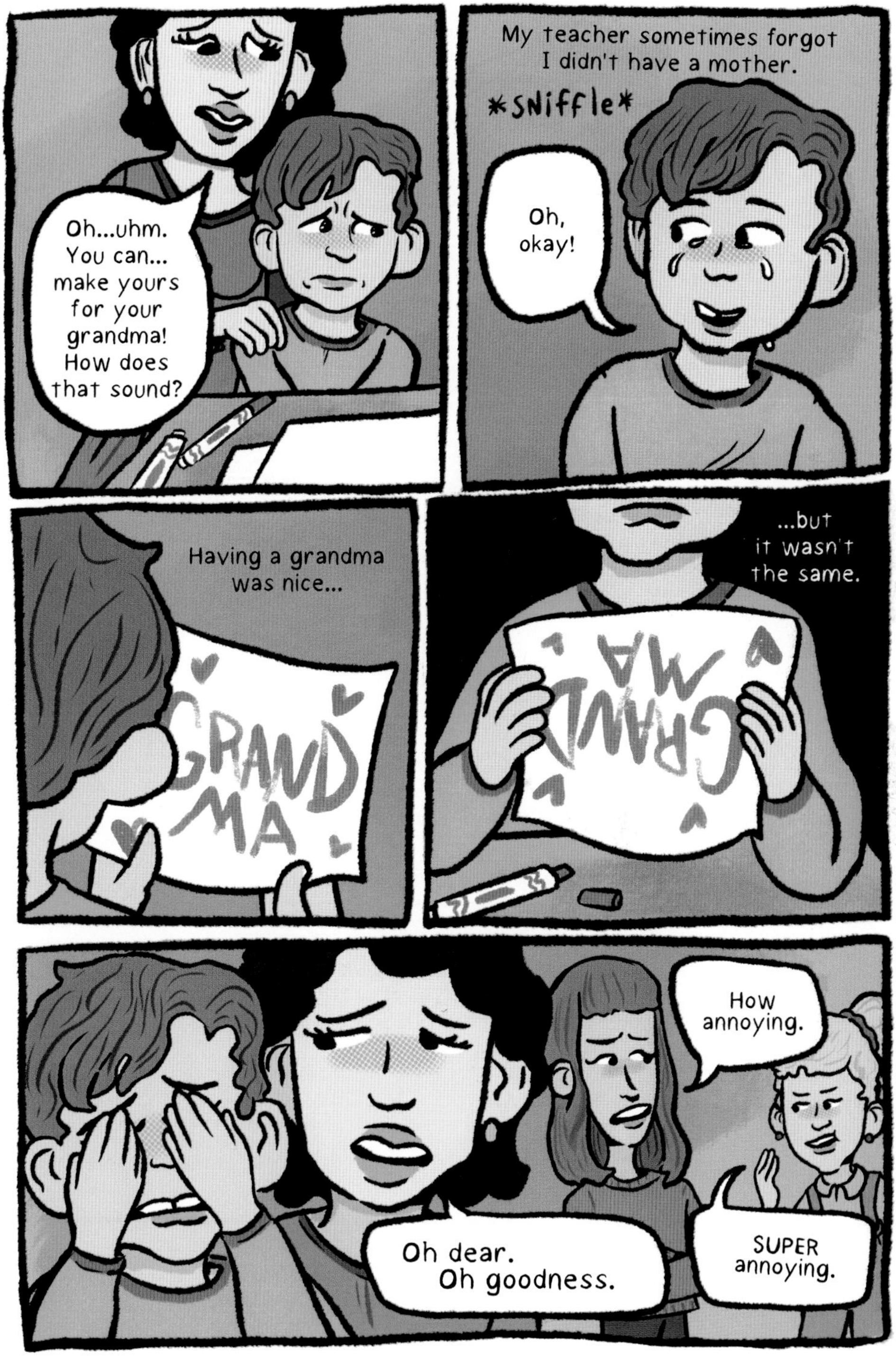
Oh...uhm. You can... make yours for your grandma! How does that sound?
My teacher sometimes forgot I didn't have a mother.
SNIFFLE
Oh, okay!
Having a grandma was nice...
GRAND MA
...but it wasn't the same.
GRAND MA
How annoying.
Oh dear. Oh goodness.
SUPER annoying.

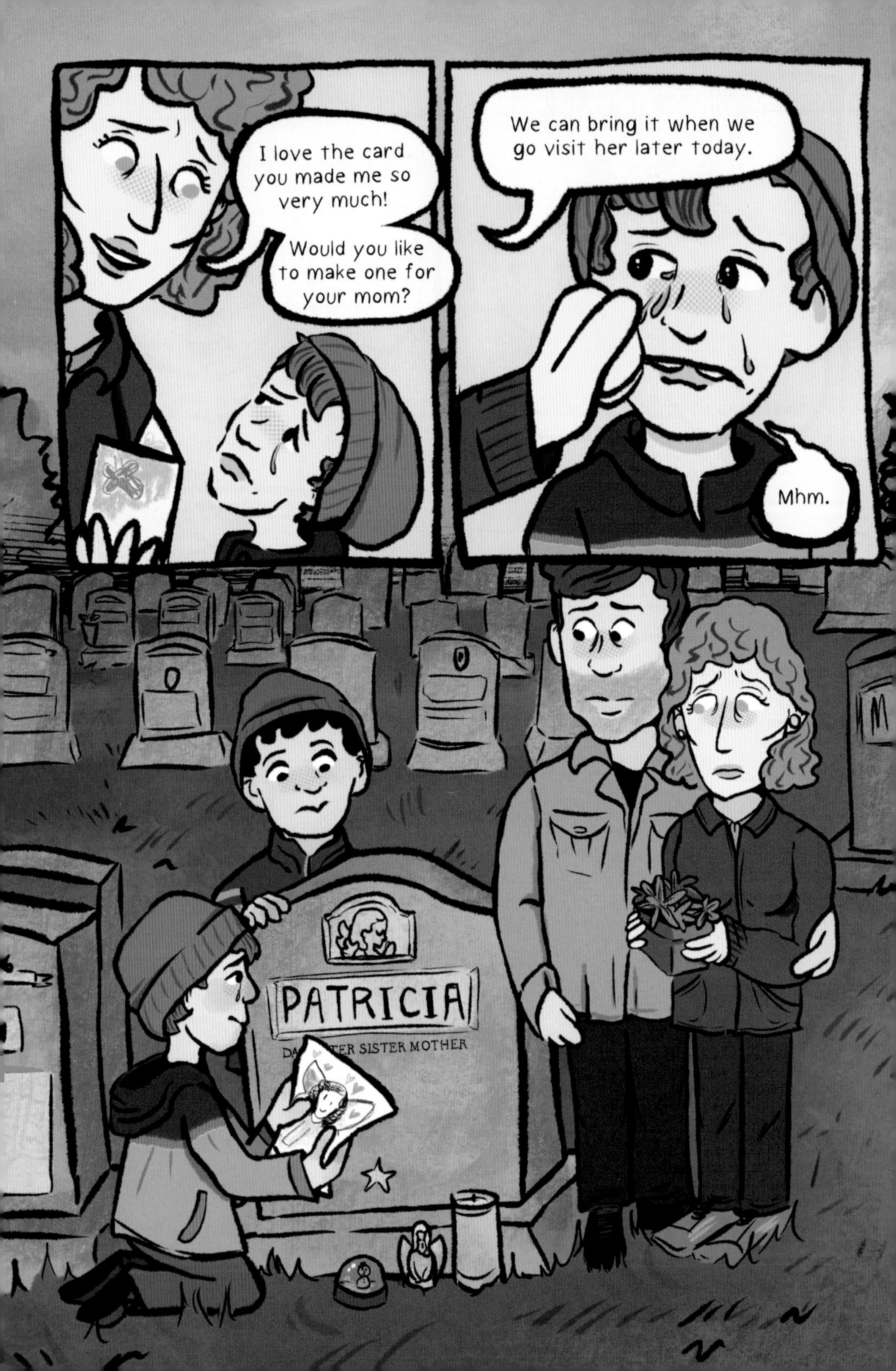
I love the card you made me so very much!
Would you like to make one for your mom?
We can bring it when we go visit her later today.
Mhm.
PATRICIA
SISTER MOTHER

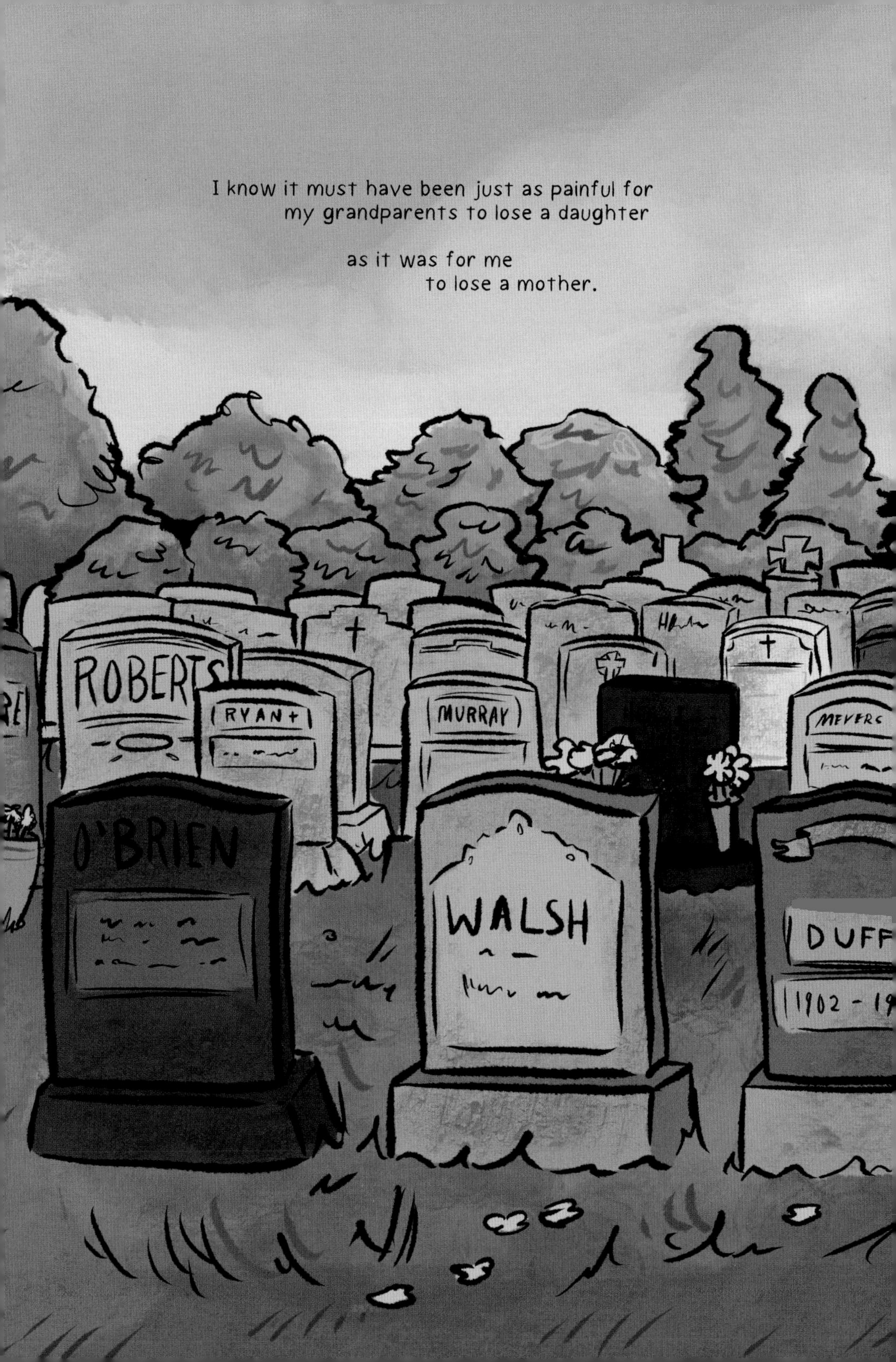
I know it must have been just as painful for my grandparents to lose a daughter
as it was for me to lose a mother.
ROBERTS
RYAN
MURRAY
MEYERS
O'BRIEN
WALSH
DUFF
1902 - 19

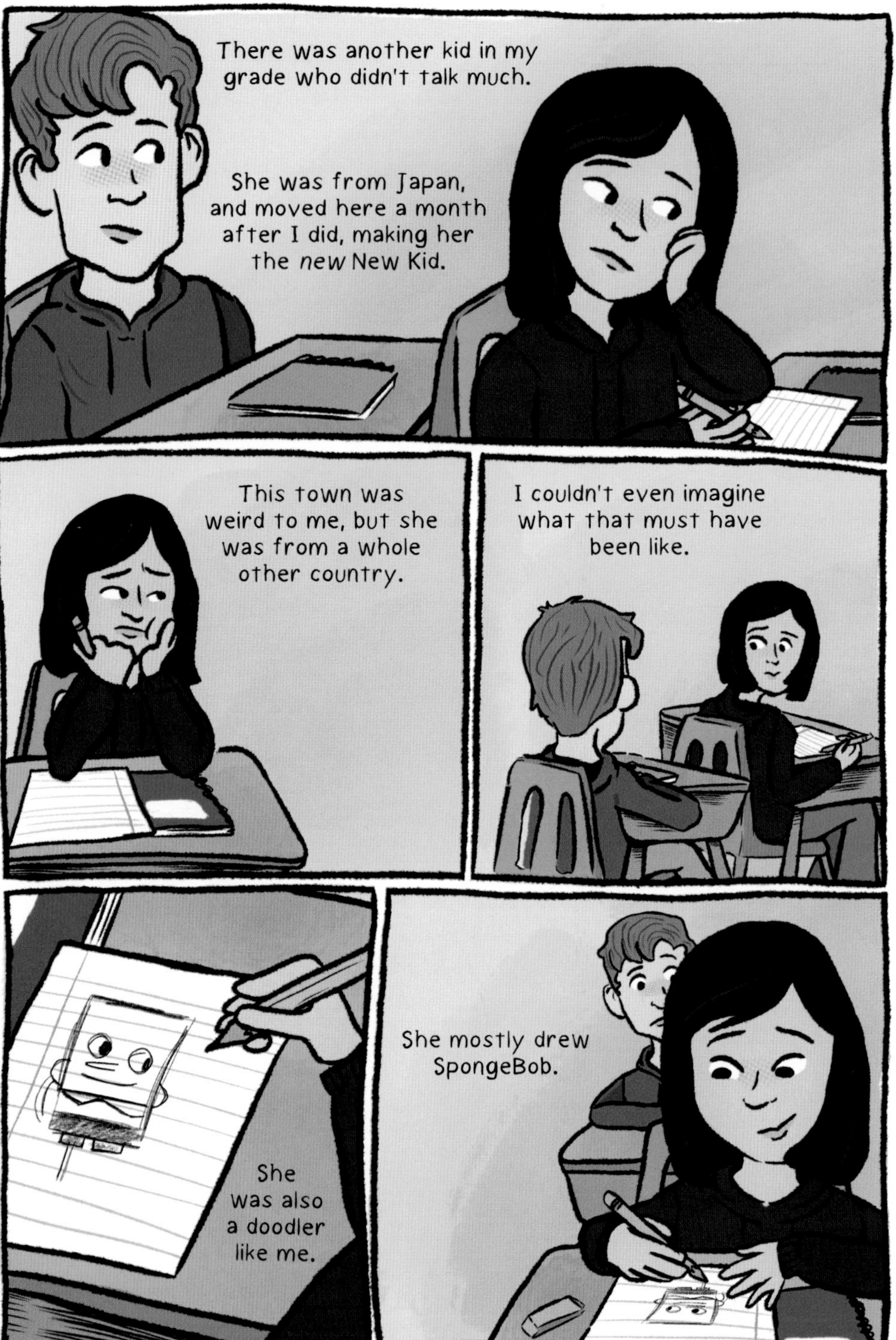
There was another kid in my grade who didn't talk much.
She was from Japan, and moved here a month after I did, making her the *new* New Kid.
This town was weird to me, but she was from a whole other country.
I couldn't even imagine what that must have been like.
She was also a doodler like me.
She mostly drew SpongeBob.

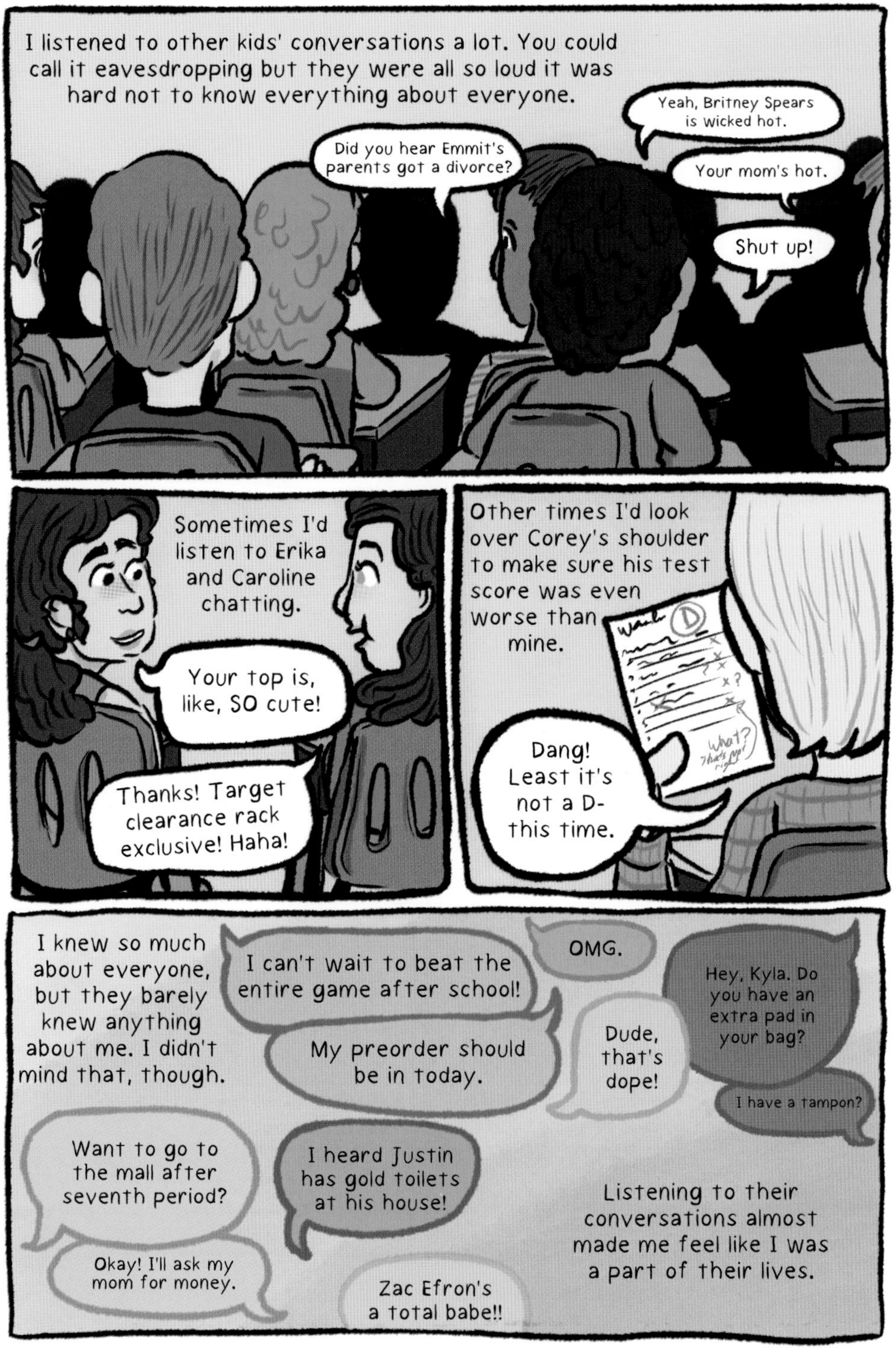
I listened to other kids' conversations a lot. You could call it eavesdropping but they were all so loud it was hard not to know everything about everyone.
Did you hear Emmit's parents got a divorce?
Yeah, Britney Spears is wicked hot.
Your mom's hot.
Shut up!
Sometimes I'd listen to Erika and Caroline chatting.
Your top is, like, SO cute!
Thanks! Target clearance rack exclusive! Haha!
Other times I'd look over Corey's shoulder to make sure his test score was even worse than mine.
Dang! Least it's not a D- this time.
I knew so much about everyone, but they barely knew anything about me. I didn't mind that, though.
I can't wait to beat the entire game after school!
My preorder should be in today.
OMG.
Dude, that's dope!
Hey, Kyla. Do you have an extra pad in your bag?
I have a tampon?
Want to go to the mall after seventh period?
Okay! I'll ask my mom for money.
I heard Justin has gold toilets at his house!
Zac Efron's a total babe!!
Listening to their conversations almost made me feel like I was a part of their lives.

Sometimes I'd look over at Max, that kid who had been nice to me on my very first day.

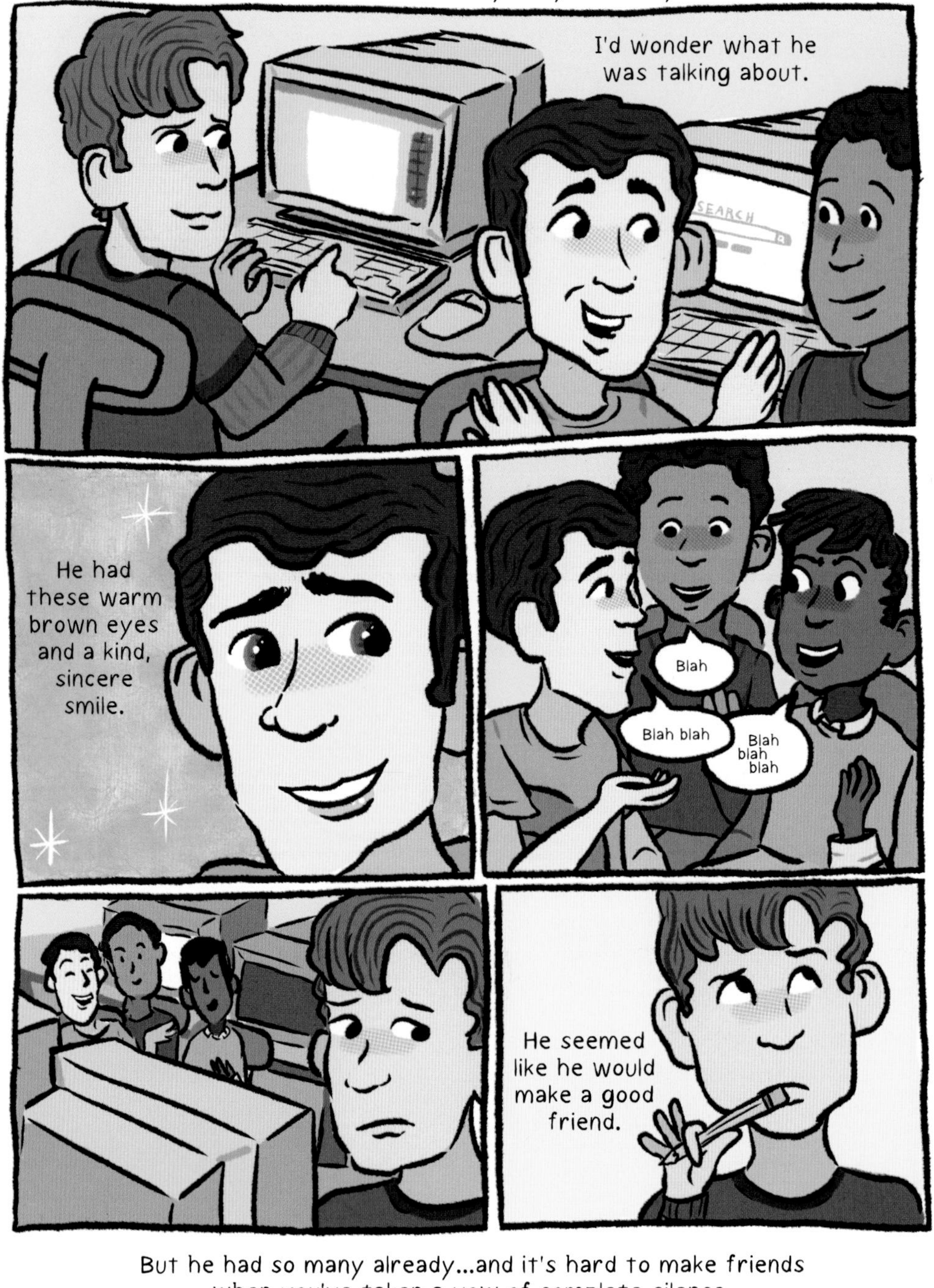
I'd wonder what he was talking about.
SEARCH
He had these warm brown eyes and a kind, sincere smile.
Blah
Blah blah
Blah blah blah
He seemed like he would make a good friend.

But he had so many already...and it's hard to make friends when you've taken a vow of complete silence.

In English class Akiko and I were paired together for a poetry assignment. Each kid had to pass it back and forth, adding a new line each time.

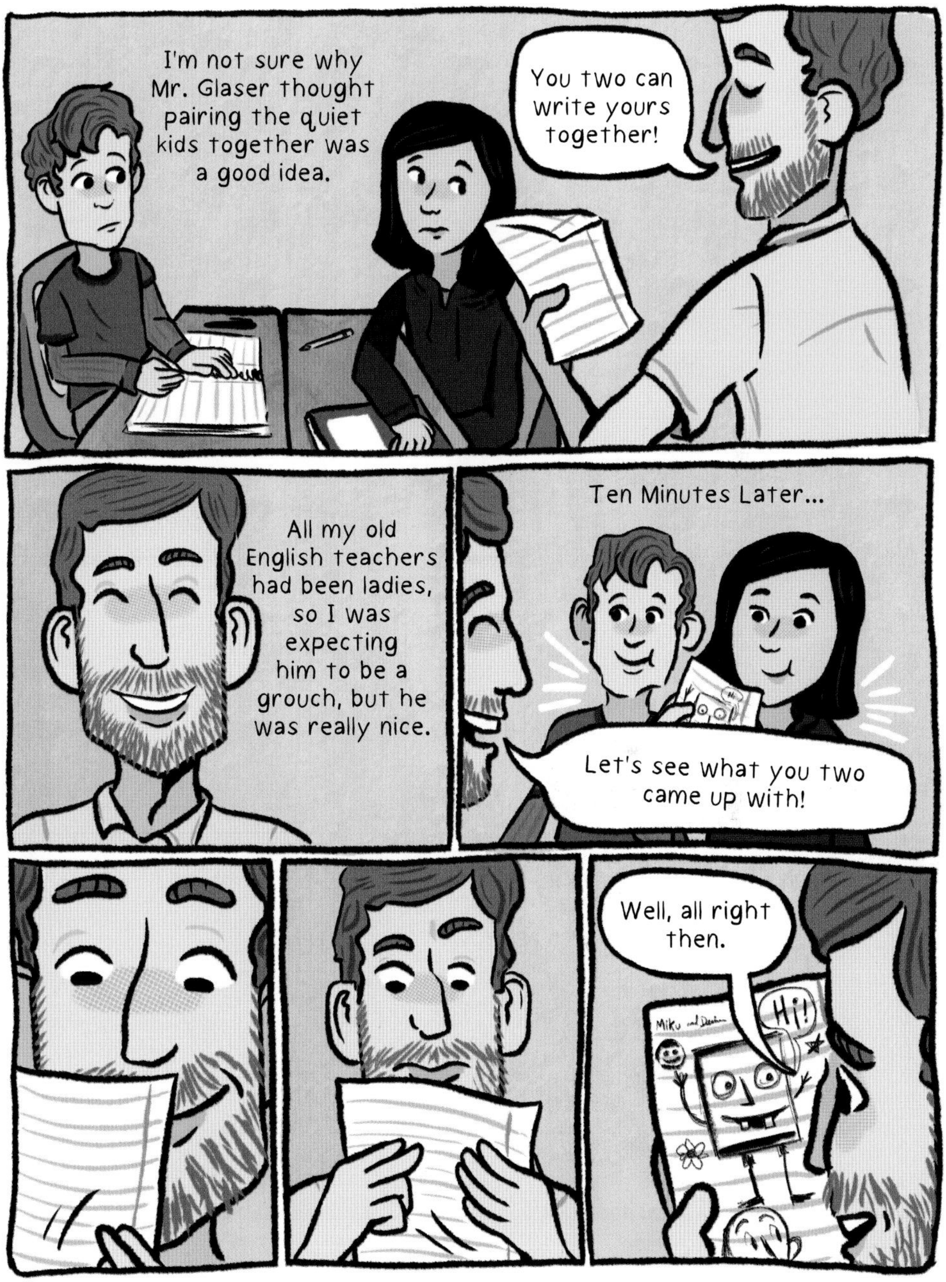

I'm not sure why Mr. Glaser thought pairing the quiet kids together was a good idea.
You two can write yours together!
All my old English teachers had been ladies, so I was expecting him to be a grouch, but he was really nice.
Ten Minutes Later...
Let's see what you two came up with!
Well, all right then.
Hi!

Technically we did add "a line" each time.

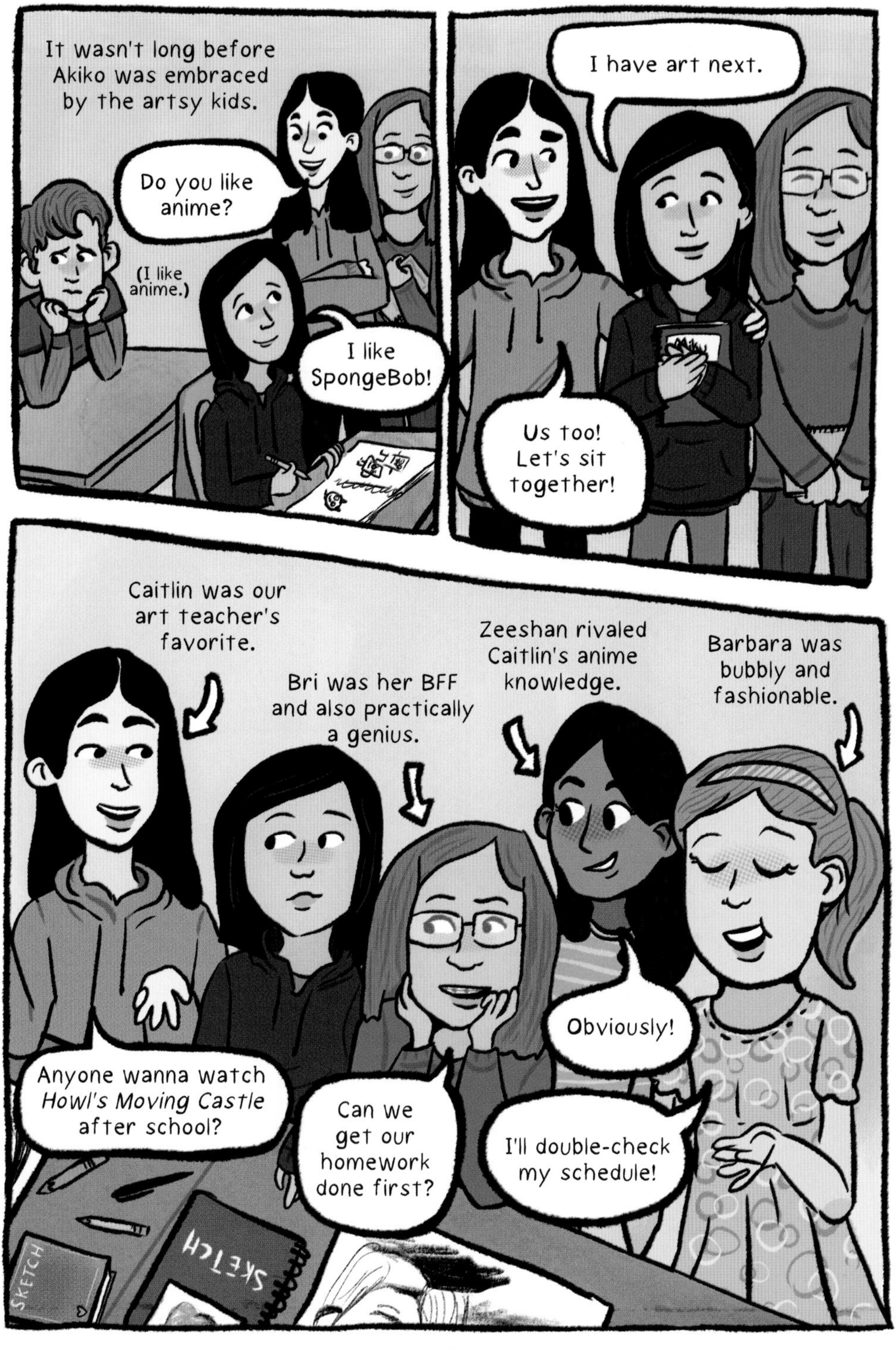

It wasn't long before Akiko was embraced by the artsy kids.
Do you like anime?
(I like anime.)
I like SpongeBob!
I have art next.
Us too! Let's sit together!
Caitlin was our art teacher's favorite.
Bri was her BFF and also practically a genius.
Zeeshan rivaled Caitlin's anime knowledge.
Barbara was bubbly and fashionable.
Anyone wanna watch *Howl's Moving Castle* after school?
Can we get our homework done first?
Obviously!
I'll double-check my schedule!
SKETCH
SKETCH

I doodled all the time, everywhere, but I didn't consider myself much of an artist. I imagined artists being people with berets and fancy paint palettes.

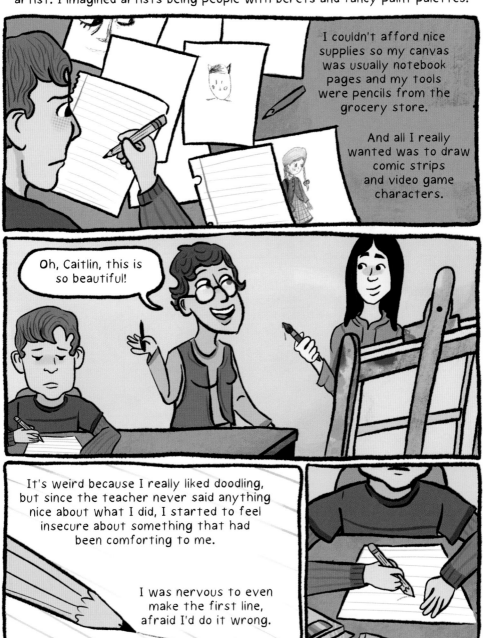

I couldn't afford nice supplies so my canvas was usually notebook pages and my tools were pencils from the grocery store.

And all I really wanted was to draw comic strips and video game characters.

Oh, Caitlin, this is so beautiful!

It's weird because I really liked doodling, but since the teacher never said anything nice about what I did, I started to feel insecure about something that had been comforting to me.

I was nervous to even make the first line, afraid I'd do it wrong.

Later, I learned even some of the artists I admired felt insecure sometimes.

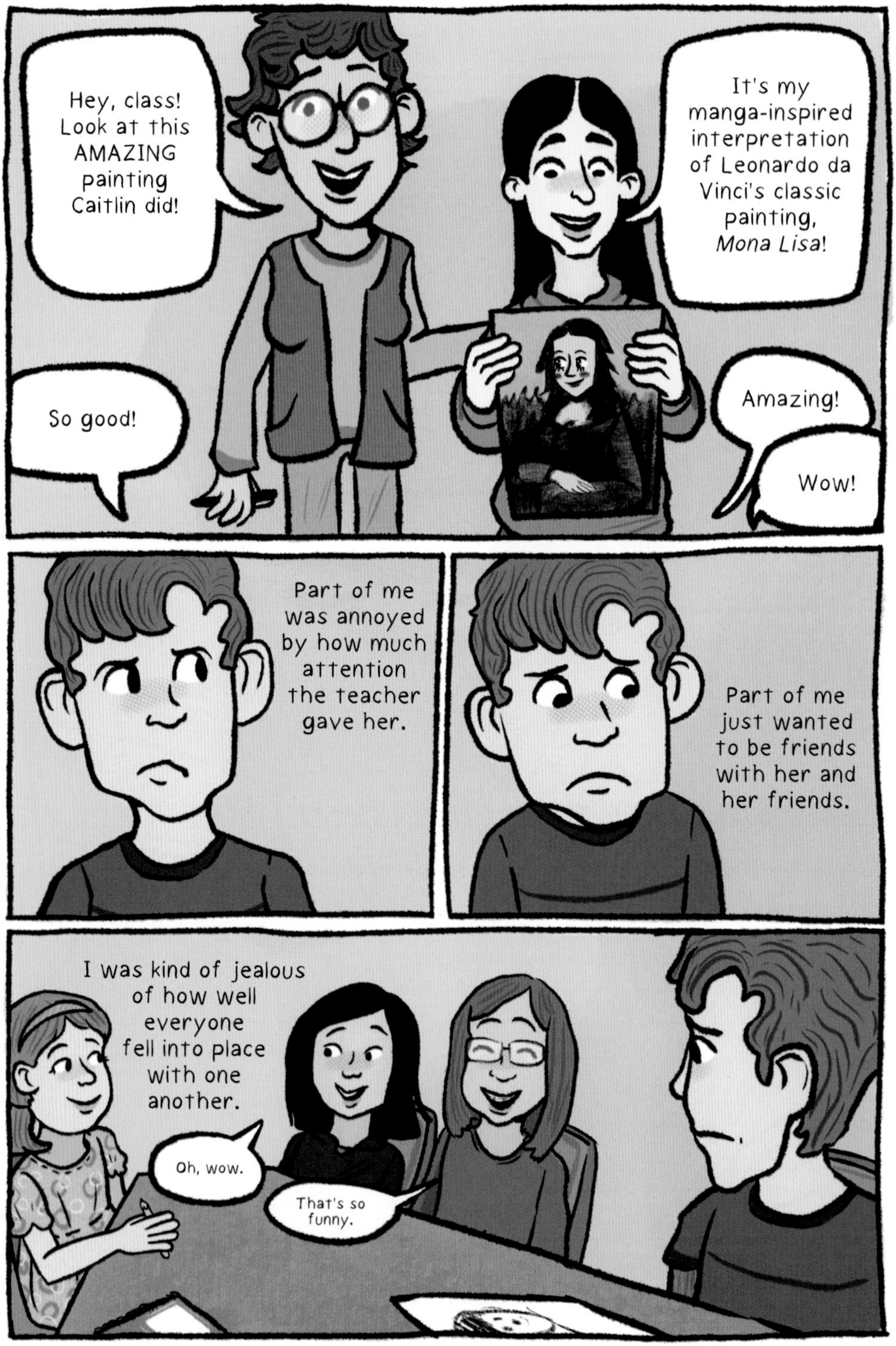
Hey, class! Look at this AMAZING painting Caitlin did!
It's my manga-inspired interpretation of Leonardo da Vinci's classic painting, *Mona Lisa*!
So good!
Amazing!
Wow!
Part of me was annoyed by how much attention the teacher gave her.
Part of me just wanted to be friends with her and her friends.
I was kind of jealous of how well everyone fell into place with one another.
Oh, wow.
That's so funny.

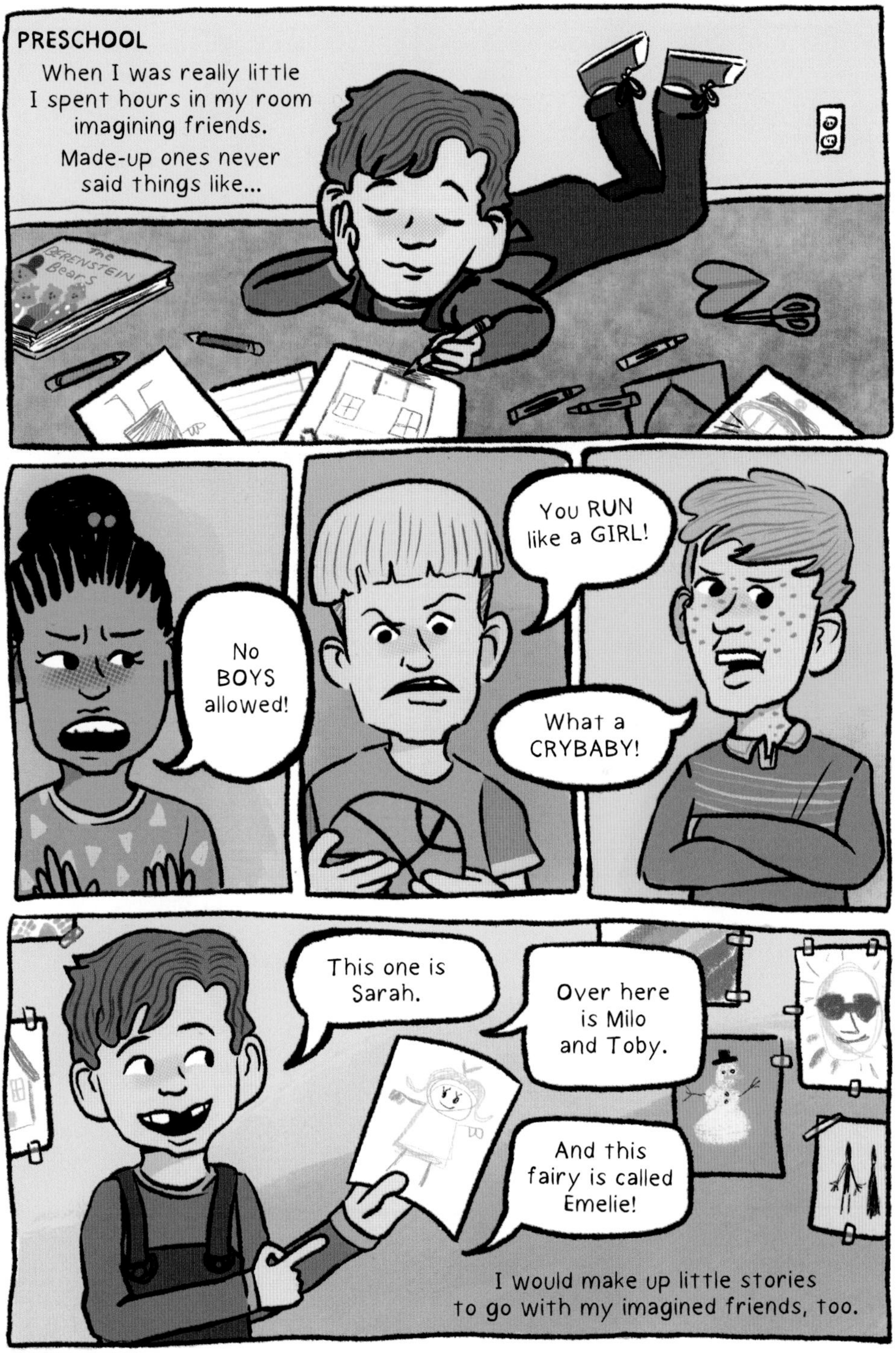

PRESCHOOL
When I was really little I spent hours in my room imagining friends.
Made-up ones never said things like...
The BERENSTEIN Bears
No BOYS allowed!
You RUN like a GIRL!
What a CRYBABY!
This one is Sarah.
Over here is Milo and Toby.
And this fairy is called Emelie!
I would make up little stories to go with my imagined friends, too.

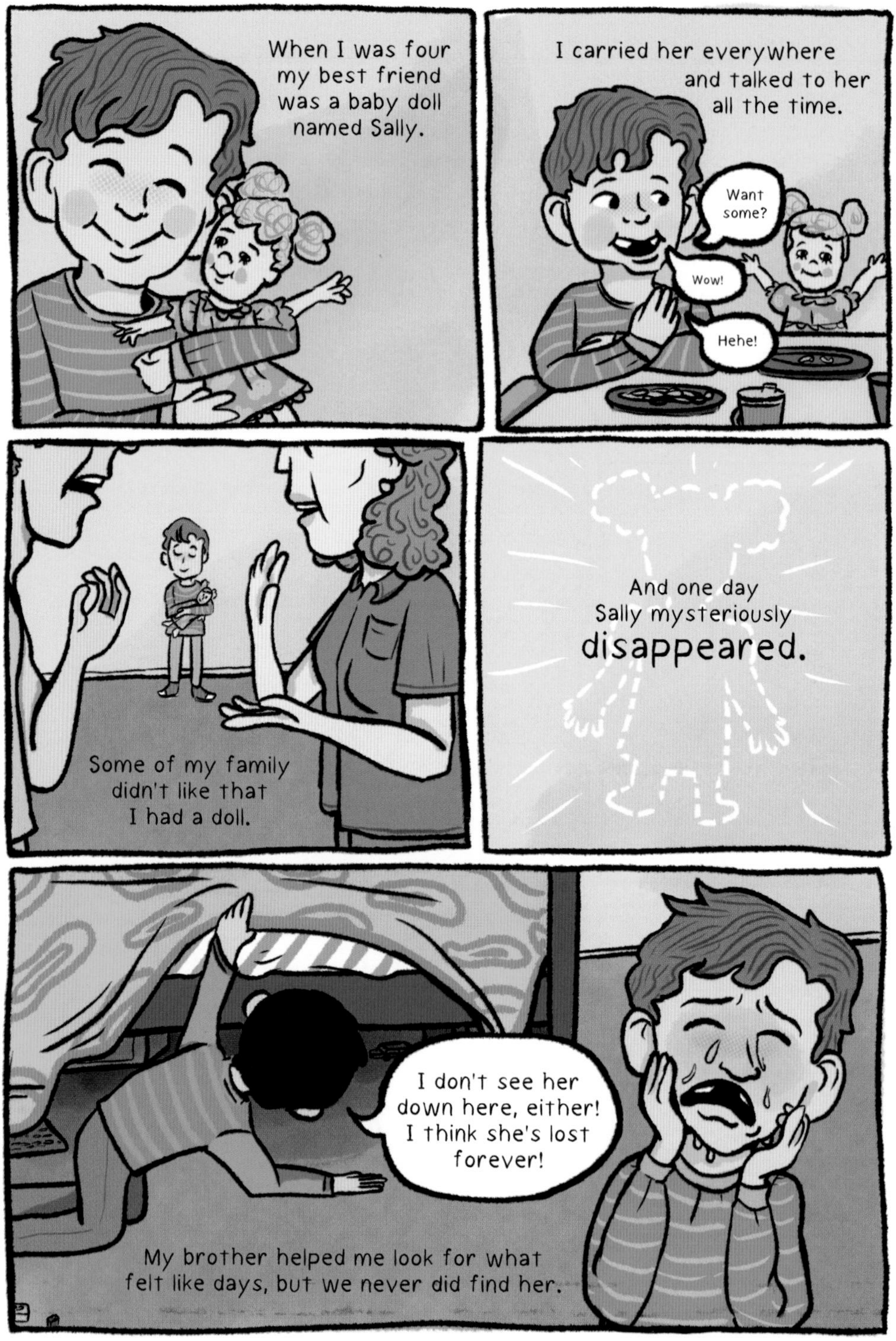

When I was four my best friend was a baby doll named Sally.
I carried her everywhere and talked to her all the time.
Want some?
Wow!
Hehe!
Some of my family didn't like that I had a doll.
And one day Sally mysteriously disappeared.
I don't see her down here, either! I think she's lost forever!
My brother helped me look for what felt like days, but we never did find her.

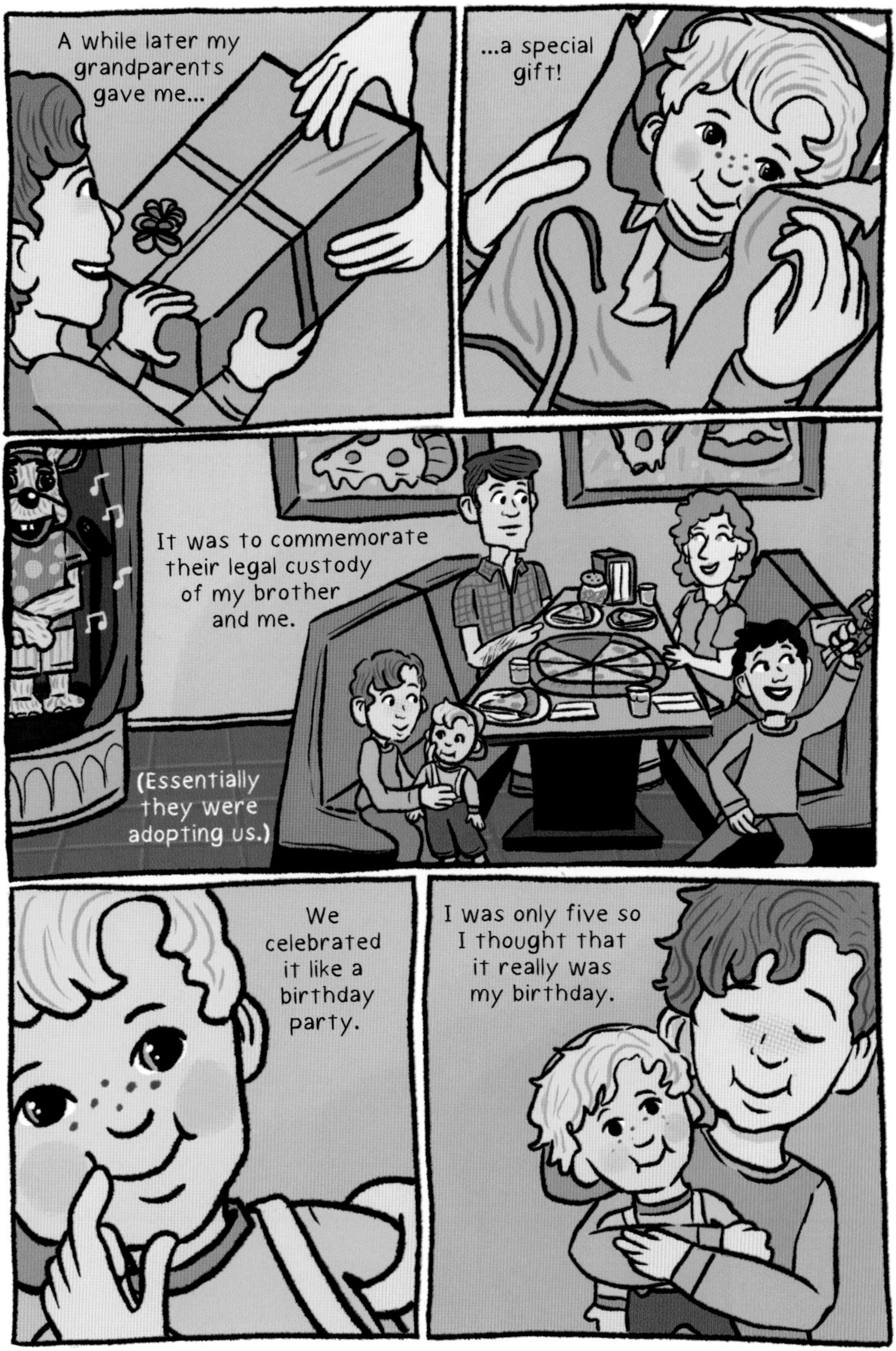
A while later my grandparents gave me...
...a special gift!
It was to commemorate their legal custody of my brother and me.
(Essentially they were adopting us.)
We celebrated it like a birthday party.
I was only five so I thought that it really was my birthday.

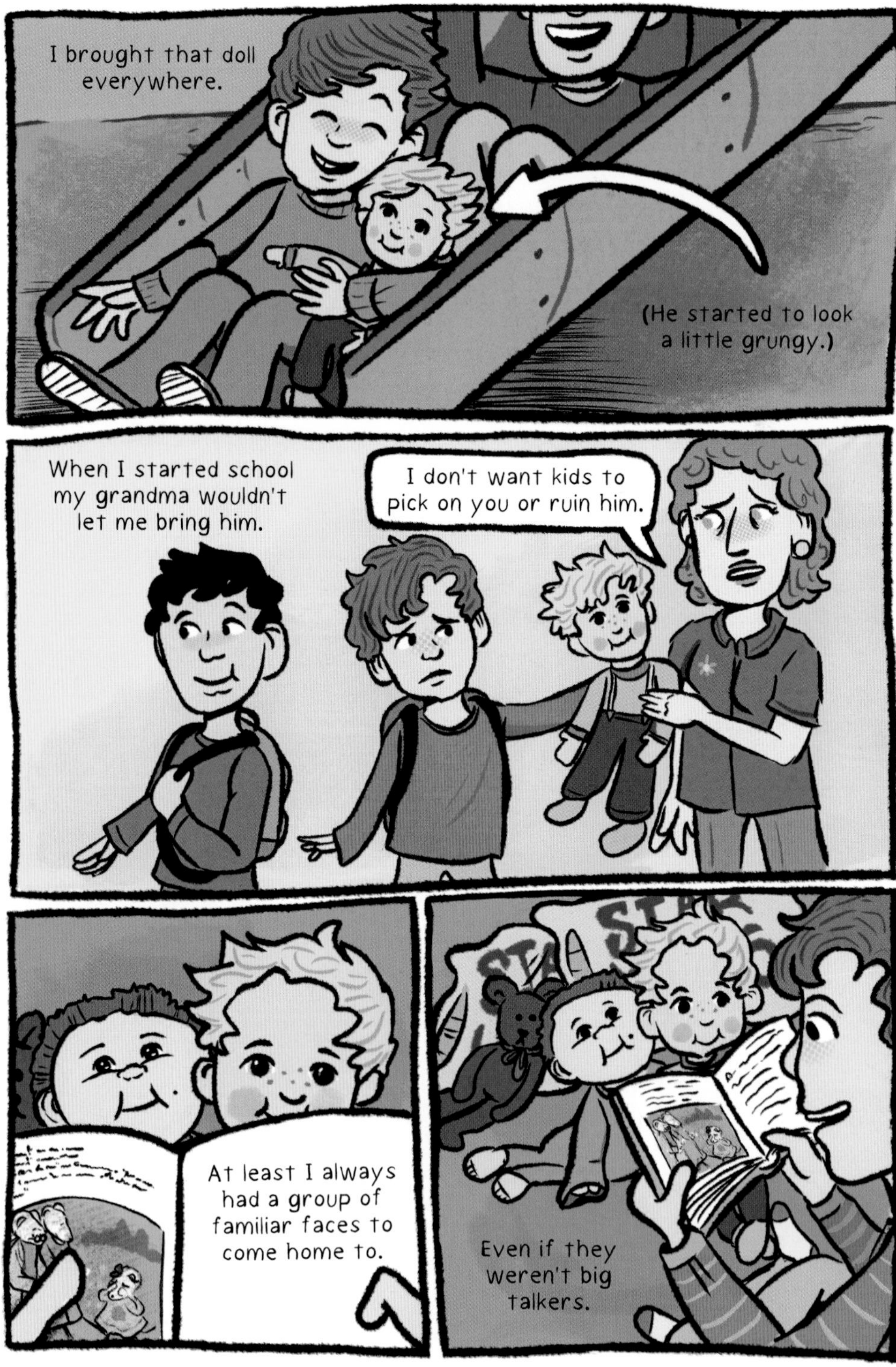
I brought that doll everywhere.
(He started to look a little grungy.)
When I started school my grandma wouldn't let me bring him.
I don't want kids to pick on you or ruin him.
At least I always had a group of familiar faces to come home to.
Even if they weren't big talkers.

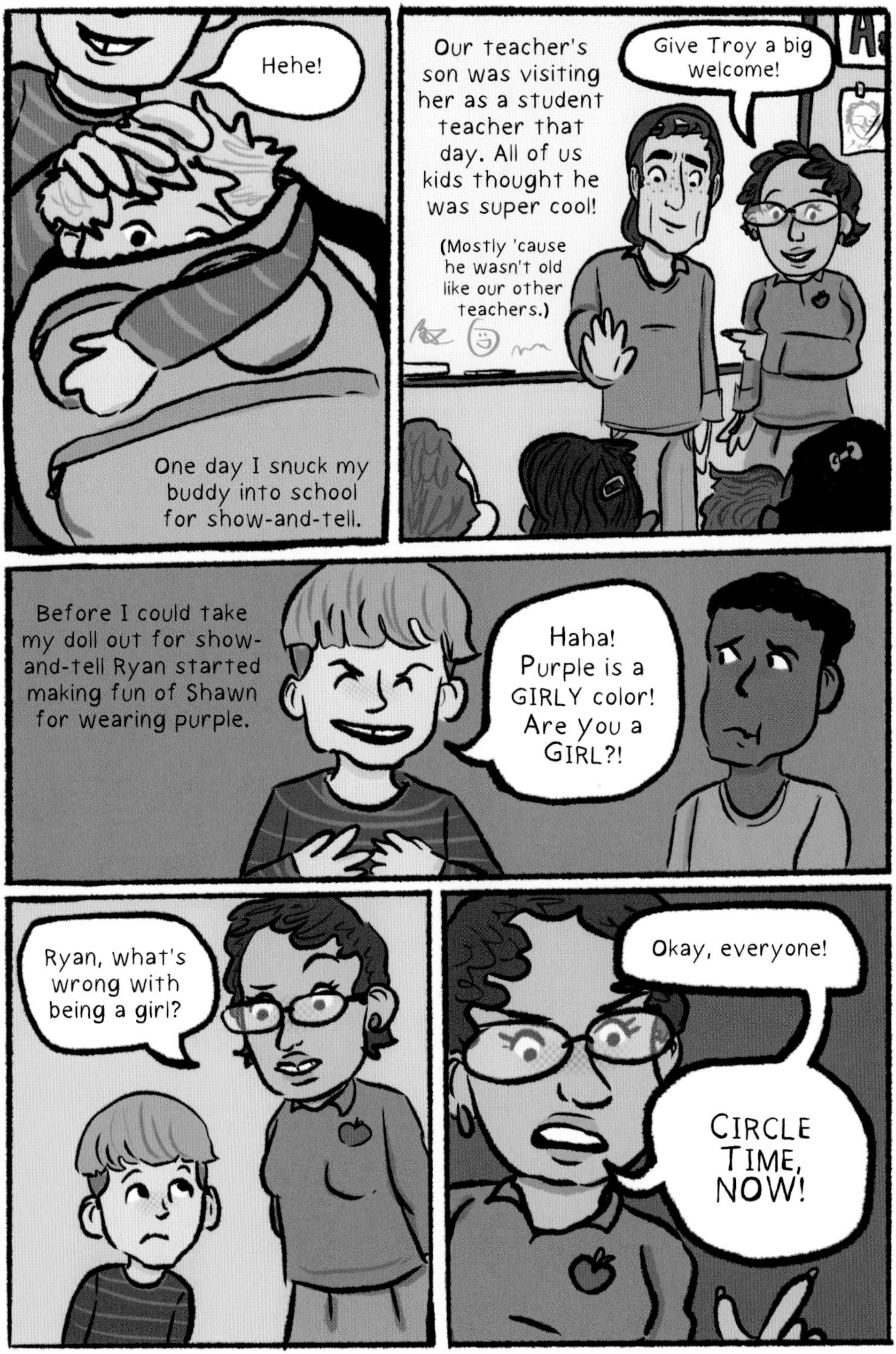

Hehe!
One day I snuck my buddy into school for show-and-tell.
Our teacher's son was visiting her as a student teacher that day. All of us kids thought he was super cool!
(Mostly 'cause he wasn't old like our other teachers.)
Give Troy a big welcome!
Before I could take my doll out for show-and-tell Ryan started making fun of Shawn for wearing purple.
Haha! Purple is a GIRLY color! Are you a GIRL?!
Ryan, what's wrong with being a girl?
Okay, everyone!
CIRCLE TIME, NOW!

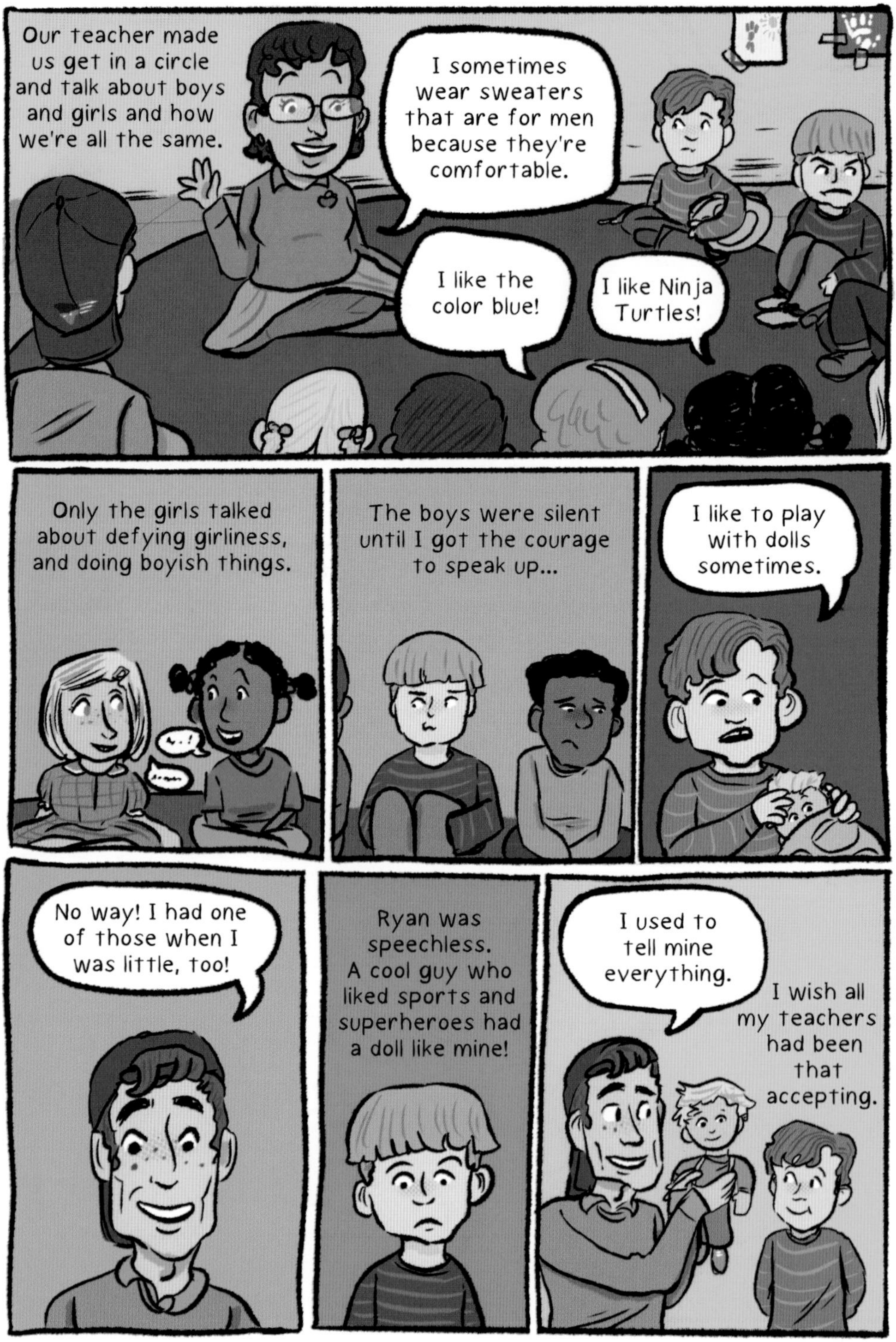

Our teacher made us get in a circle and talk about boys and girls and how we're all the same.
I sometimes wear sweaters that are for men because they're comfortable.
I like the color blue!
I like Ninja Turtles!
Only the girls talked about defying girliness, and doing boyish things.
The boys were silent until I got the courage to speak up...
I like to play with dolls sometimes.
No way! I had one of those when I was little, too!
Ryan was speechless. A cool guy who liked sports and superheroes had a doll like mine!
I used to tell mine everything.
I wish all my teachers had been that accepting.

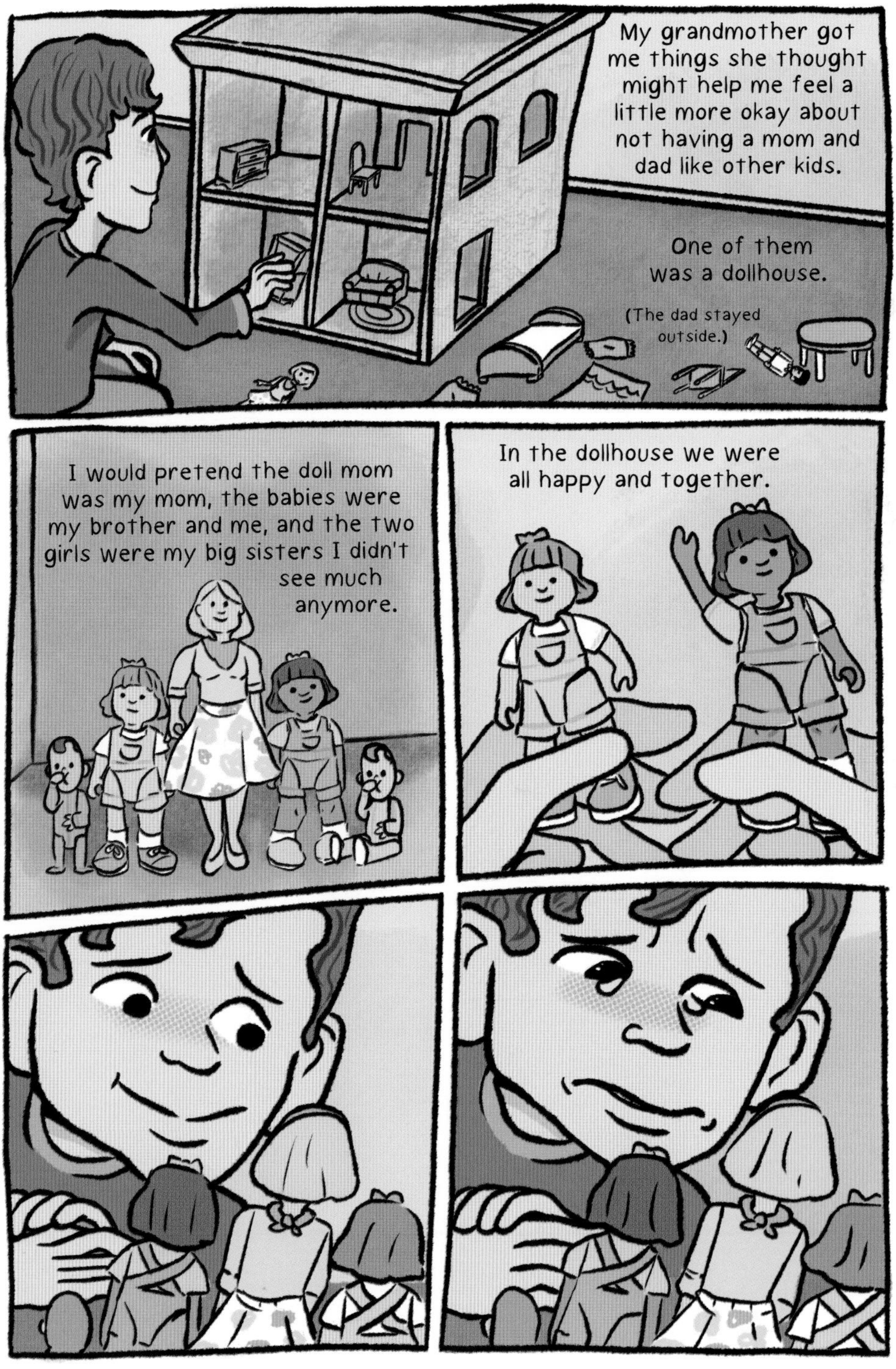
My grandmother got me things she thought might help me feel a little more okay about not having a mom and dad like other kids.
One of them was a dollhouse.
(The dad stayed outside.)
I would pretend the doll mom was my mom, the babies were my brother and me, and the two girls were my big sisters I didn't see much anymore.
In the dollhouse we were all happy and together.

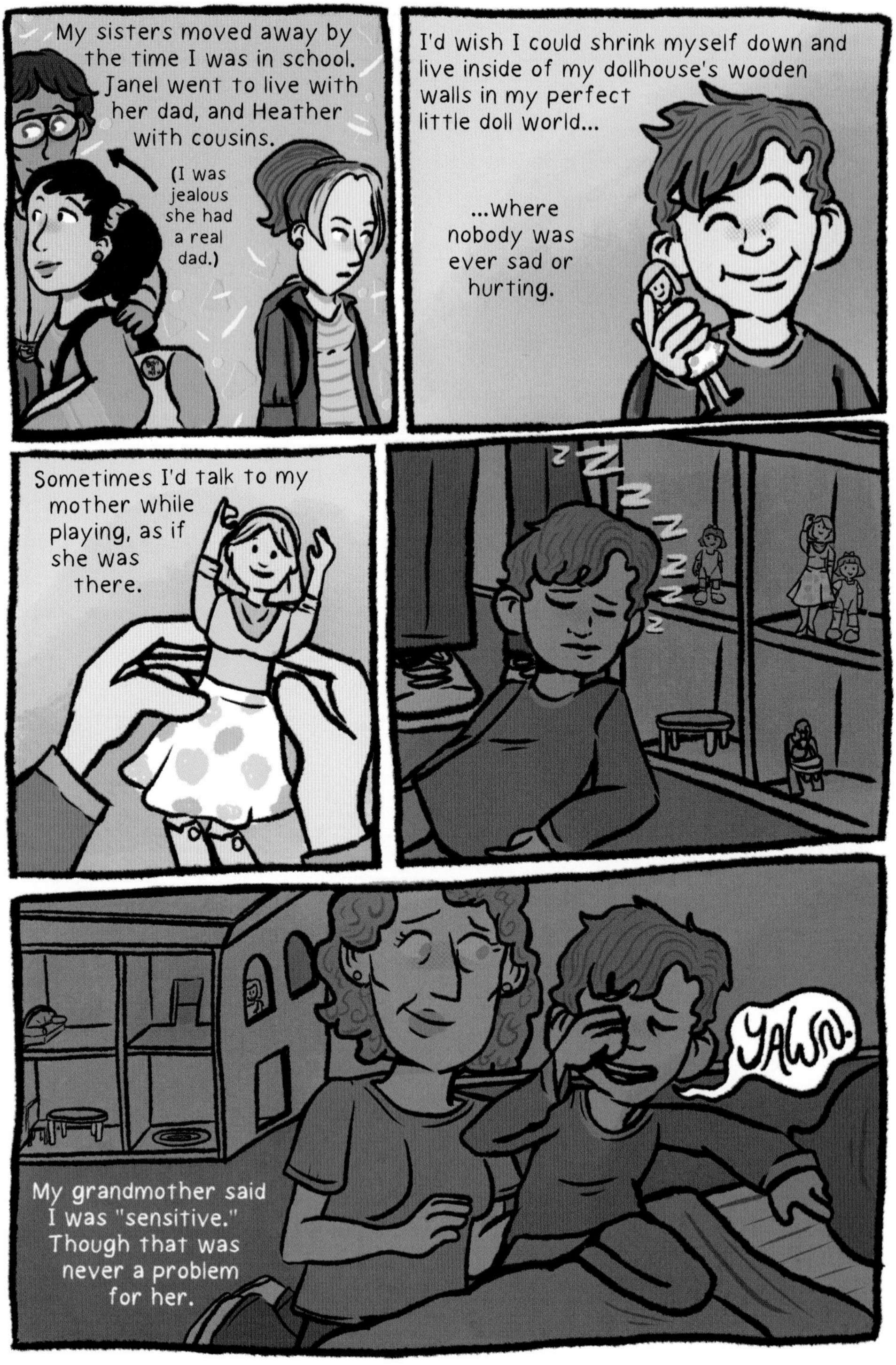

My sisters moved away by the time I was in school. Janel went to live with her dad, and Heather with cousins.
(I was jealous she had a real dad.)
I'd wish I could shrink myself down and live inside of my dollhouse's wooden walls in my perfect little doll world...
...where nobody was ever sad or hurting.
Sometimes I'd talk to my mother while playing, as if she was there.
Z Z Z Z Z Z Z
My grandmother said I was "sensitive." Though that was never a problem for her.
YAWN.

There was talk over whether I should be allowed to play with dolls or a dollhouse.

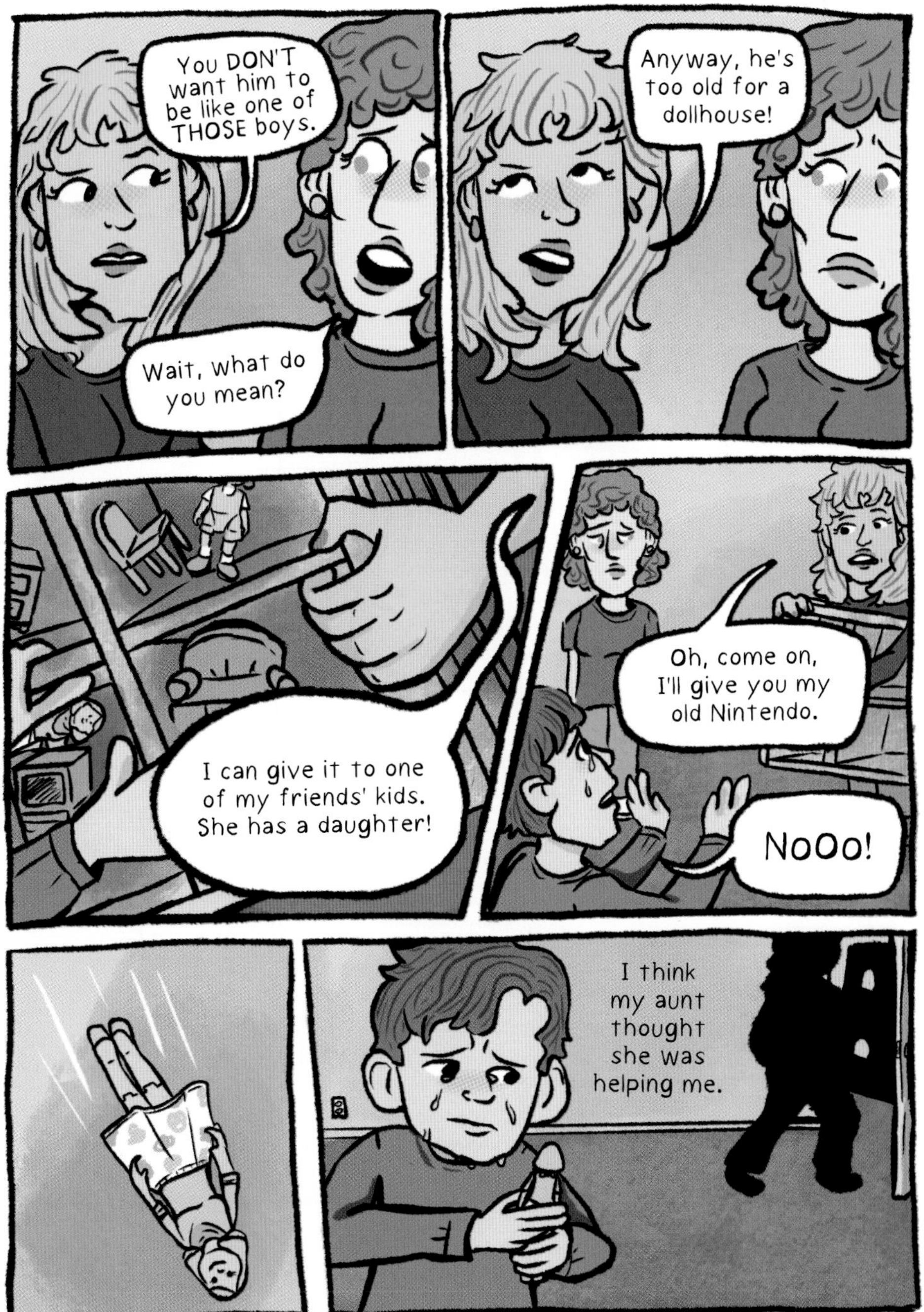

You DON'T want him to be like one of THOSE boys.
Wait, what do you mean?
Anyway, he's too old for a dollhouse!
I can give it to one of my friends' kids. She has a daughter!
Oh, come on, I'll give you my old Nintendo.
NoOo!
I think my aunt thought she was helping me.

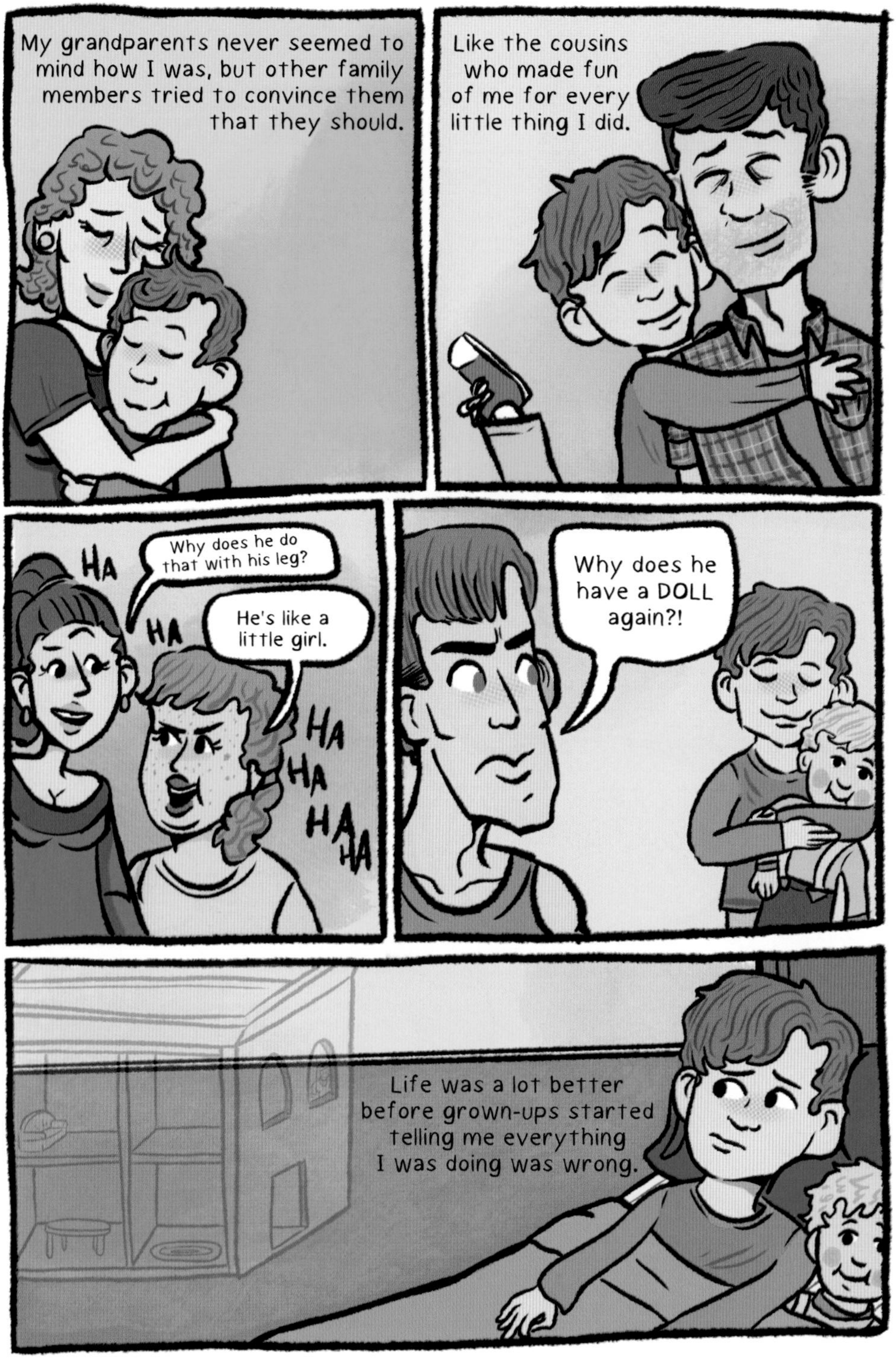
My grandparents never seemed to mind how I was, but other family members tried to convince them that they should.
Like the cousins who made fun of me for every little thing I did.
HA
Why does he do that with his leg?
HA
He's like a little girl.
HA
HA
HA
HA
Why does he have a DOLL again?!
Life was a lot better before grown-ups started telling me everything I was doing was wrong.

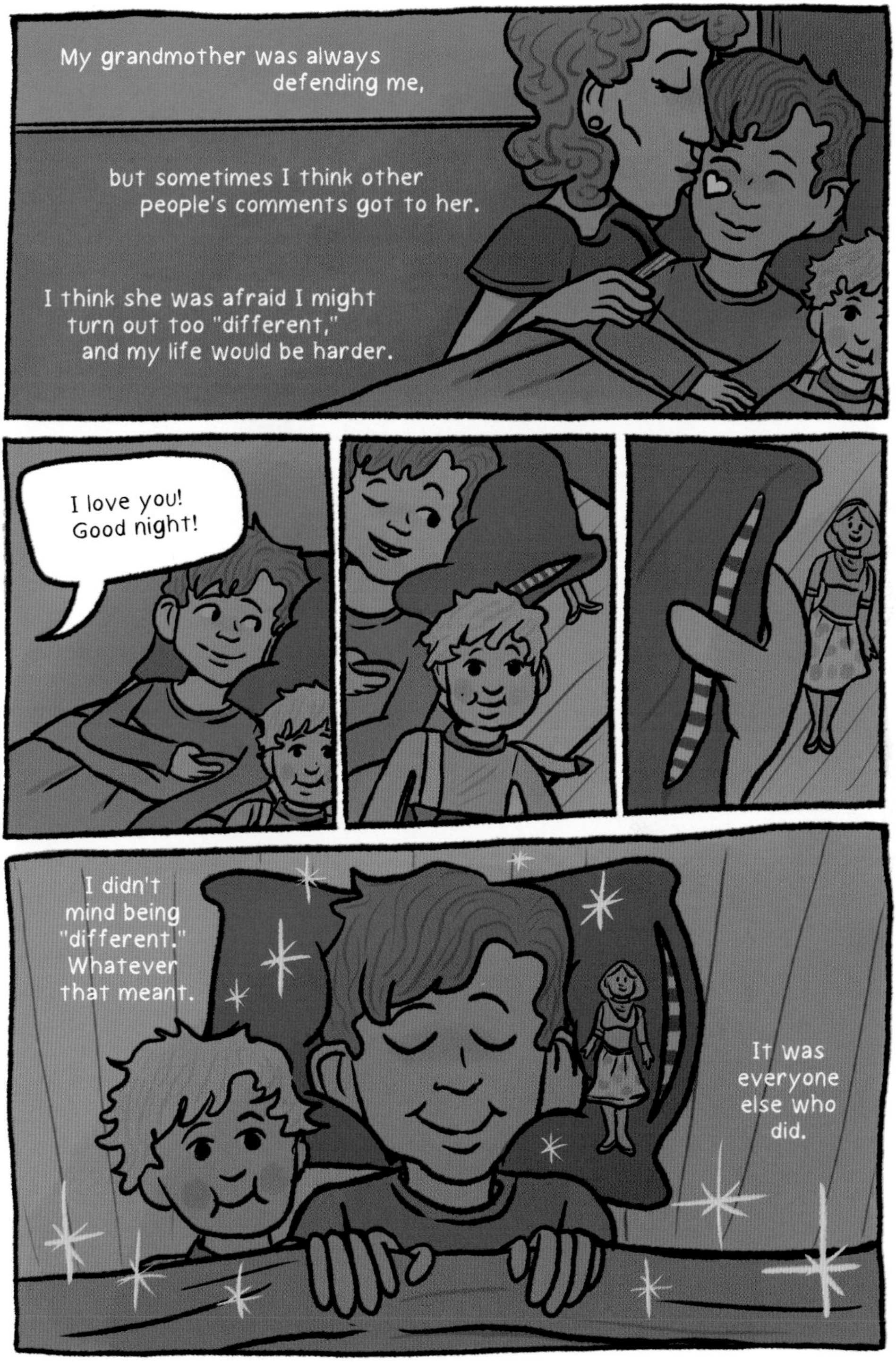
My grandmother was always defending me,
but sometimes I think other people's comments got to her.
I think she was afraid I might turn out too "different," and my life would be harder.
I love you! Good night!
I didn't mind being "different." Whatever that meant.
It was everyone else who did.

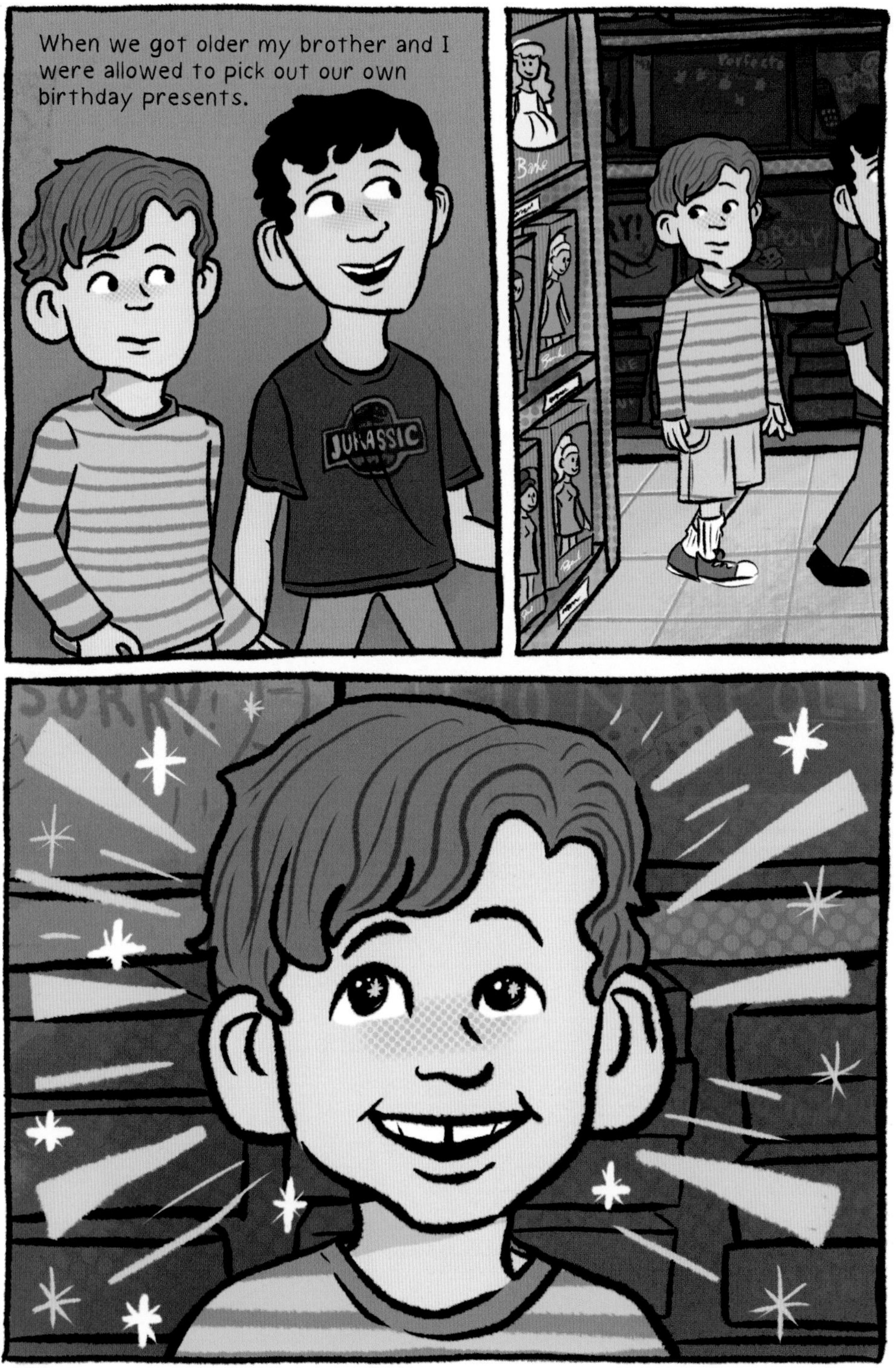
When we got older my brother and I were allowed to pick out our own birthday presents.
JURASSIC

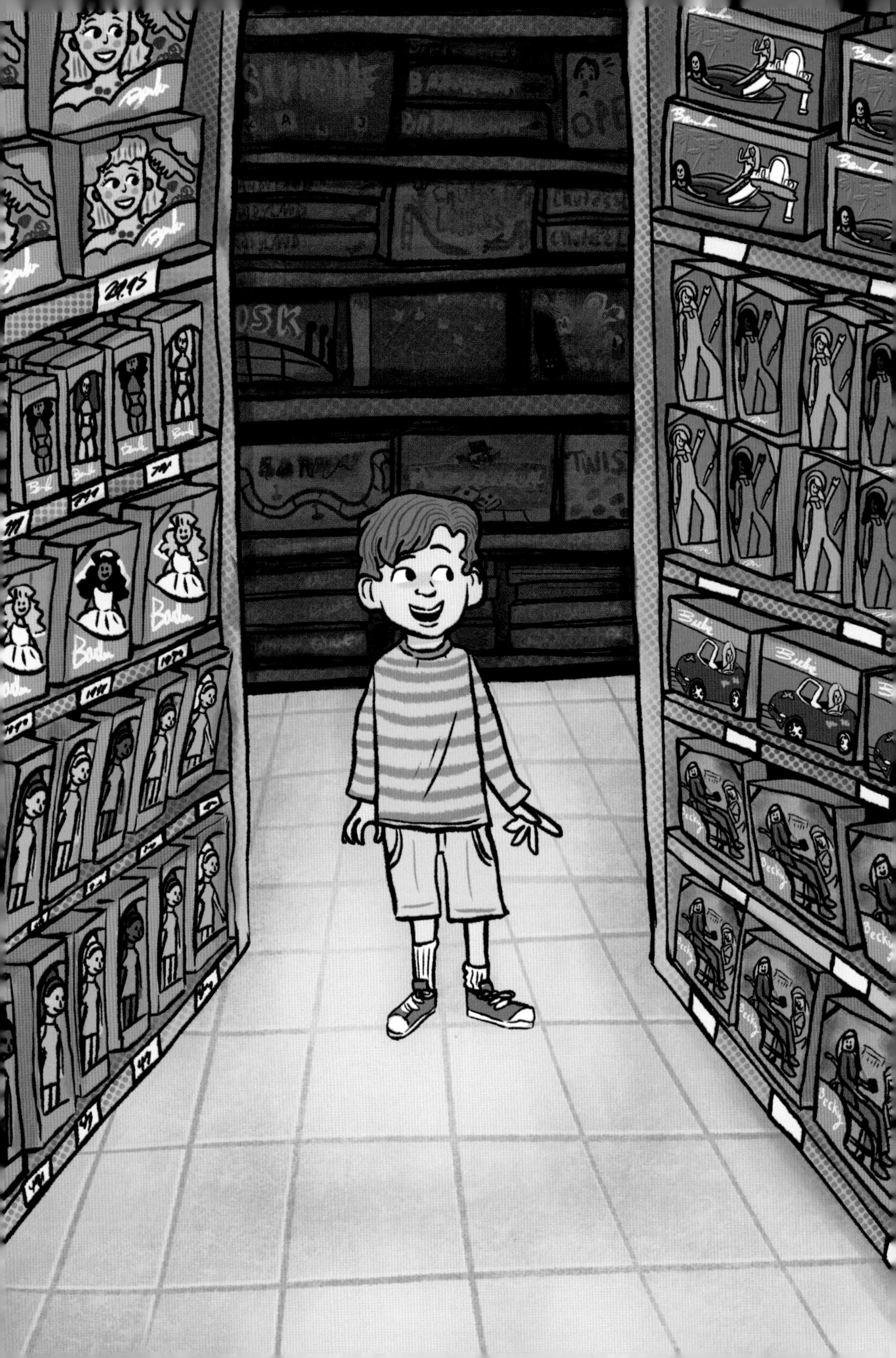
Becky

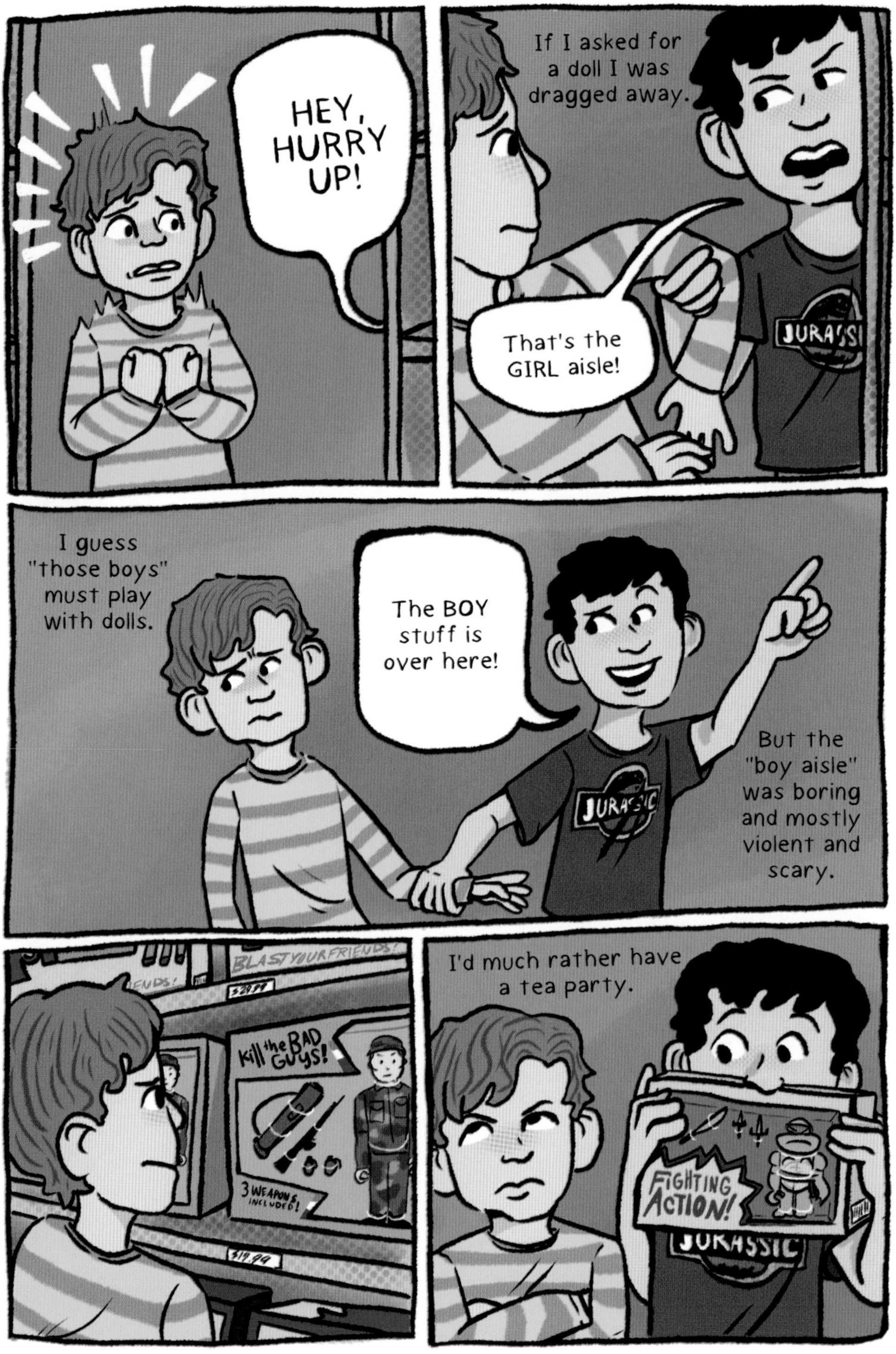
HEY, HURRY UP!
If I asked for a doll I was dragged away.
That's the GIRL aisle!
JURASSI
I guess "those boys" must play with dolls.
The BOY stuff is over here!
But the "boy aisle" was boring and mostly violent and scary.
JURASSIC
BLAST YOUR FRIENDS!
kill the BAD GUYS!
3 WEAPONS INCLUDED!
I'd much rather have a tea party.
FIGHTING ACTION!
JURASSIC

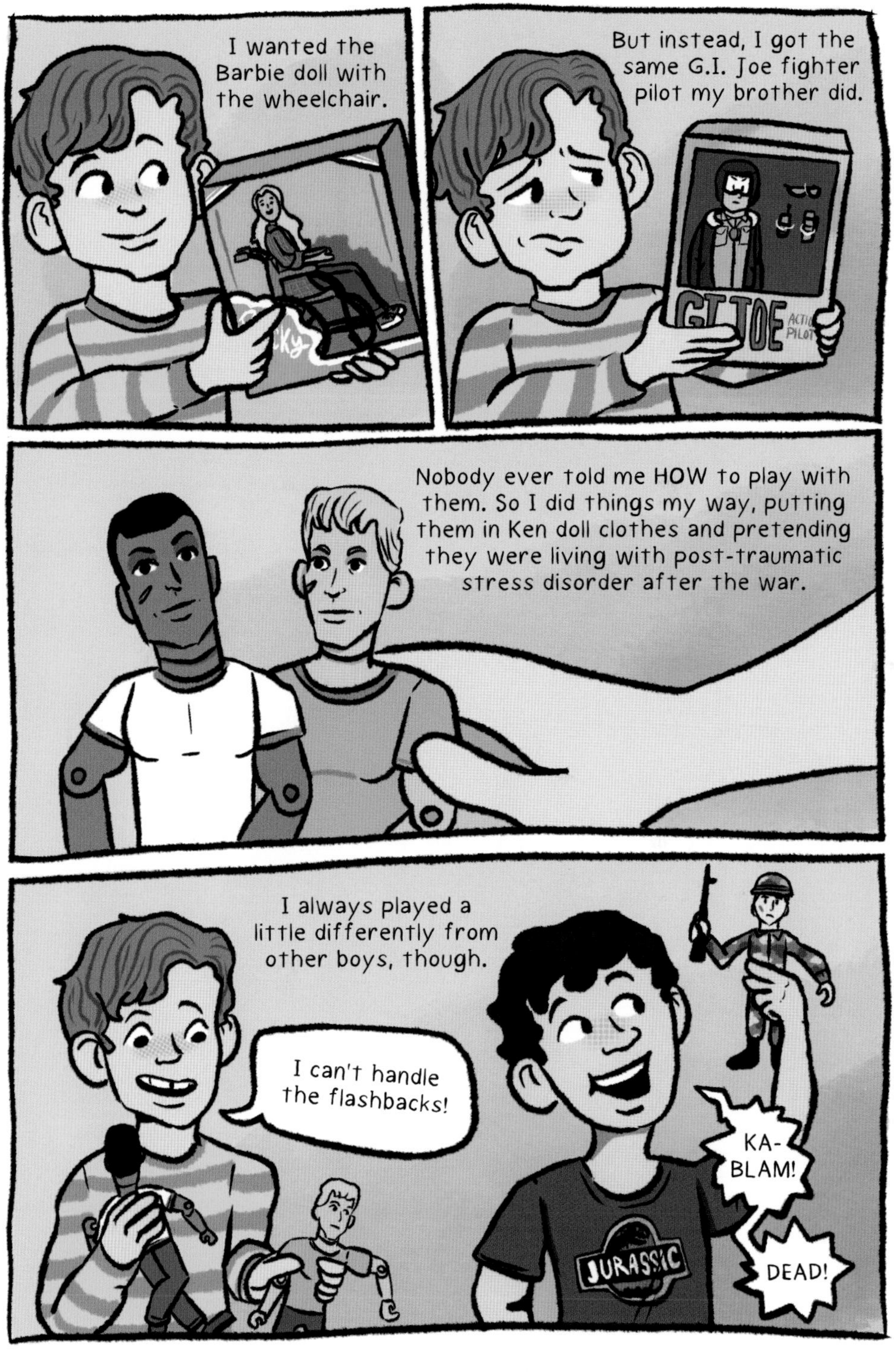
I wanted the Barbie doll with the wheelchair.
But instead, I got the same G.I. Joe fighter pilot my brother did.
GI JOE
Nobody ever told me HOW to play with them. So I did things my way, putting them in Ken doll clothes and pretending they were living with post-traumatic stress disorder after the war.
I always played a little differently from other boys, though.
I can't handle the flashbacks!
KA-BLAM!
DEAD!
JURASSIC

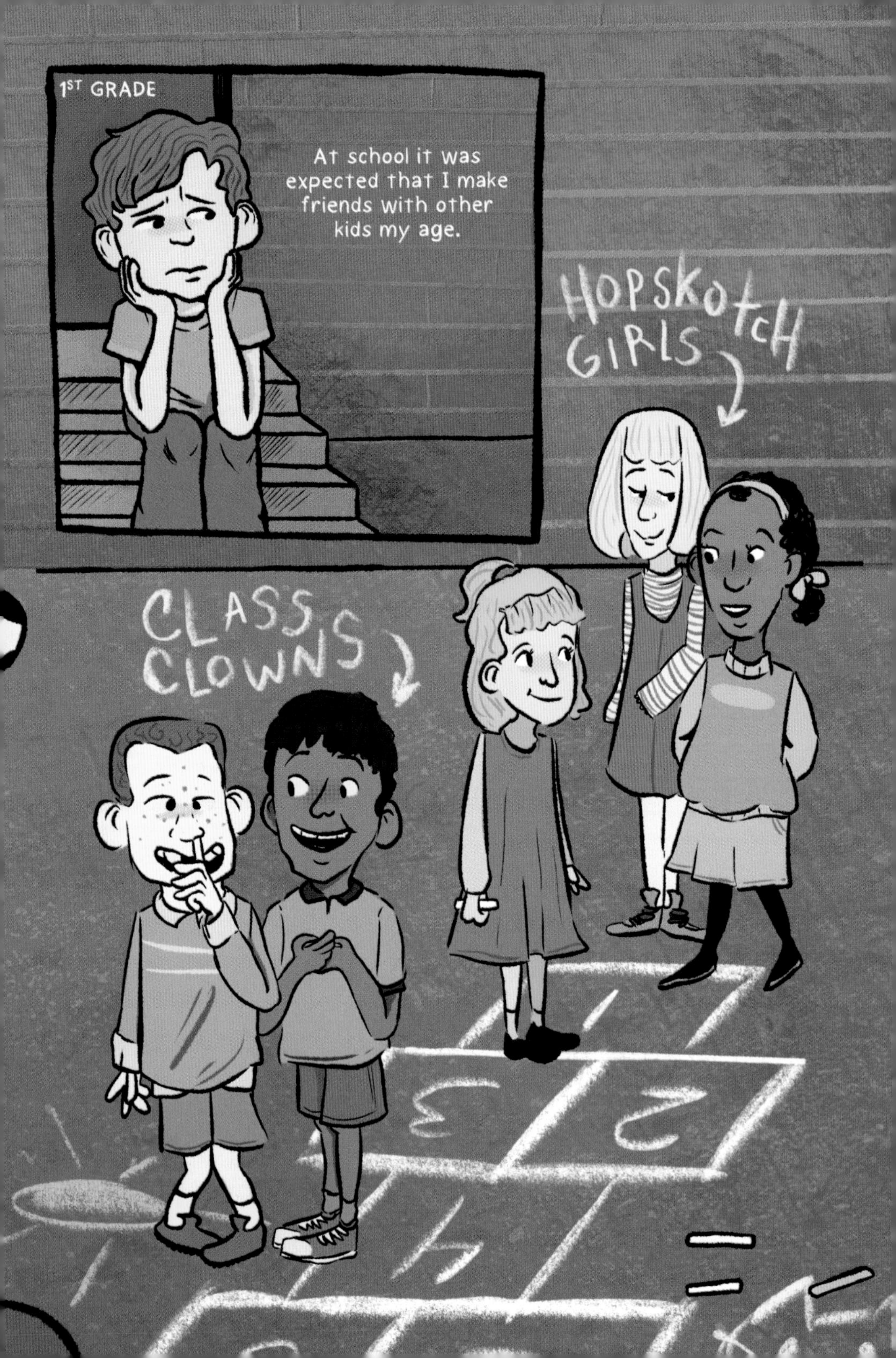
1ST GRADE
At school it was expected that I make friends with other kids my age.
HOPSKOTCH GIRLS
CLASS CLOWNS
3
2
4

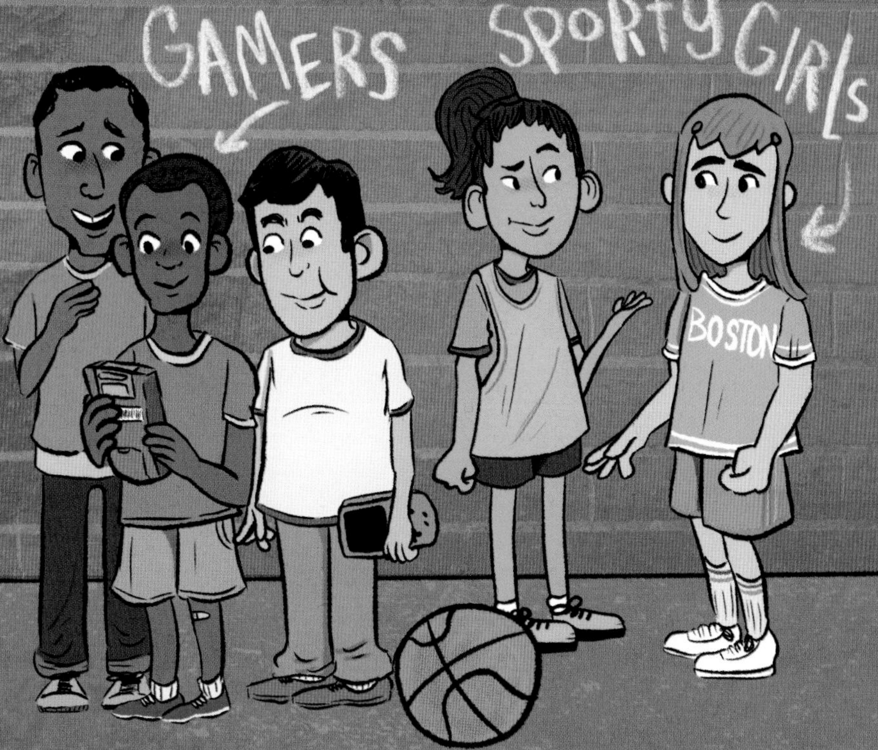
GAMERS
SPORTY GIRLS
BOSTON

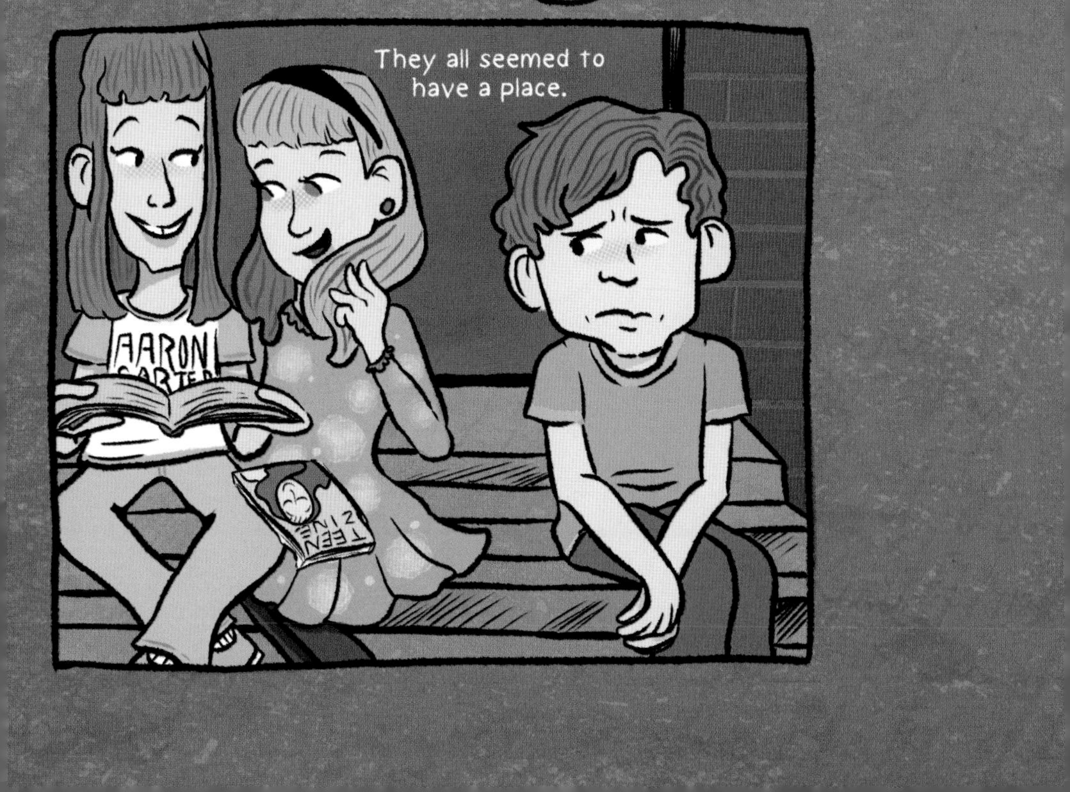
They all seemed to have a place.
AARON

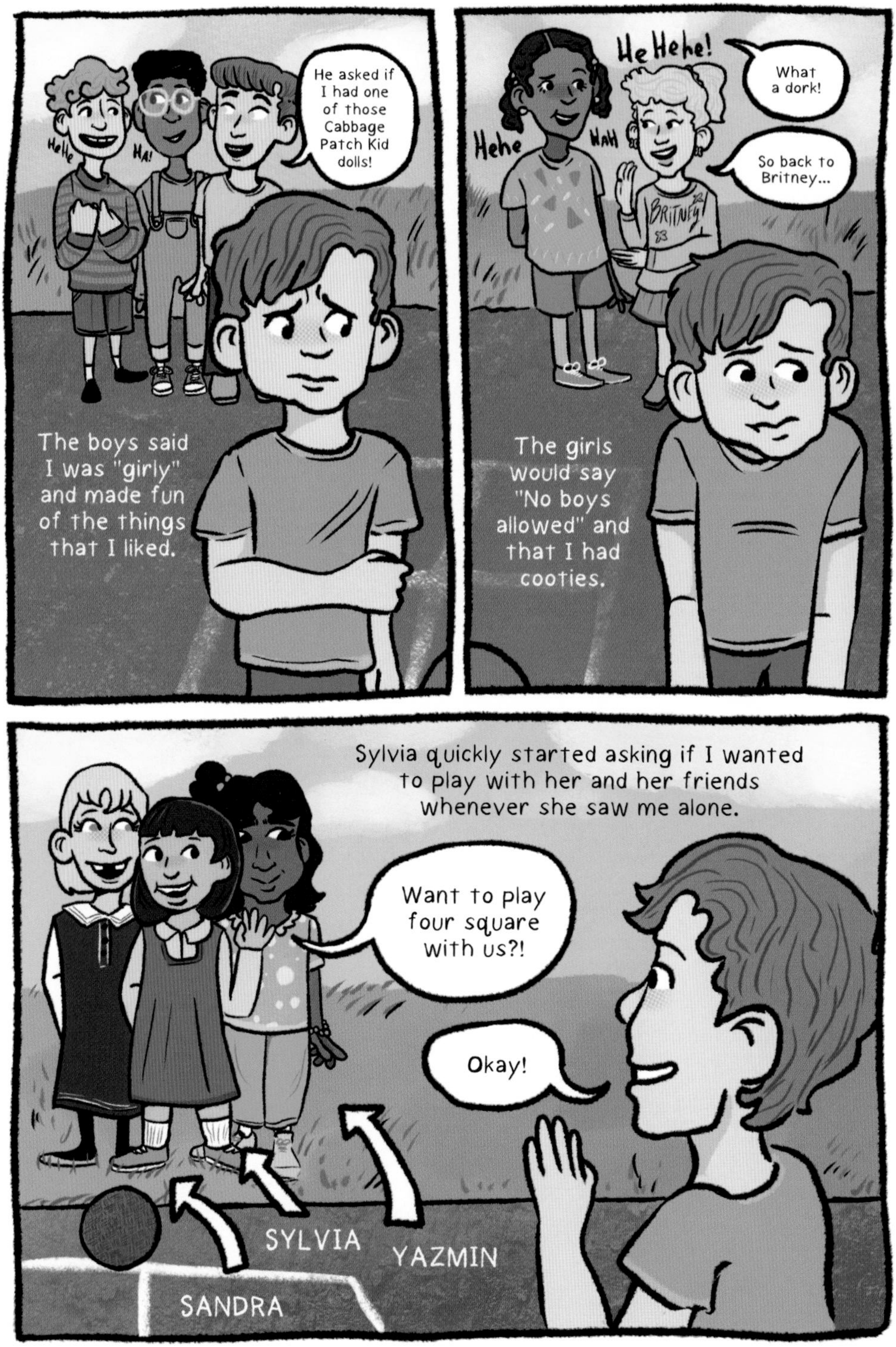
HeHe
HA!
He asked if I had one of those Cabbage Patch Kid dolls!
The boys said I was "girly" and made fun of the things that I liked.
He Hehe!
What a dork!
Hehe
WAH
So back to Britney...
BRITNEY
The girls would say "No boys allowed" and that I had cooties.
Sylvia quickly started asking if I wanted to play with her and her friends whenever she saw me alone.
Want to play four square with us?!
Okay!
SYLVIA
YAZMIN
SANDRA

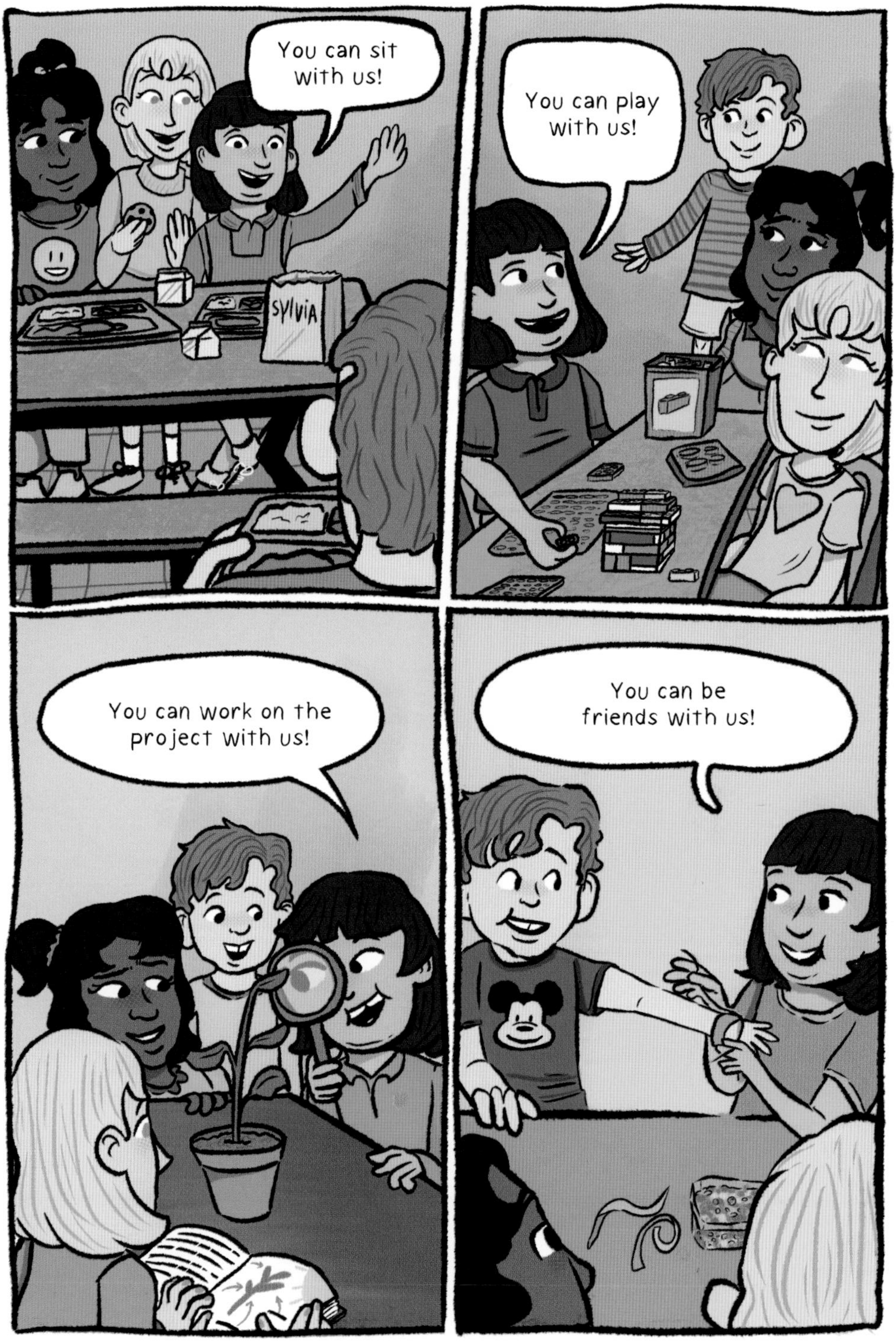
You can sit with us!
SYLVIA
You can play with us!
You can work on the project with us!
You can be friends with us!

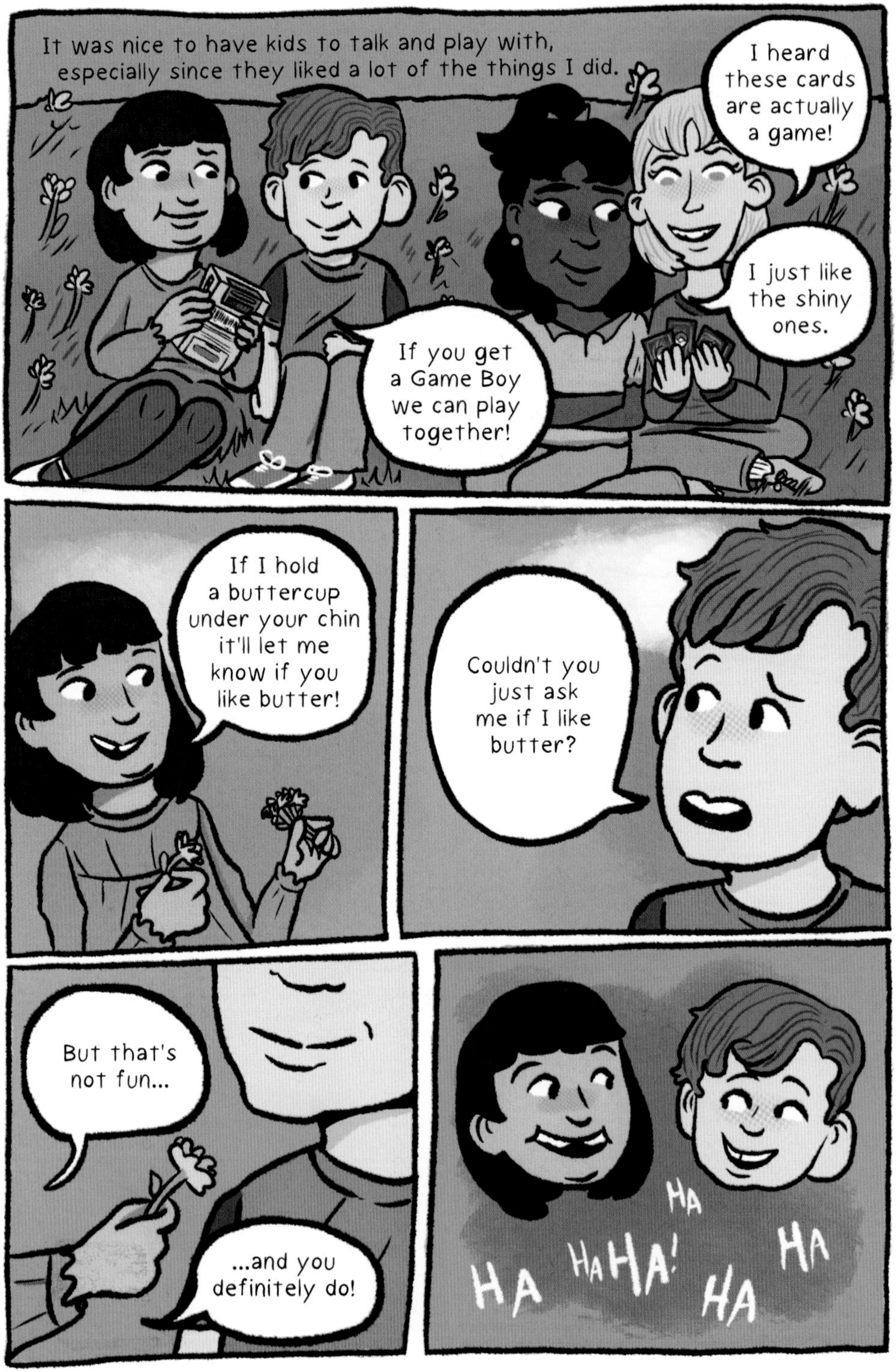

It was nice to have kids to talk and play with, especially since they liked a lot of the things I did.
I heard these cards are actually a game!
I just like the shiny ones.
If you get a Game Boy we can play together!
If I hold a buttercup under your chin it'll let me know if you like butter!
Couldn't you just ask me if I like butter?
But that's not fun...
...and you definitely do!
HA
HA HA HA!
HA
HA
HA

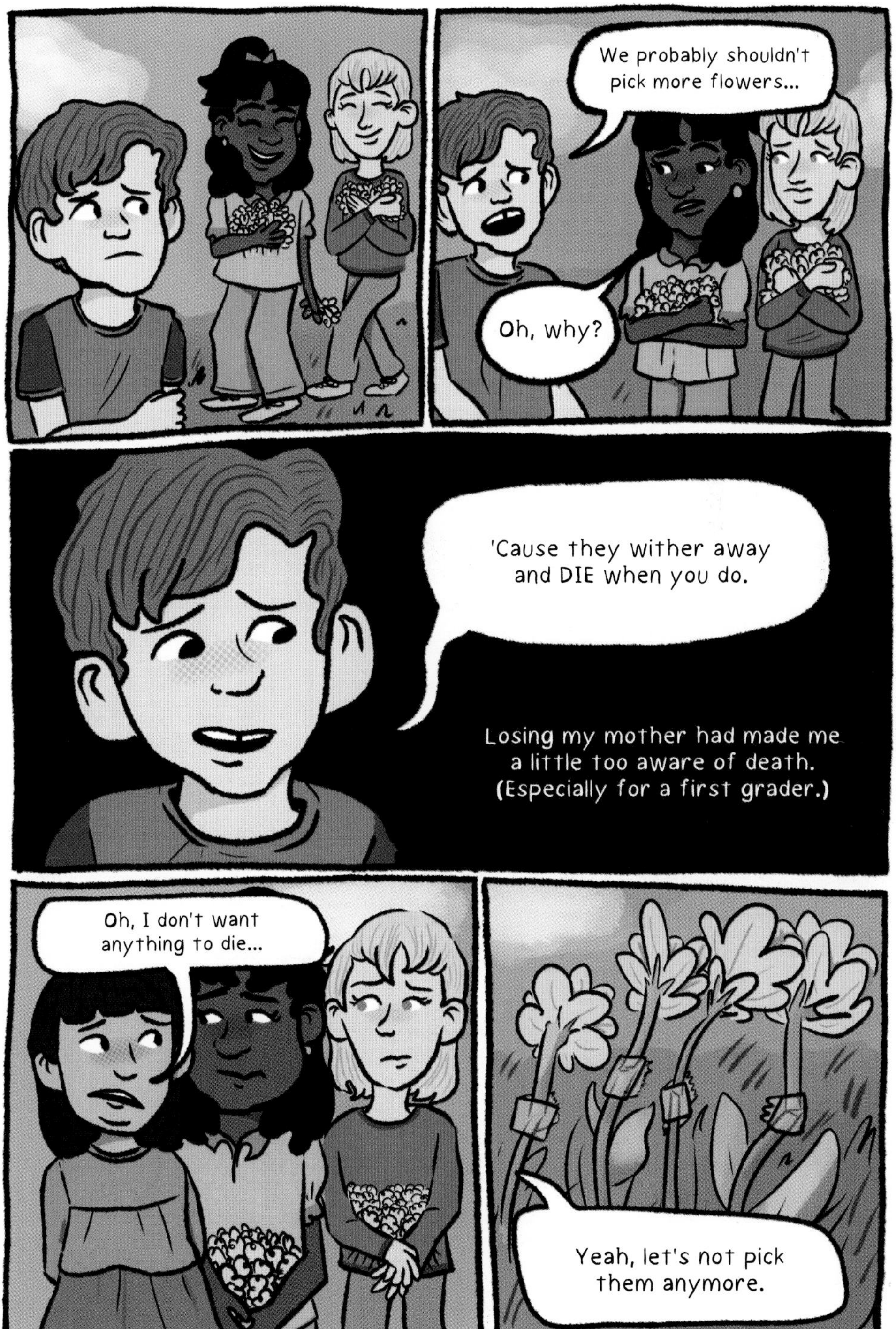
We probably shouldn't pick more flowers...
Oh, why?
'Cause they wither away and DIE when you do.
Losing my mother had made me a little too aware of death. (Especially for a first grader.)
Oh, I don't want anything to die...
Yeah, let's not pick them anymore.

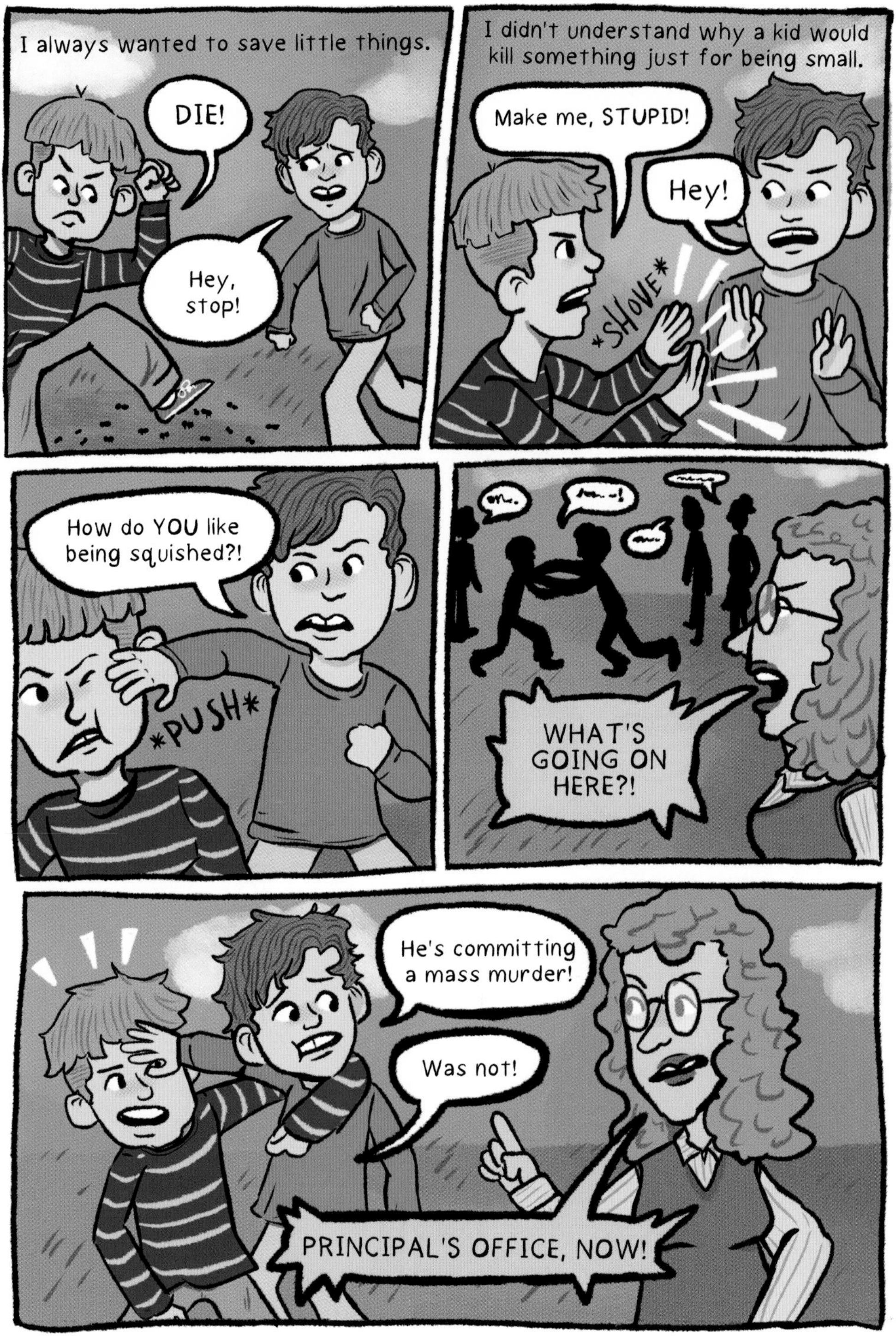
I always wanted to save little things.
DIE!
Hey, stop!
I didn't understand why a kid would kill something just for being small.
Make me, STUPID!
Hey!
SHOVE
How do YOU like being squished?!
PUSH
WHAT'S GOING ON HERE?!
He's committing a mass murder!
Was not!
PRINCIPAL'S OFFICE, NOW!

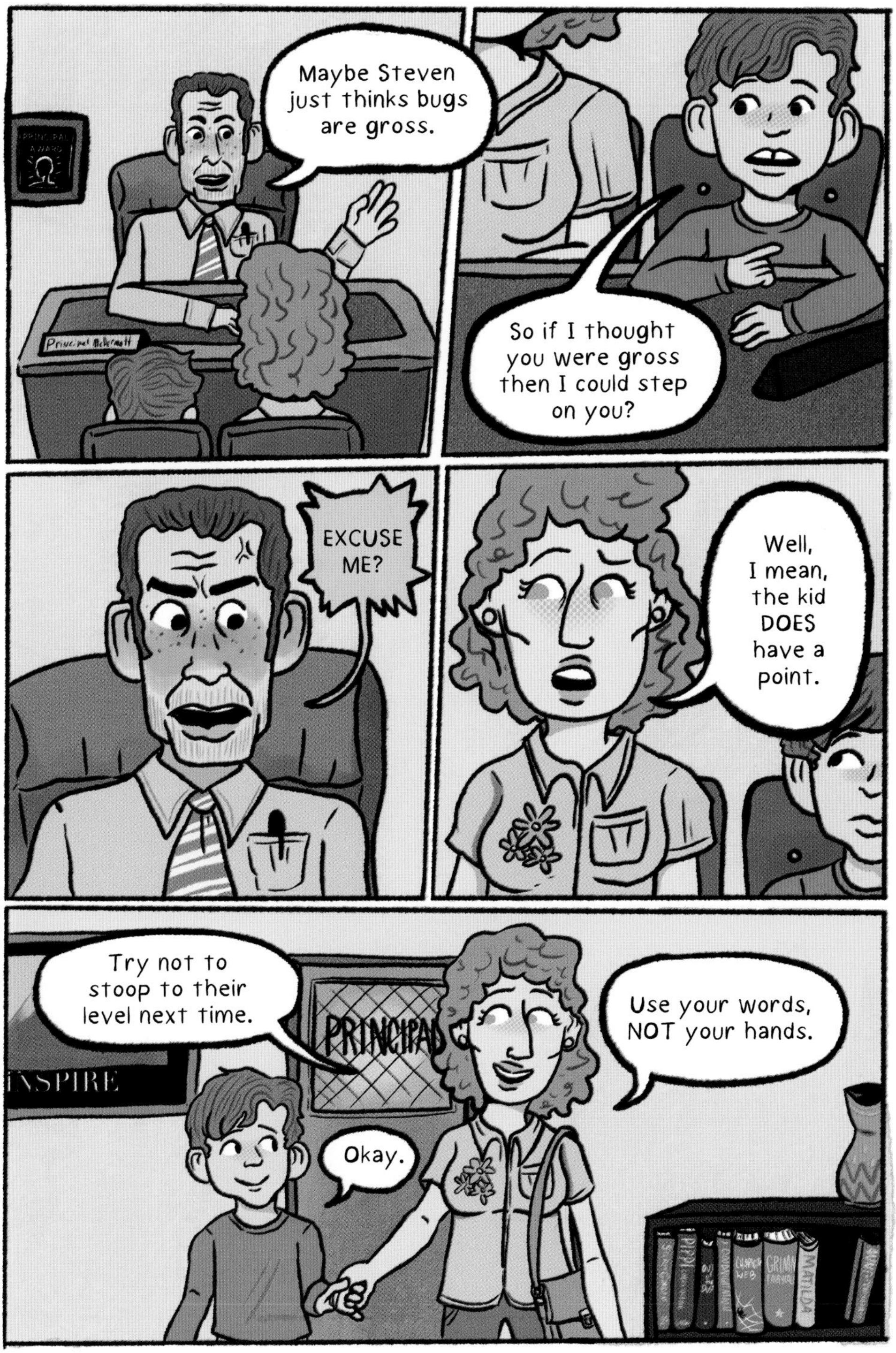
PRINCIPAL AWARD
Maybe Steven just thinks bugs are gross.
Principal McDermott
So if I thought you were gross then I could step on you?
EXCUSE ME?
Well, I mean, the kid DOES have a point.
Try not to stoop to their level next time.
PRINCIPAL
INSPIRE
Use your words, NOT your hands.
Okay.
CHARLOTTE'S WEB
MATILDA

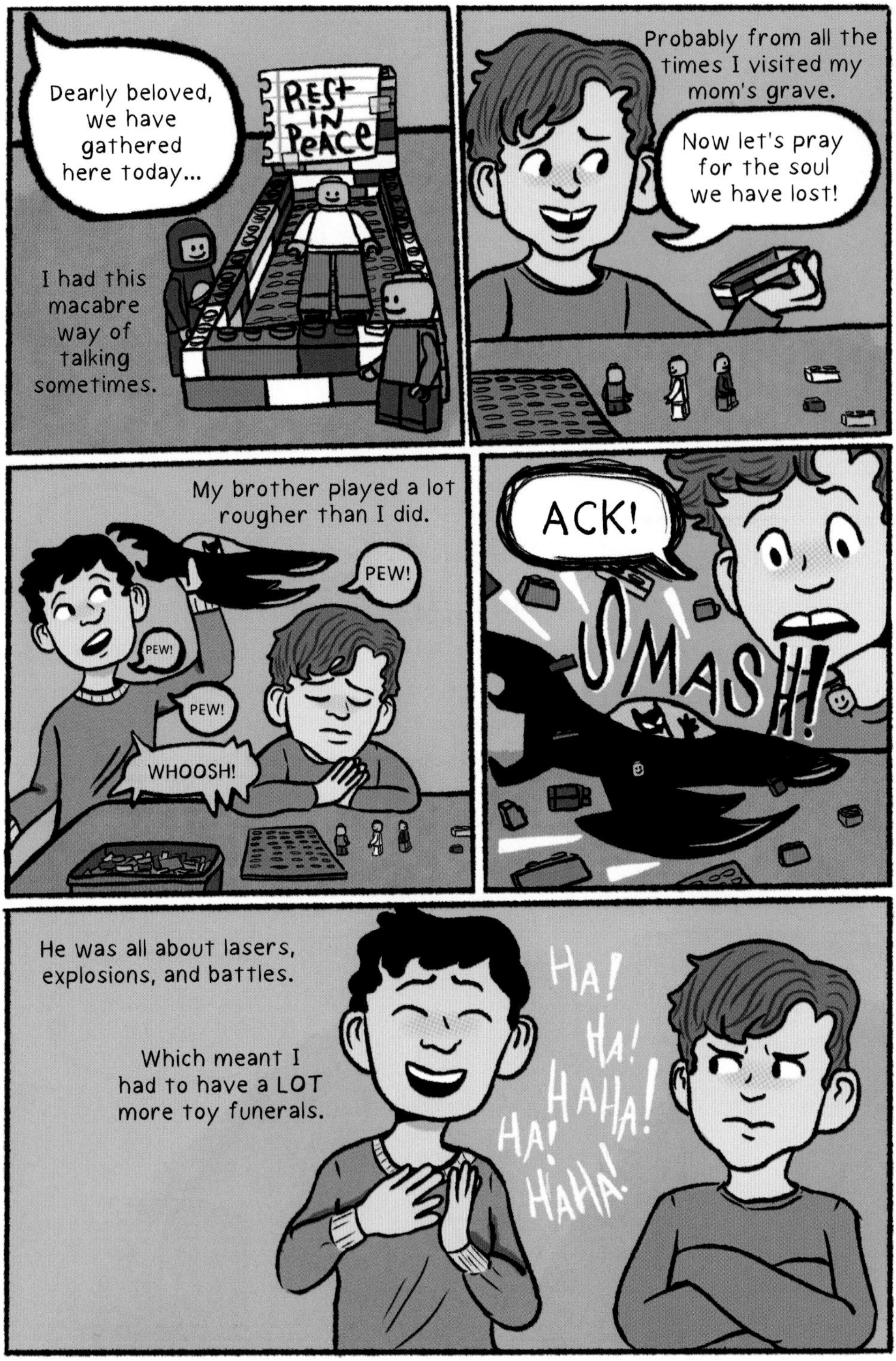
Dearly beloved, we have gathered here today...
REST IN PEACE
I had this macabre way of talking sometimes.
Probably from all the times I visited my mom's grave.
Now let's pray for the soul we have lost!
My brother played a lot rougher than I did.
PEW!
PEW!
PEW!
WHOOSH!
ACK!
SMASH!
He was all about lasers, explosions, and battles.
Which meant I had to have a LOT more toy funerals.
HA! HA! HAHA! HA! HAHA!

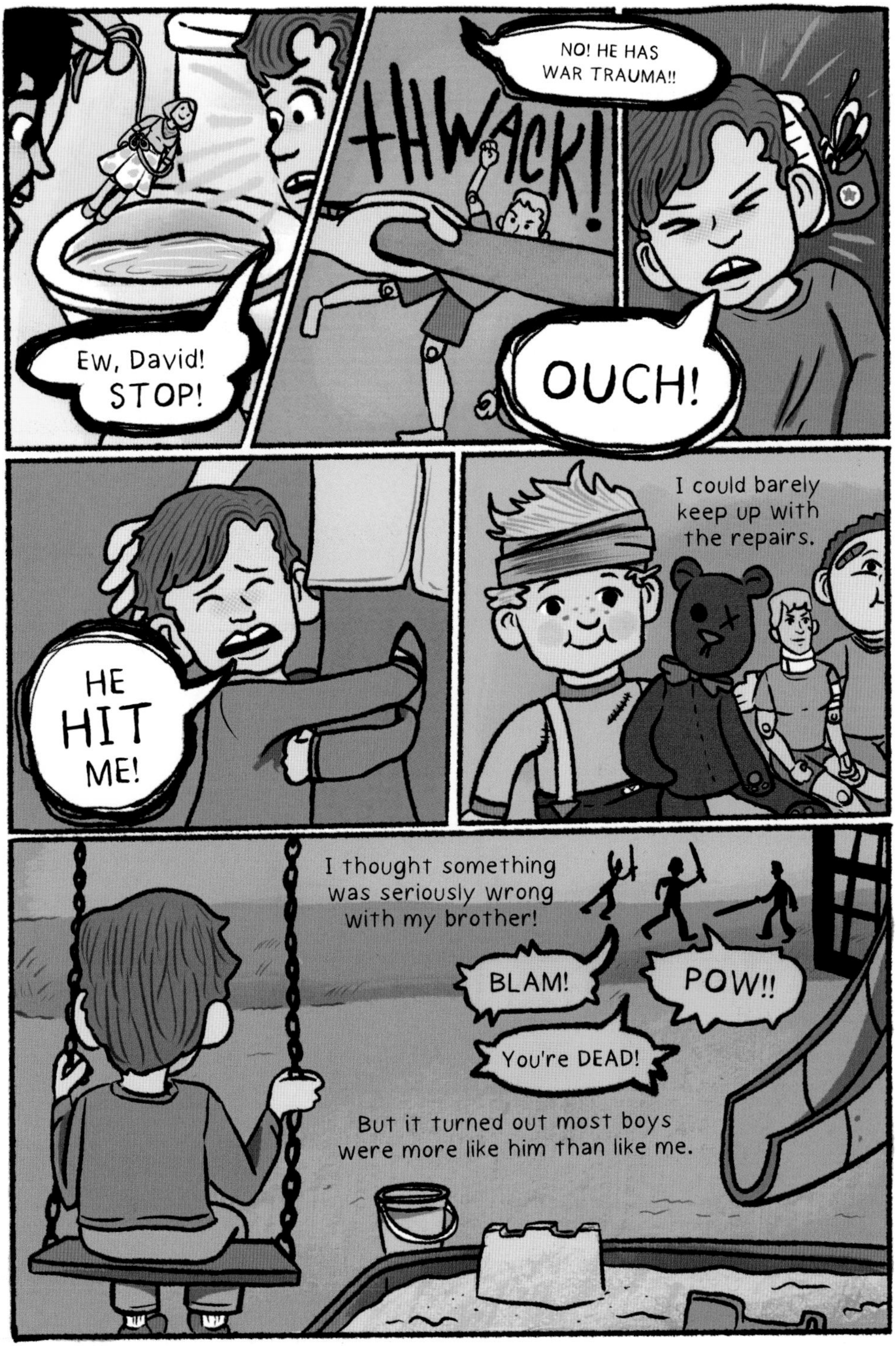
Ew, David! STOP!
THWACK!
NO! HE HAS WAR TRAUMA!!
OUCH!
HE HIT ME!
I could barely keep up with the repairs.
I thought something was seriously wrong with my brother!
BLAM!
POW!!
You're DEAD!
But it turned out most boys were more like him than like me.

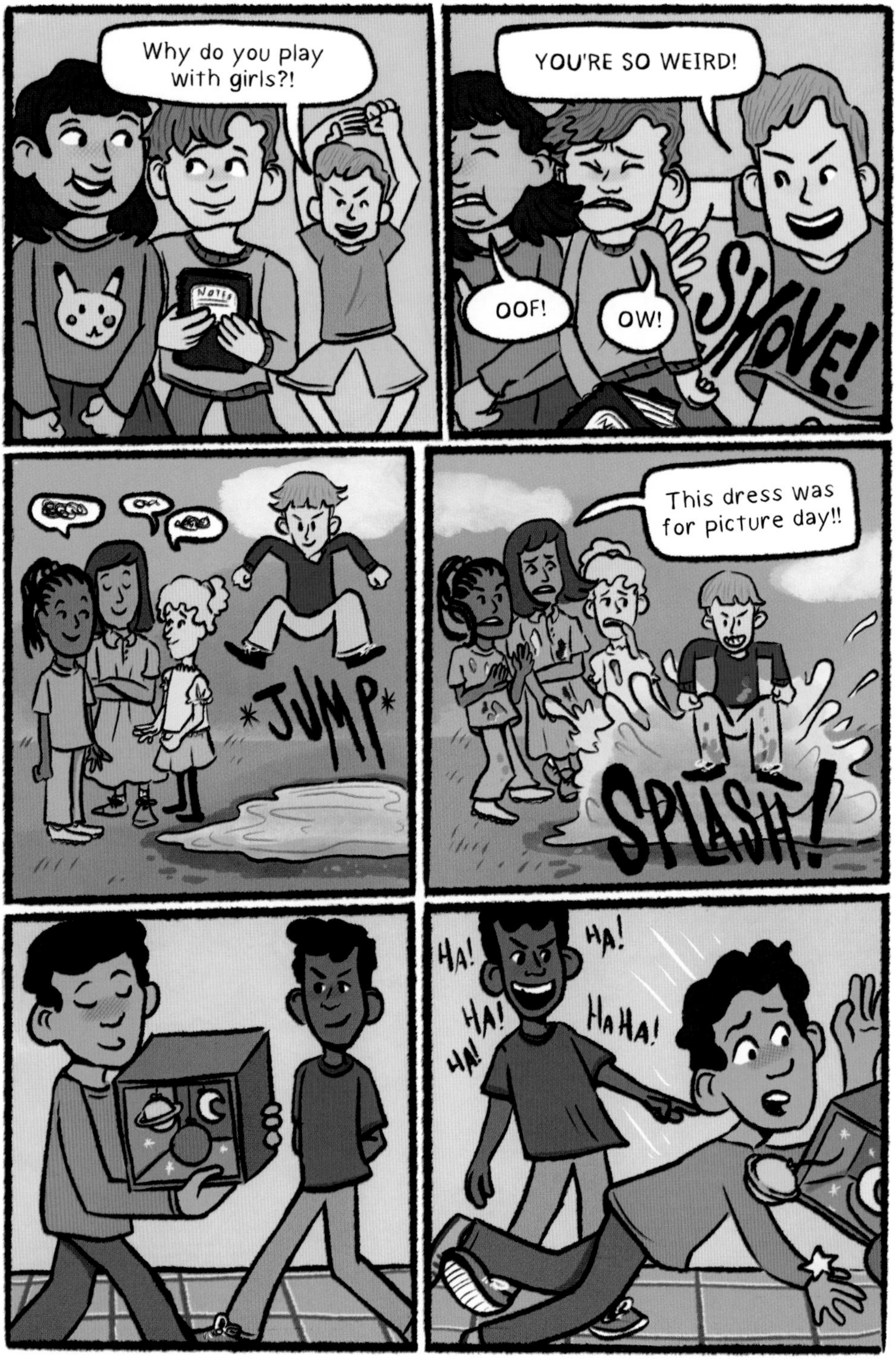
Why do you play with girls?!
YOU'RE SO WEIRD!
OOF!
OW!
SHOVE!
JUMP
This dress was for picture day!!
SPLASH!
HA!
HA!
HA!
HAHA!
HA!

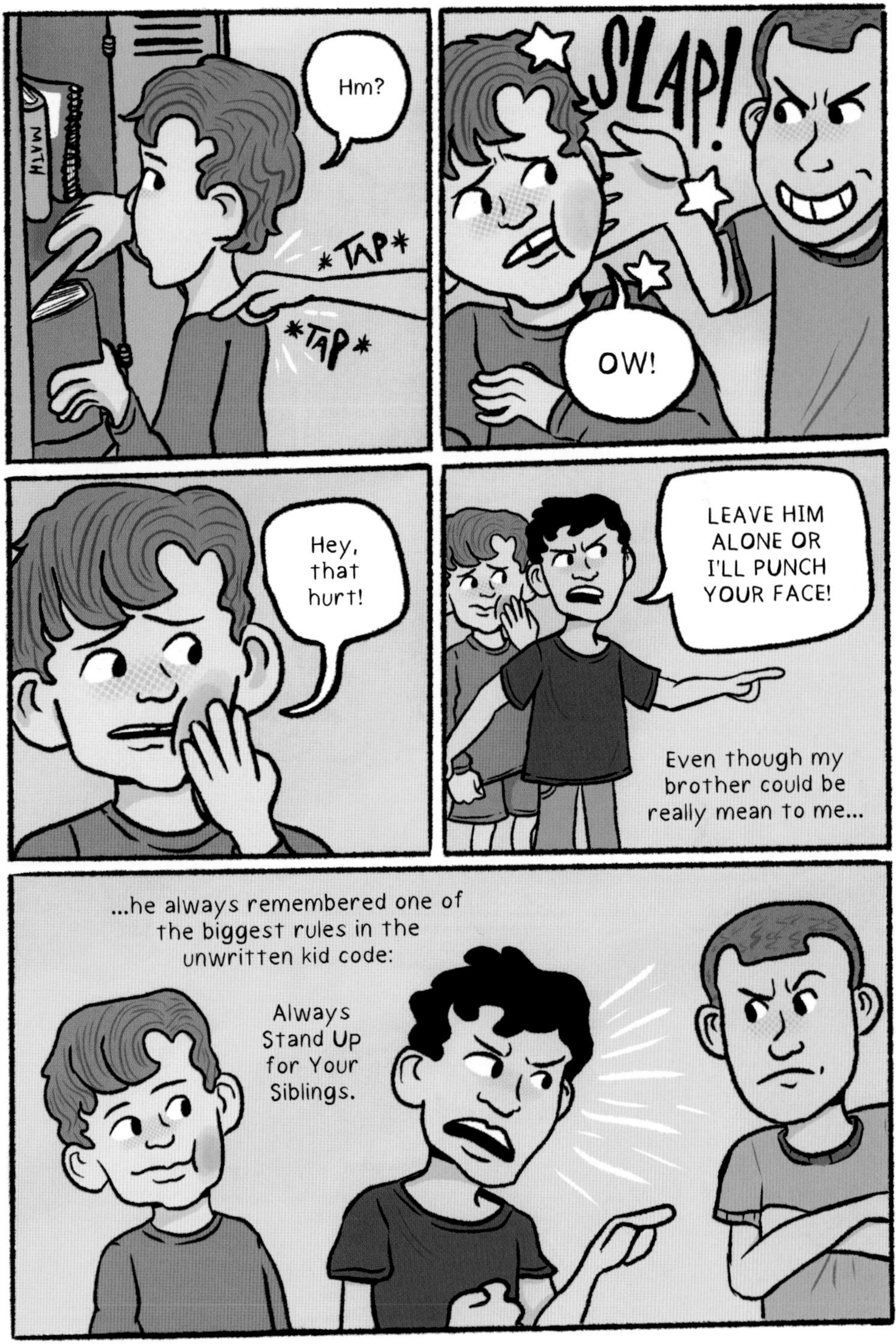
Hm?
TAP
TAP
SLAP!
OW!
Hey, that hurt!
LEAVE HIM ALONE OR I'LL PUNCH YOUR FACE!
Even though my brother could be really mean to me...
...he always remembered one of the biggest rules in the unwritten kid code:
Always Stand Up for Your Siblings.

Anytime a boy did something cruddy, a grown-up would say:

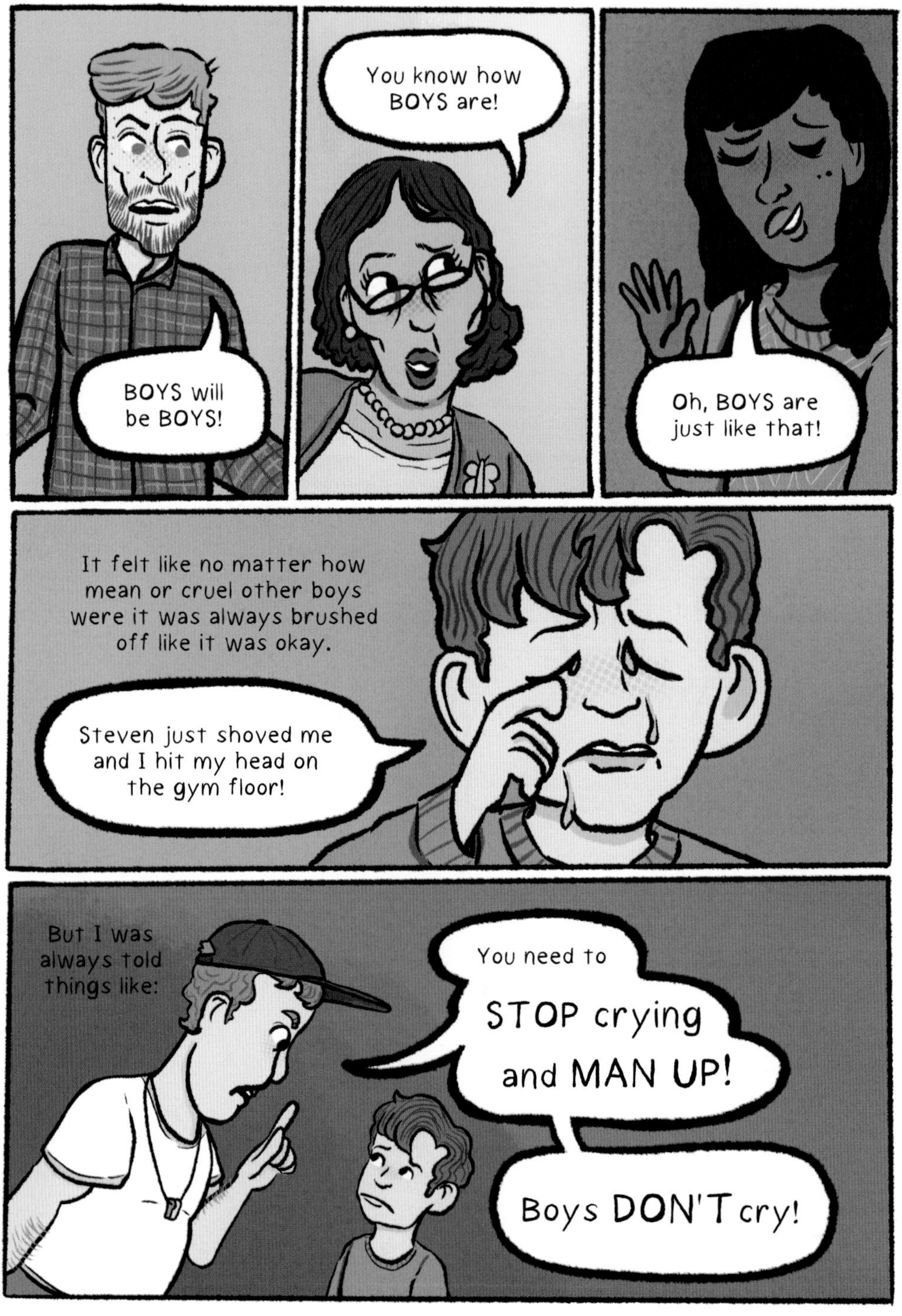
BOYS will be BOYS!
You know how BOYS are!
Oh, BOYS are just like that!
It felt like no matter how mean or cruel other boys were it was always brushed off like it was okay.
Steven just shoved me and I hit my head on the gym floor!
But I was always told things like:
You need to STOP crying and MAN UP!
Boys DON'T cry!

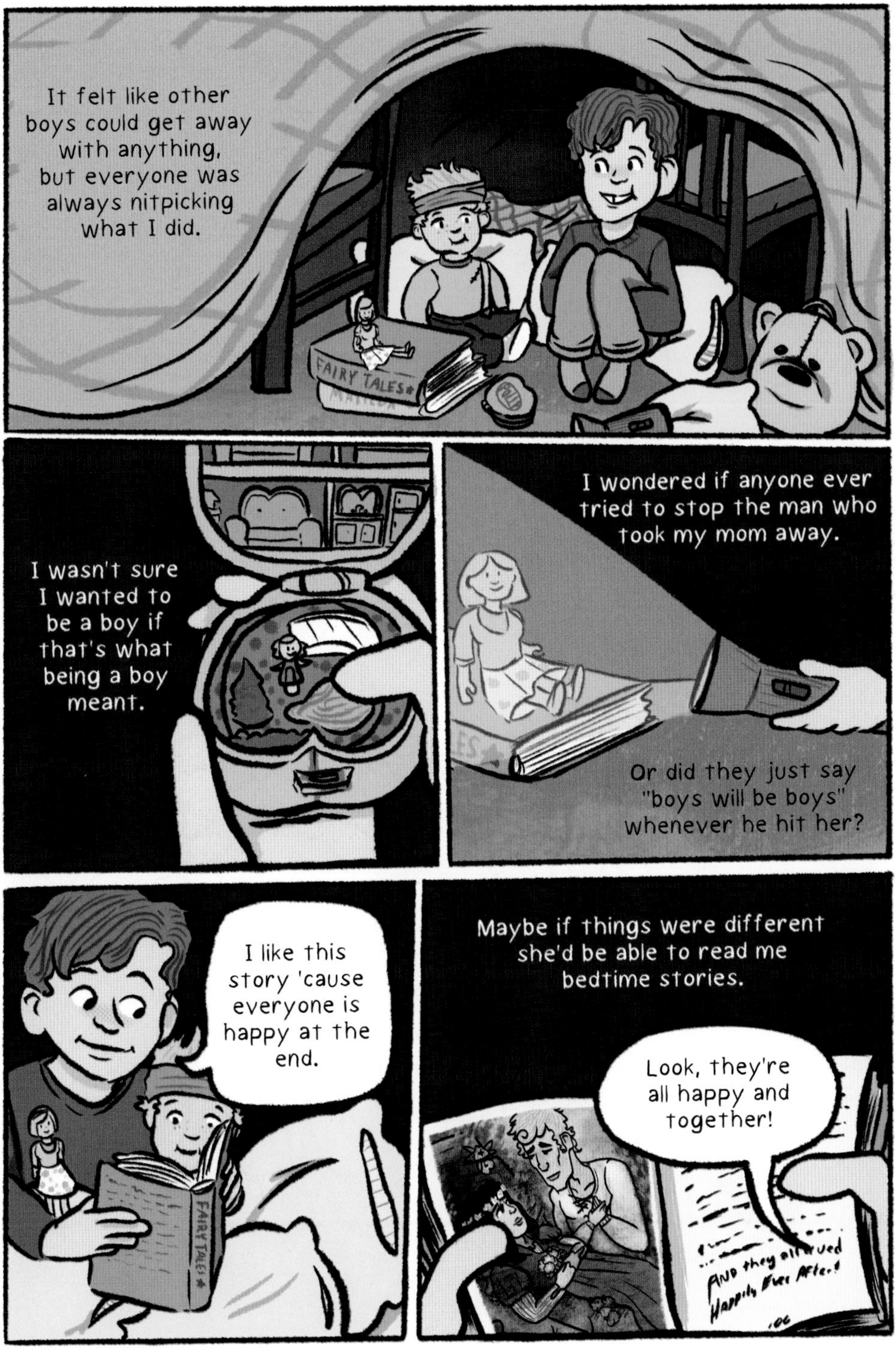
It felt like other boys could get away with anything, but everyone was always nitpicking what I did.
FAIRY TALES
I wasn't sure I wanted to be a boy if that's what being a boy meant.
I wondered if anyone ever tried to stop the man who took my mom away.
Or did they just say "boys will be boys" whenever he hit her?
I like this story 'cause everyone is happy at the end.
FAIRY TALES
Maybe if things were different she'd be able to read me bedtime stories.
Look, they're all happy and together!

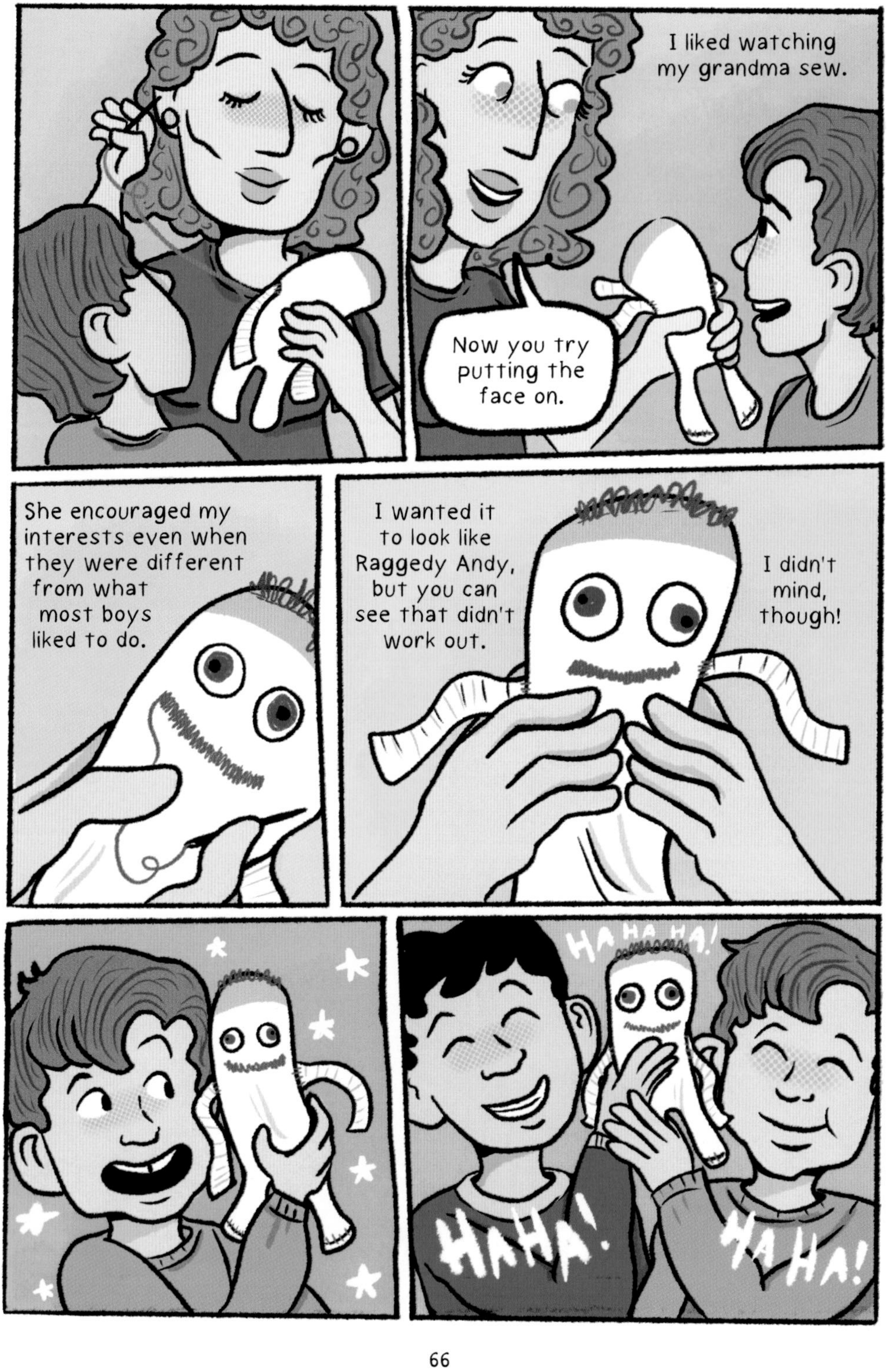
I liked watching my grandma sew.
Now you try putting the face on.
She encouraged my interests even when they were different from what most boys liked to do.
I wanted it to look like Raggedy Andy, but you can see that didn't work out.
I didn't mind, though!
HA HA HA!
HAHA!
HA HA!

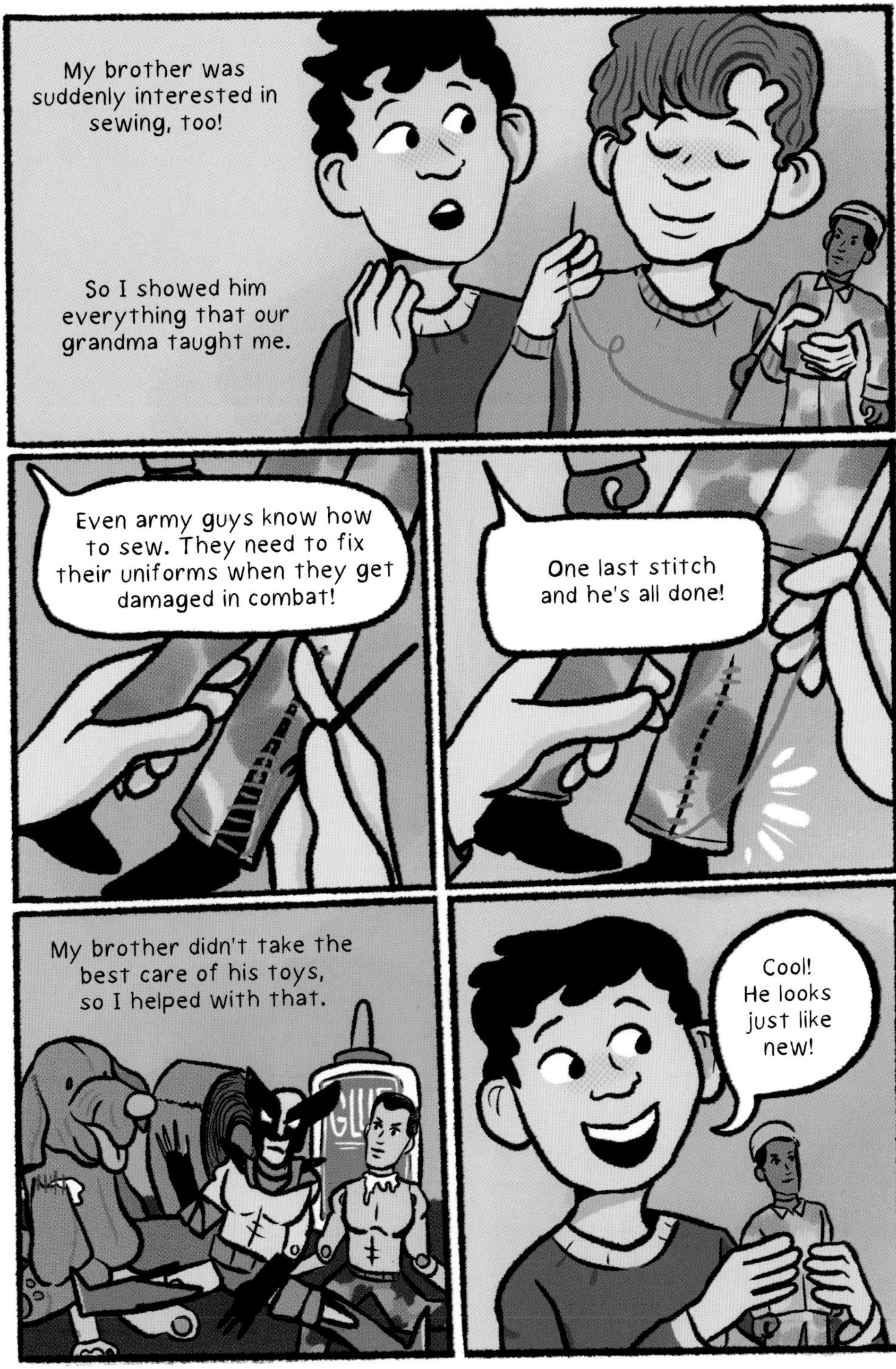
My brother was suddenly interested in sewing, too!
So I showed him everything that our grandma taught me.
Even army guys know how to sew. They need to fix their uniforms when they get damaged in combat!
One last stitch and he's all done!
My brother didn't take the best care of his toys, so I helped with that.
GLUE
Cool! He looks just like new!

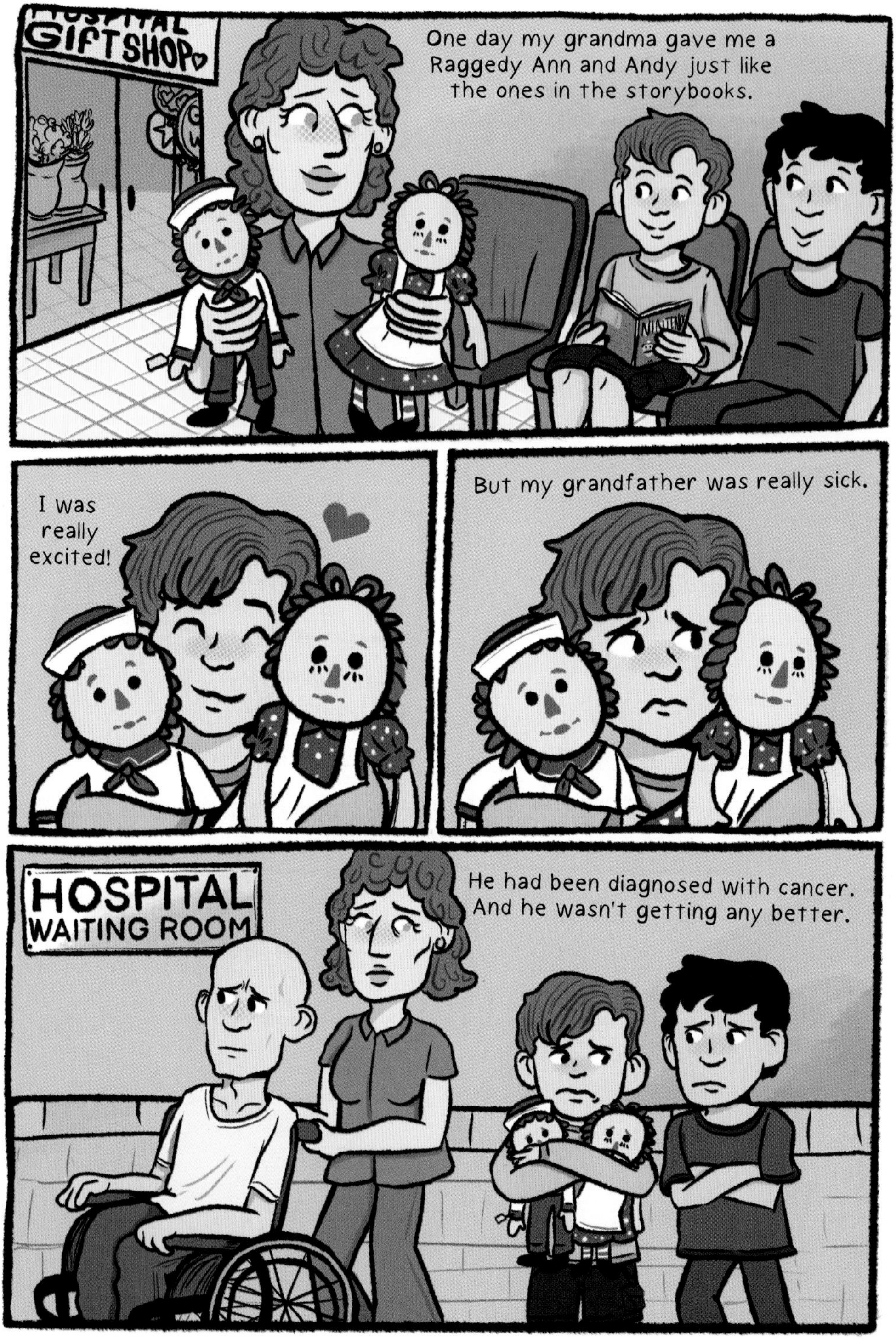
GIFTSHOP
One day my grandma gave me a Raggedy Ann and Andy just like the ones in the storybooks.
I was really excited!
But my grandfather was really sick.
HOSPITAL WAITING ROOM
He had been diagnosed with cancer. And he wasn't getting any better.

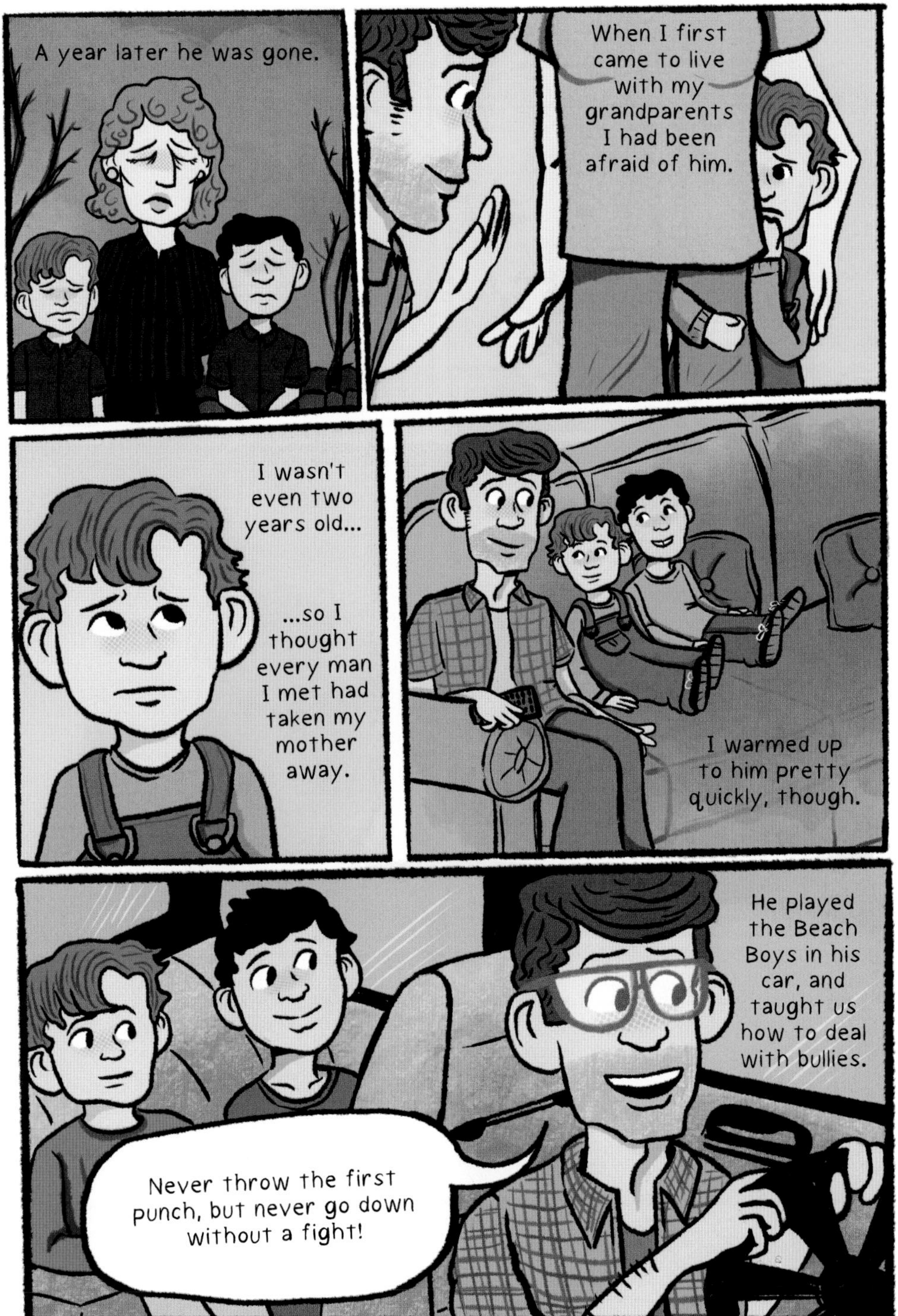
A year later he was gone.
When I first came to live with my grandparents I had been afraid of him.
I wasn't even two years old...
...so I thought every man I met had taken my mother away.
I warmed up to him pretty quickly, though.
He played the Beach Boys in his car, and taught us how to deal with bullies.
Never throw the first punch, but never go down without a fight!

He made the best dinners for us.

And he always took care of us if we got hurt playing outside.

My brother and I would wait to see how long it would take for him to fall asleep at the movies.

Sometimes he barely made it through the opening credits.

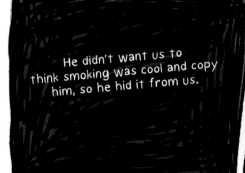

He didn't want us to think smoking was cool and copy him, so he hid it from us.

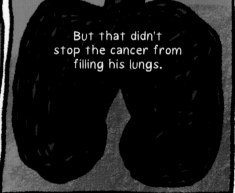

But that didn't stop the cancer from filling his lungs.

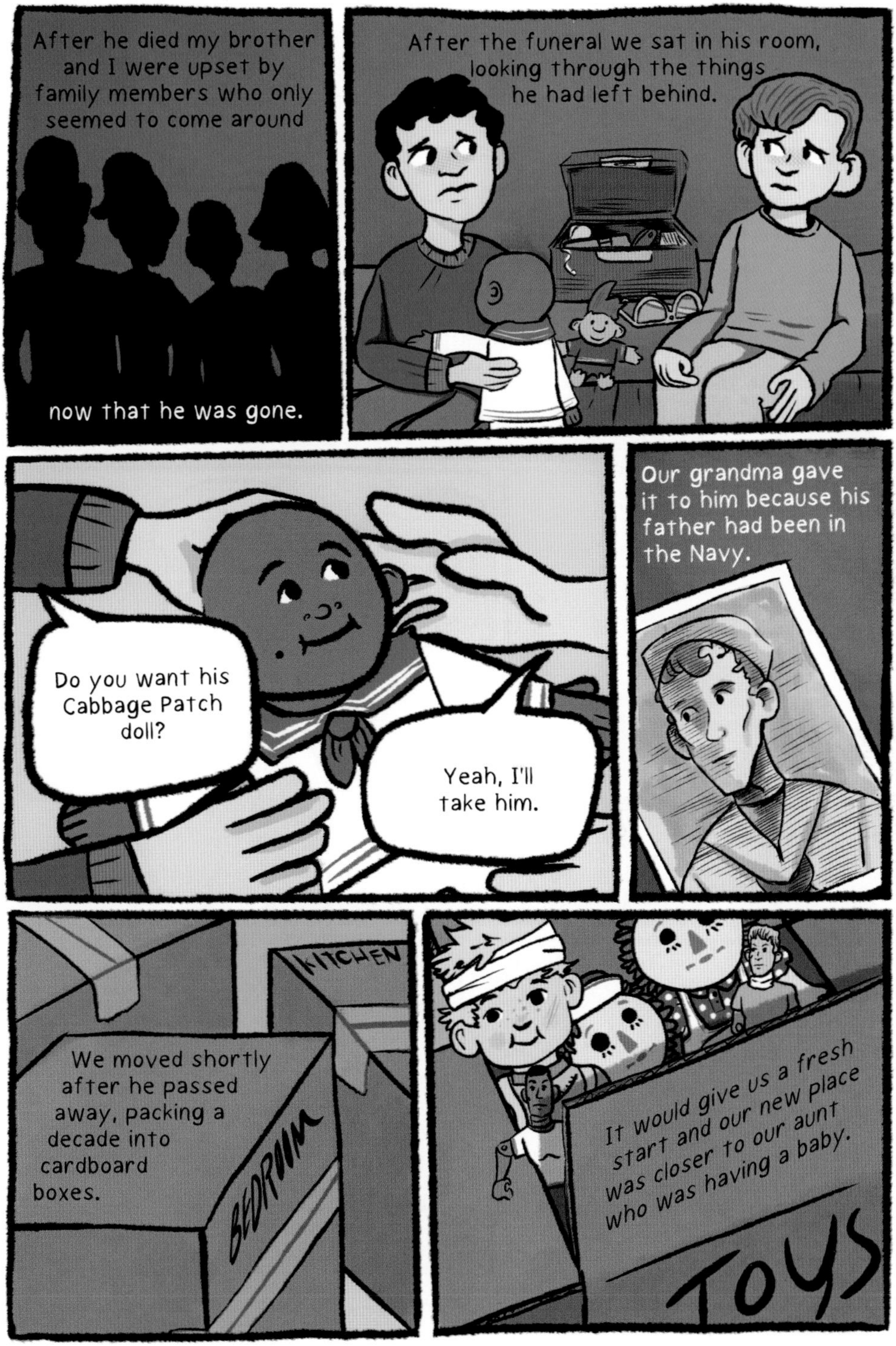
After he died my brother and I were upset by family members who only seemed to come around
now that he was gone.
After the funeral we sat in his room, looking through the things he had left behind.
Do you want his Cabbage Patch doll?
Yeah, I'll take him.
Our grandma gave it to him because his father had been in the Navy.
KITCHEN
We moved shortly after he passed away, packing a decade into cardboard boxes.
BEDROOM
It would give us a fresh start and our new place was closer to our aunt who was having a baby.
TOYS

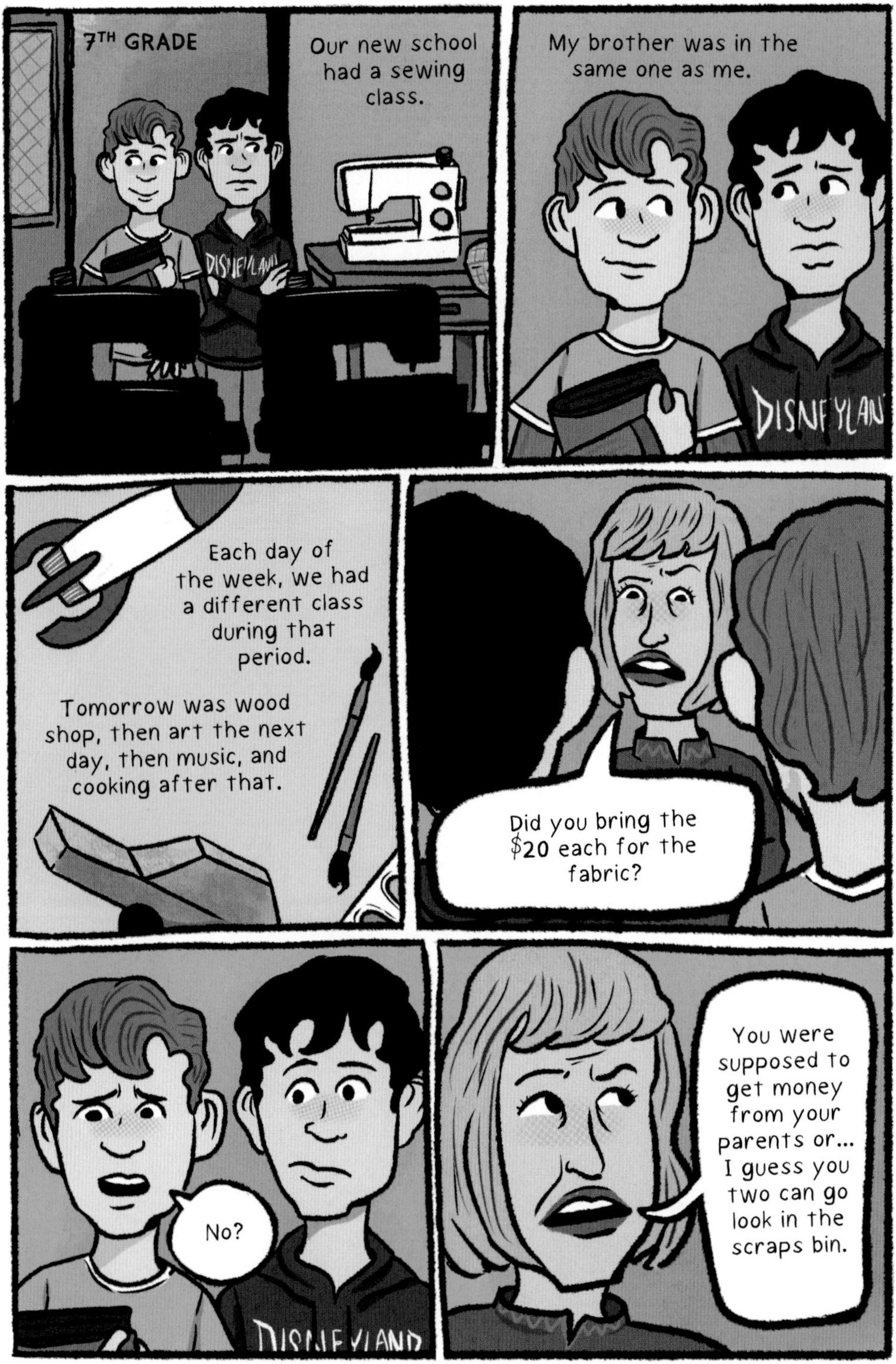
7TH GRADE
Our new school had a sewing class.
DISNEYLAND
My brother was in the same one as me.
DISNEYLAND
Each day of the week, we had a different class during that period.
Tomorrow was wood shop, then art the next day, then music, and cooking after that.
Did you bring the $20 each for the fabric?
No?
DISNEYLAND
You were supposed to get money from your parents or... I guess you two can go look in the scraps bin.

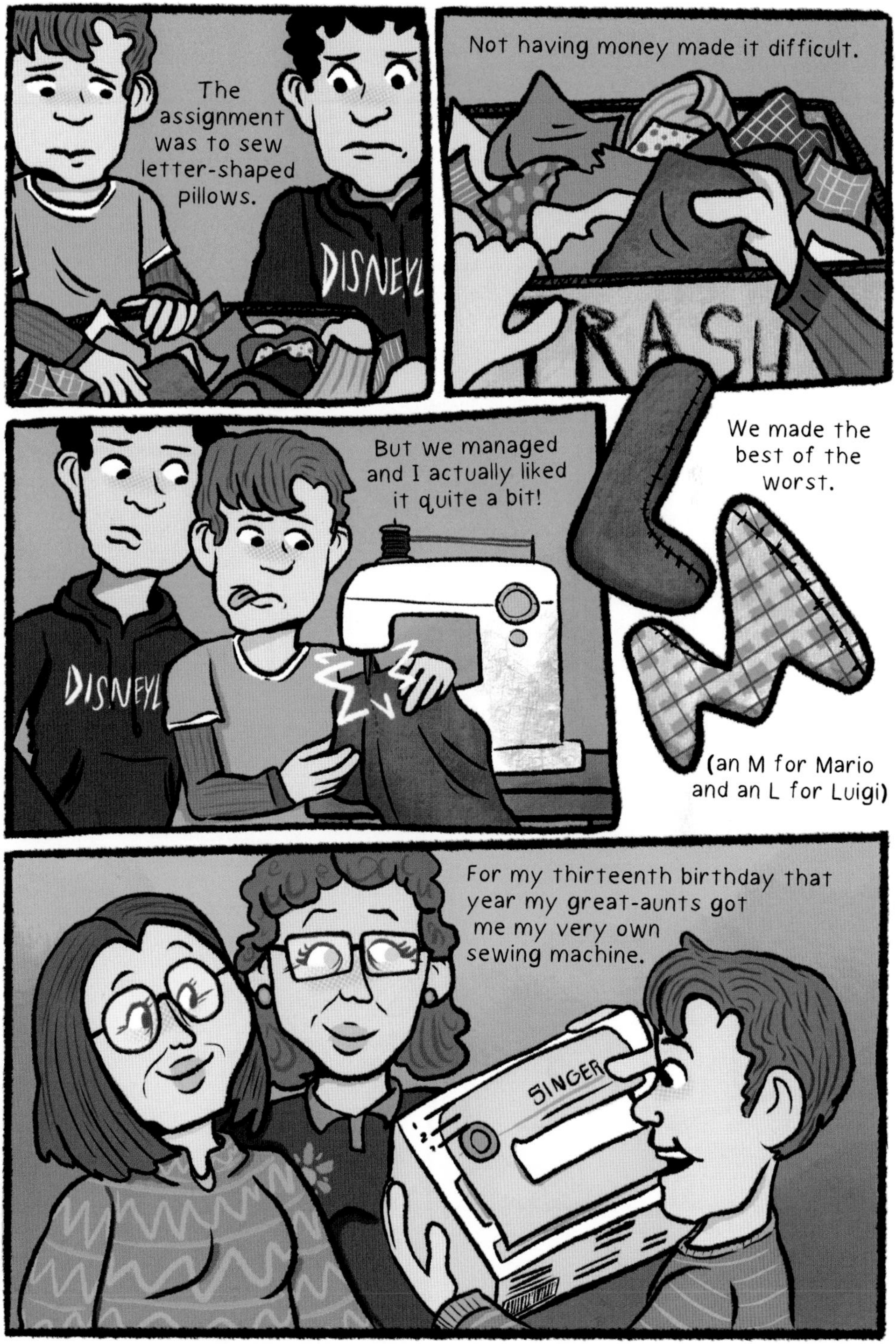
The assignment was to sew letter-shaped pillows.
DISNEYL
Not having money made it difficult.
TRASH
But we managed and I actually liked it quite a bit!
DISNEYL
We made the best of the worst.
(an M for Mario and an L for Luigi)
For my thirteenth birthday that year my great-aunts got me my very own sewing machine.
SINGER

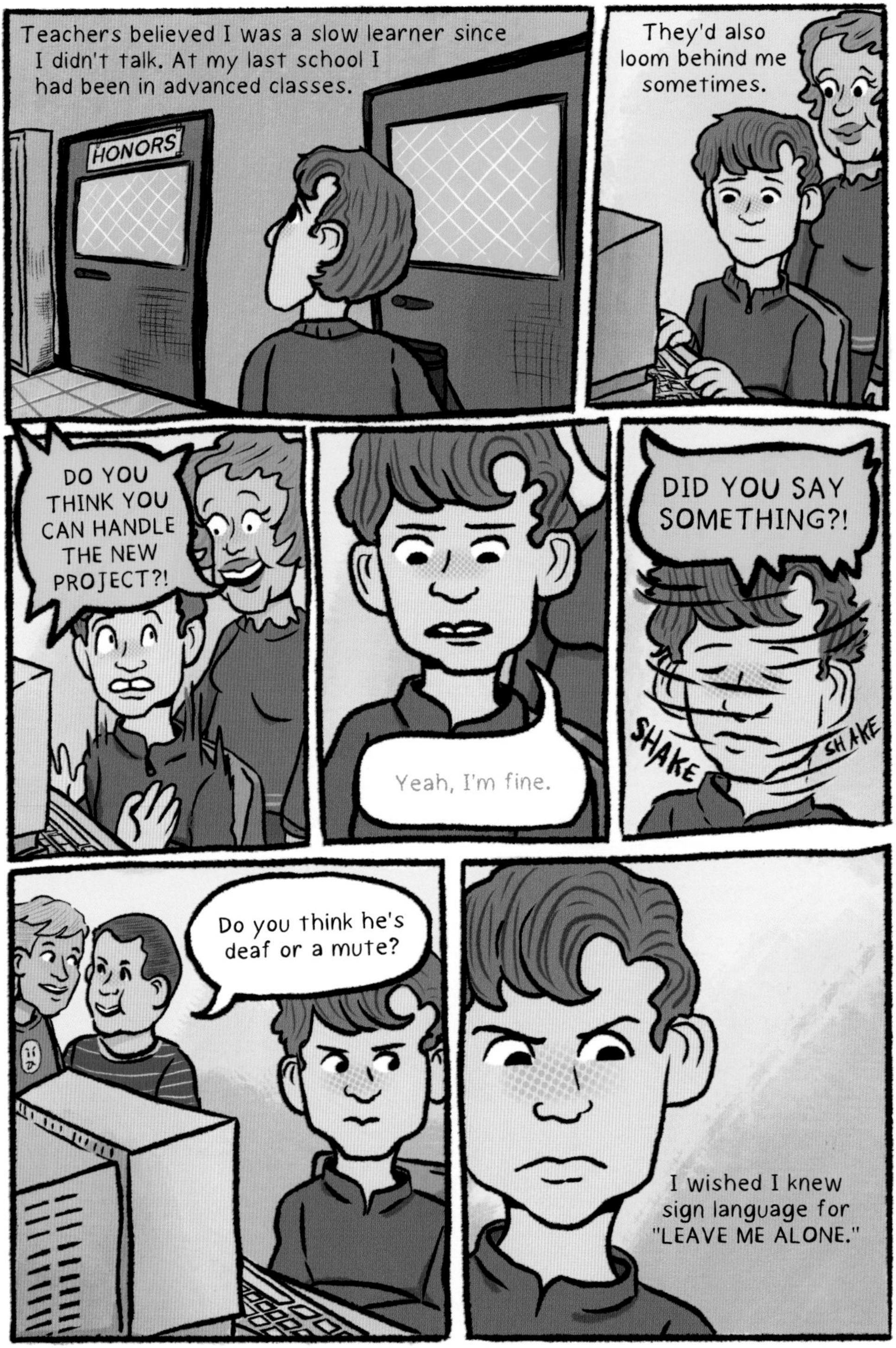
Teachers believed I was a slow learner since I didn't talk. At my last school I had been in advanced classes.
HONORS
They'd also loom behind me sometimes.
DO YOU THINK YOU CAN HANDLE THE NEW PROJECT?!
Yeah, I'm fine.
DID YOU SAY SOMETHING?!
SHAKE
SHAKE
Do you think he's deaf or a mute?
I wished I knew sign language for "LEAVE ME ALONE."

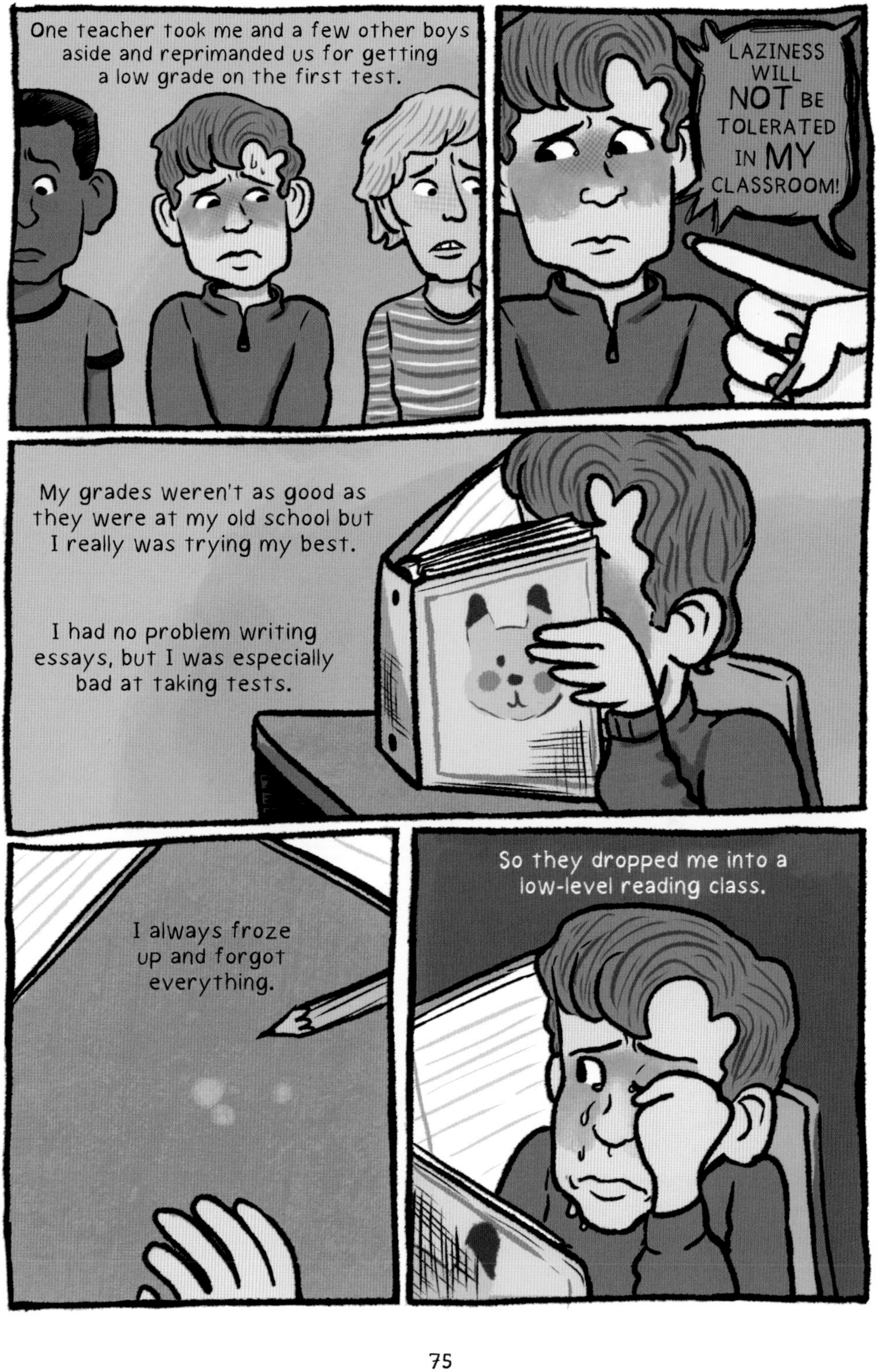
One teacher took me and a few other boys aside and reprimanded us for getting a low grade on the first test.
LAZINESS WILL NOT BE TOLERATED IN MY CLASSROOM!
My grades weren't as good as they were at my old school but I really was trying my best.
I had no problem writing essays, but I was especially bad at taking tests.
I always froze up and forgot everything.
So they dropped me into a low-level reading class.

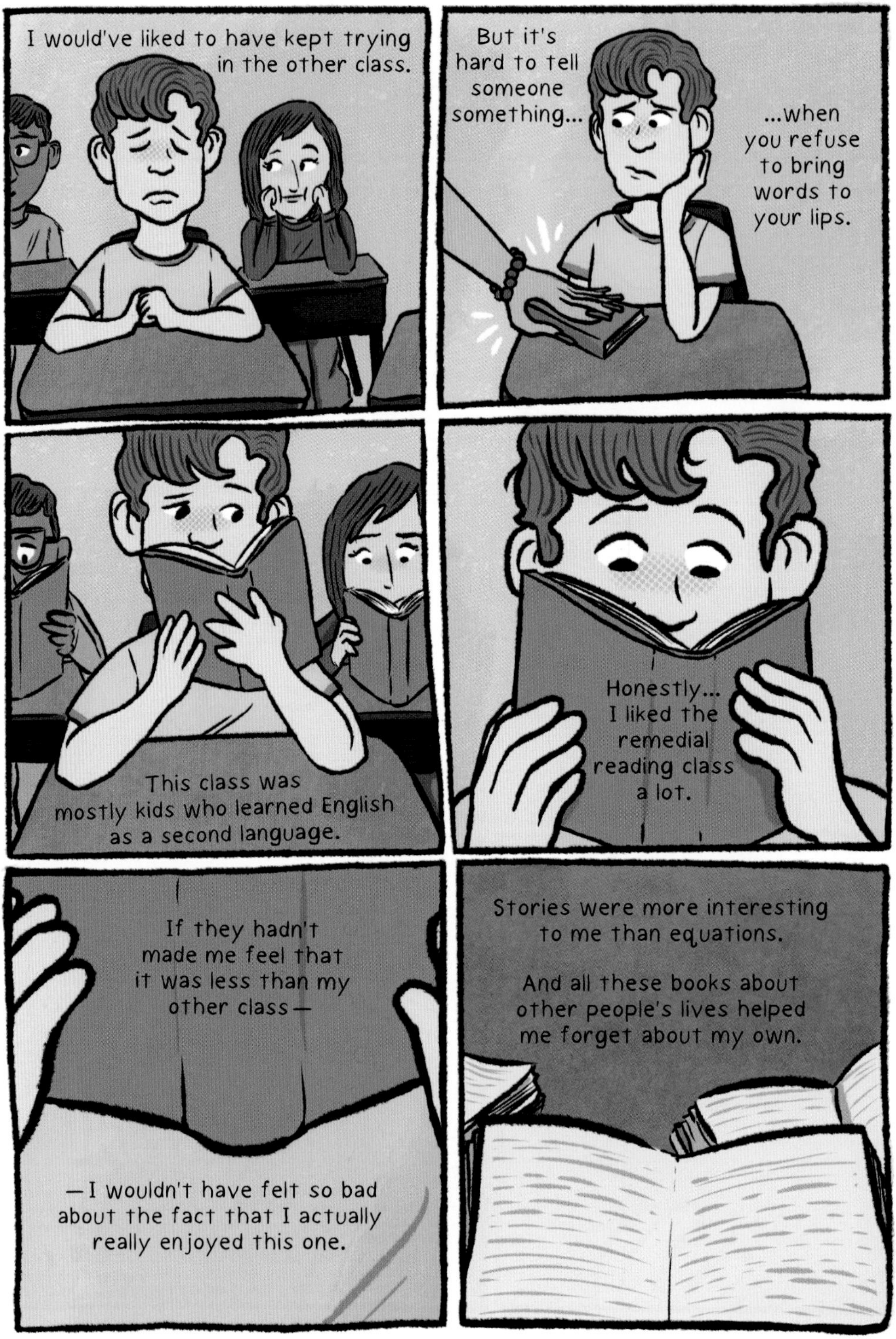
I would've liked to have kept trying in the other class.
But it's hard to tell someone something...
...when you refuse to bring words to your lips.
This class was mostly kids who learned English as a second language.
Honestly... I liked the remedial reading class a lot.
If they hadn't made me feel that it was less than my other class—
—I wouldn't have felt so bad about the fact that I actually really enjoyed this one.
Stories were more interesting to me than equations.
And all these books about other people's lives helped me forget about my own.

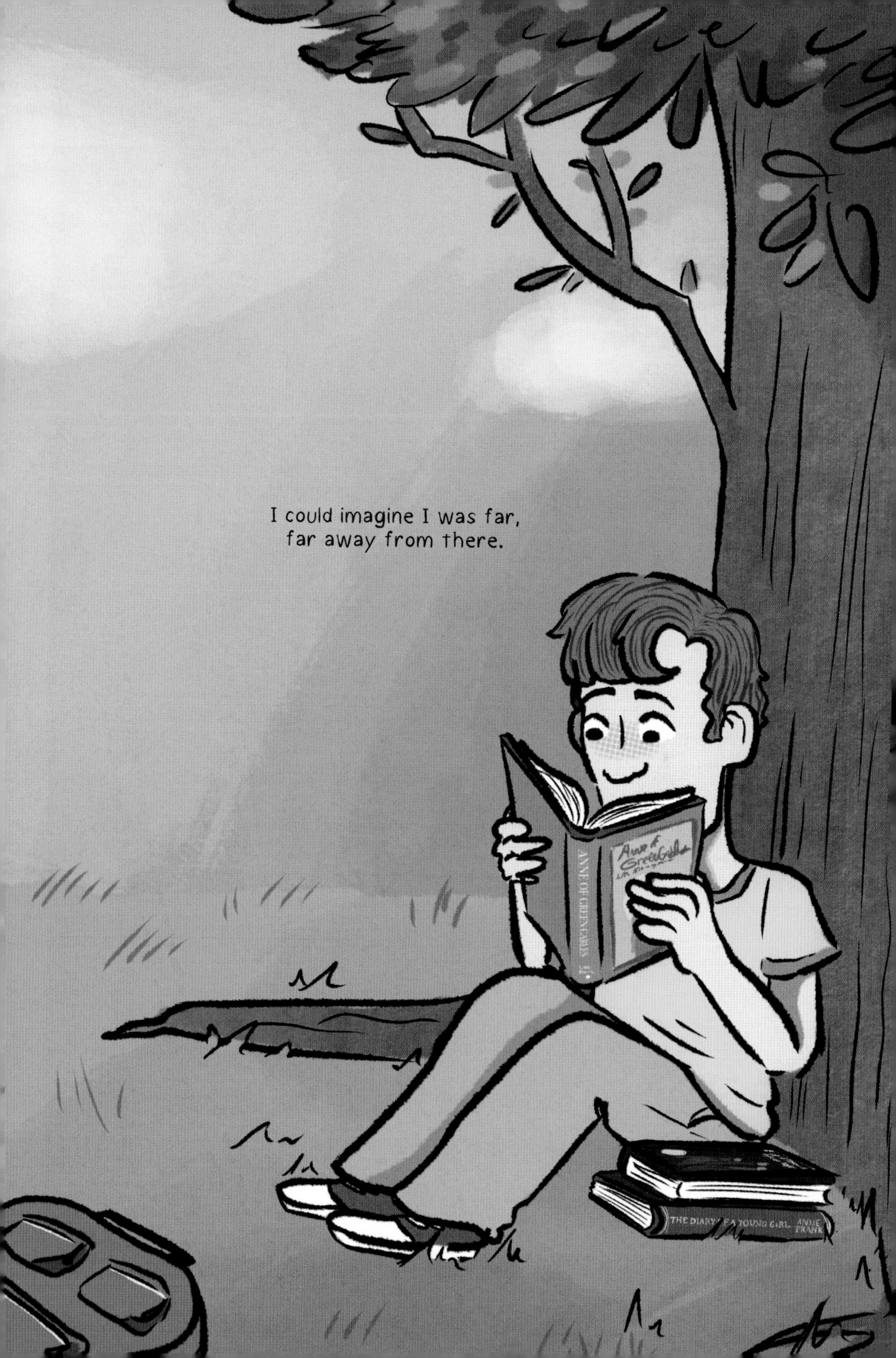
I could imagine I was far, far away from there.
ANNE OF GREEN GABLES
ANNE FRANK

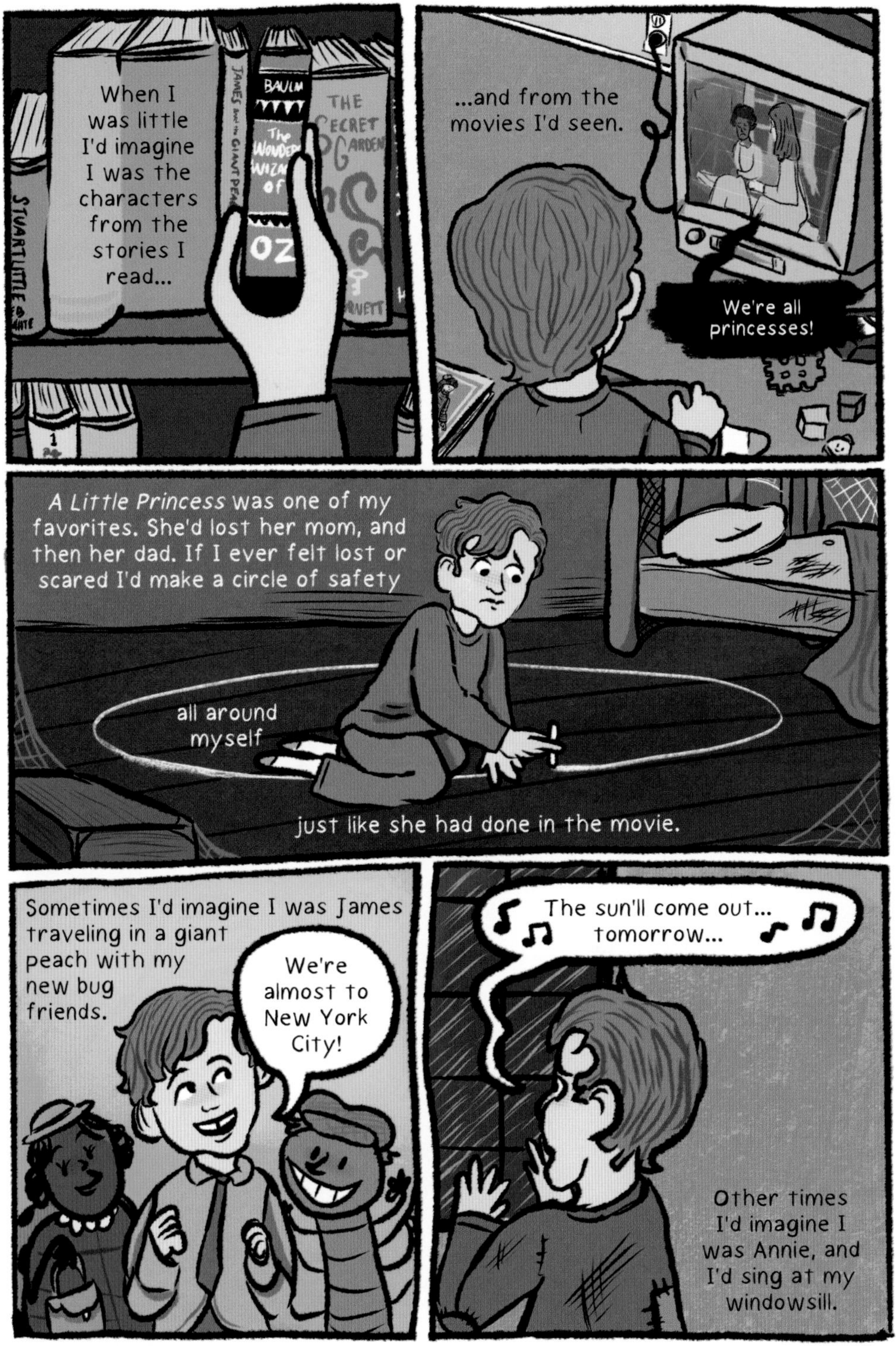
When I was little I'd imagine I was the characters from the stories I read...
STUART LITTLE
JAMES and the GIANT PEACH
BAUM
The Wonderful Wizard of OZ
THE SECRET GARDEN
...and from the movies I'd seen.
We're all princesses!
A Little Princess was one of my favorites. She'd lost her mom, and then her dad. If I ever felt lost or scared I'd make a circle of safety
all around myself
just like she had done in the movie.
Sometimes I'd imagine I was James traveling in a giant peach with my new bug friends.
We're almost to New York City!
The *sun'll* come out... tomorrow...
Other times I'd imagine I was Annie, and I'd sing at my windowsill.

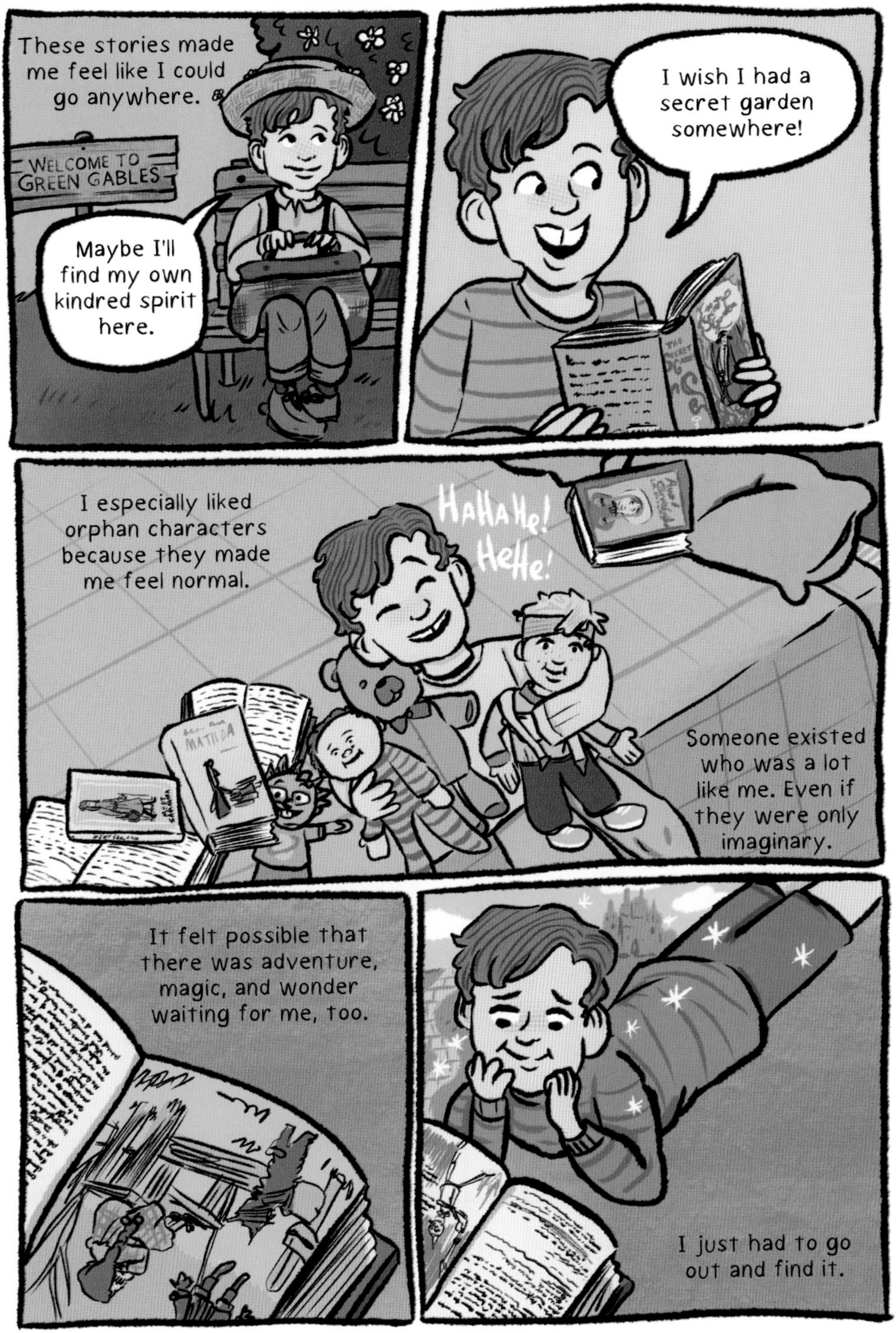

These stories made me feel like I could go anywhere.
WELCOME TO GREEN GABLES
Maybe I'll find my own kindred spirit here.
I wish I had a secret garden somewhere!
THE SECRET GARDEN
I especially liked orphan characters because they made me feel normal.
HaHaHe! HeHe!
MATILDA
Someone existed who was a lot like me. Even if they were only imaginary.
It felt possible that there was adventure, magic, and wonder waiting for me, too.
I just had to go out and find it.

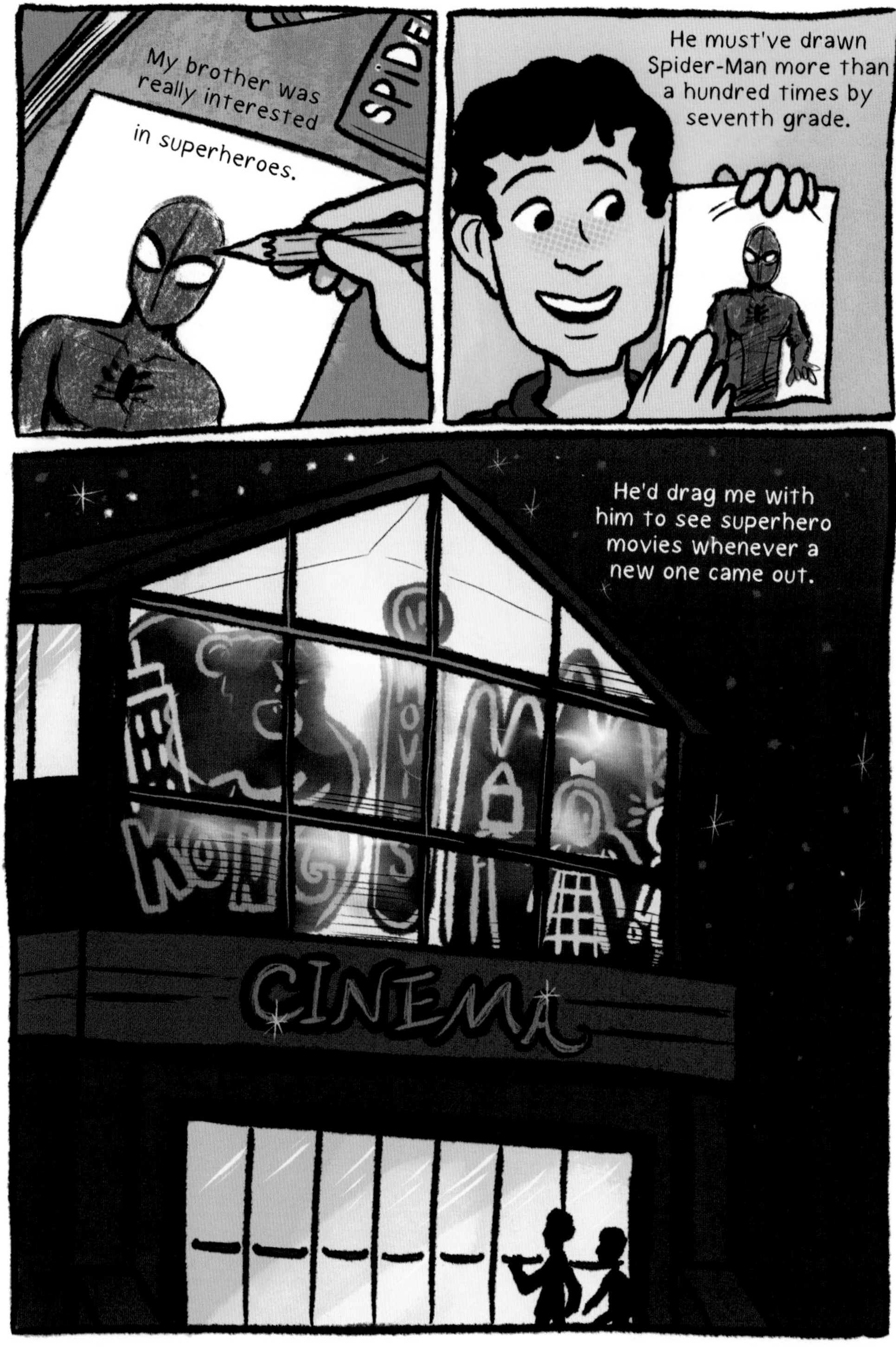
My brother was really interested
in superheroes.
SPIDE
He must've drawn Spider-Man more than a hundred times by seventh grade.
He'd drag me with him to see superhero movies whenever a new one came out.
CINEMA

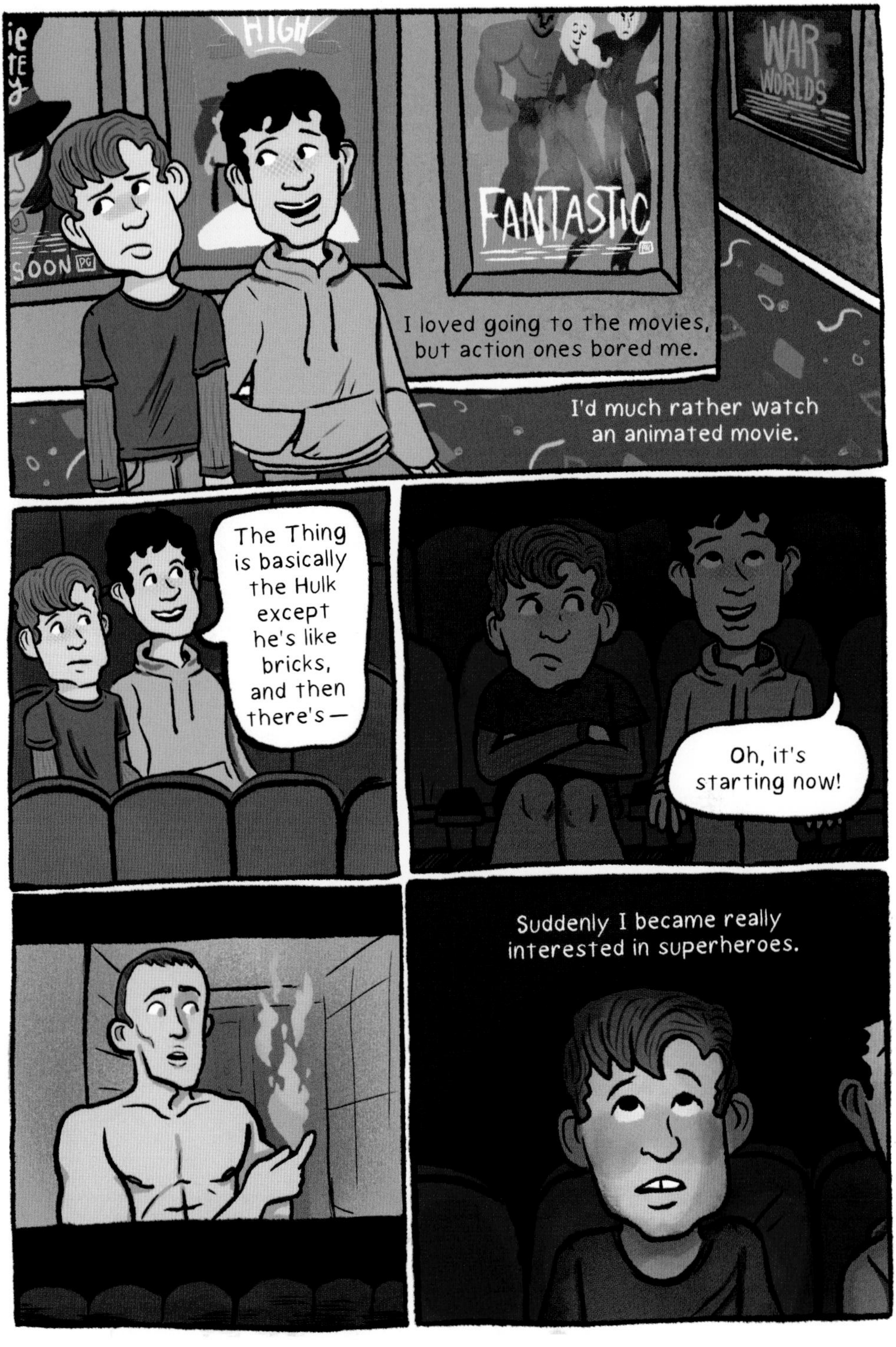

HIGH
WAR WORLDS
FANTASTIC
SOON
I loved going to the movies, but action ones bored me.
I'd much rather watch an animated movie.
The Thing is basically the Hulk except he's like bricks, and then there's—
Oh, it's starting now!
Suddenly I became really interested in superheroes.

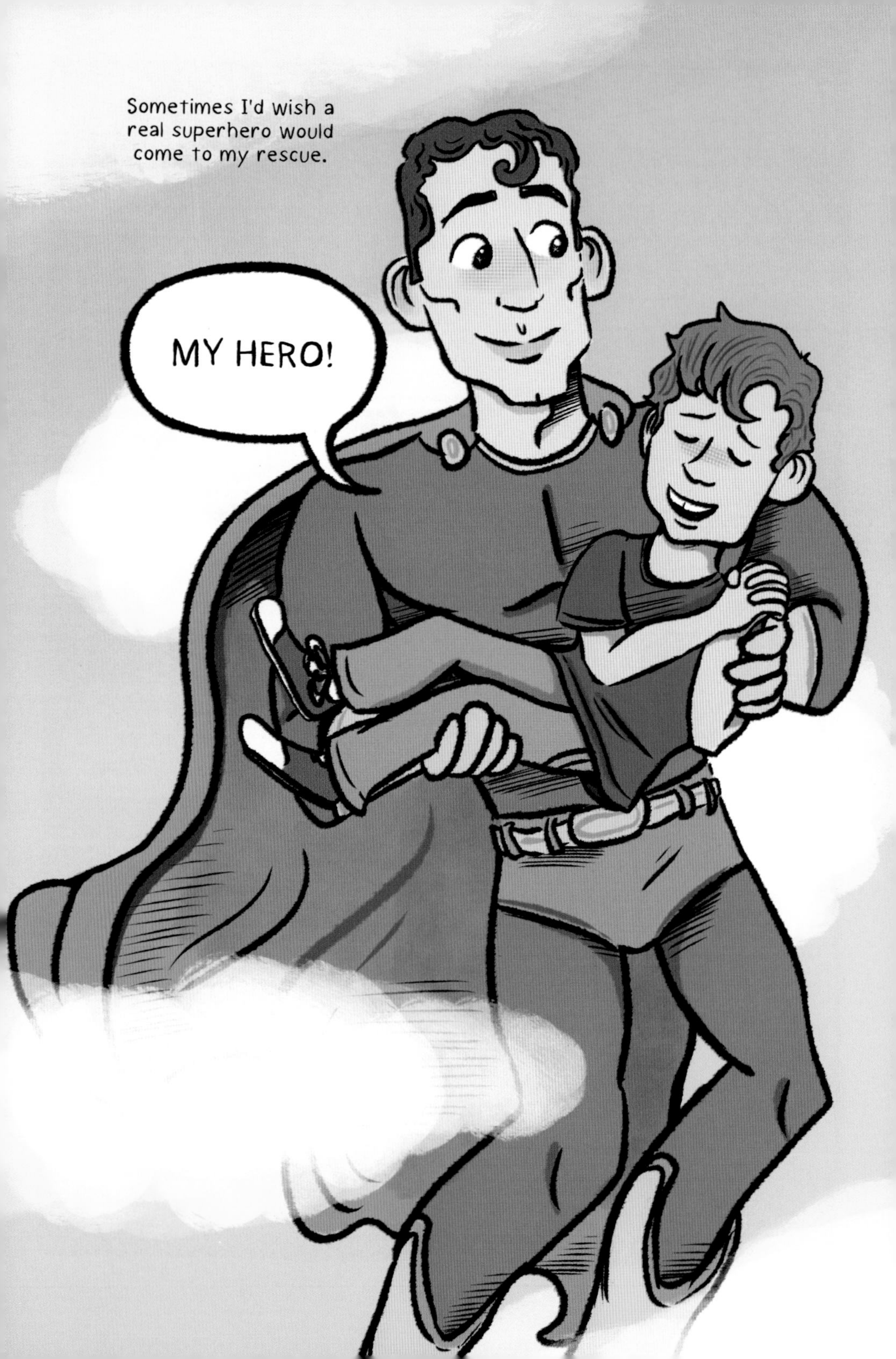
Sometimes I'd wish a real superhero would come to my rescue.
MY HERO!

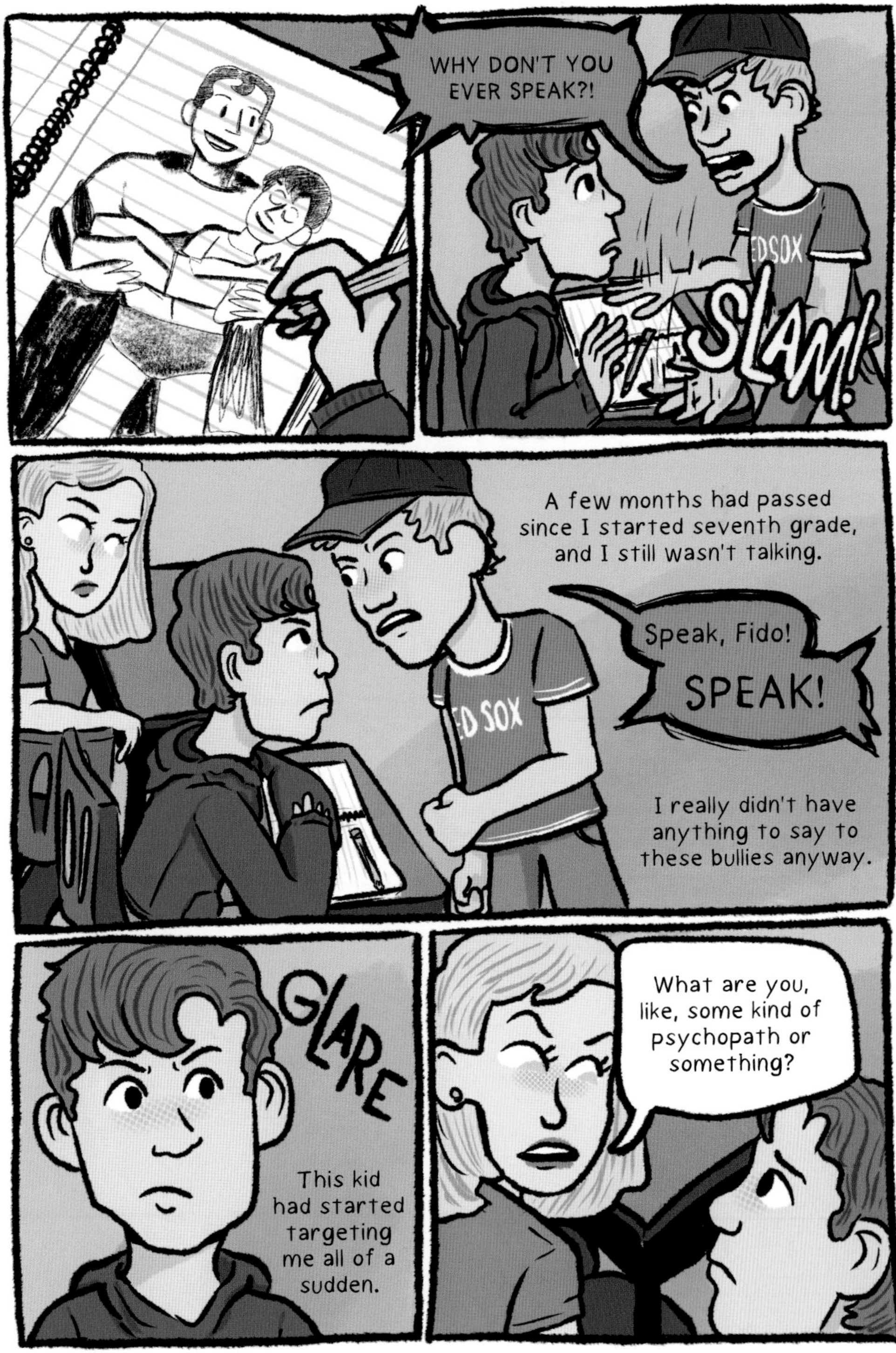
WHY DON'T YOU EVER SPEAK?!
EDSOX
SLAM!
A few months had passed since I started seventh grade, and I still wasn't talking.
ED SOX
Speak, Fido!
SPEAK!
I really didn't have anything to say to these bullies anyway.
GLARE
This kid had started targeting me all of a sudden.
What are you, like, some kind of psychopath or something?

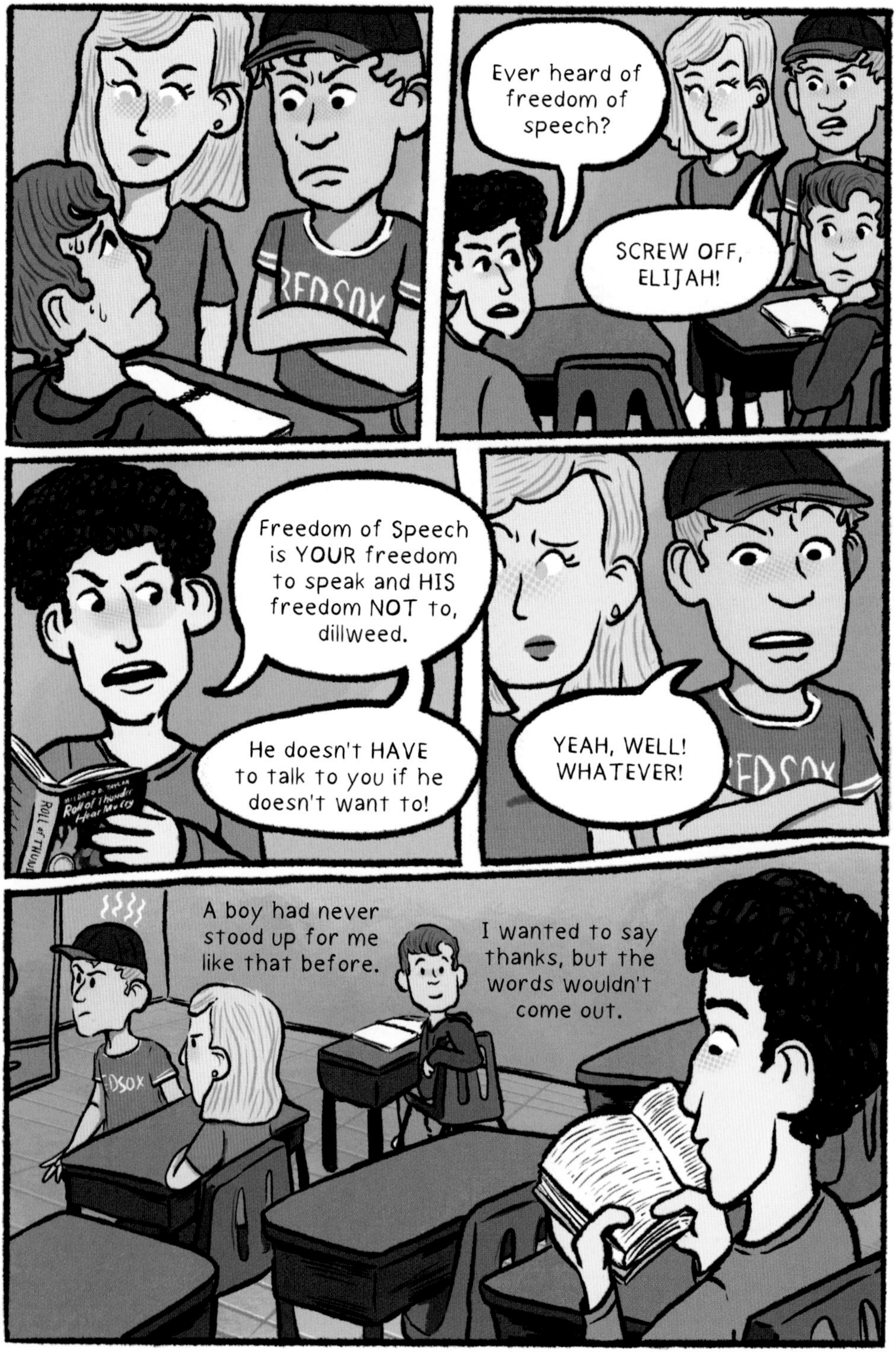
Ever heard of freedom of speech?
SCREW OFF, ELIJAH!
Freedom of Speech is YOUR freedom to speak and HIS freedom NOT to, dillweed.
He doesn't HAVE to talk to you if he doesn't want to!
YEAH, WELL! WHATEVER!
A boy had never stood up for me like that before.
I wanted to say thanks, but the words wouldn't come out.

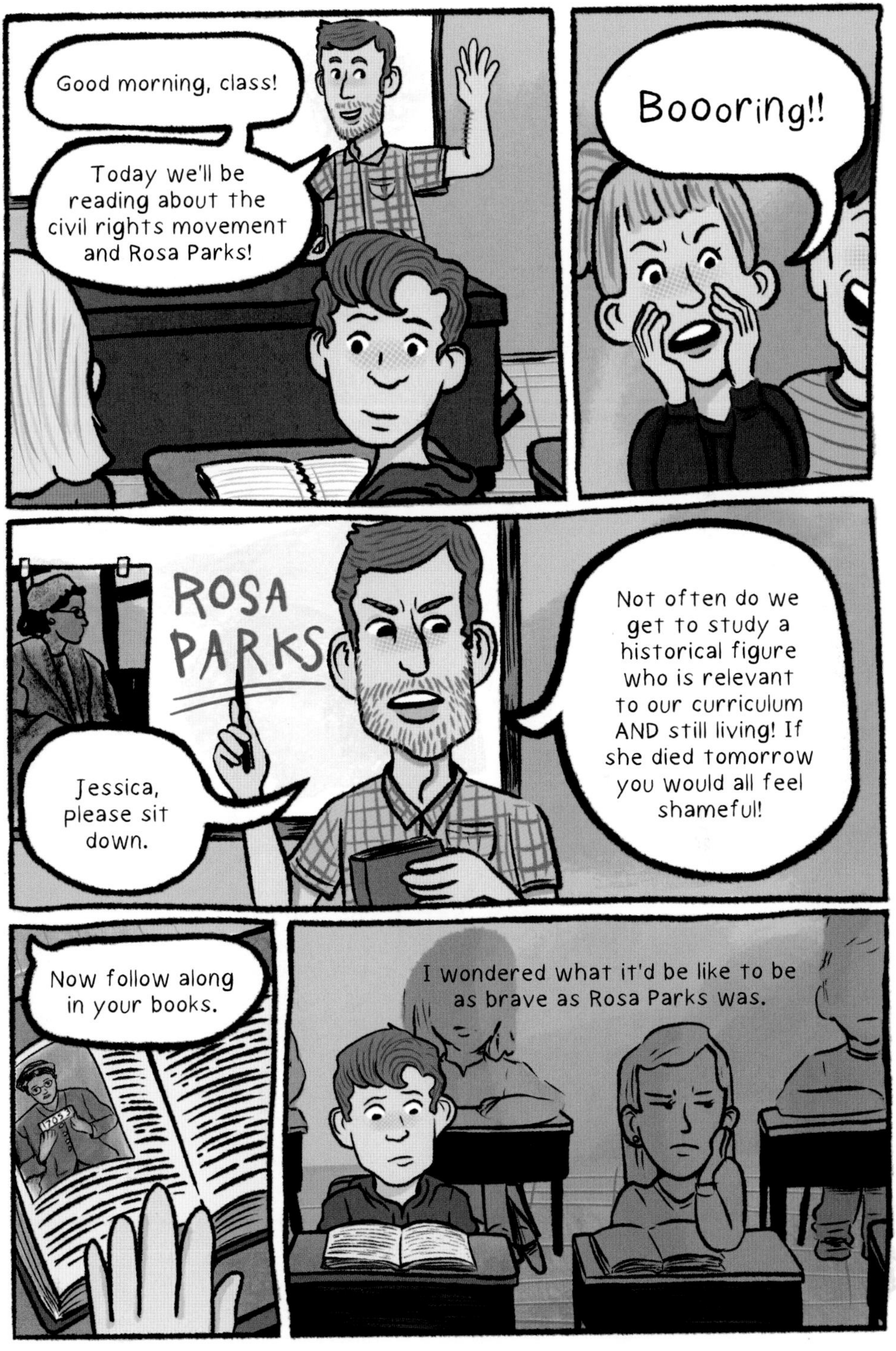
Good morning, class!
Today we'll be reading about the civil rights movement and Rosa Parks!
Booring!!
ROSA PARKS
Not often do we get to study a historical figure who is relevant to our curriculum AND still living! If she died tomorrow you would all feel shameful!
Jessica, please sit down.
Now follow along in your books.
I wondered what it'd be like to be as brave as Rosa Parks was.

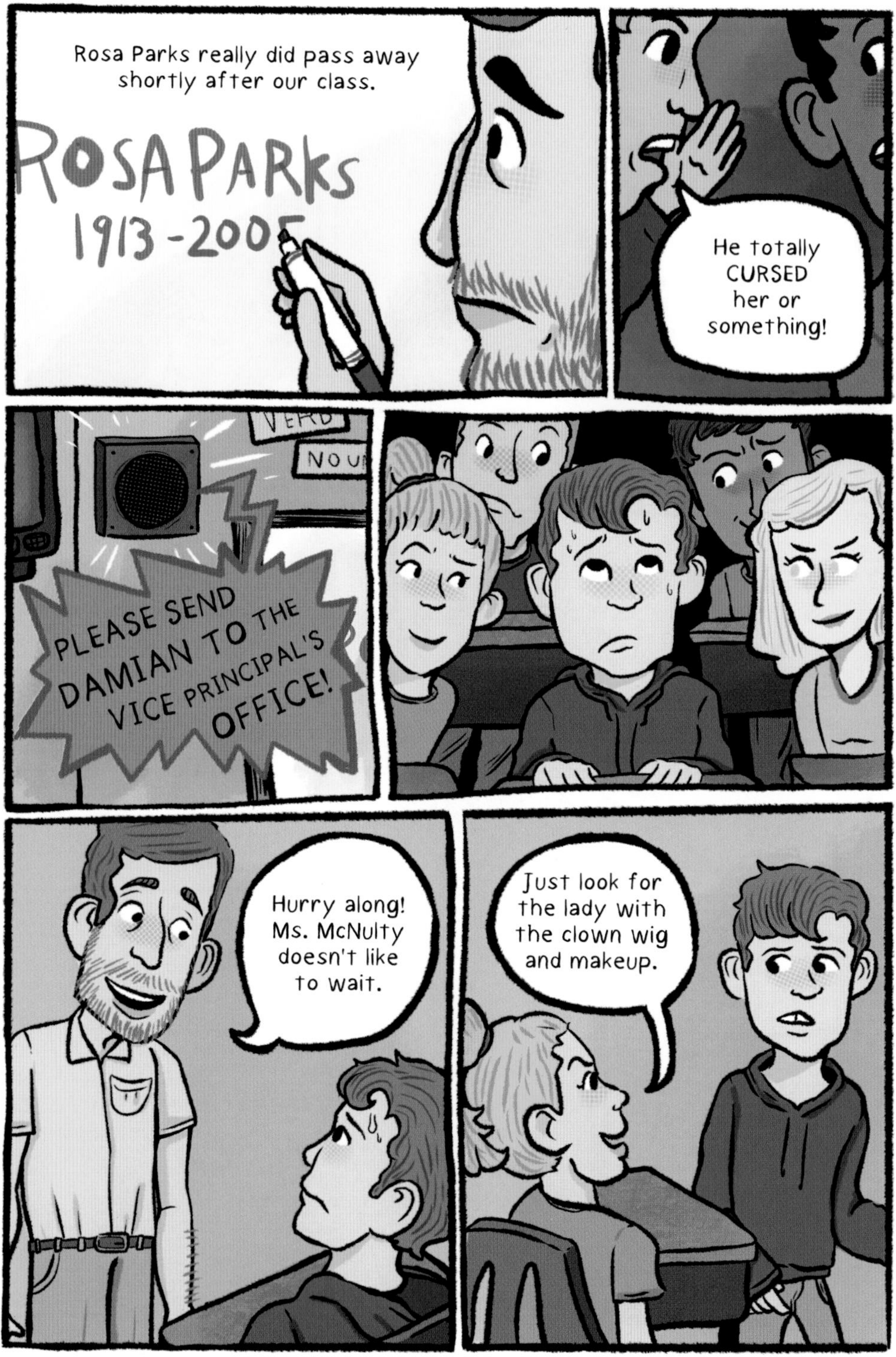
Rosa Parks really did pass away shortly after our class.
ROSA PARKS
1913-2005
He totally CURSED her or something!
VERB
NOUN
PLEASE SEND DAMIAN TO THE VICE PRINCIPAL'S OFFICE!
Hurry along! Ms. McNulty doesn't like to wait.
Just look for the lady with the clown wig and makeup.

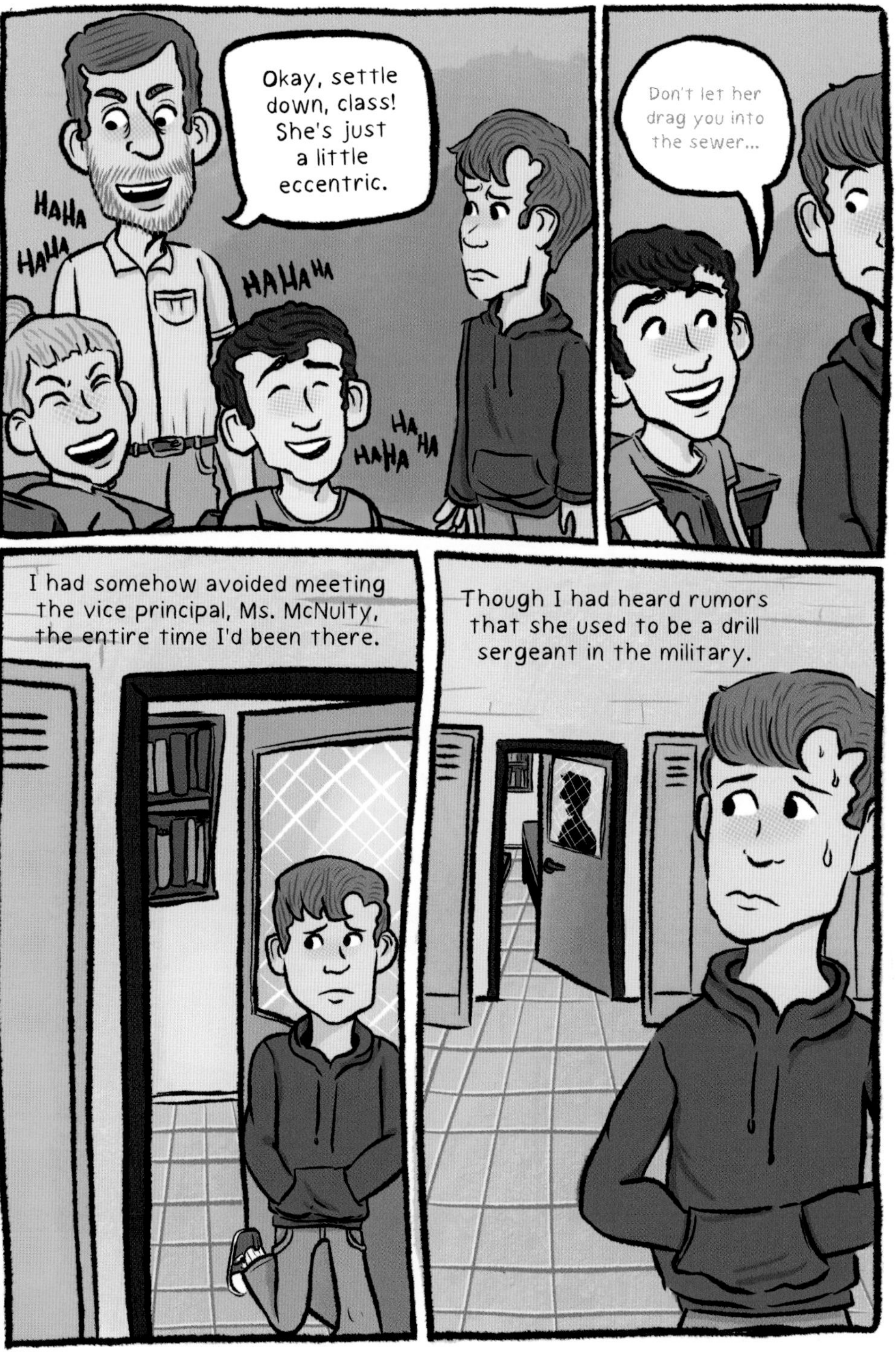
Okay, settle down, class! She's just a little eccentric.
HAHA
HAHA
HAHAHA
HAHA
HAHA
Don't let her drag you into the sewer...
I had somehow avoided meeting the vice principal, Ms. McNulty, the entire time I'd been there.
Though I had heard rumors that she used to be a drill sergeant in the military.

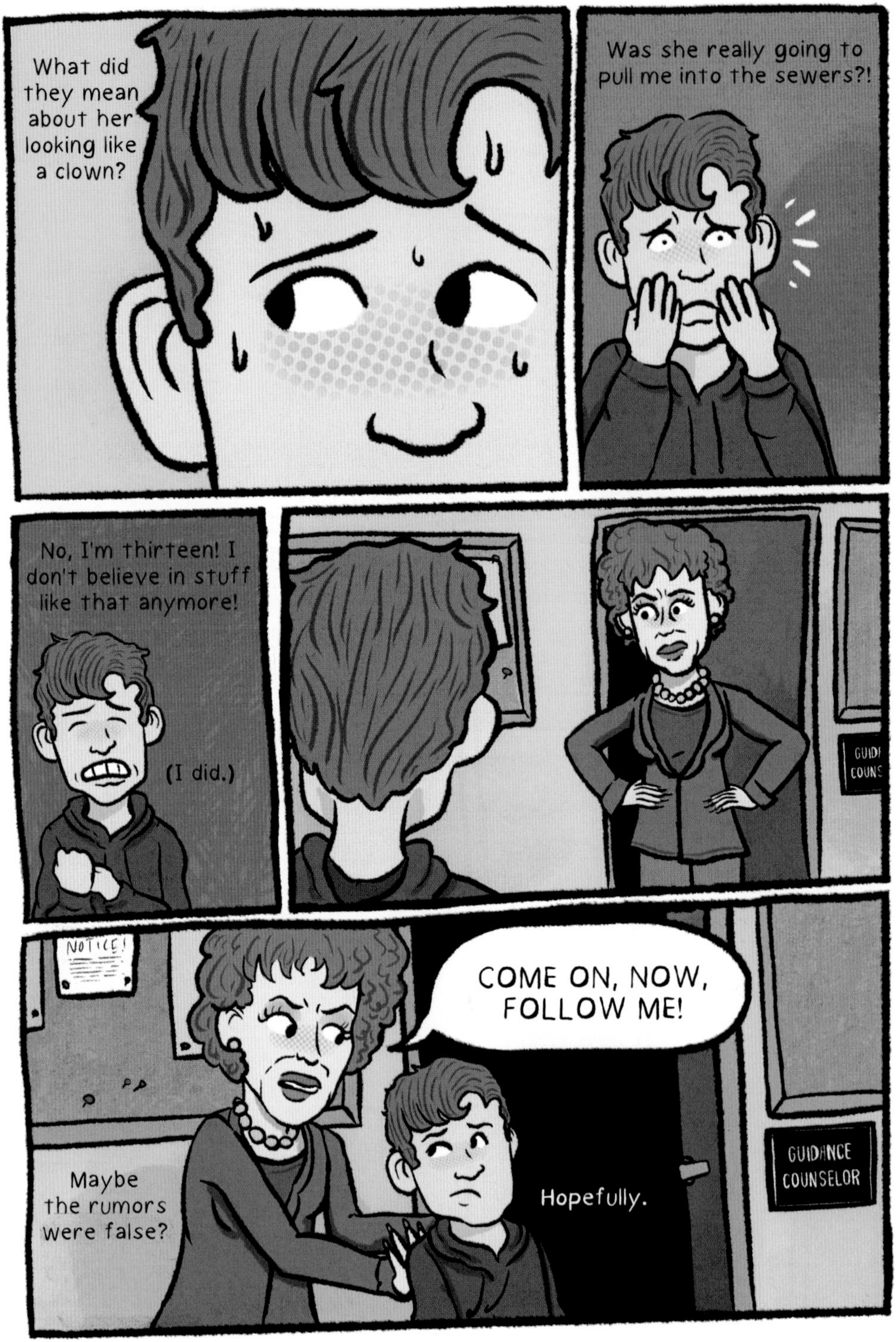
What did they mean about her looking like a clown?
Was she really going to pull me into the sewers?!
No, I'm thirteen! I don't believe in stuff like that anymore!
(I did.)
GUIDA
COUNS
NOTICE!
COME ON, NOW, FOLLOW ME!
Maybe the rumors were false?
Hopefully.
GUIDANCE COUNSELOR

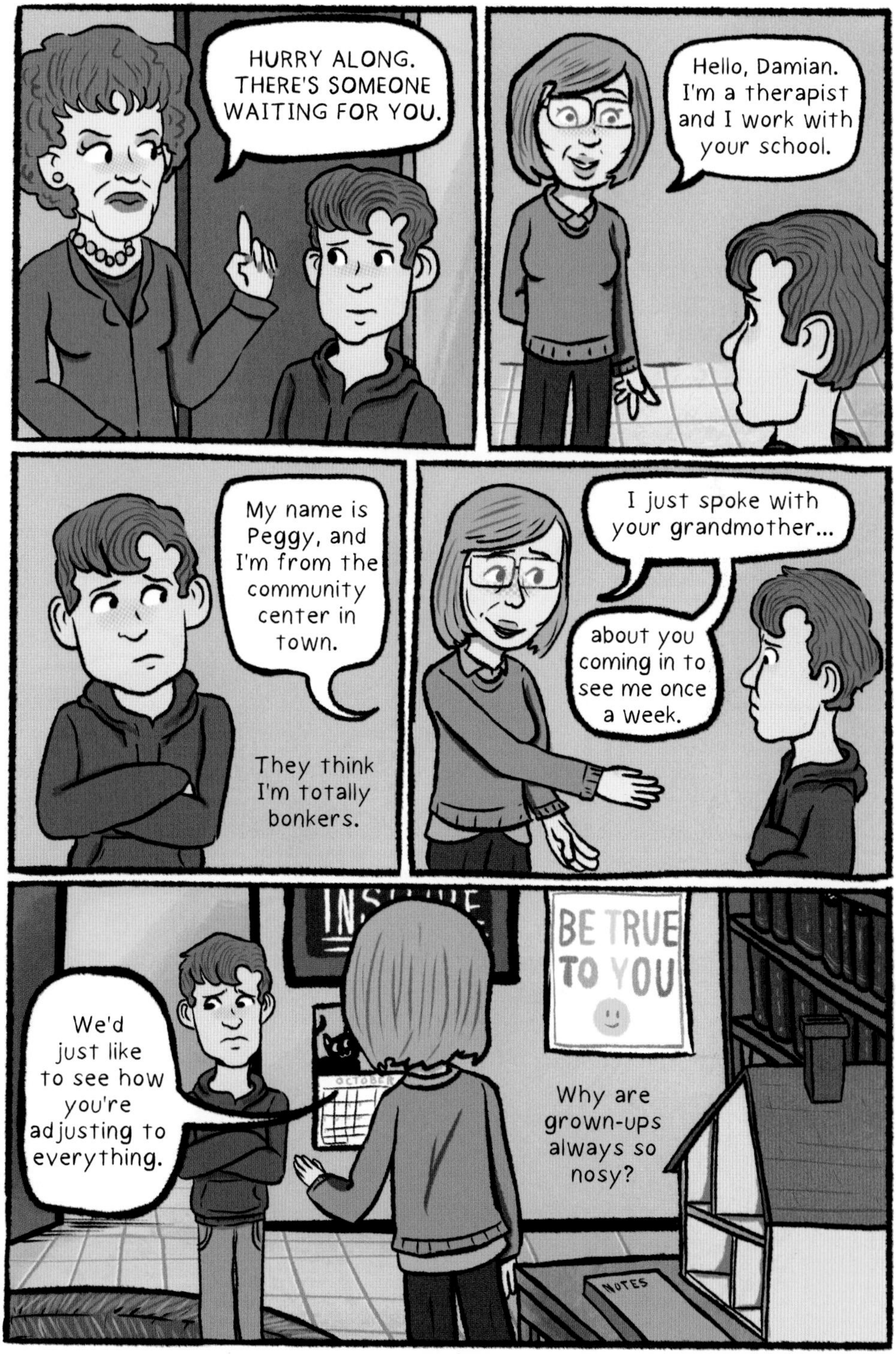
HURRY ALONG. THERE'S SOMEONE WAITING FOR YOU.
Hello, Damian. I'm a therapist and I work with your school.
My name is Peggy, and I'm from the community center in town.
They think I'm totally bonkers.
I just spoke with your grandmother...
about you coming in to see me once a week.
We'd just like to see how you're adjusting to everything.
BE TRUE TO YOU
OCTOBER
Why are grown-ups always so nosy?
NOTES

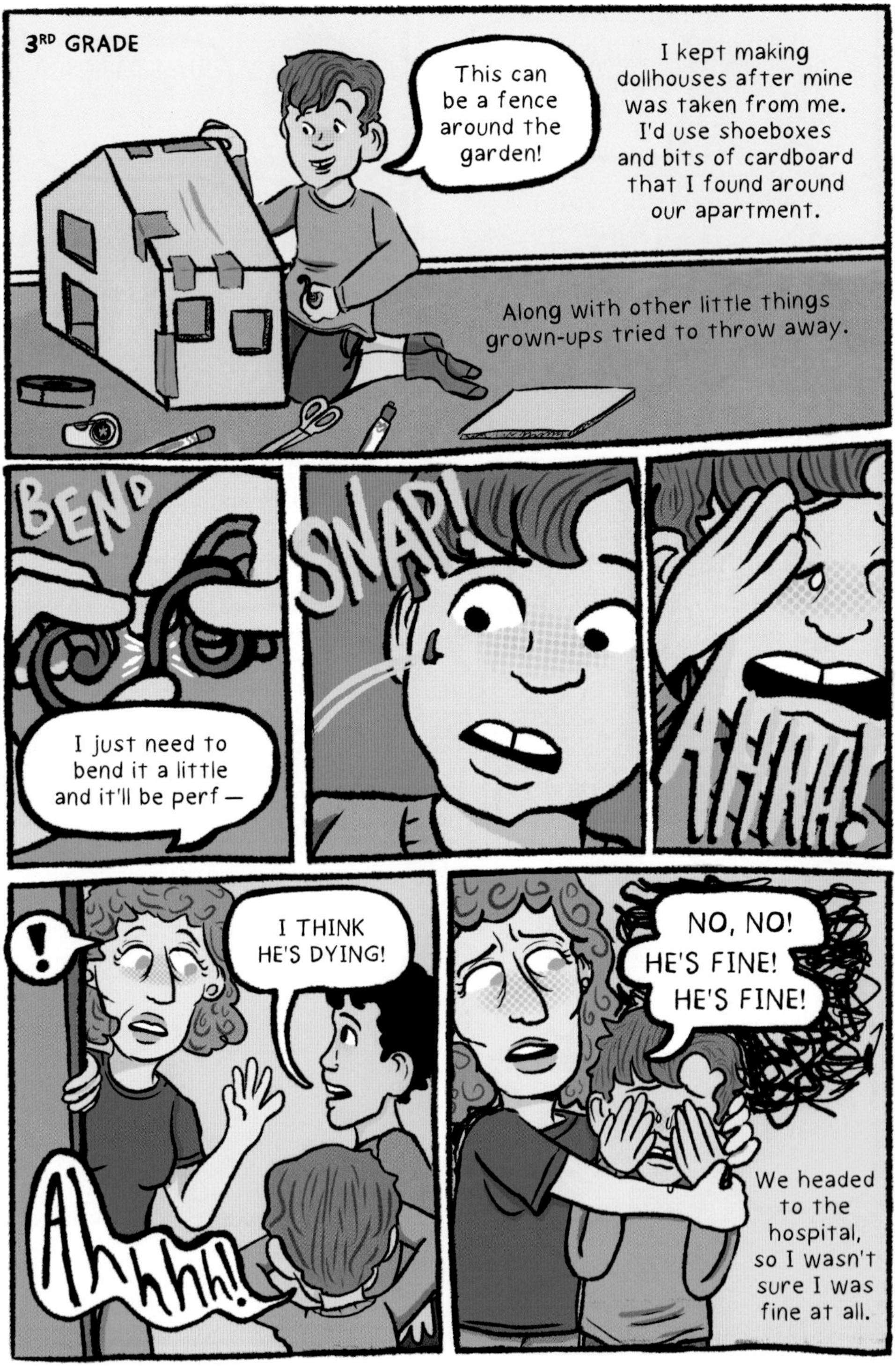
3RD GRADE
This can be a fence around the garden!
I kept making dollhouses after mine was taken from me. I'd use shoeboxes and bits of cardboard that I found around our apartment.
Along with other little things grown-ups tried to throw away.
BEND
I just need to bend it a little and it'll be perf—
SNAP!
AHHH!
!
I THINK HE'S DYING!
Ahhhh!
NO, NO! HE'S FINE! HE'S FINE!
We headed to the hospital, so I wasn't sure I was fine at all.

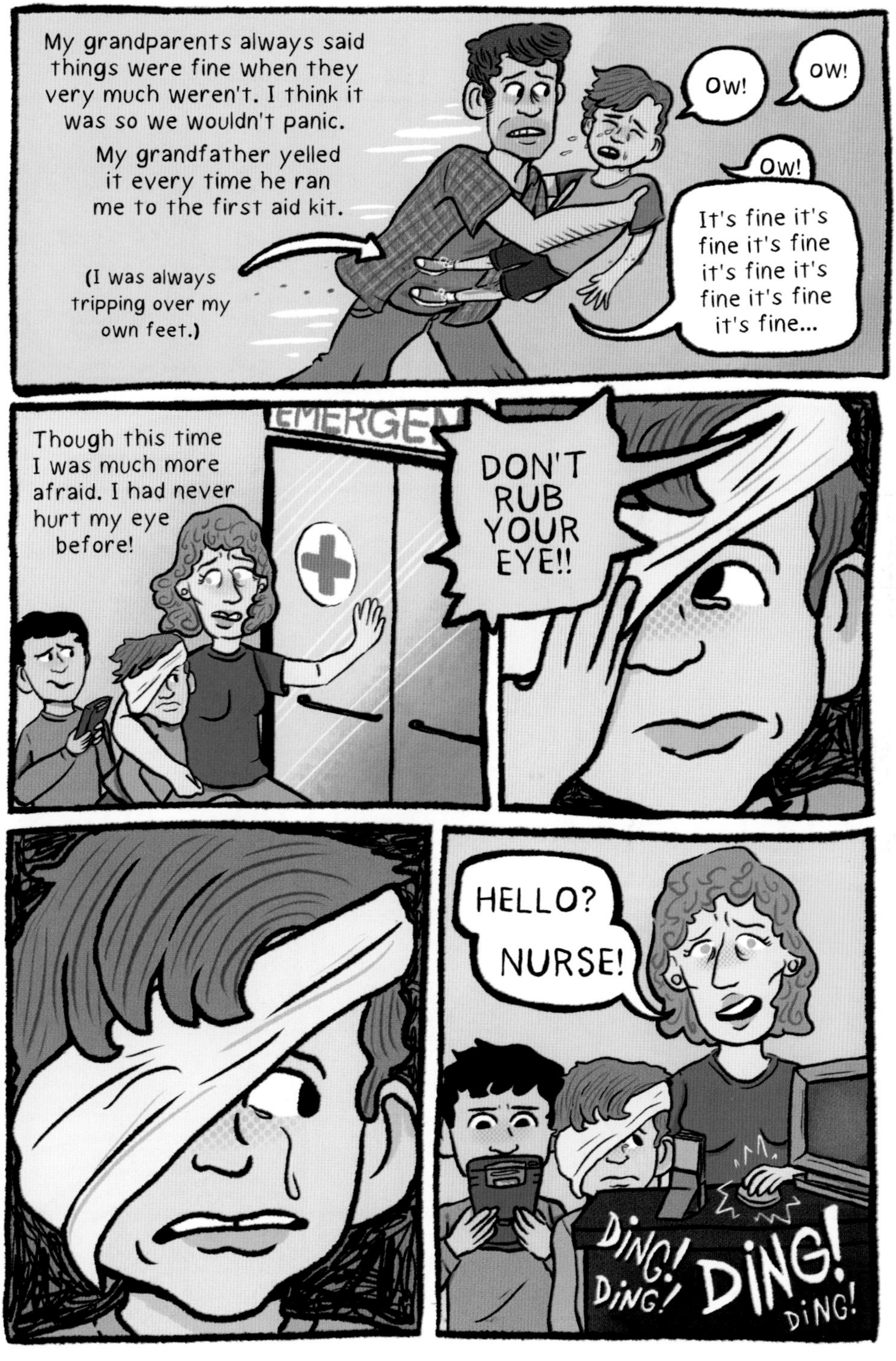
My grandparents always said things were fine when they very much weren't. I think it was so we wouldn't panic.
My grandfather yelled it every time he ran me to the first aid kit.
(I was always tripping over my own feet.)
OW!
OW!
OW!
It's fine it's fine it's fine it's fine it's fine it's fine it's fine it's fine...
Though this time I was much more afraid. I had never hurt my eye before!
EMERGEN
DON'T RUB YOUR EYE!!
HELLO?
NURSE!
DING! DING! DING! DING!

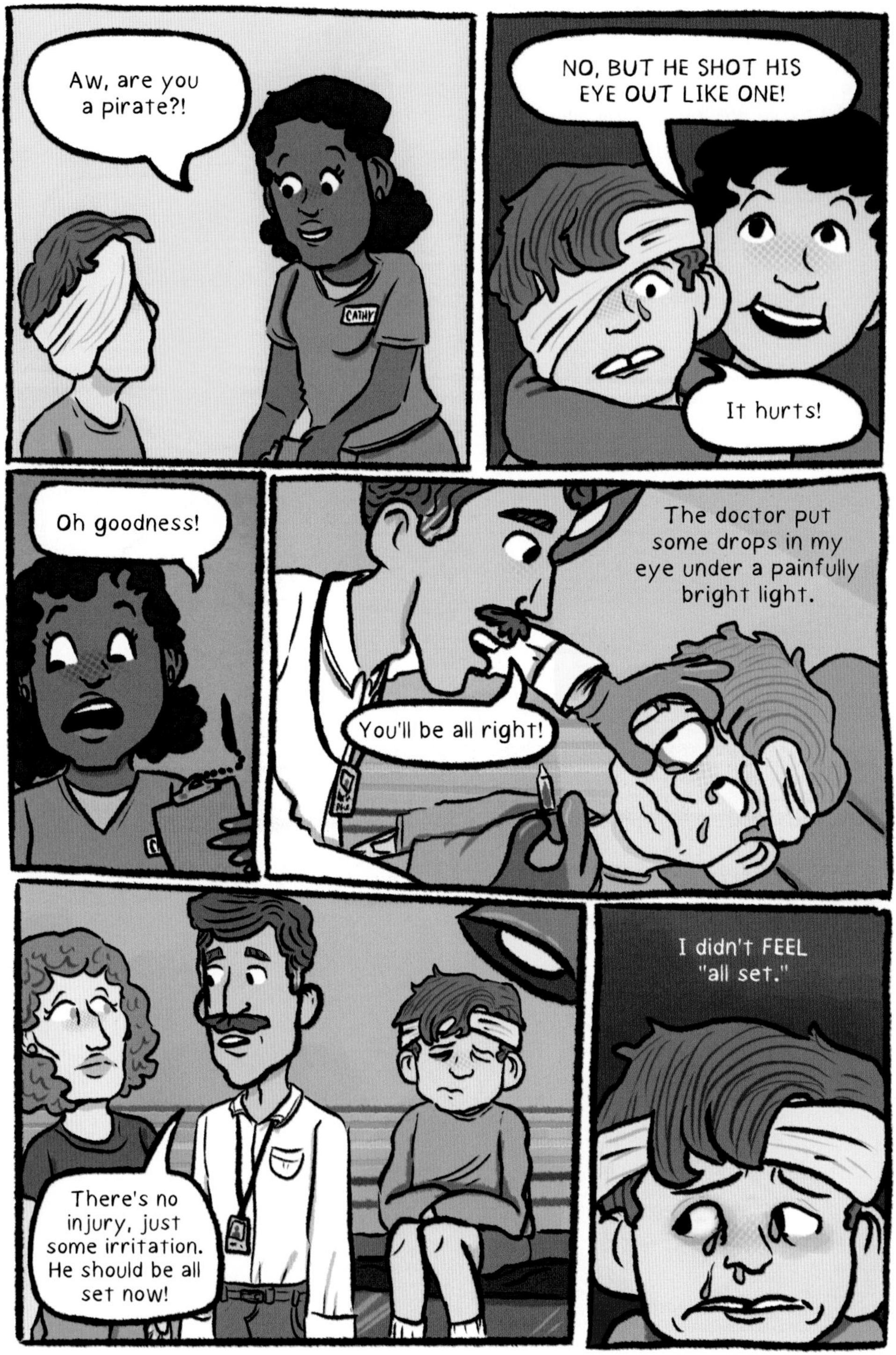
Aw, are you a pirate?!
CATHY
NO, BUT HE SHOT HIS EYE OUT LIKE ONE!
It hurts!
Oh goodness!
The doctor put some drops in my eye under a painfully bright light.
You'll be all right!
There's no injury, just some irritation. He should be all set now!
I didn't FEEL "all set."

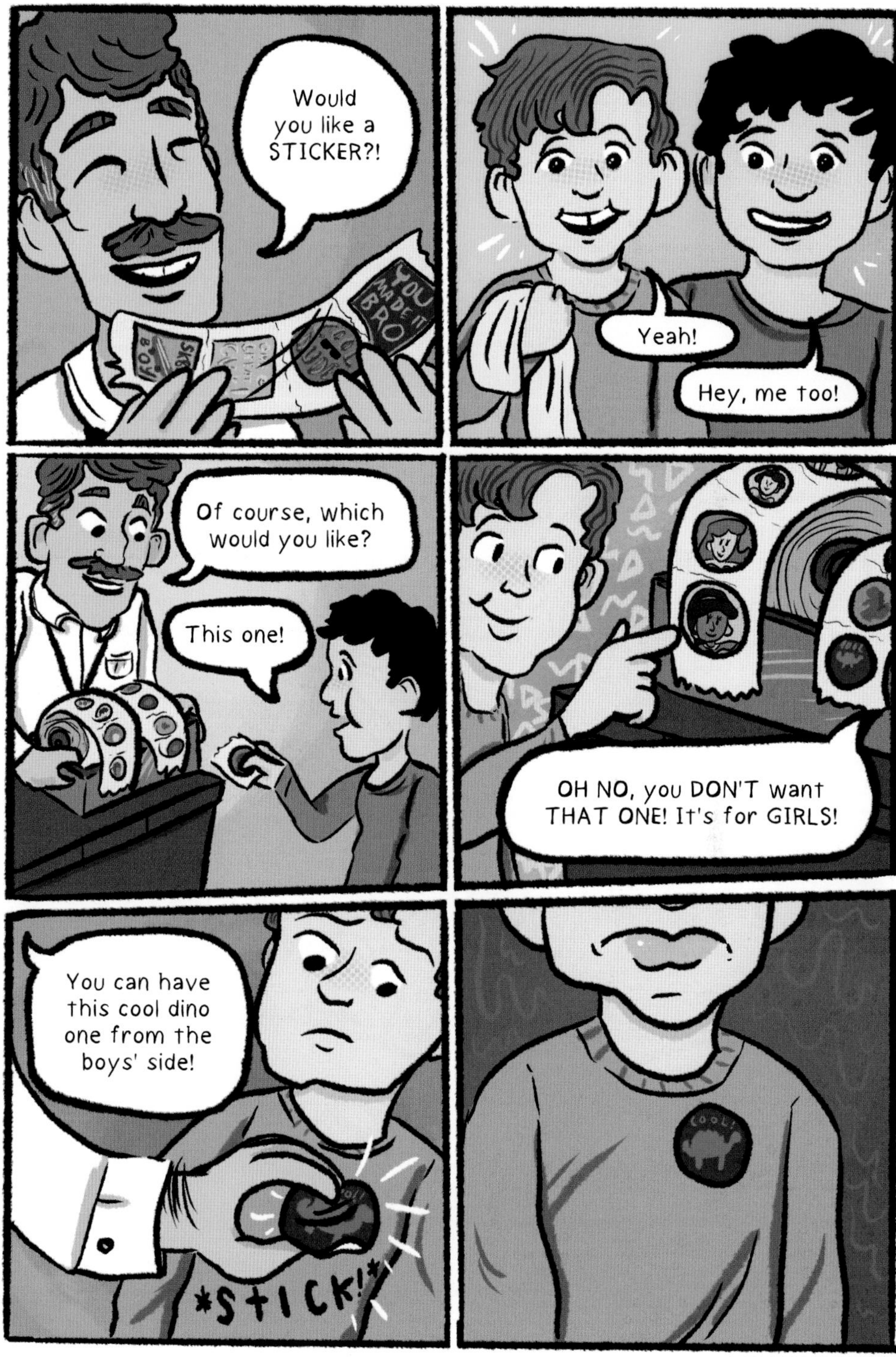

Would you like a STICKER?!
YOU MADE IT BRO
Yeah!
Hey, me too!
Of course, which would you like?
This one!
OH NO, you DON'T want THAT ONE! It's for GIRLS!
You can have this cool dino one from the boys' side!
STICK!
COOL!

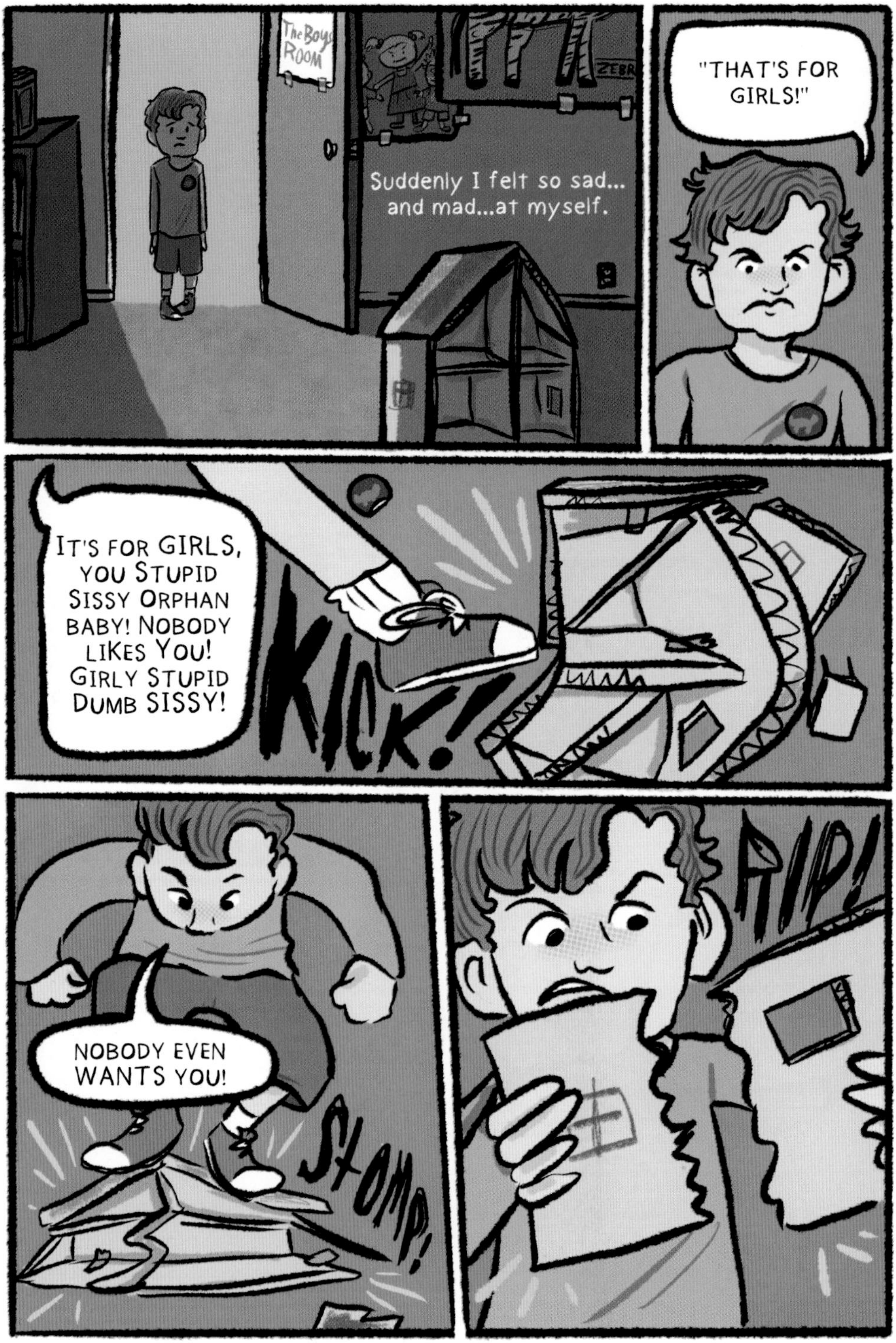

The Boys ROOM
ZEBR
Suddenly I felt so sad... and mad...at myself.
"THAT'S FOR GIRLS!"
IT'S FOR GIRLS, YOU STUPID SISSY ORPHAN BABY! NOBODY LIKES YOU! GIRLY STUPID DUMB SISSY!
KICK!!
NOBODY EVEN WANTS YOU!
STOMP!
RIP!

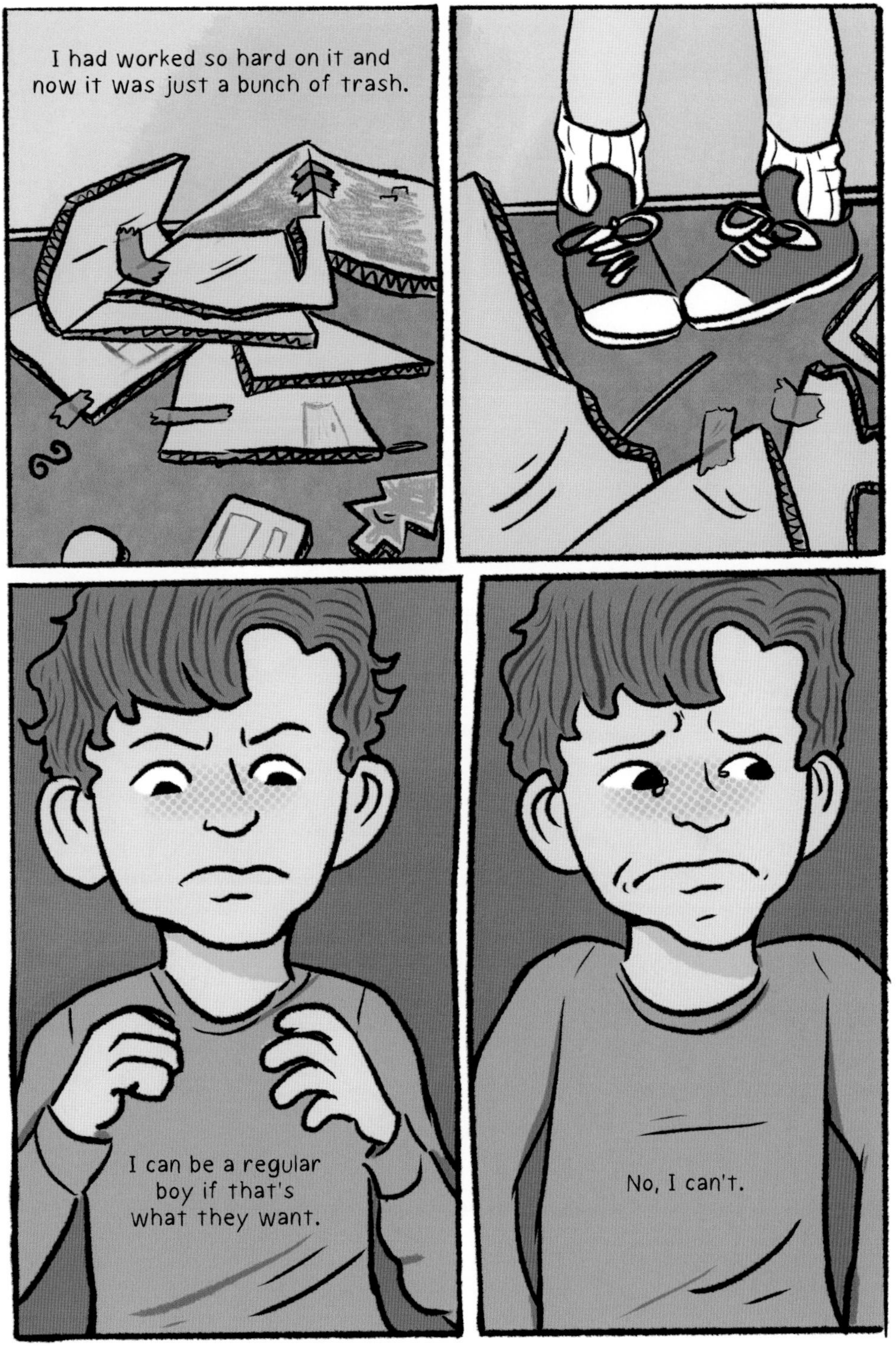

I had worked so hard on it and now it was just a bunch of trash.
I can be a regular boy if that's what they want.
No, I can't.

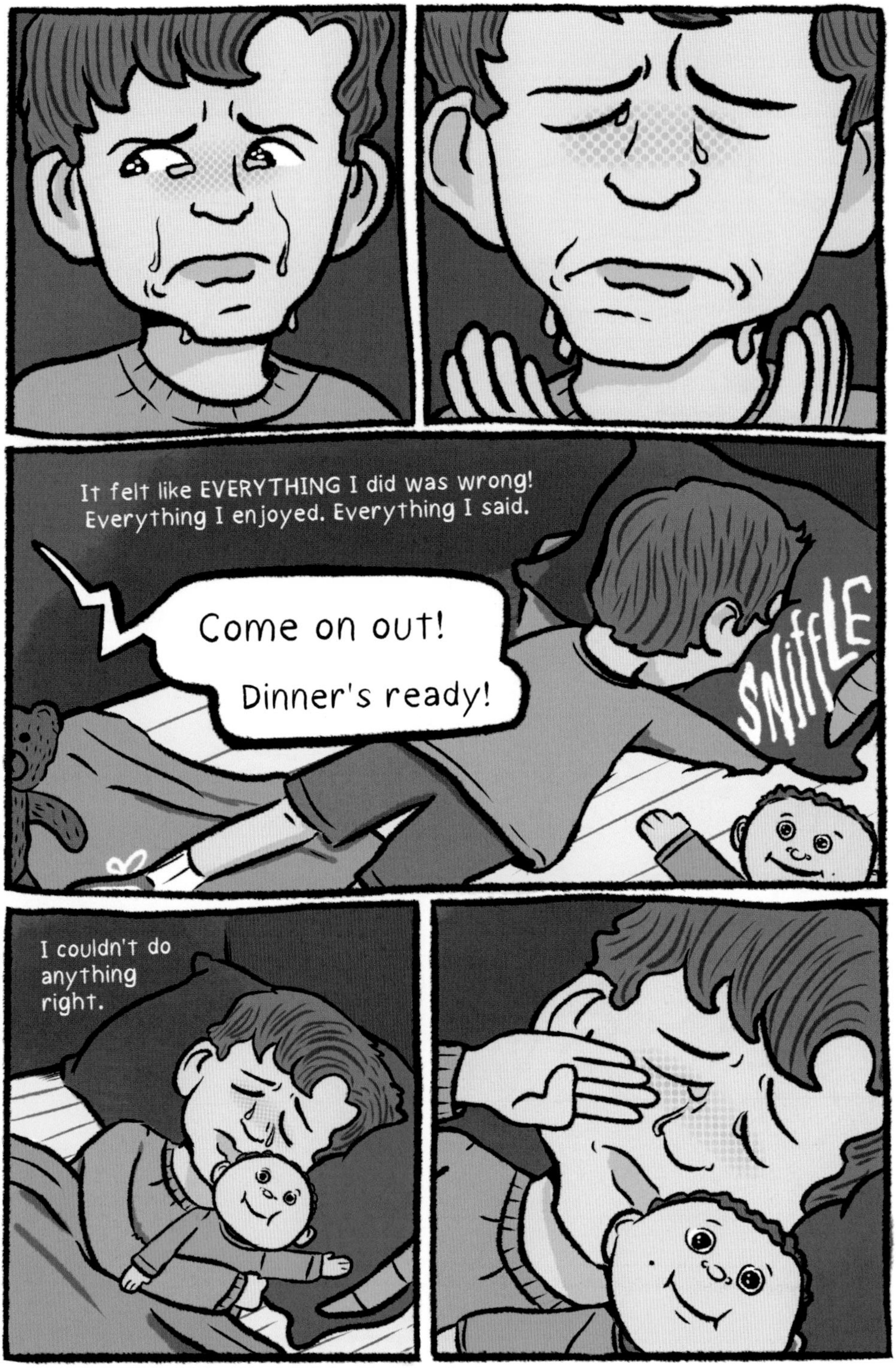
It felt like EVERYTHING I did was wrong! Everything I enjoyed. Everything I said.
Come on out!
Dinner's ready!
SNIFFLE
I couldn't do anything right.

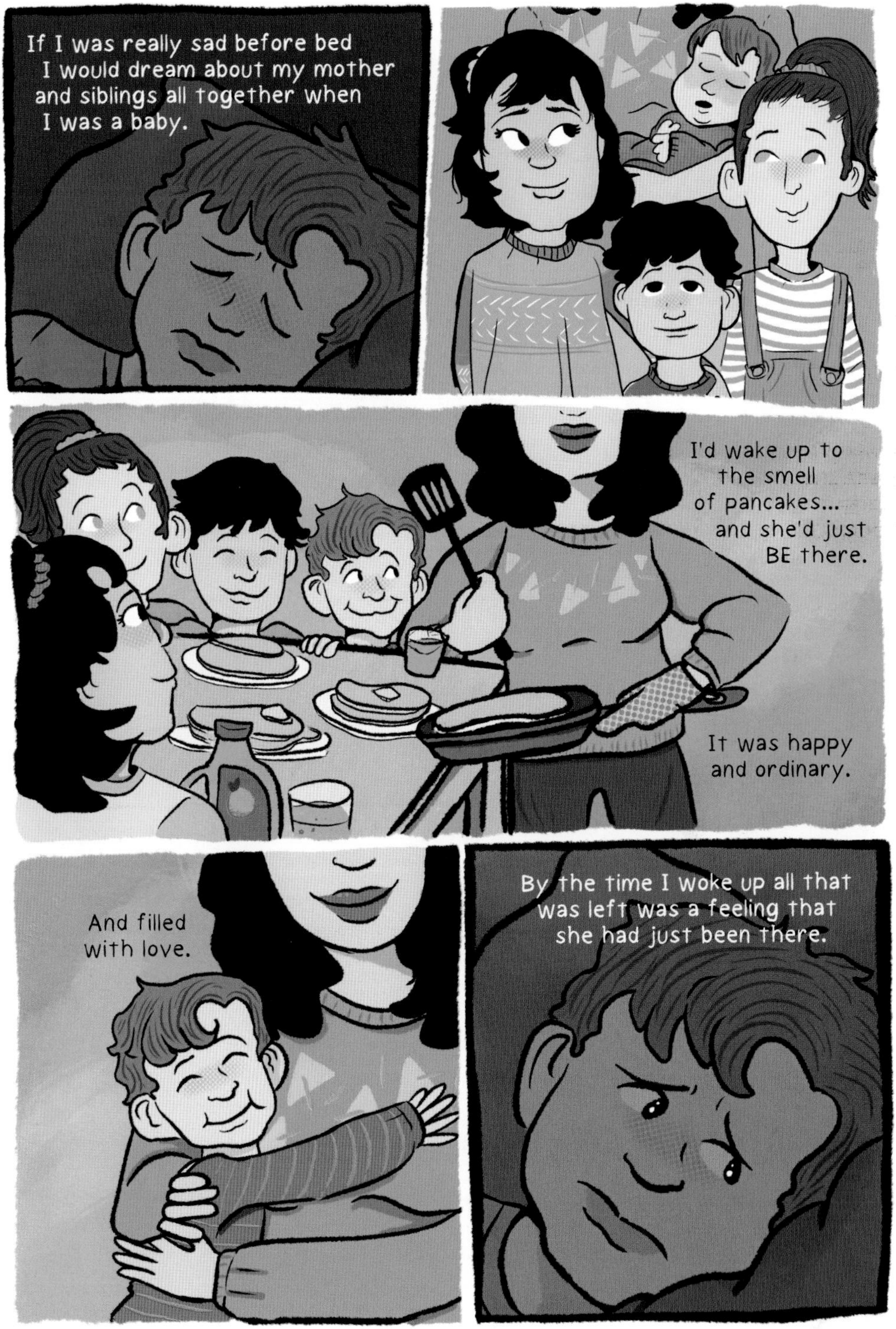
If I was really sad before bed I would dream about my mother and siblings all together when I was a baby.
I'd wake up to the smell of pancakes... and she'd just BE there.
It was happy and ordinary.
And filled with love.
By the time I woke up all that was left was a feeling that she had just been there.

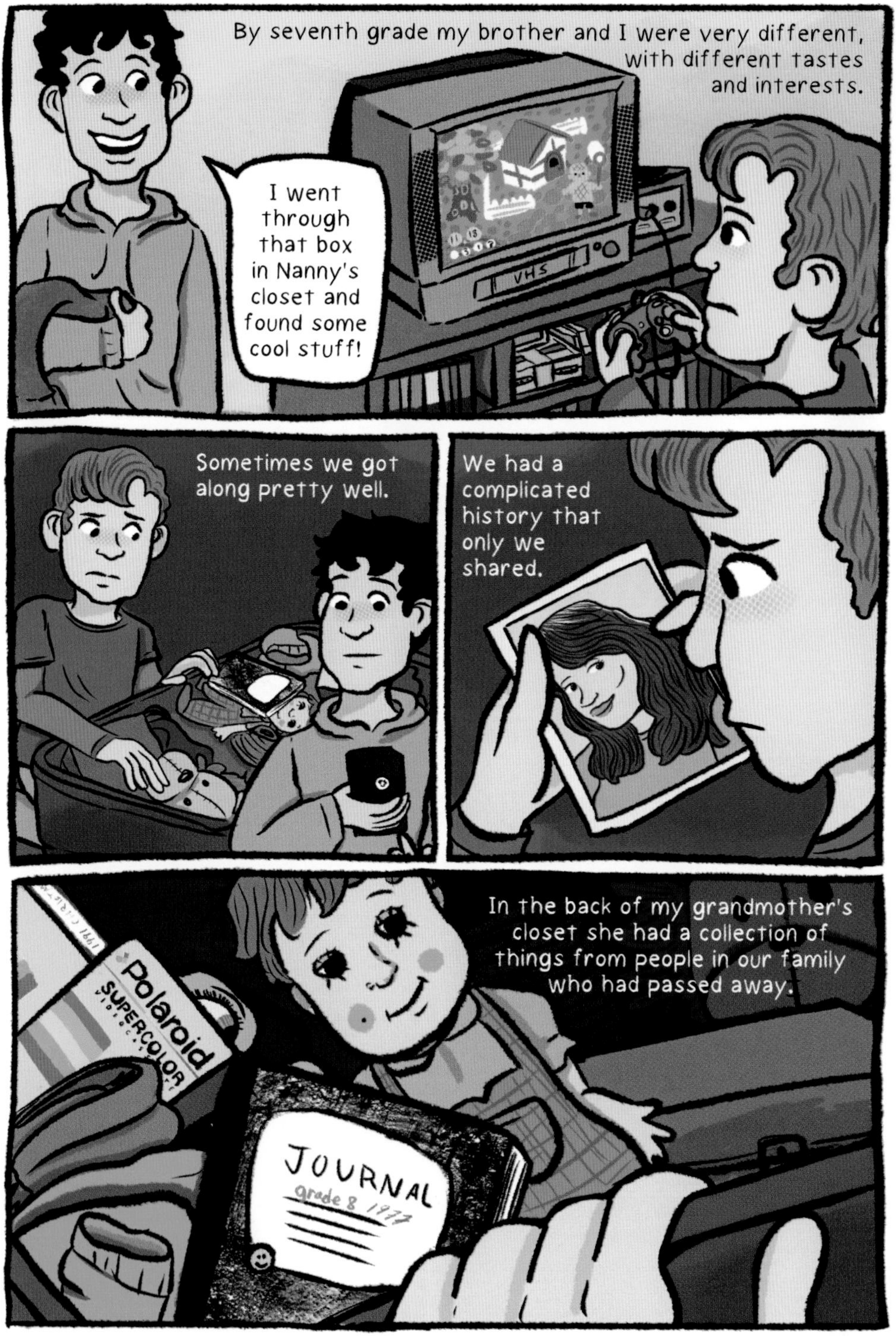

By seventh grade my brother and I were very different, with different tastes and interests.
I went through that box in Nanny's closet and found some cool stuff!
VHS
Sometimes we got along pretty well.
We had a complicated history that only we shared.
In the back of my grandmother's closet she had a collection of things from people in our family who had passed away.
Polaroid
SUPERCOLOR
JOURNAL
grade 8 1977

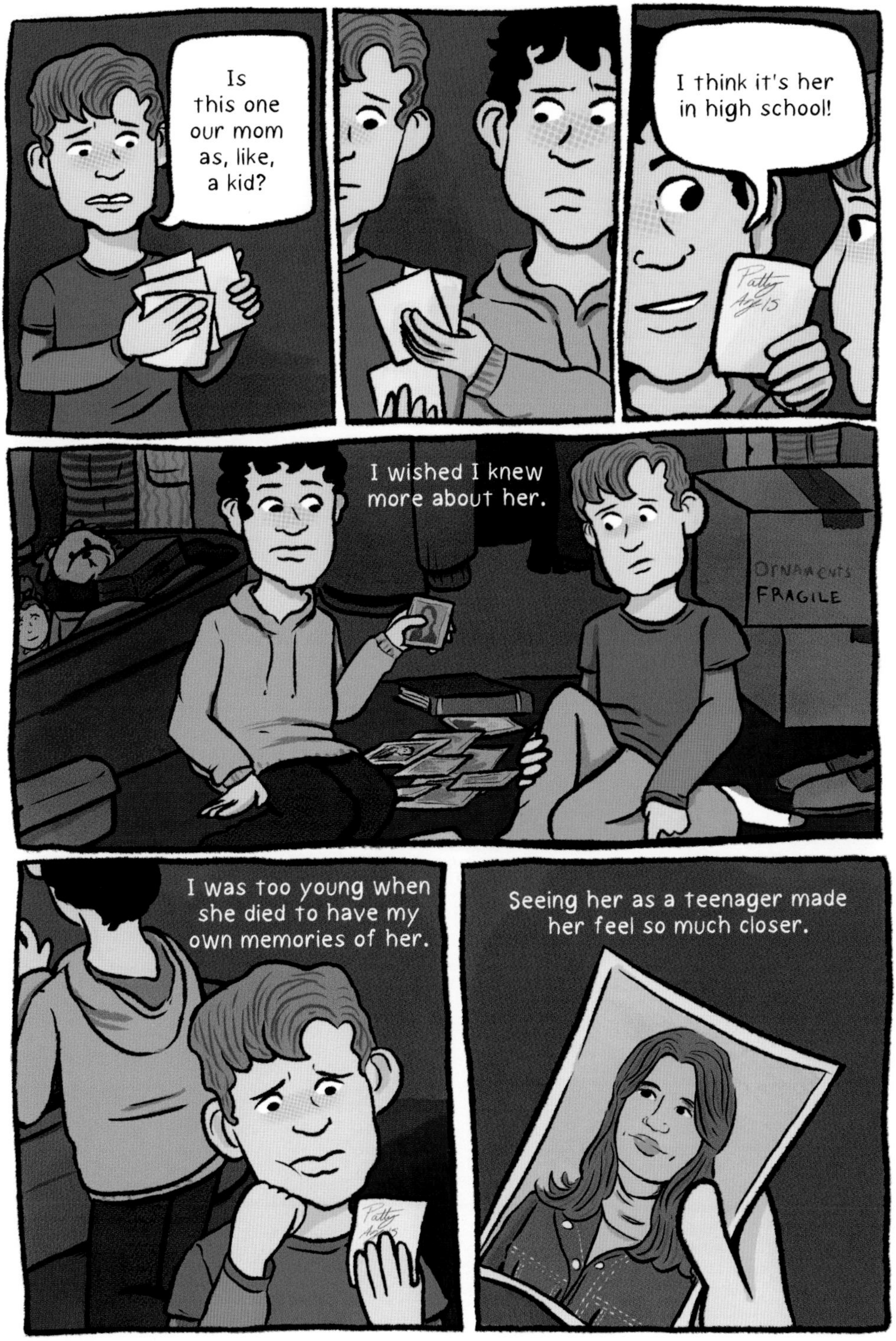
Is this one our mom as, like, a kid?
I think it's her in high school!
Patty Age 15
I wished I knew more about her.
ORNAMENTS FRAGILE
I was too young when she died to have my own memories of her.
Seeing her as a teenager made her feel so much closer.

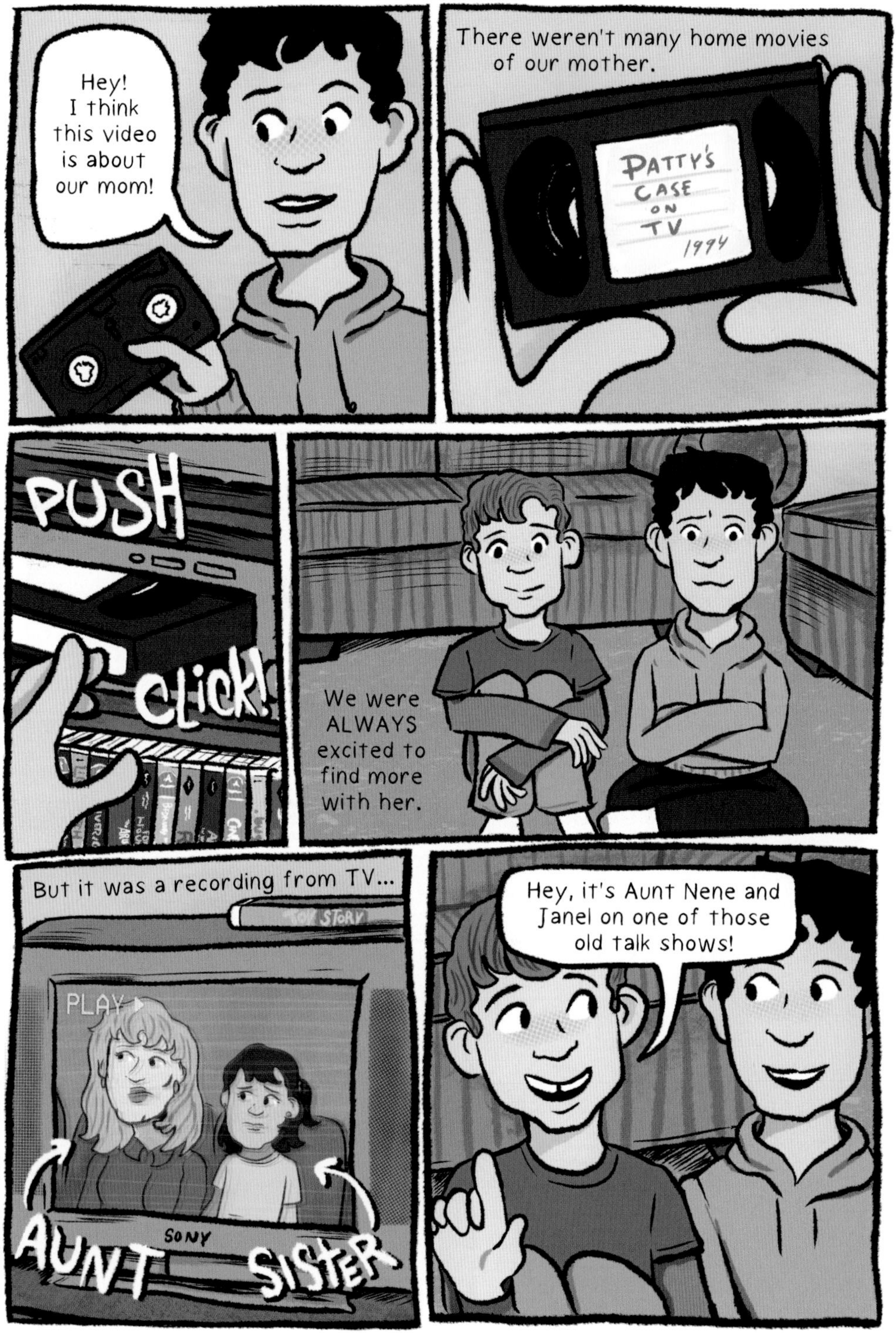
Hey!
I think
this video
is about
our mom!
There weren't many home movies of our mother.
PATTY'S CASE ON TV 1994
PUSH
CLICK!
We were ALWAYS excited to find more with her.
But it was a recording from TV...
TOY STORY
PLAY
SONY
AUNT
SISTER
Hey, it's Aunt Nene and Janel on one of those old talk shows!

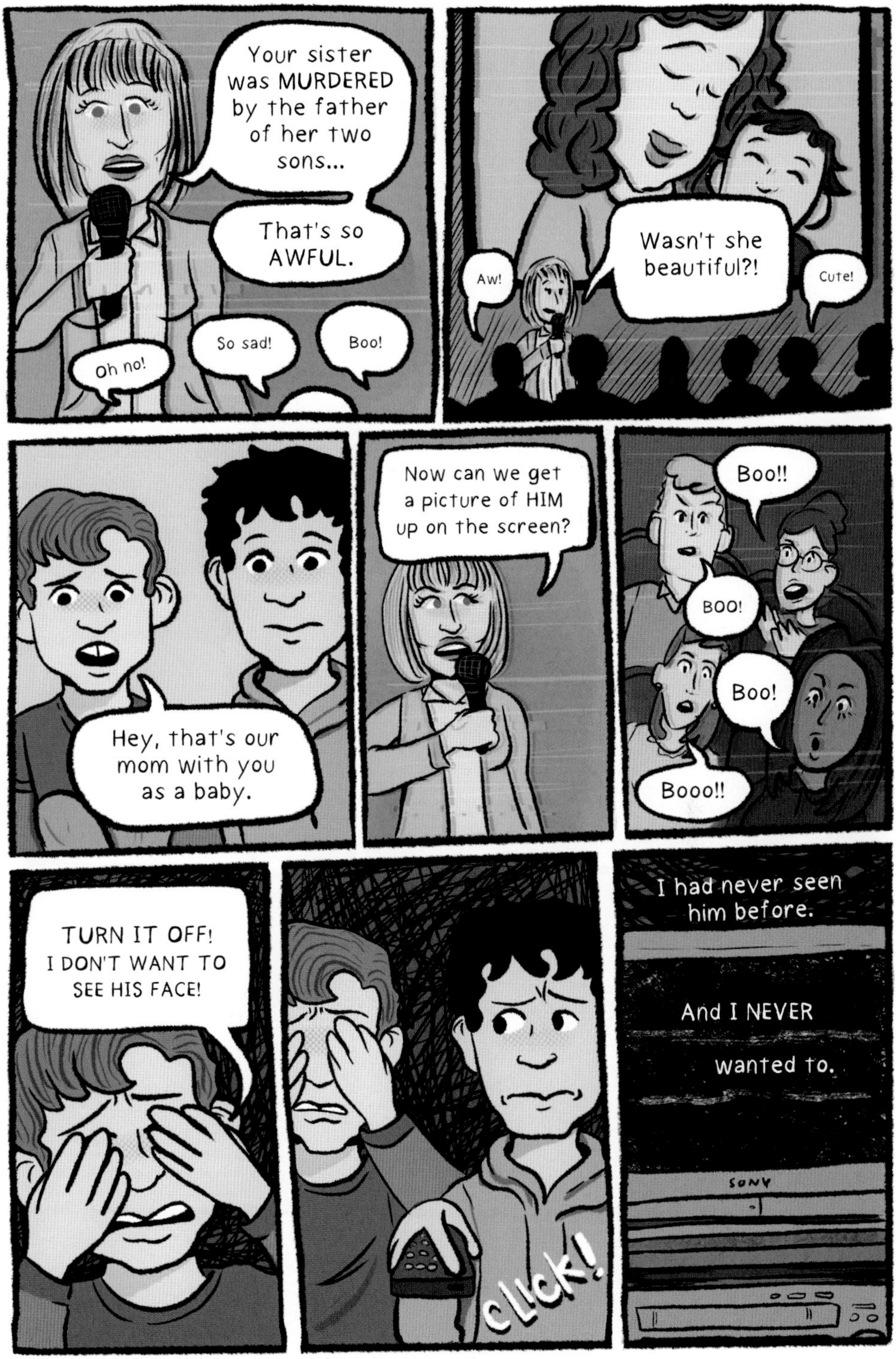
Your sister was MURDERED by the father of her two sons...
That's so AWFUL.
Oh no!
So sad!
Boo!
Aw!
Wasn't she beautiful?!
Cute!
Hey, that's our mom with you as a baby.
Now can we get a picture of HIM up on the screen?
Boo!!
BOO!
Boo!
Booo!!
TURN IT OFF! I DON'T WANT TO SEE HIS FACE!
CLICK!
I had never seen him before.
And I NEVER
wanted to.
SONY

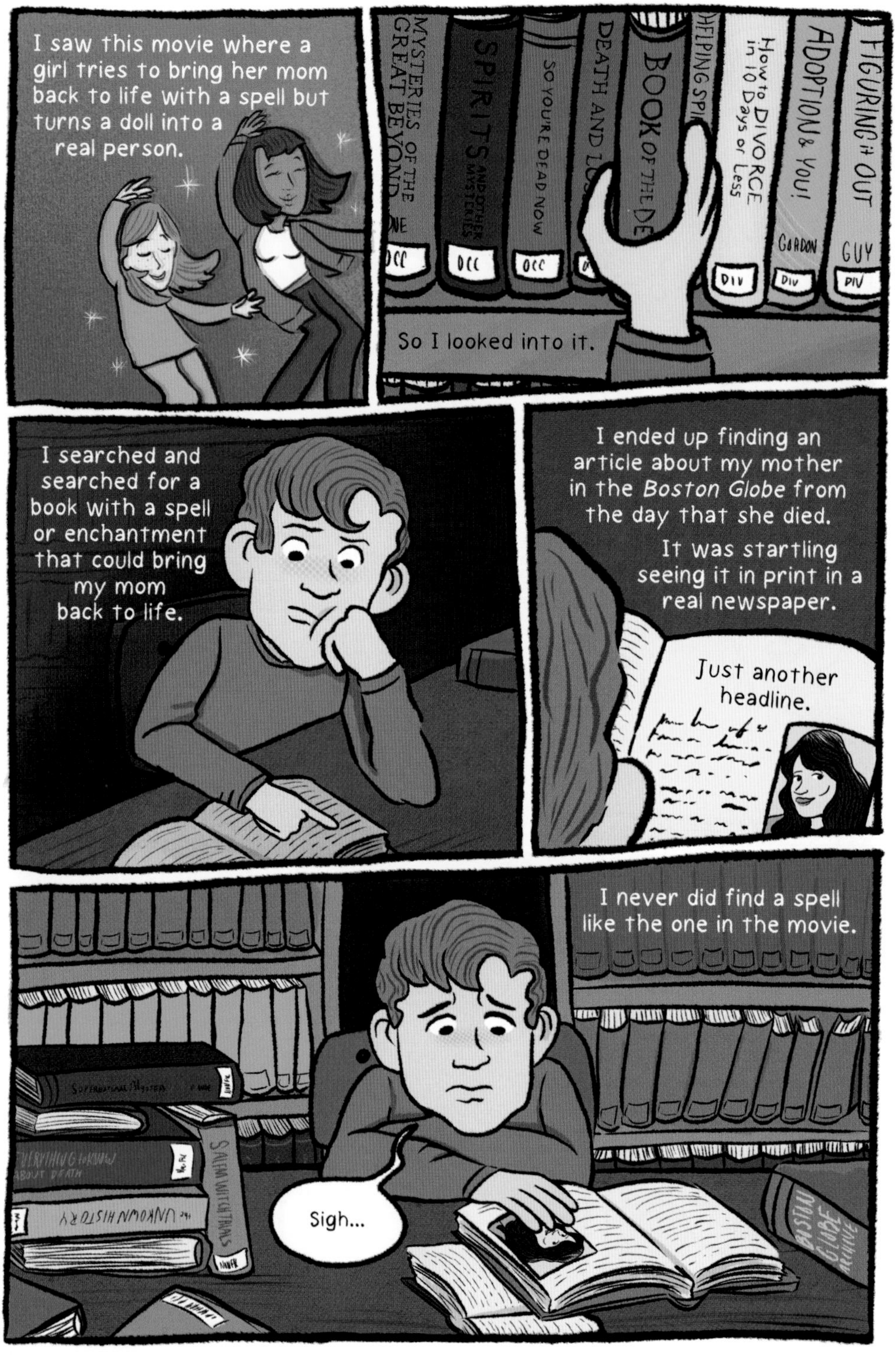
I saw this movie where a girl tries to bring her mom back to life with a spell but turns a doll into a real person.
MYSTERIES OF THE GREAT BEYOND
SPIRITS AND OTHER MYSTERIES
SO YOU'RE DEAD NOW
DEATH AND
How to DIVORCE in 10 Days or Less
ADOPTION & YOU!
GORDON
FIGURING IT OUT
GUY
So I looked into it.
I searched and searched for a book with a spell or enchantment that could bring my mom back to life.
I ended up finding an article about my mother in the *Boston Globe* from the day that she died.
It was startling seeing it in print in a real newspaper.
Just another headline.
I never did find a spell like the one in the movie.
SALEM WITCH TRIALS
THE UNKOWN HISTORY
Sigh...

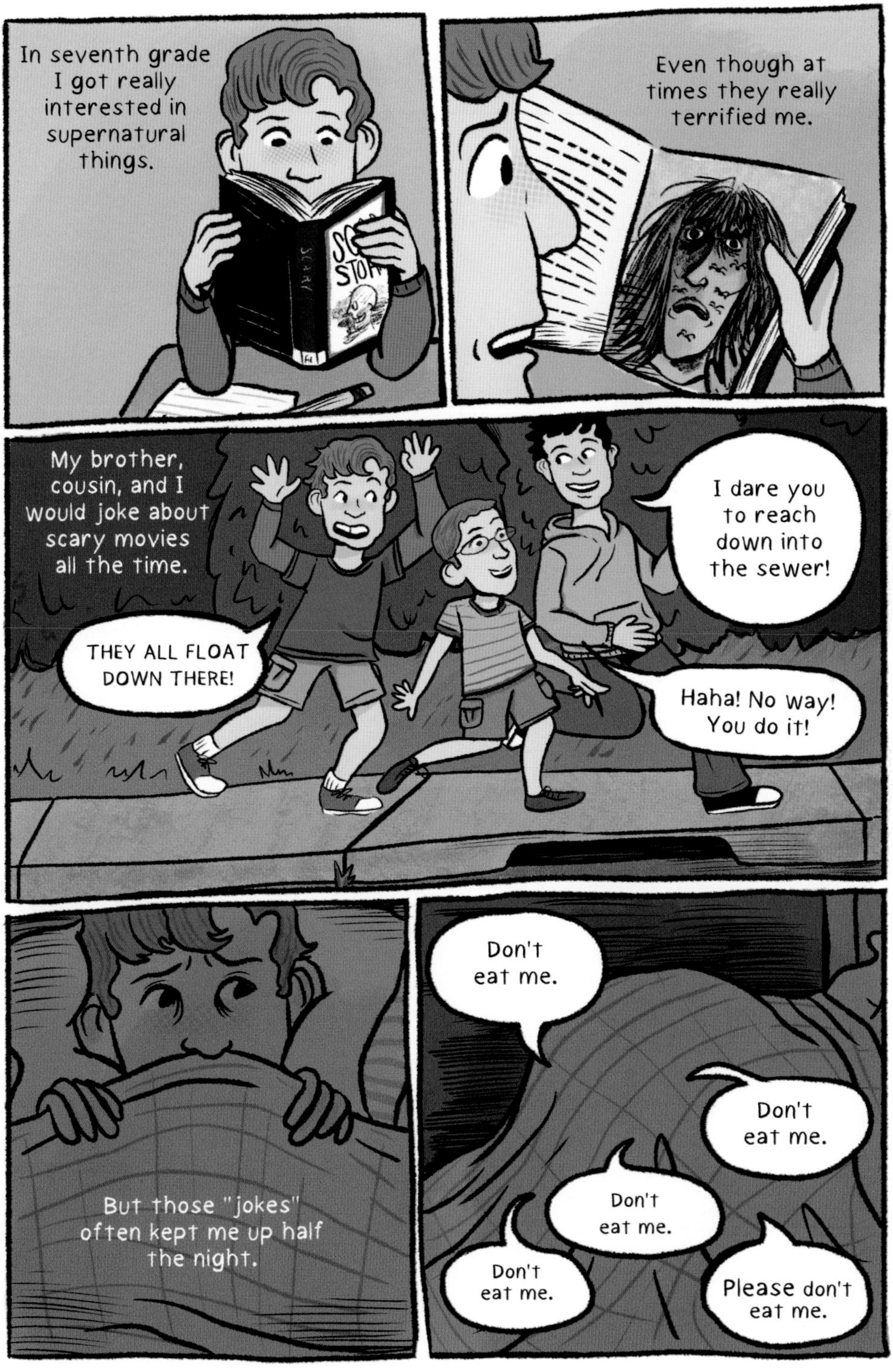
In seventh grade I got really interested in supernatural things.
SCARY
Even though at times they really terrified me.
My brother, cousin, and I would joke about scary movies all the time.
I dare you to reach down into the sewer!
THEY ALL FLOAT DOWN THERE!
Haha! No way! You do it!
But those "jokes" often kept me up half the night.
Don't eat me.
Don't eat me.
Don't eat me.
Don't eat me.
Please don't eat me.

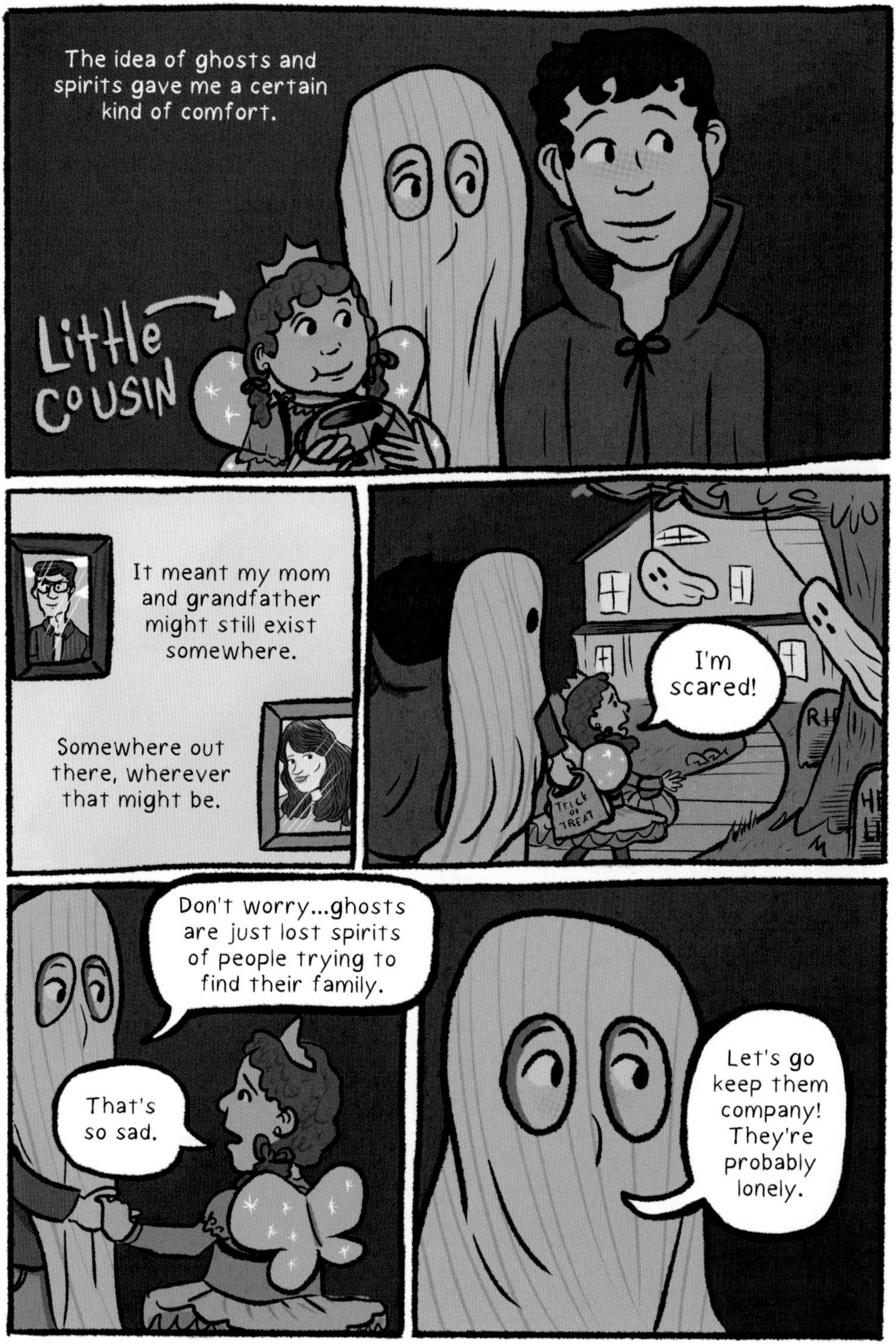

The idea of ghosts and spirits gave me a certain kind of comfort.
Little Cousin
It meant my mom and grandfather might still exist somewhere.
Somewhere out there, wherever that might be.
I'm scared!
Trick or Treat
RIP
Don't worry...ghosts are just lost spirits of people trying to find their family.
That's so sad.
Let's go keep them company! They're probably lonely.

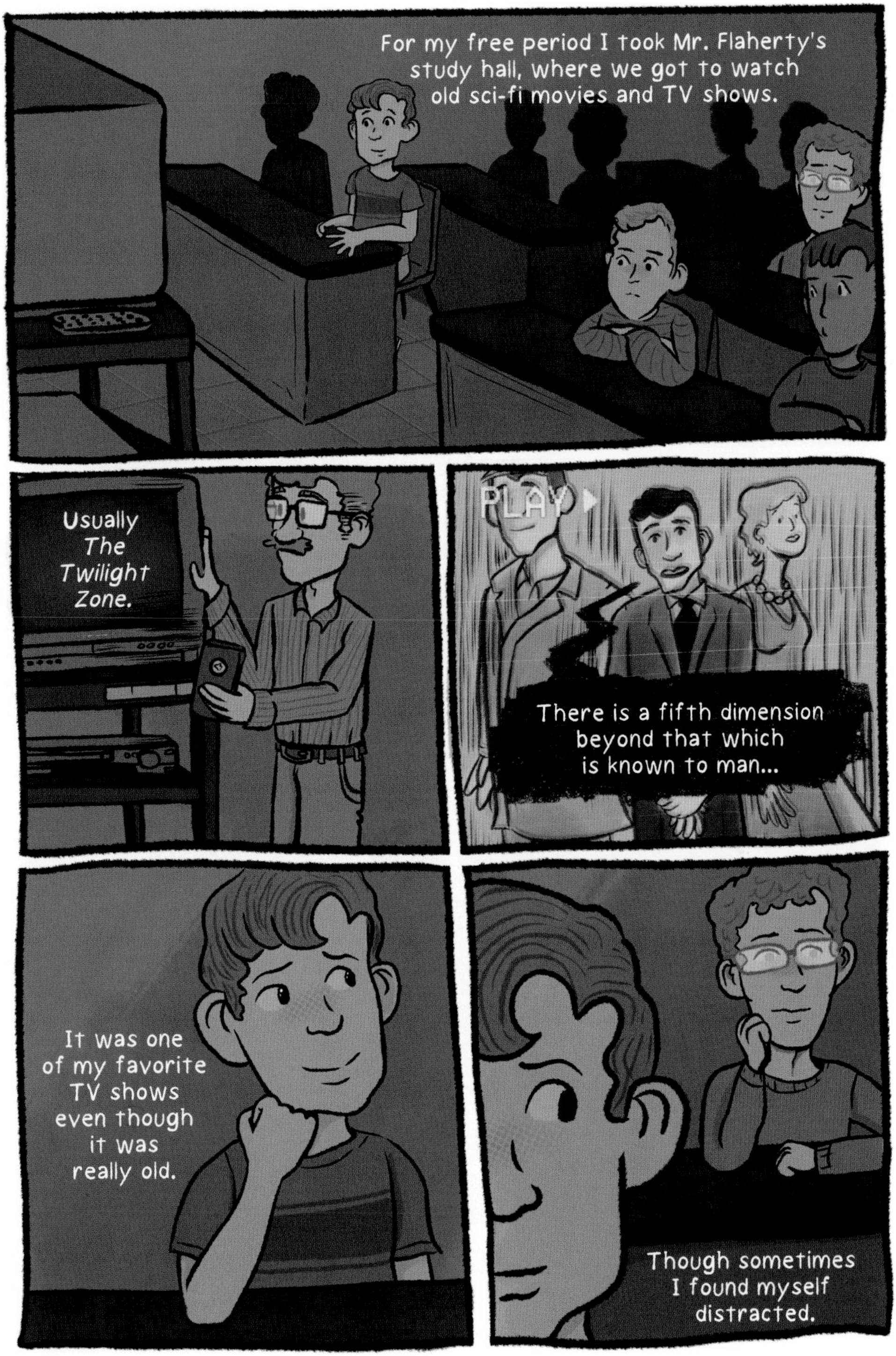
For my free period I took Mr. Flaherty's study hall, where we got to watch old sci-fi movies and TV shows.
Usually *The Twilight Zone.*
PLAY
There is a fifth dimension beyond that which is known to man...
It was one of my favorite TV shows even though it was really old.
Though sometimes I found myself distracted.

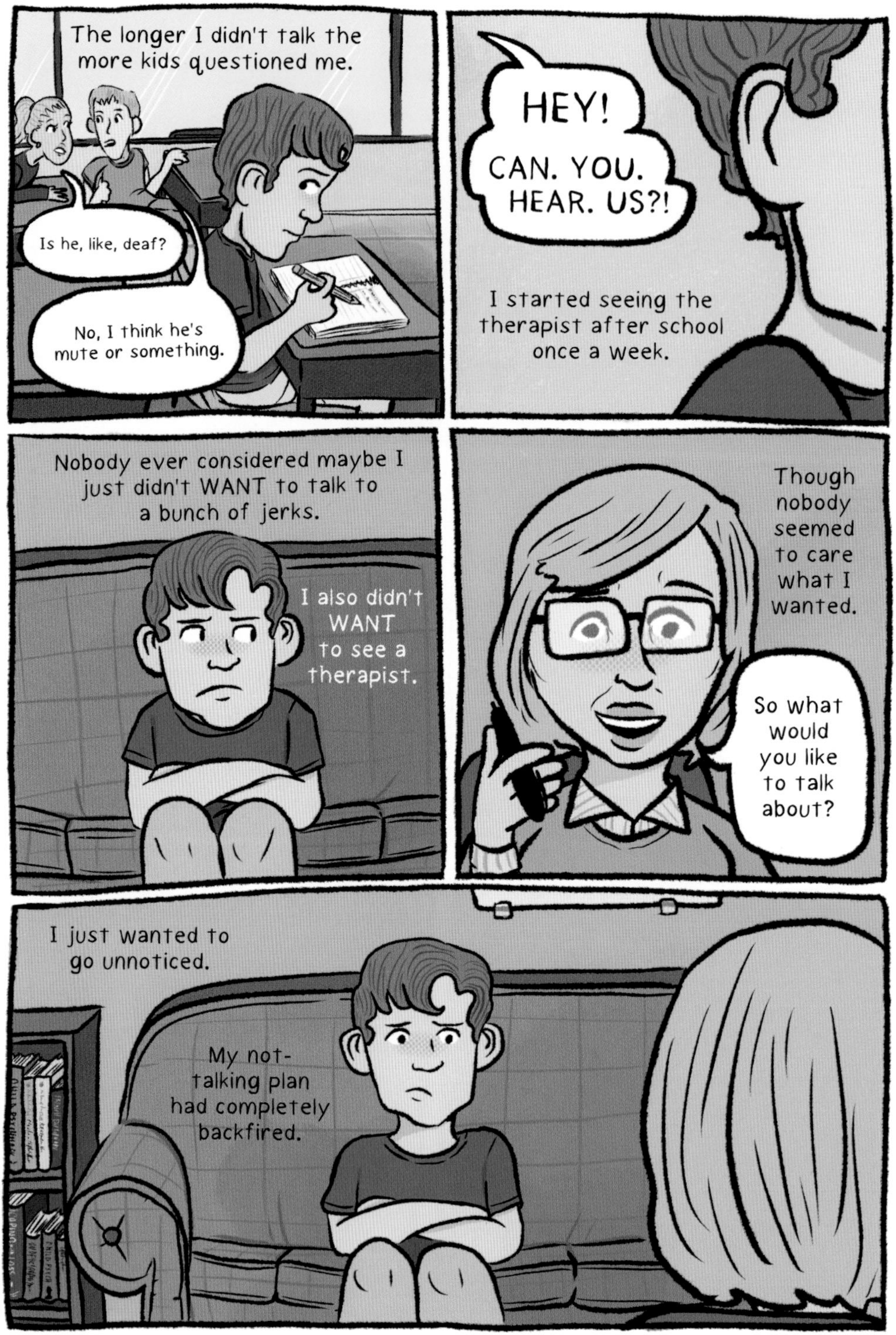
The longer I didn't talk the more kids questioned me.
Is he, like, deaf?
No, I think he's mute or something.
HEY!
CAN. YOU. HEAR. US?!
I started seeing the therapist after school once a week.
Nobody ever considered maybe I just didn't WANT to talk to a bunch of jerks.
I also didn't WANT to see a therapist.
Though nobody seemed to care what I wanted.
So what would you like to talk about?
I just wanted to go unnoticed.
My not-talking plan had completely backfired.

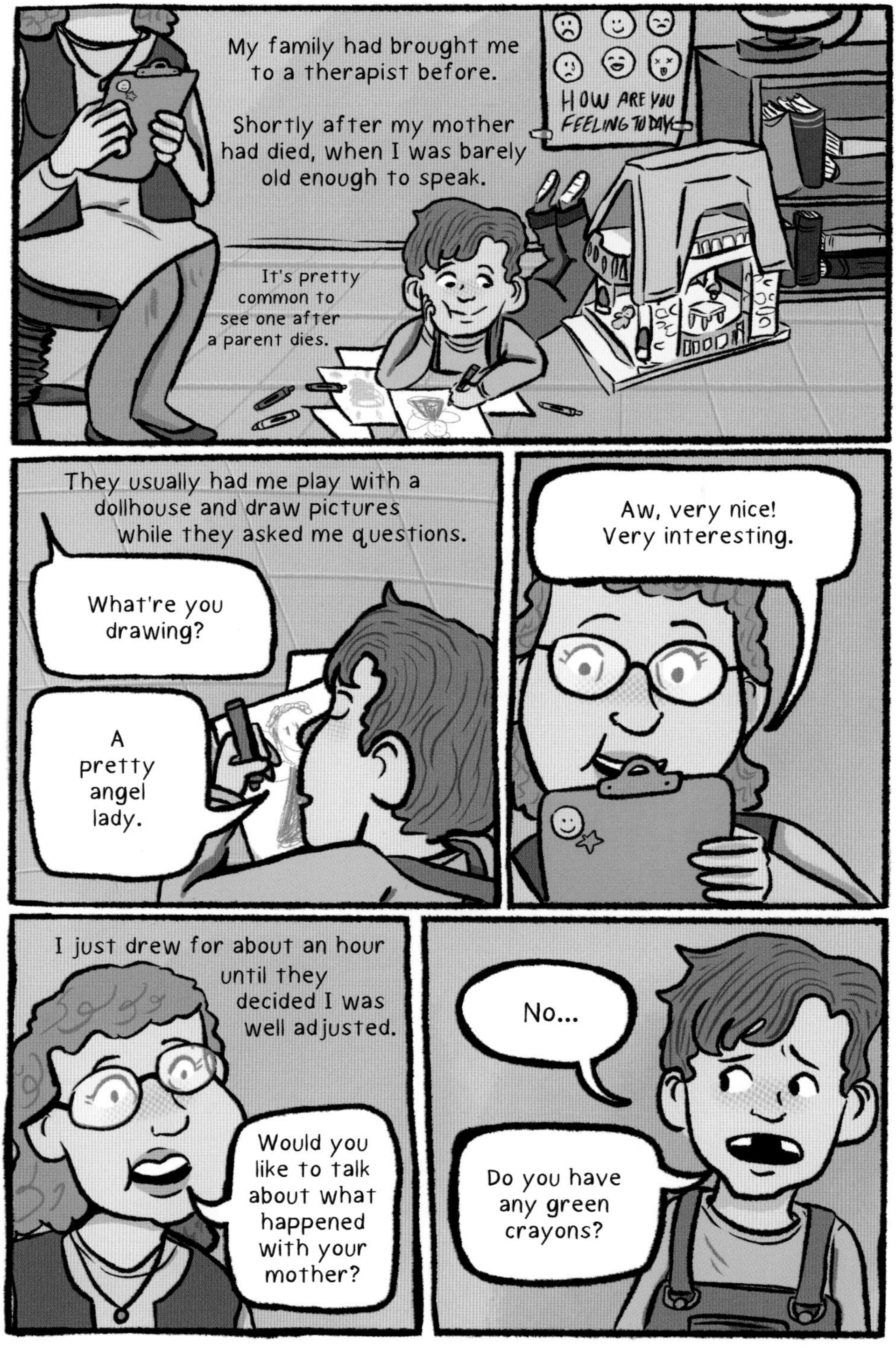

HOW ARE YOU FEELING TODAY
My family had brought me to a therapist before.
Shortly after my mother had died, when I was barely old enough to speak.
It's pretty common to see one after a parent dies.
They usually had me play with a dollhouse and draw pictures while they asked me questions.
What're you drawing?
A pretty angel lady.
Aw, very nice! Very interesting.
I just drew for about an hour until they decided I was well adjusted.
Would you like to talk about what happened with your mother?
No...
Do you have any green crayons?

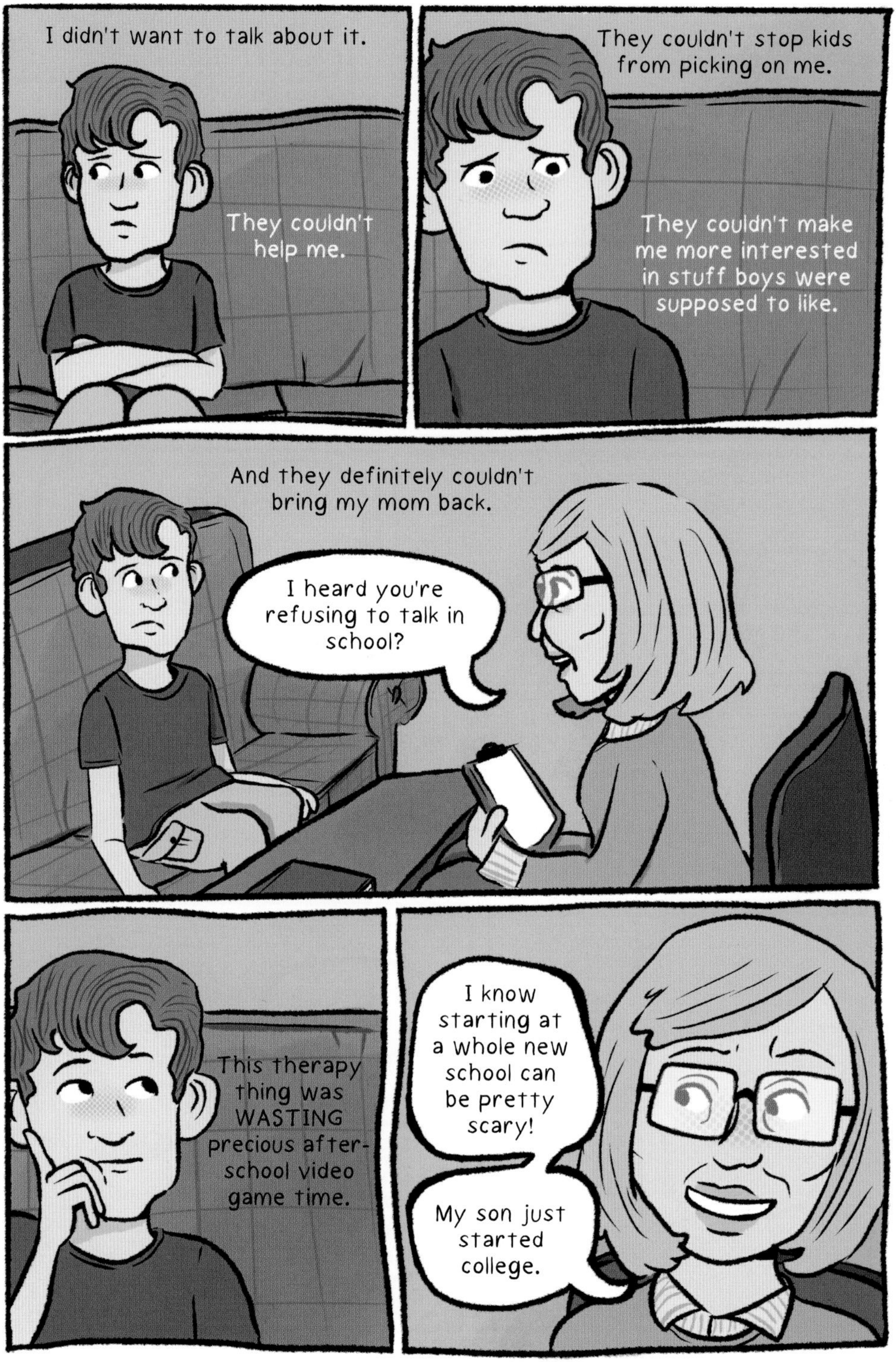
I didn't want to talk about it.
They couldn't help me.
They couldn't stop kids from picking on me.
They couldn't make me more interested in stuff boys were supposed to like.
And they definitely couldn't bring my mom back.
I heard you're refusing to talk in school?
This therapy thing was WASTING precious after-school video game time.
I know starting at a whole new school can be pretty scary!
My son just started college.

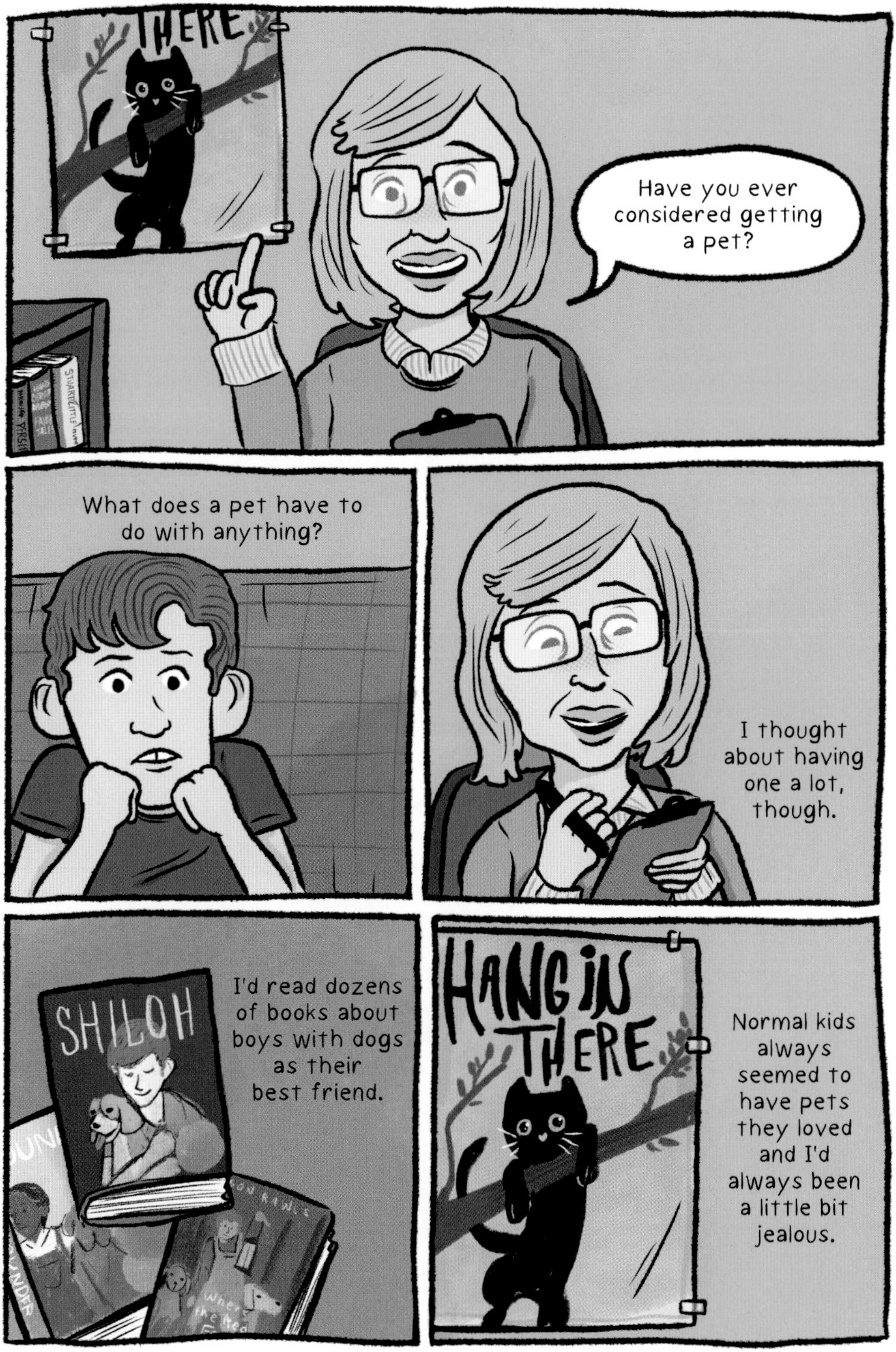
THERE
Have you ever considered getting a pet?
What does a pet have to do with anything?
I thought about having one a lot, though.
SHILOH
I'd read dozens of books about boys with dogs as their best friend.
HANG IN THERE
Normal kids always seemed to have pets they loved and I'd always been a little bit jealous.

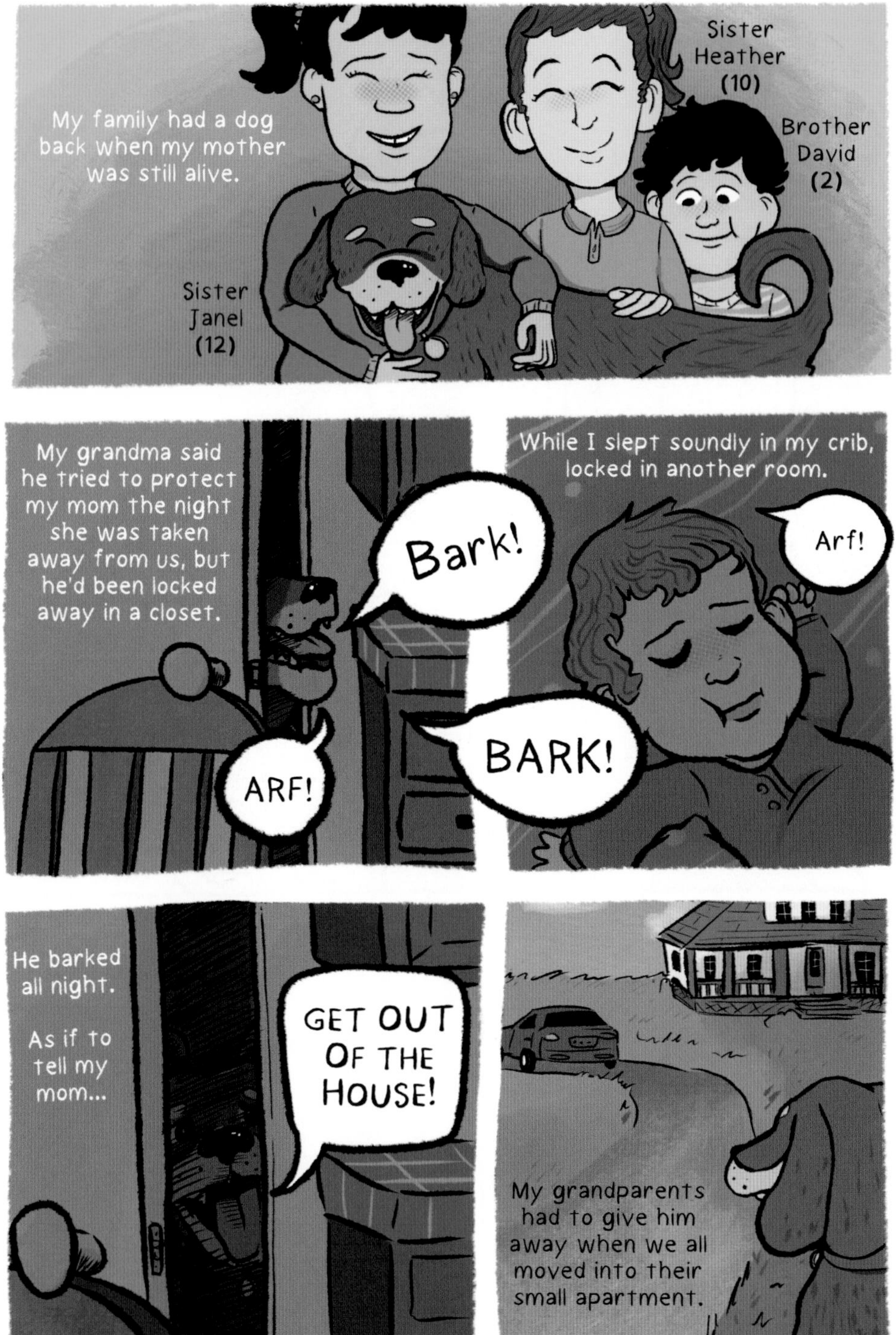

My family had a dog back when my mother was still alive.
Sister Heather (10)
Brother David (2)
Sister Janel (12)
My grandma said he tried to protect my mom the night she was taken away from us, but he'd been locked away in a closet.
Bark!
ARF!
While I slept soundly in my crib, locked in another room.
Arf!
BARK!
He barked all night.
As if to tell my mom...
GET OUT OF THE HOUSE!
My grandparents had to give him away when we all moved into their small apartment.

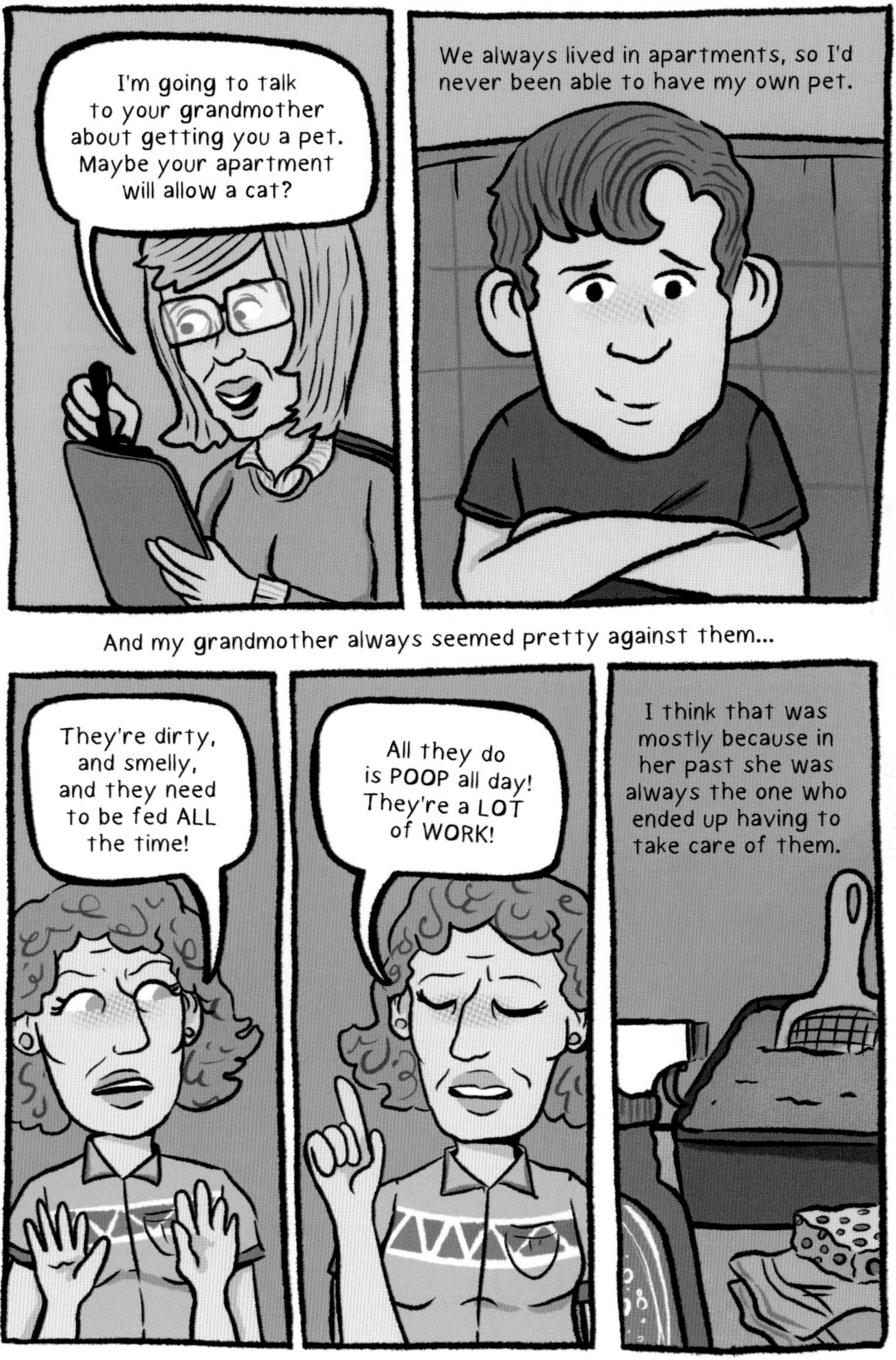
I'm going to talk to your grandmother about getting you a pet. Maybe your apartment will allow a cat?
We always lived in apartments, so I'd never been able to have my own pet.
And my grandmother always seemed pretty against them...
They're dirty, and smelly, and they need to be fed ALL the time!
All they do is POOP all day! They're a LOT of WORK!
I think that was mostly because in her past she was always the one who ended up having to take care of them.

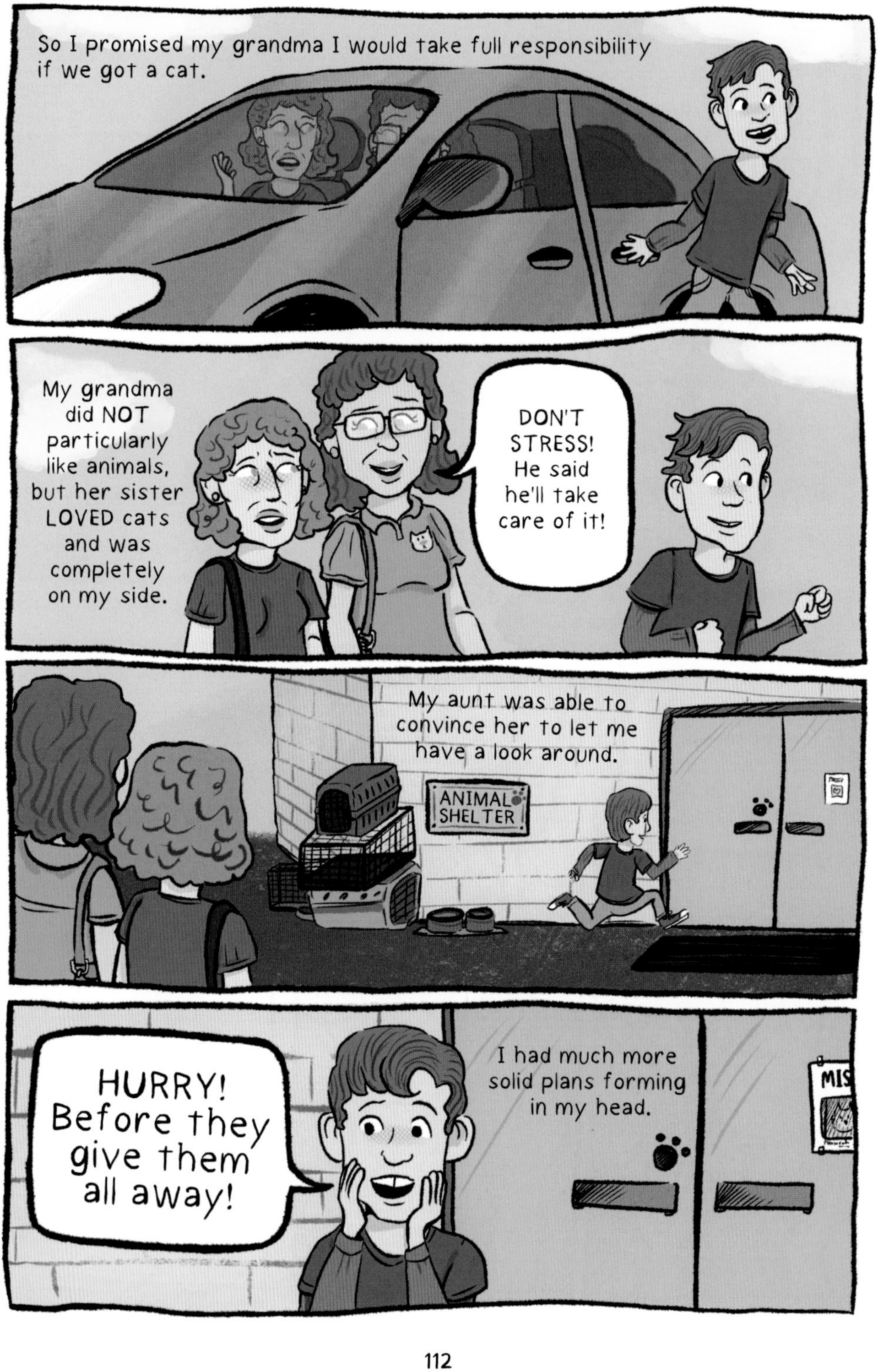

So I promised my grandma I would take full responsibility if we got a cat.
My grandma did NOT particularly like animals, but her sister LOVED cats and was completely on my side.
DON'T STRESS! He said he'll take care of it!
My aunt was able to convince her to let me have a look around.
ANIMAL SHELTER
HURRY! Before they give them all away!
I had much more solid plans forming in my head.

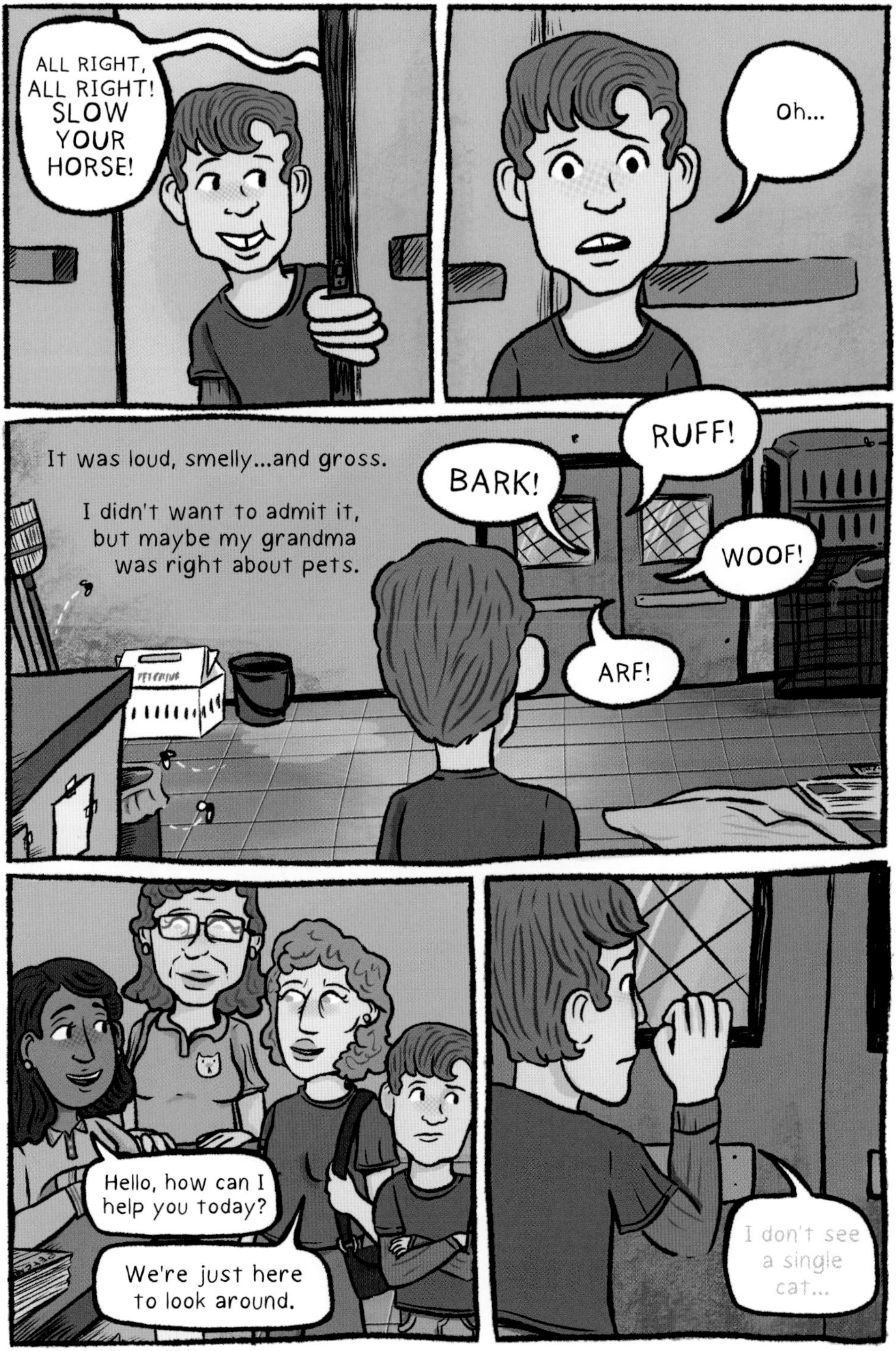
ALL RIGHT, ALL RIGHT! SLOW YOUR HORSE!
Oh...
It was loud, smelly...and gross.
I didn't want to admit it, but maybe my grandma was right about pets.
BARK!
RUFF!
WOOF!
ARF!
Hello, how can I help you today?
We're just here to look around.
I don't see a single cat...

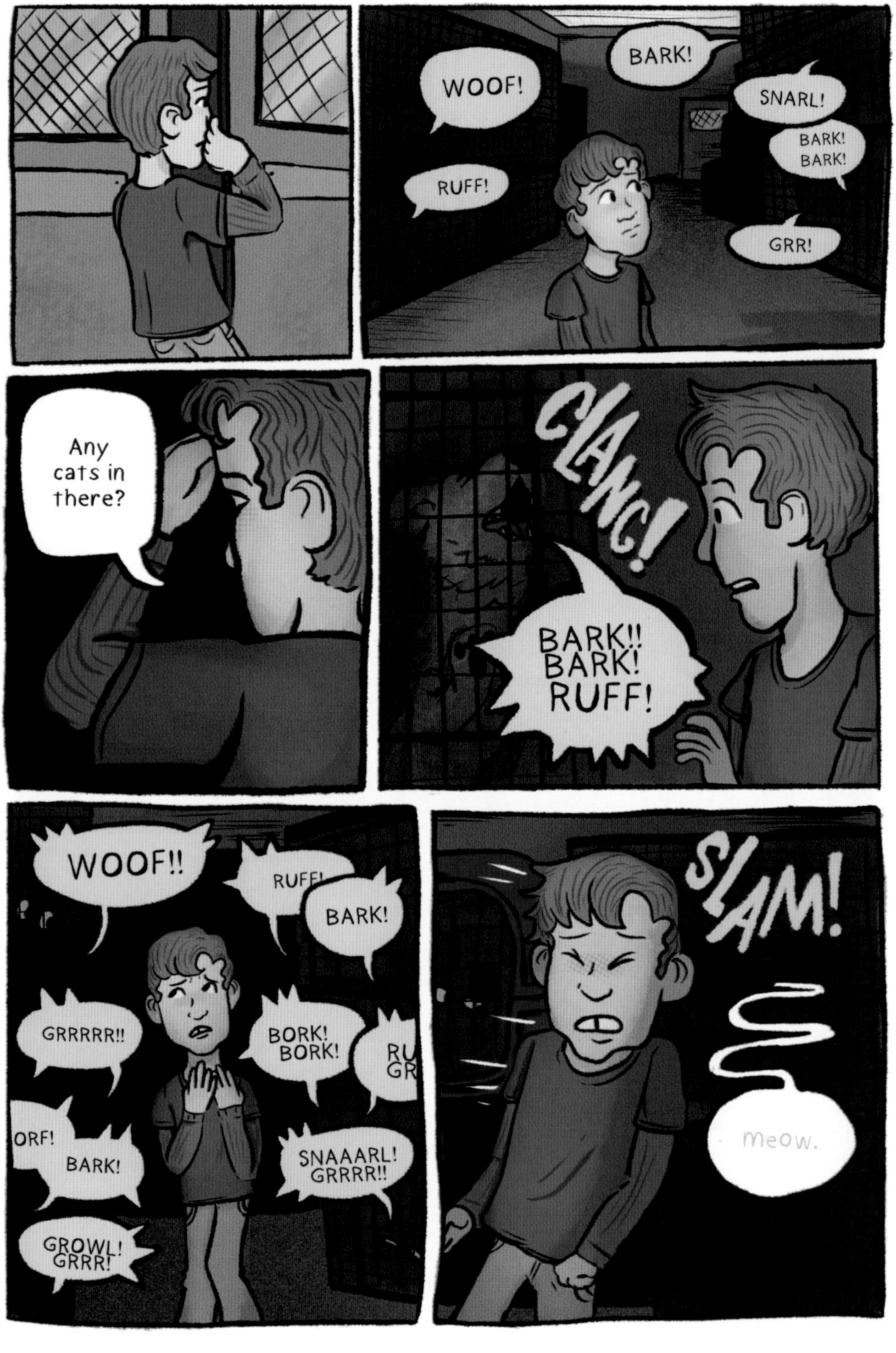

WOOF!
BARK!
SNARL!
BARK! BARK!
RUFF!
GRR!
Any cats in there?
CLANG!
BARK!! BARK! RUFF!
WOOF!!
BARK!
GRRRRR!!
BORK! BORK!
BARK!
SNAAARL! GRRRR!!
GROWL! GRRR!
SLAM!
meow.

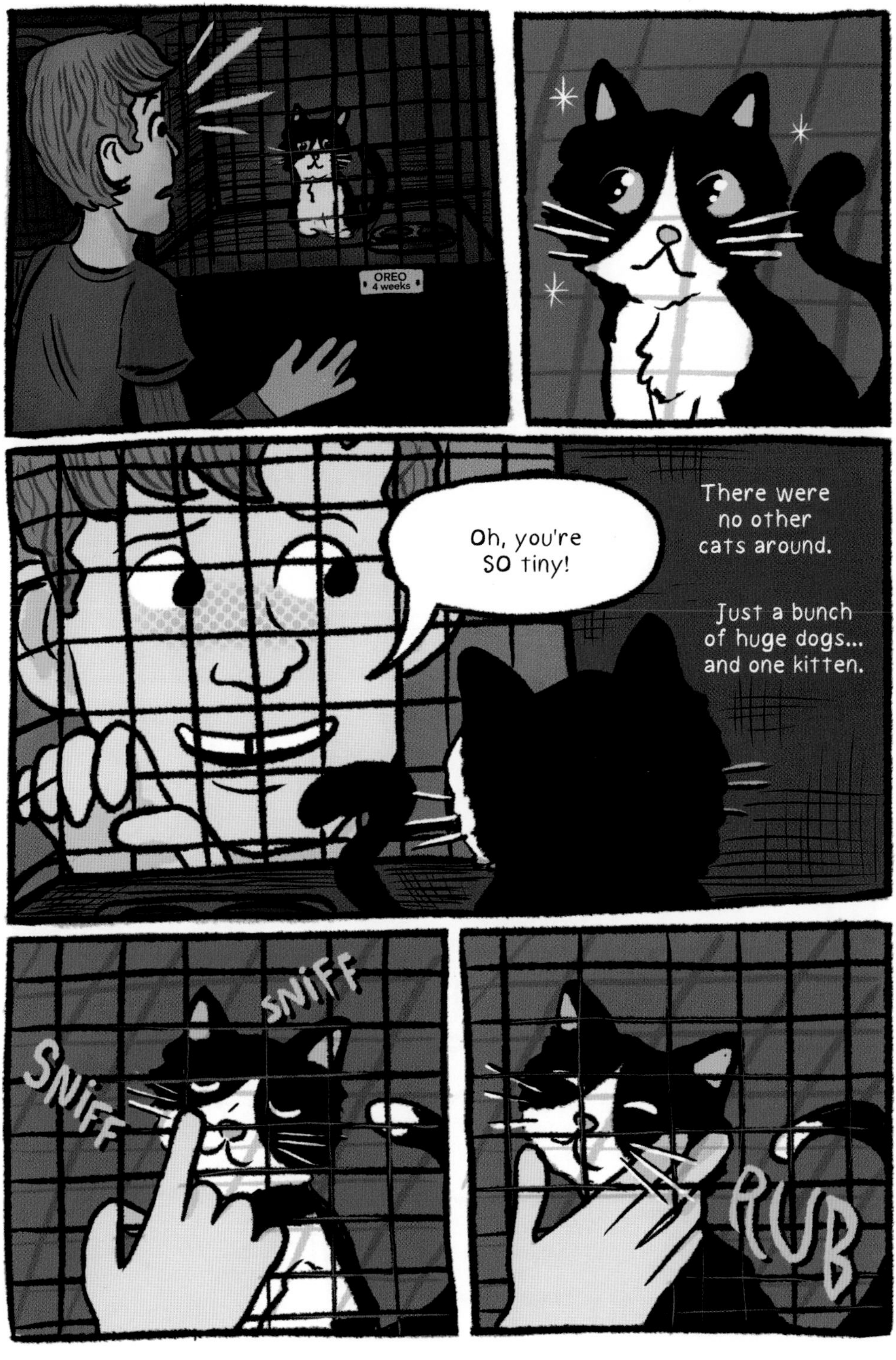
OREO
4 weeks
Oh, you're SO tiny!
There were no other cats around.
Just a bunch of huge dogs... and one kitten.
SNIFF
SNIFF
RUB

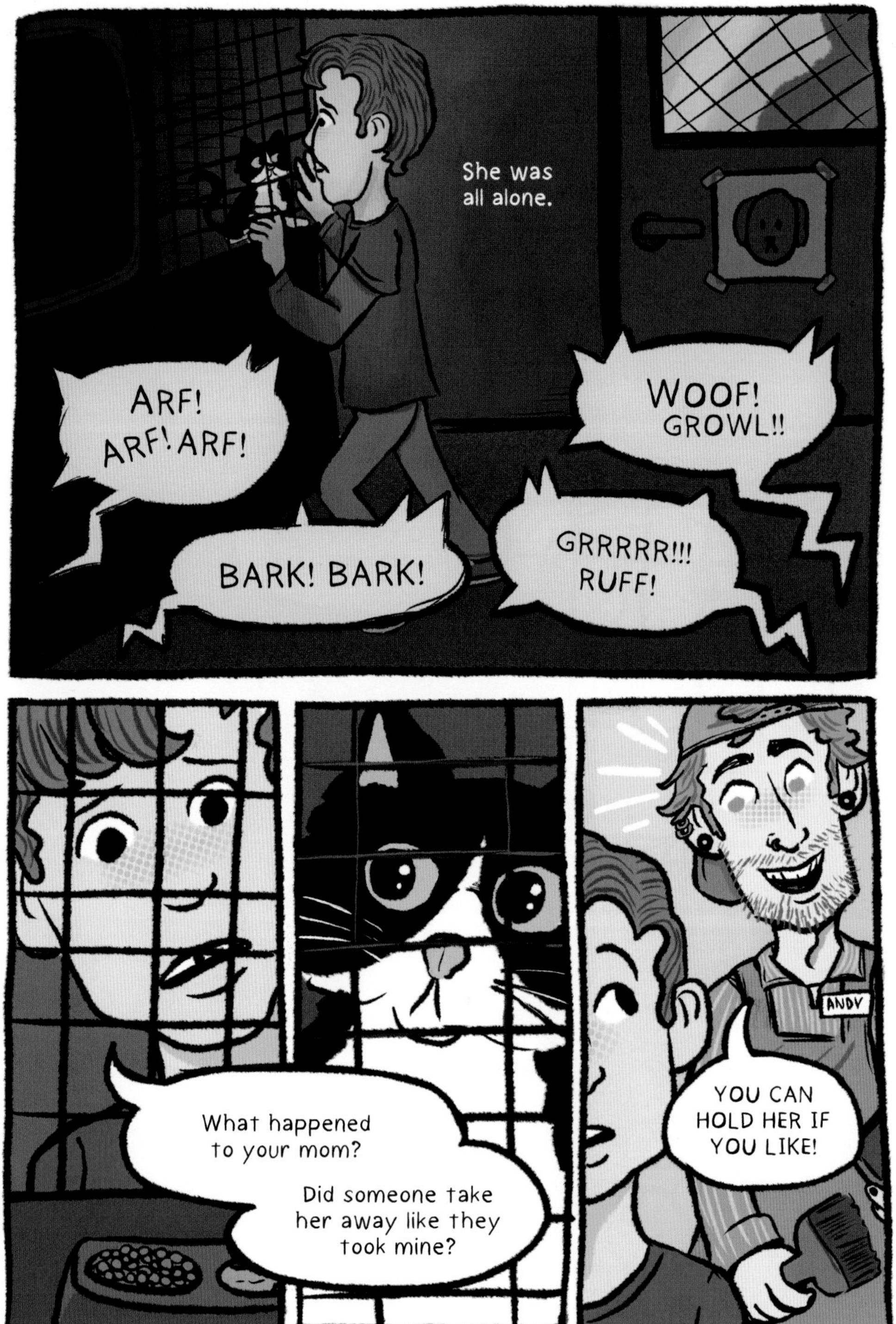
She was all alone.
ARF! ARF! ARF!
WOOF! GROWL!!
BARK! BARK!
GRRRRR!!! RUFF!
ANDY
What happened to your mom?
Did someone take her away like they took mine?
YOU CAN HOLD HER IF YOU LIKE!

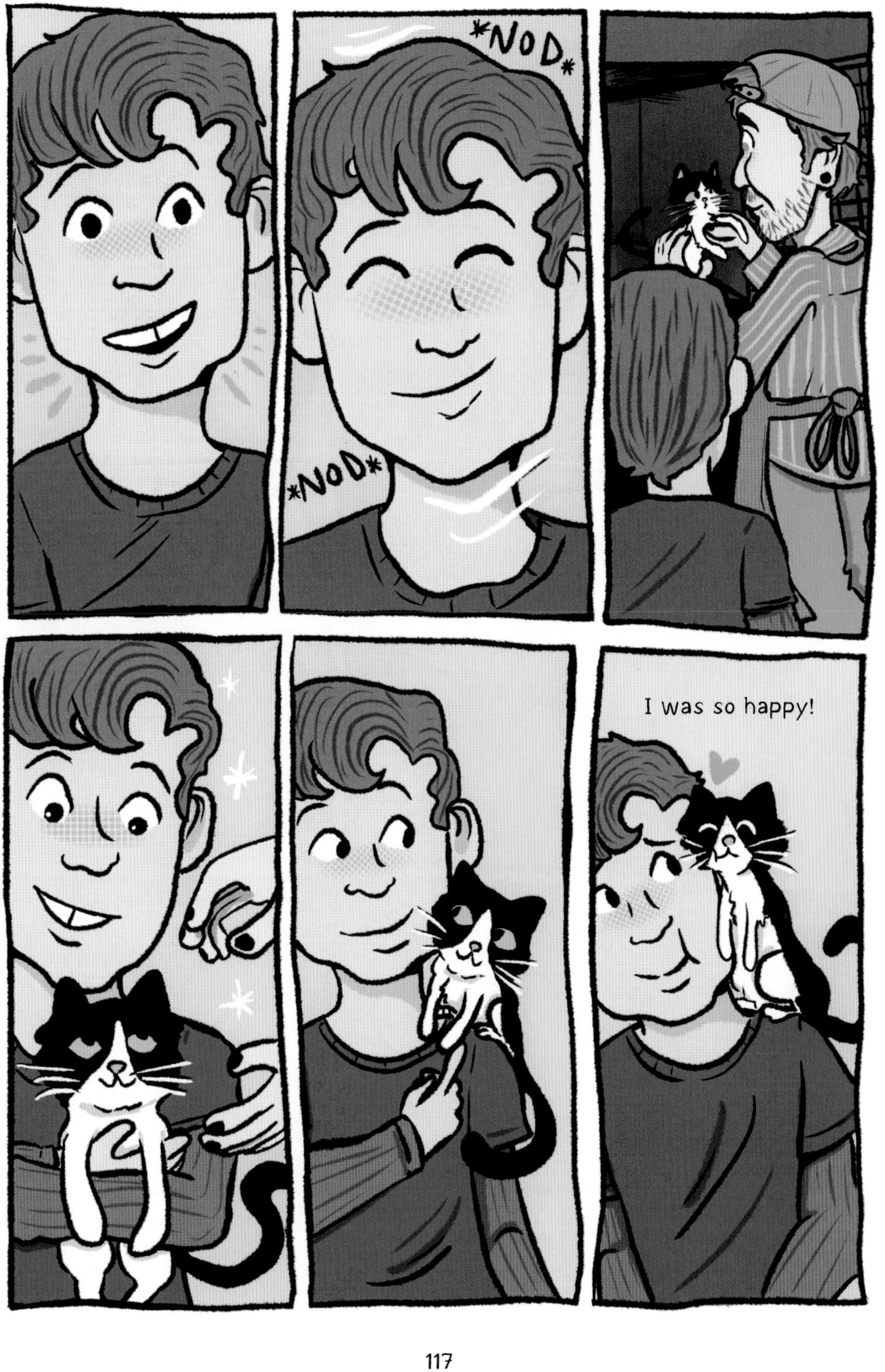
NOD
NOD
I was so happy!

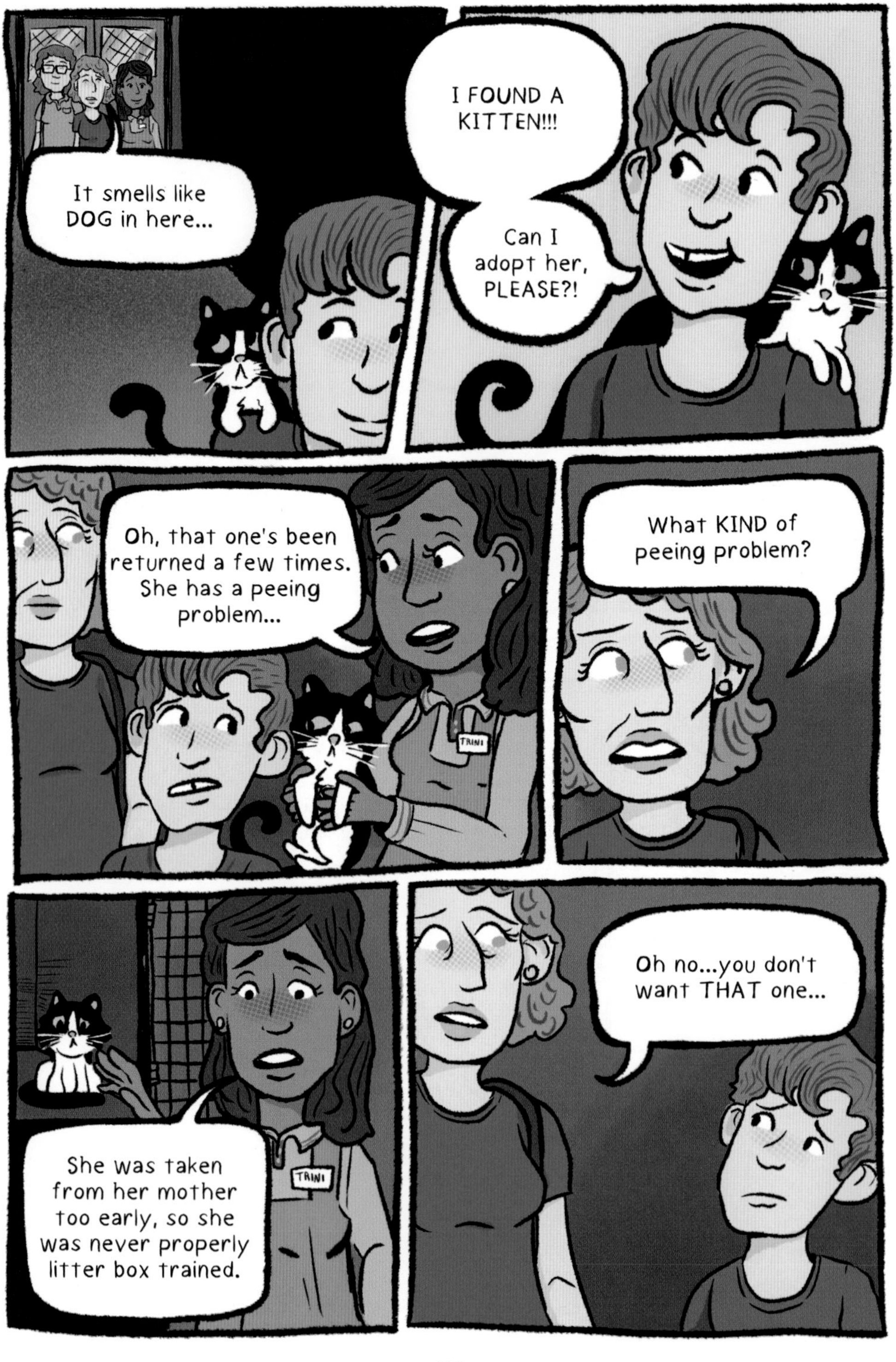
It smells like DOG in here...
I FOUND A KITTEN!!!
Can I adopt her, PLEASE?!
Oh, that one's been returned a few times. She has a peeing problem...
TRINI
What KIND of peeing problem?
She was taken from her mother too early, so she was never properly litter box trained.
TRINI
Oh no...you don't want THAT one...

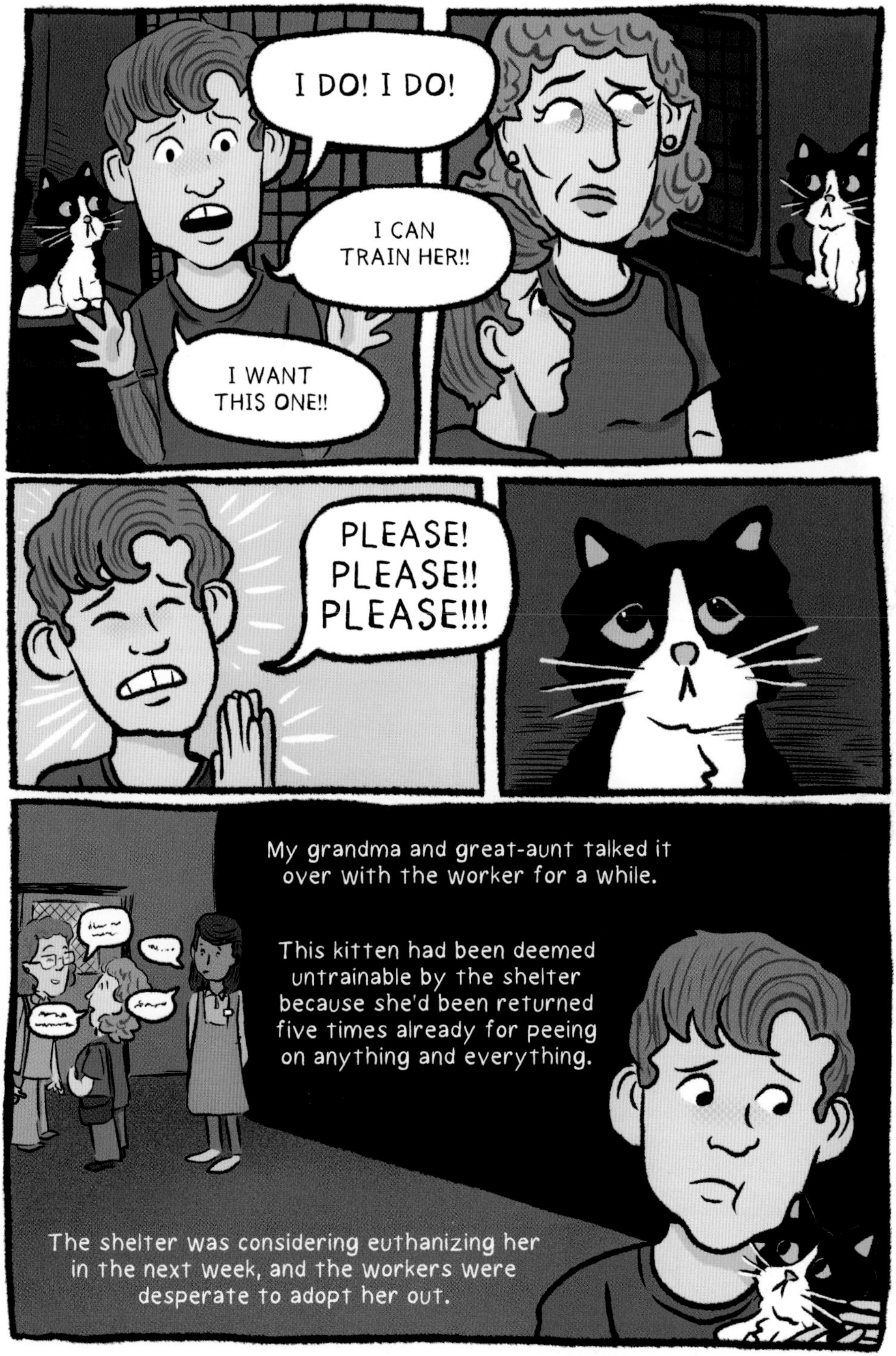
I DO! I DO!
I CAN TRAIN HER!!
I WANT THIS ONE!!
PLEASE! PLEASE!! PLEASE!!!
My grandma and great-aunt talked it over with the worker for a while.
This kitten had been deemed untrainable by the shelter because she'd been returned five times already for peeing on anything and everything.
The shelter was considering euthanizing her in the next week, and the workers were desperate to adopt her out.

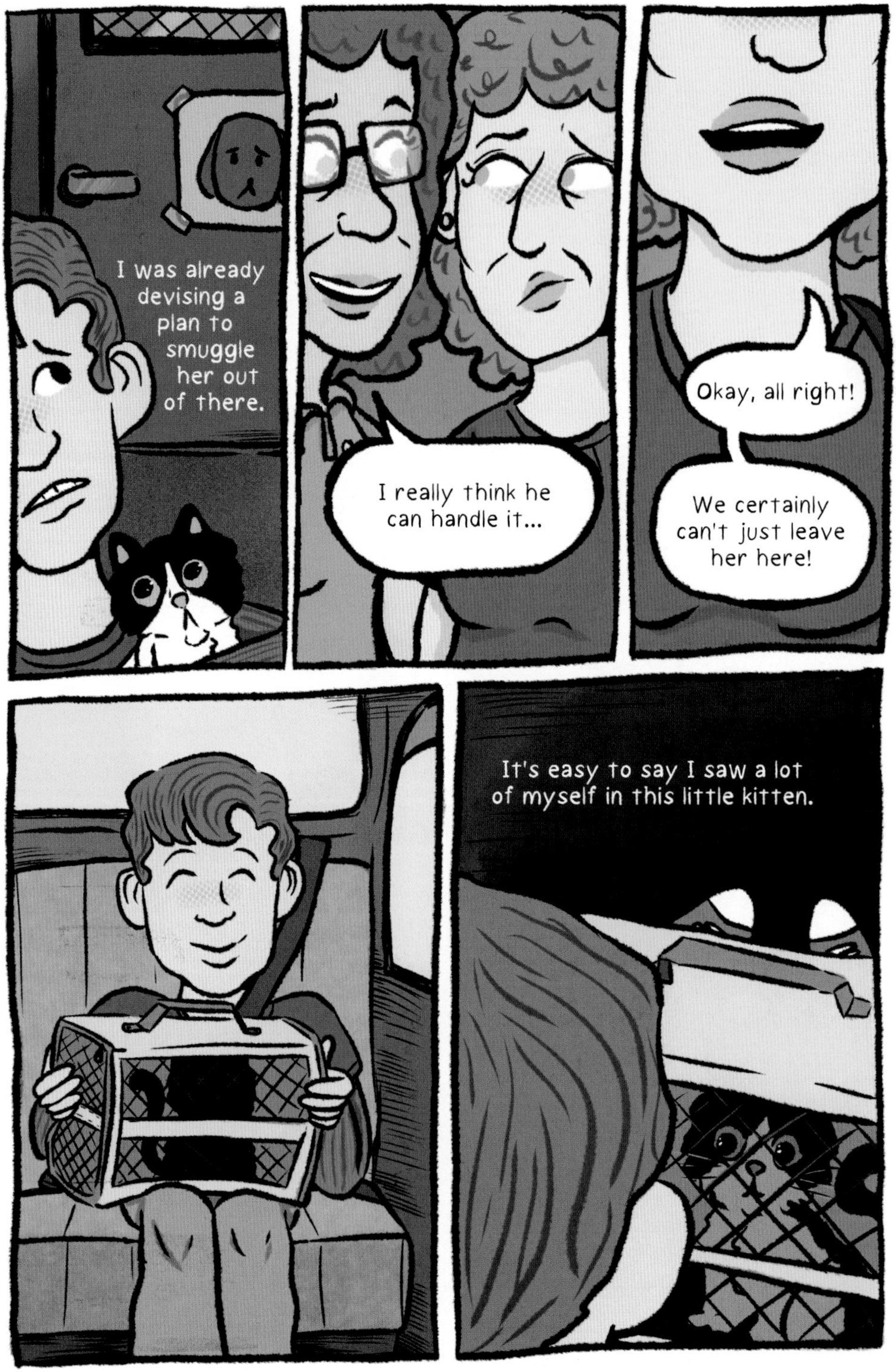
I was already devising a plan to smuggle her out of there.
I really think he can handle it...
Okay, all right!
We certainly can't just leave her here!
It's easy to say I saw a lot of myself in this little kitten.

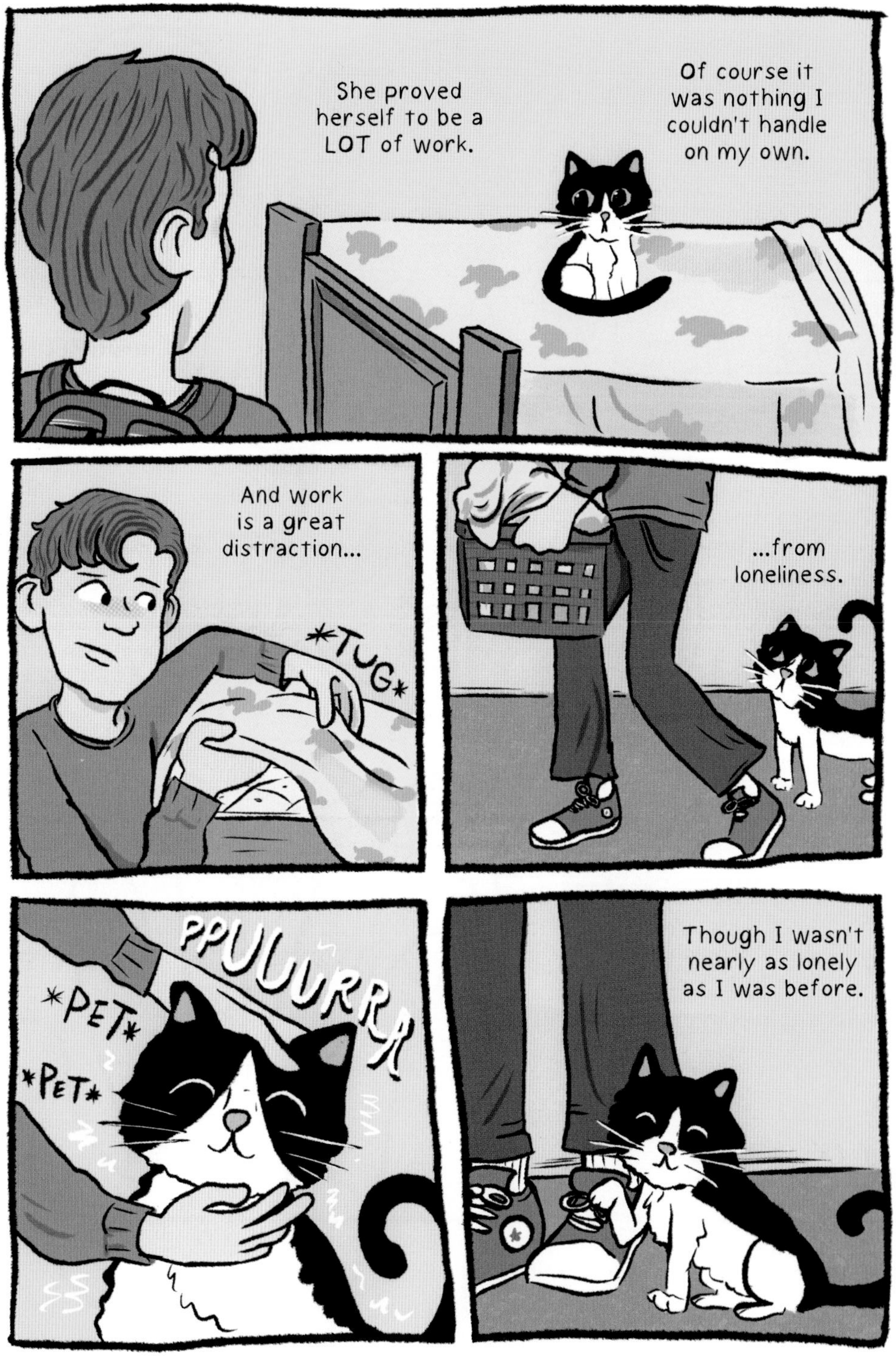
She proved herself to be a LOT of work.
Of course it was nothing I couldn't handle on my own.
And work is a great distraction...
TUG
...from loneliness.
PPUUUURRRR
PET
PET
Though I wasn't nearly as lonely as I was before.

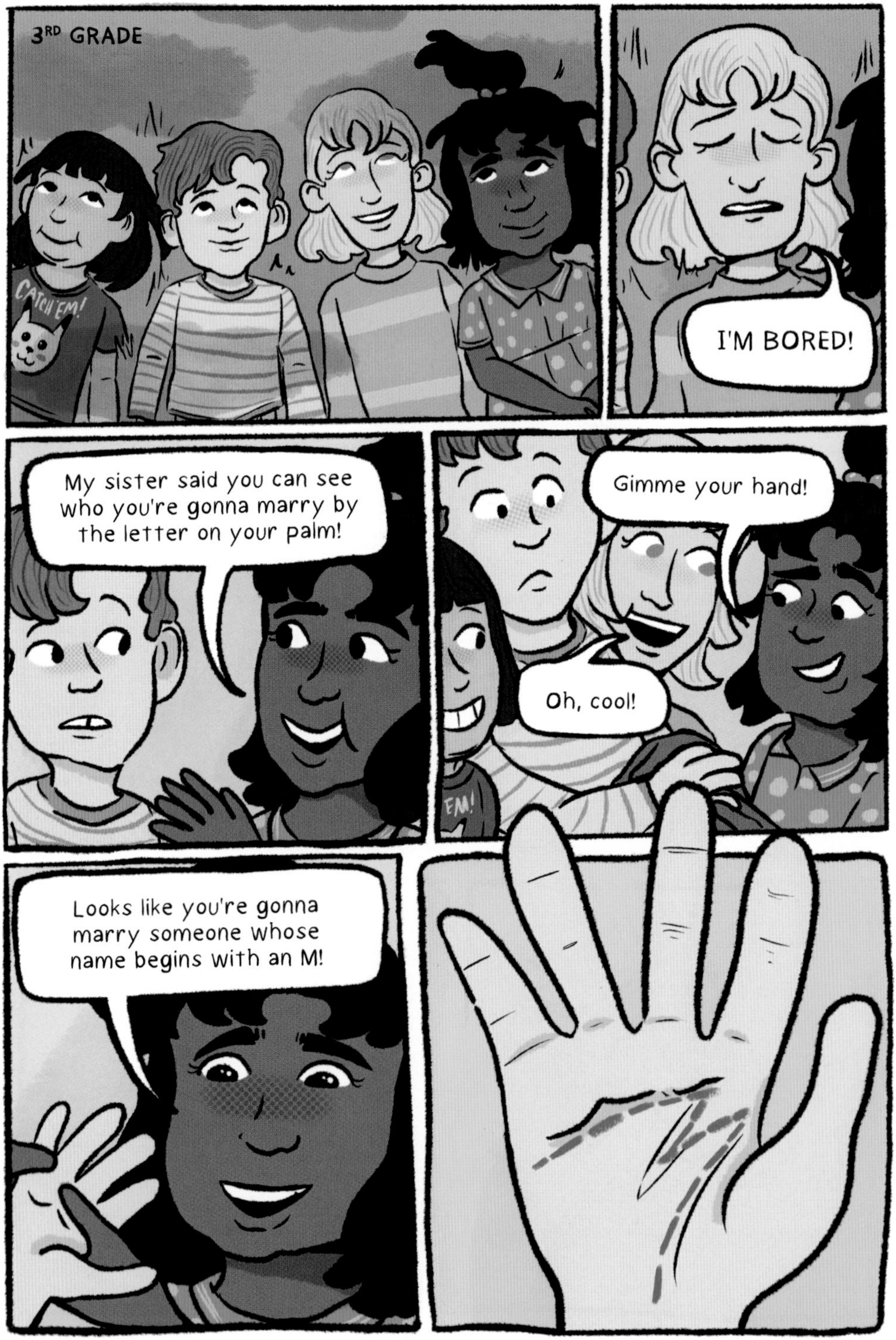
3RD GRADE
CATCH 'EM!
I'M BORED!
My sister said you can see who you're gonna marry by the letter on your palm!
Gimme your hand!
Oh, cool!
Looks like you're gonna marry someone whose name begins with an M!

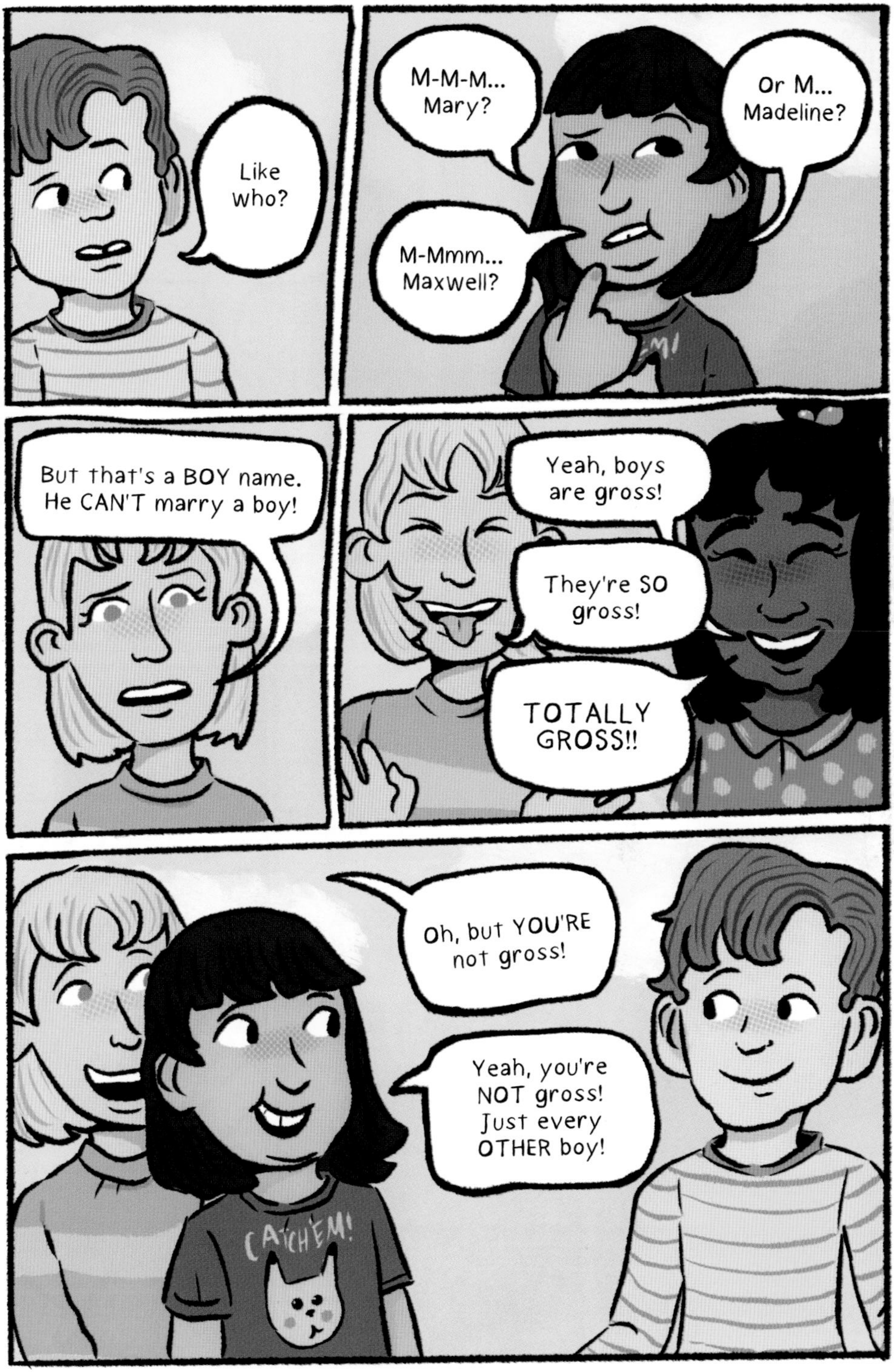
Like who?
M-M-M... Mary?
Or M... Madeline?
M-Mmm... Maxwell?
But that's a BOY name. He CAN'T marry a boy!
Yeah, boys are gross!
They're SO gross!
TOTALLY GROSS!!
Oh, but YOU'RE not gross!
Yeah, you're NOT gross! Just every OTHER boy!
CATCH'EM!

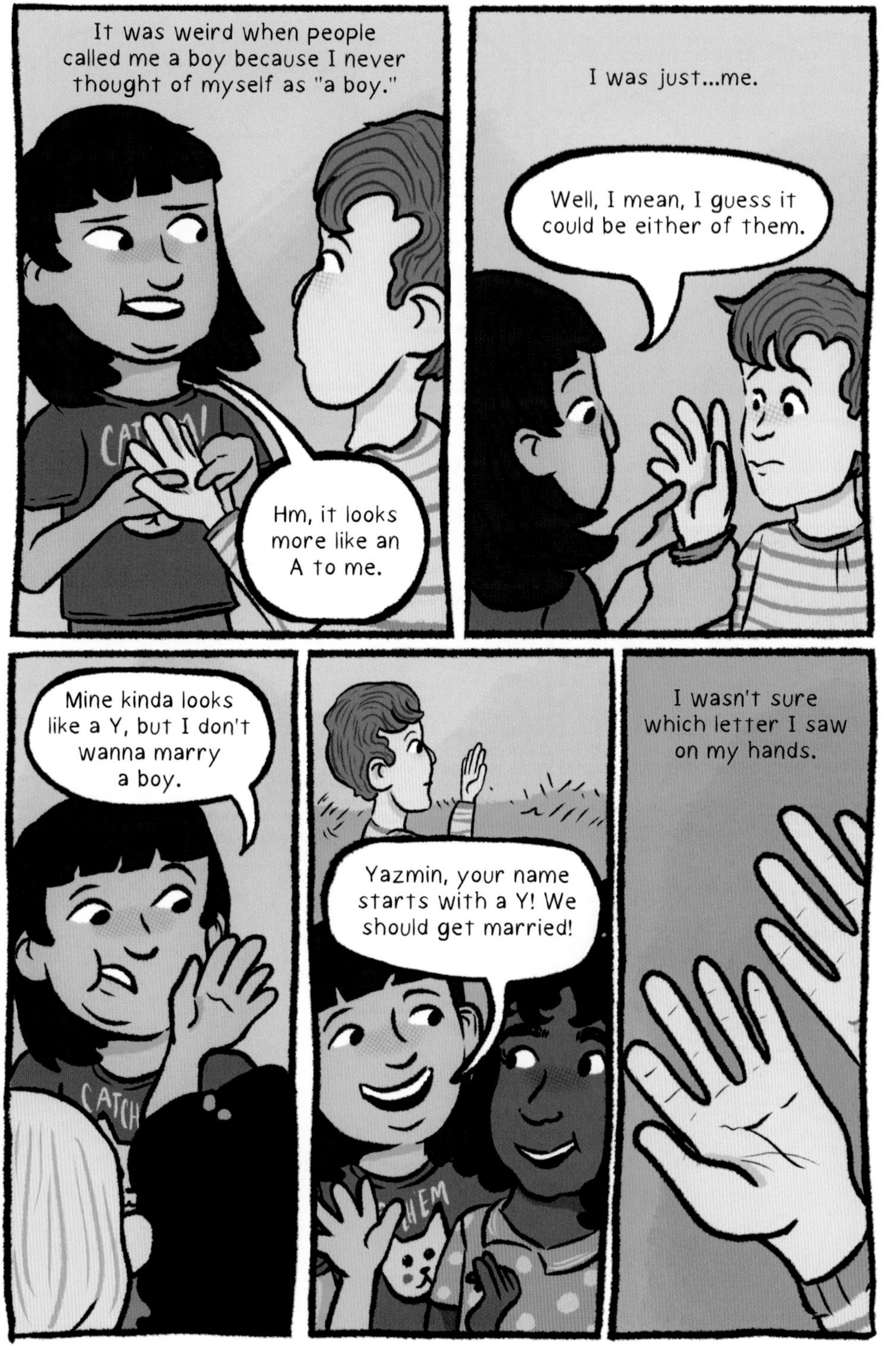
It was weird when people called me a boy because I never thought of myself as "a boy."
Hm, it looks more like an A to me.
I was just...me.
Well, I mean, I guess it could be either of them.
Mine kinda looks like a Y, but I don't wanna marry a boy.
Yazmin, your name starts with a Y! We should get married!
I wasn't sure which letter I saw on my hands.

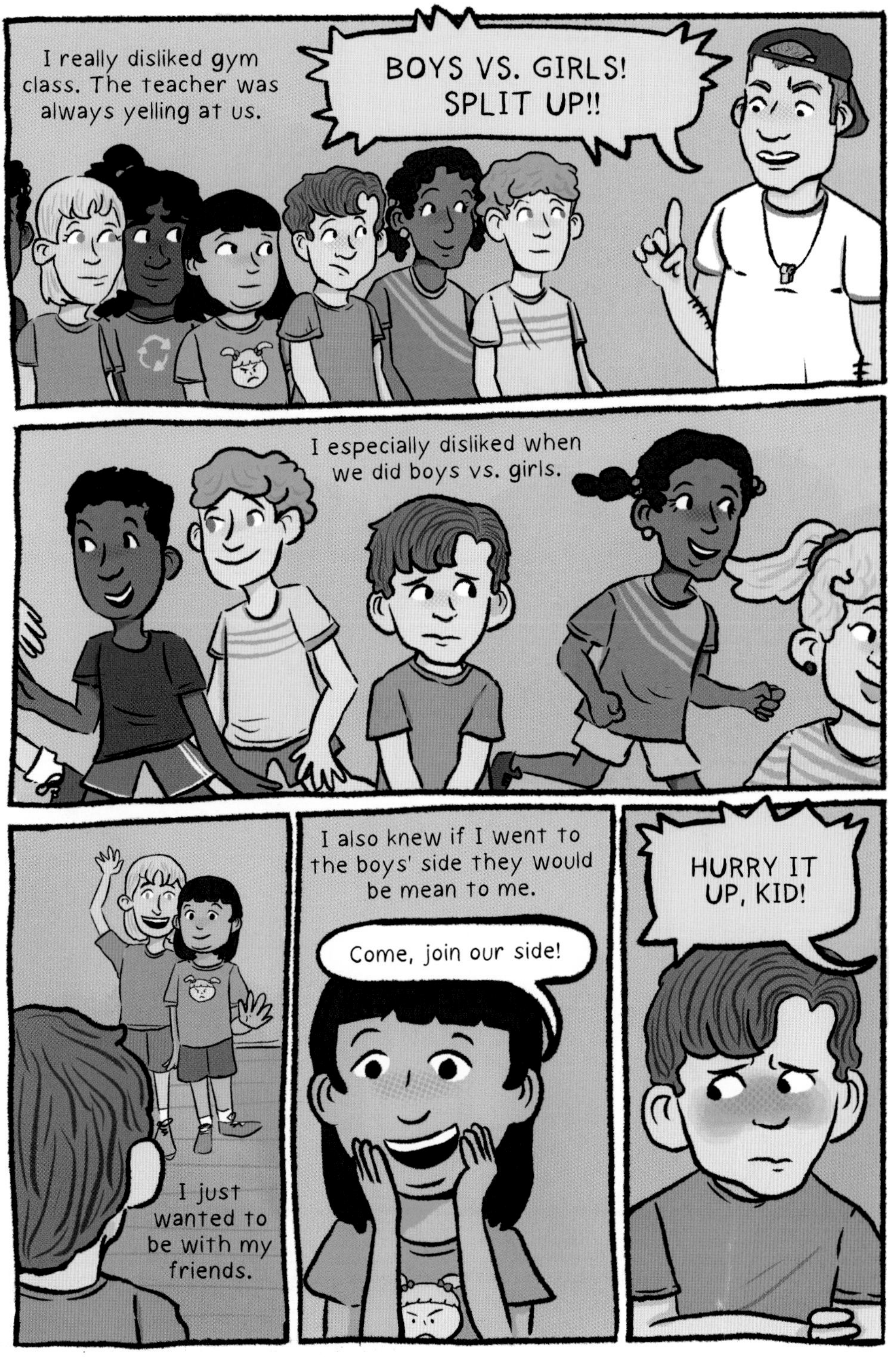
I really disliked gym class. The teacher was always yelling at us.
BOYS VS. GIRLS! SPLIT UP!!
I especially disliked when we did boys vs. girls.
I just wanted to be with my friends.
I also knew if I went to the boys' side they would be mean to me.
Come, join our side!
HURRY IT UP, KID!

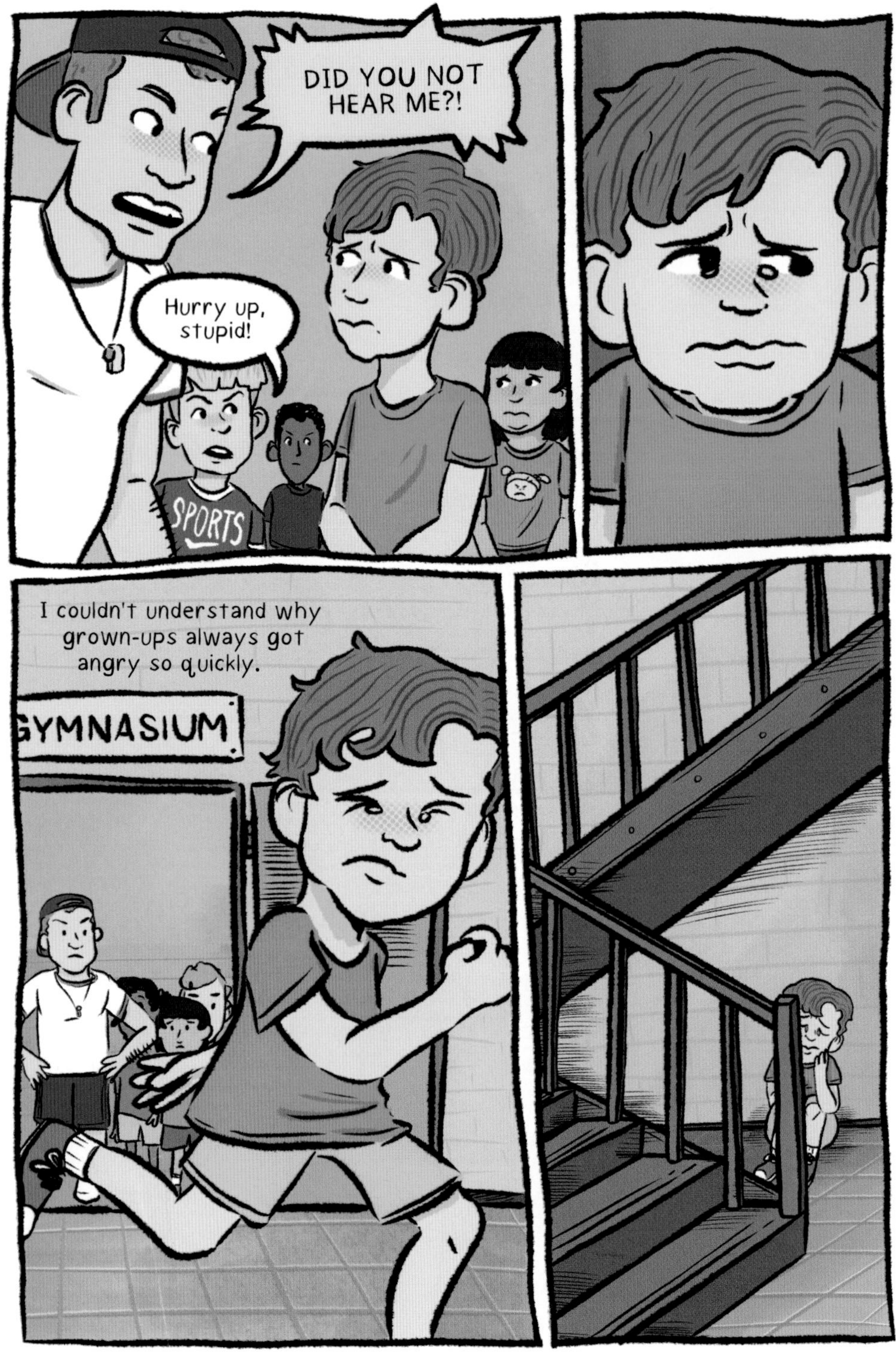
DID YOU NOT HEAR ME?!
Hurry up, stupid!
SPORTS
I couldn't understand why grown-ups always got angry so quickly.
GYMNASIUM

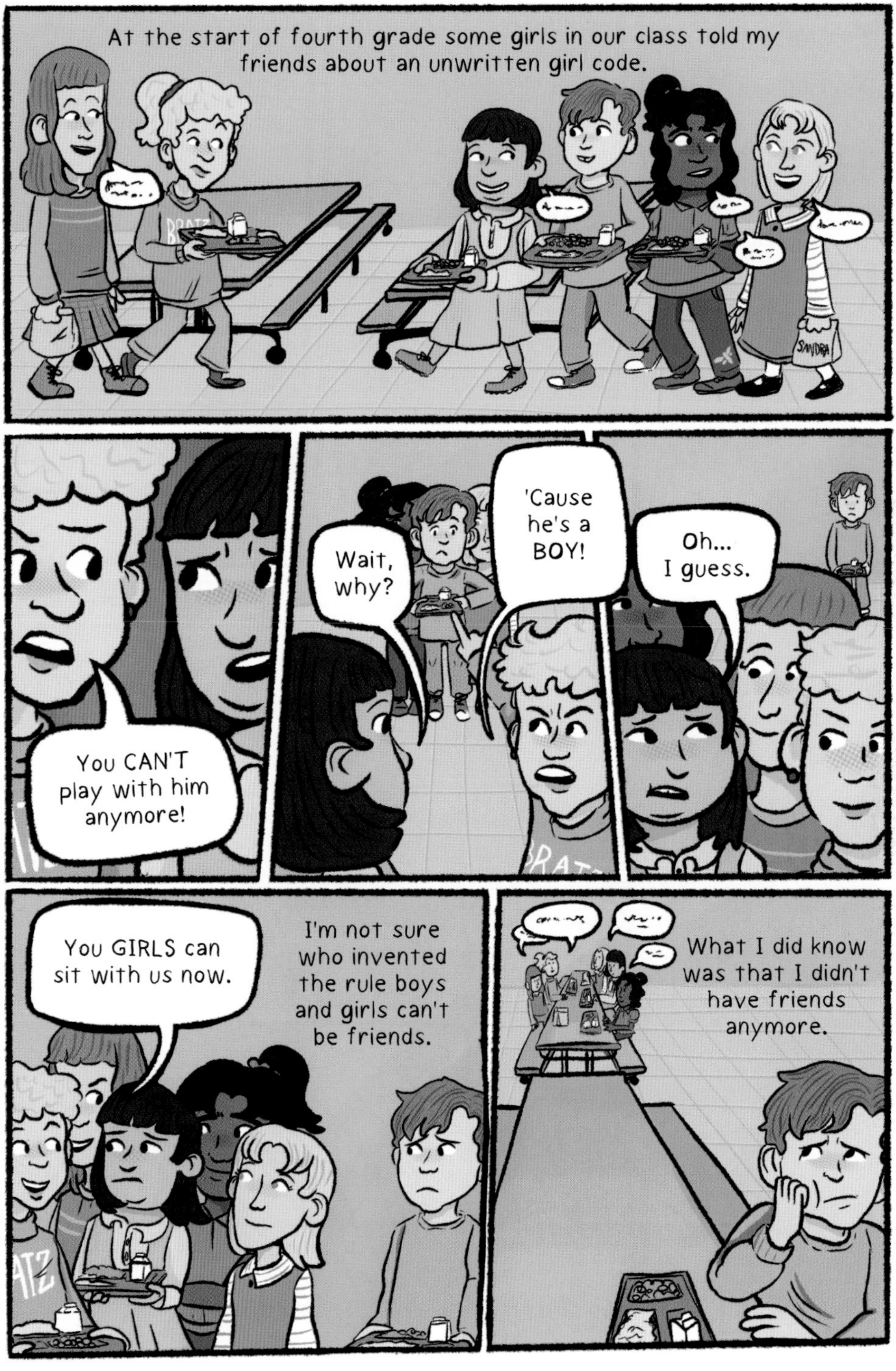
At the start of fourth grade some girls in our class told my friends about an unwritten girl code.
SANDRA
BRATZ
You CAN'T play with him anymore!
Wait, why?
'Cause he's a BOY!
Oh... I guess.
You GIRLS can sit with us now.
I'm not sure who invented the rule boys and girls can't be friends.
What I did know was that I didn't have friends anymore.

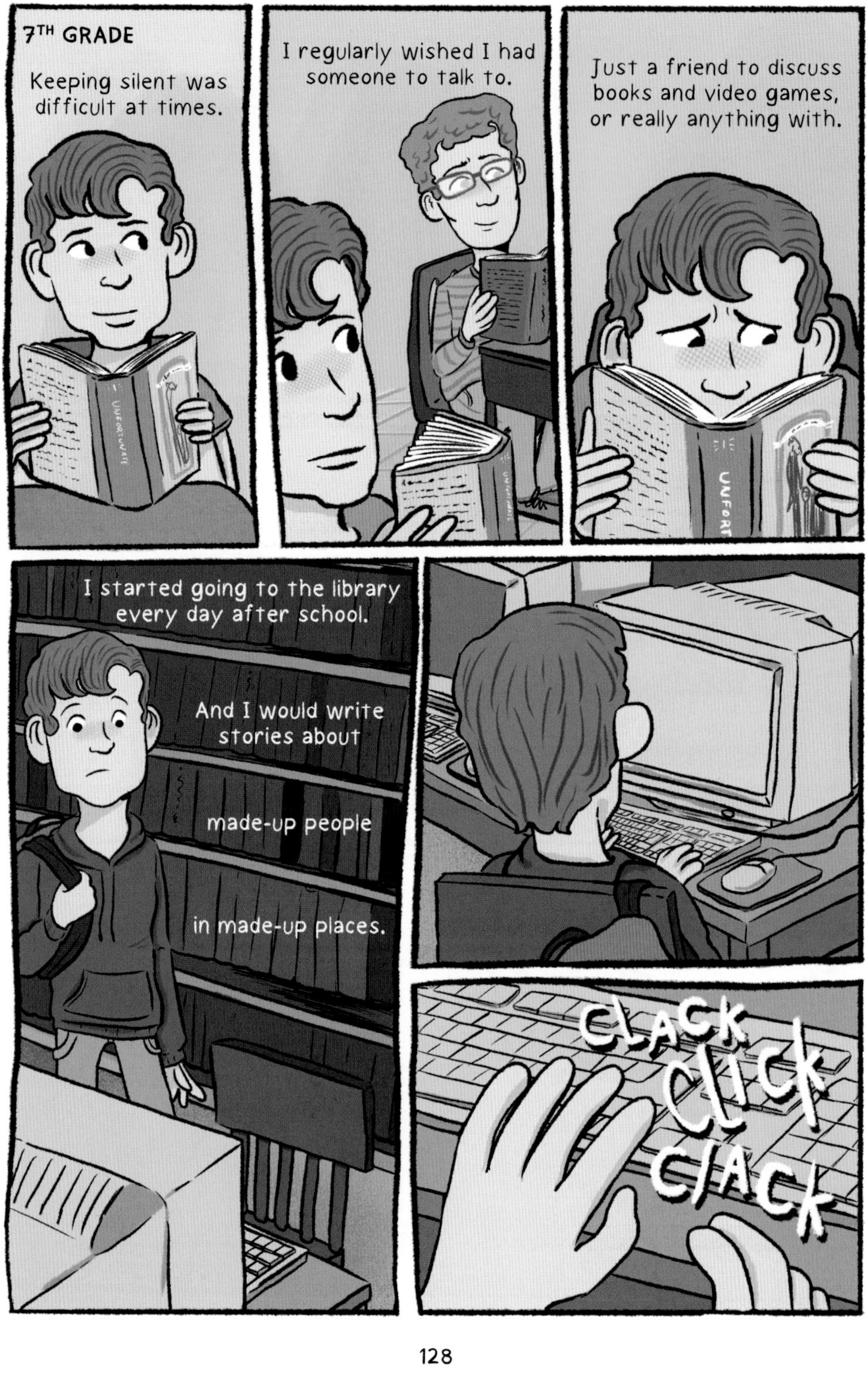
7TH GRADE
Keeping silent was difficult at times.
I regularly wished I had someone to talk to.
Just a friend to discuss books and video games, or really anything with.
I started going to the library every day after school.
And I would write stories about
made-up people
in made-up places.
CLACK
CLICK
CLACK

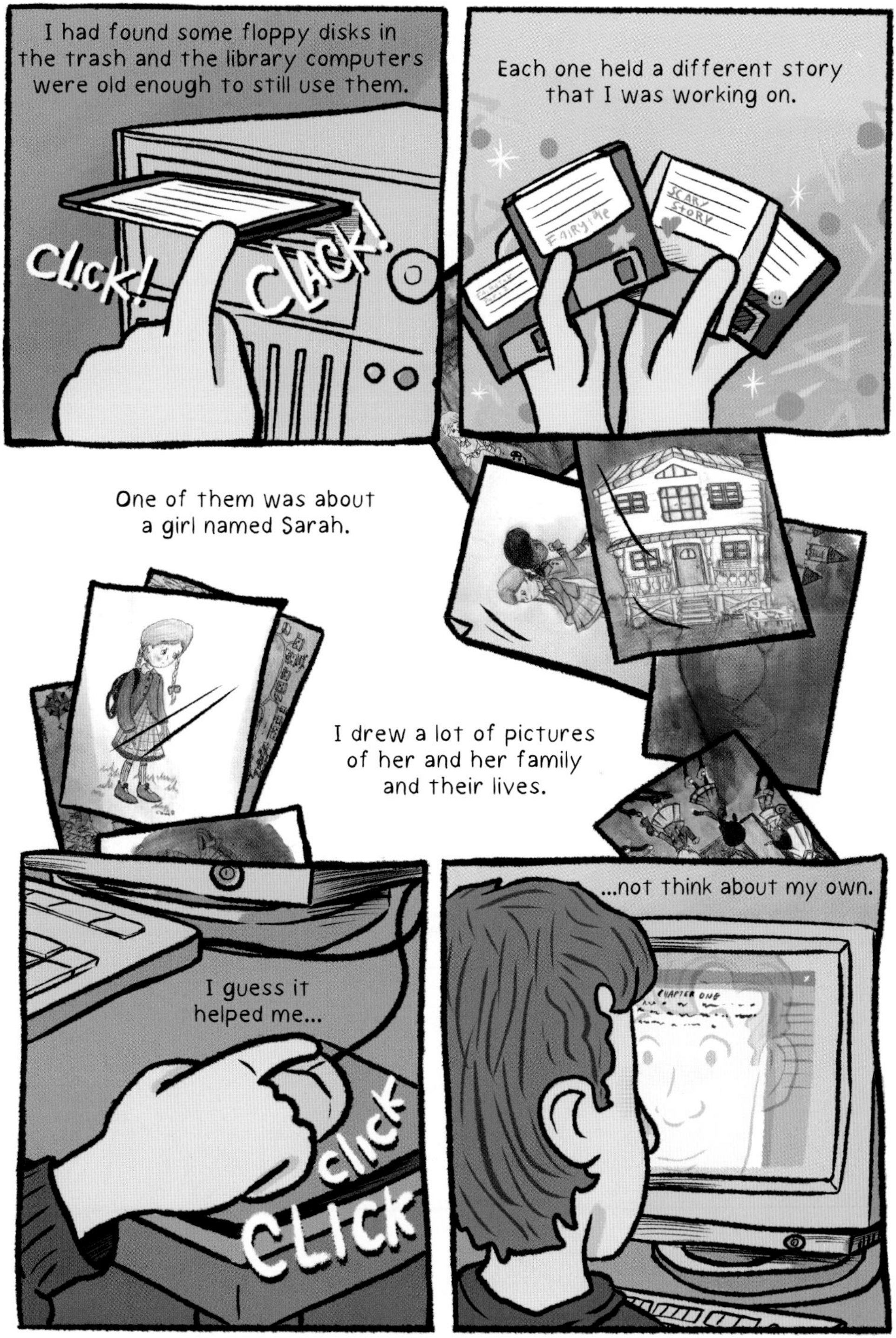
I had found some floppy disks in the trash and the library computers were old enough to still use them.
CLICK!
CLACK!
Each one held a different story that I was working on.
SCARY STORY
FAIRYTALE
One of them was about a girl named Sarah.
I drew a lot of pictures of her and her family and their lives.
I guess it helped me...
click
CLICK
...not think about my own.
CHAPTER ONE

Most of my afternoons were spent with this character.

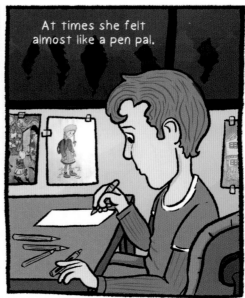

At times she felt almost like a pen pal.

She lived somewhere far away, though I was never sure exactly where.

It felt an awful lot like here.

She had two brothers who got on her nerves a lot like mine did.

Also like me, her mother had passed away when she was very young.

And she didn't have any friends because

all the kids at school thought she was a weirdo.

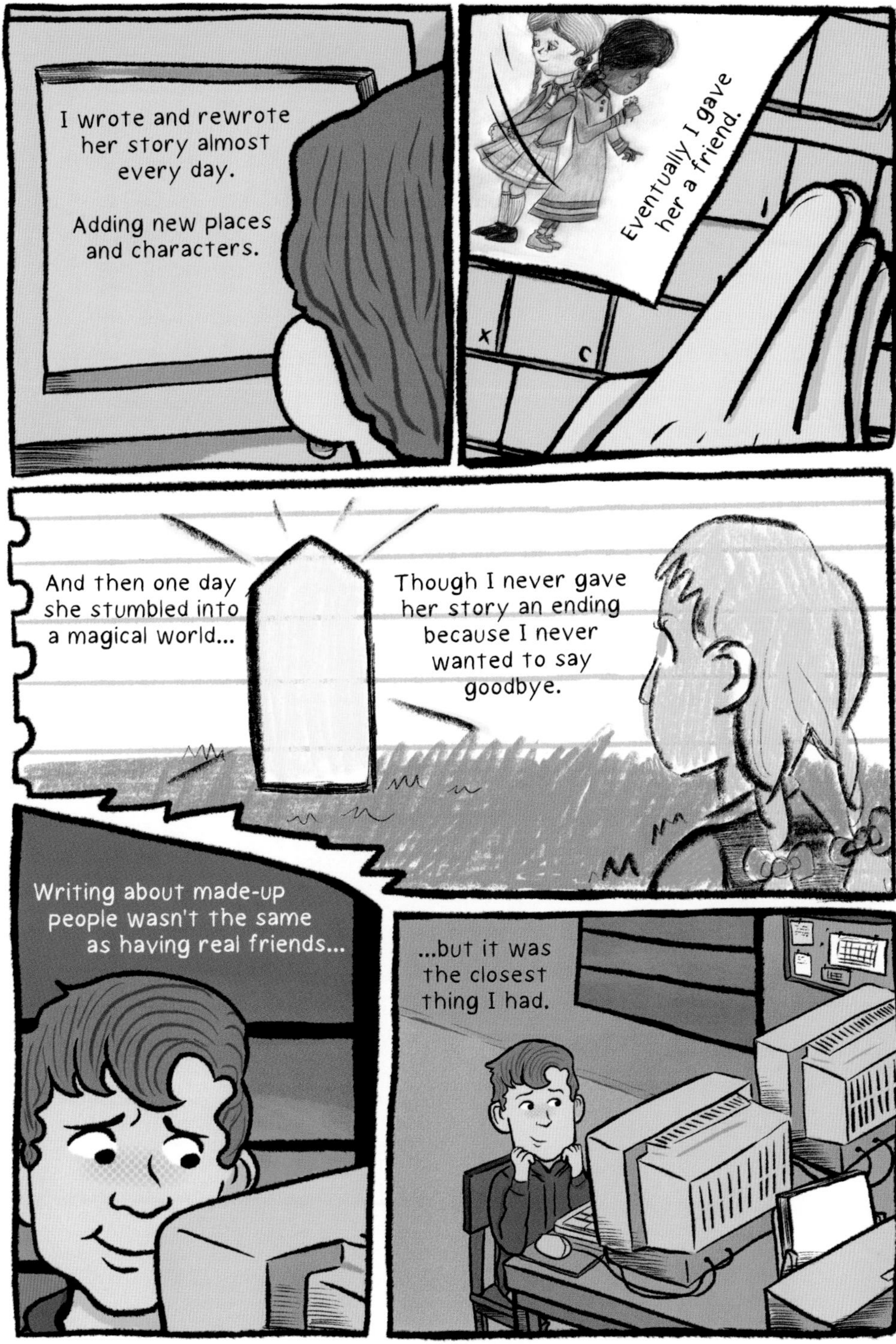
I wrote and rewrote her story almost every day.
Adding new places and characters.
Eventually I gave her a friend.
And then one day she stumbled into a magical world...
Though I never gave her story an ending because I never wanted to say goodbye.
Writing about made-up people wasn't the same as having real friends...
...but it was the closest thing I had.

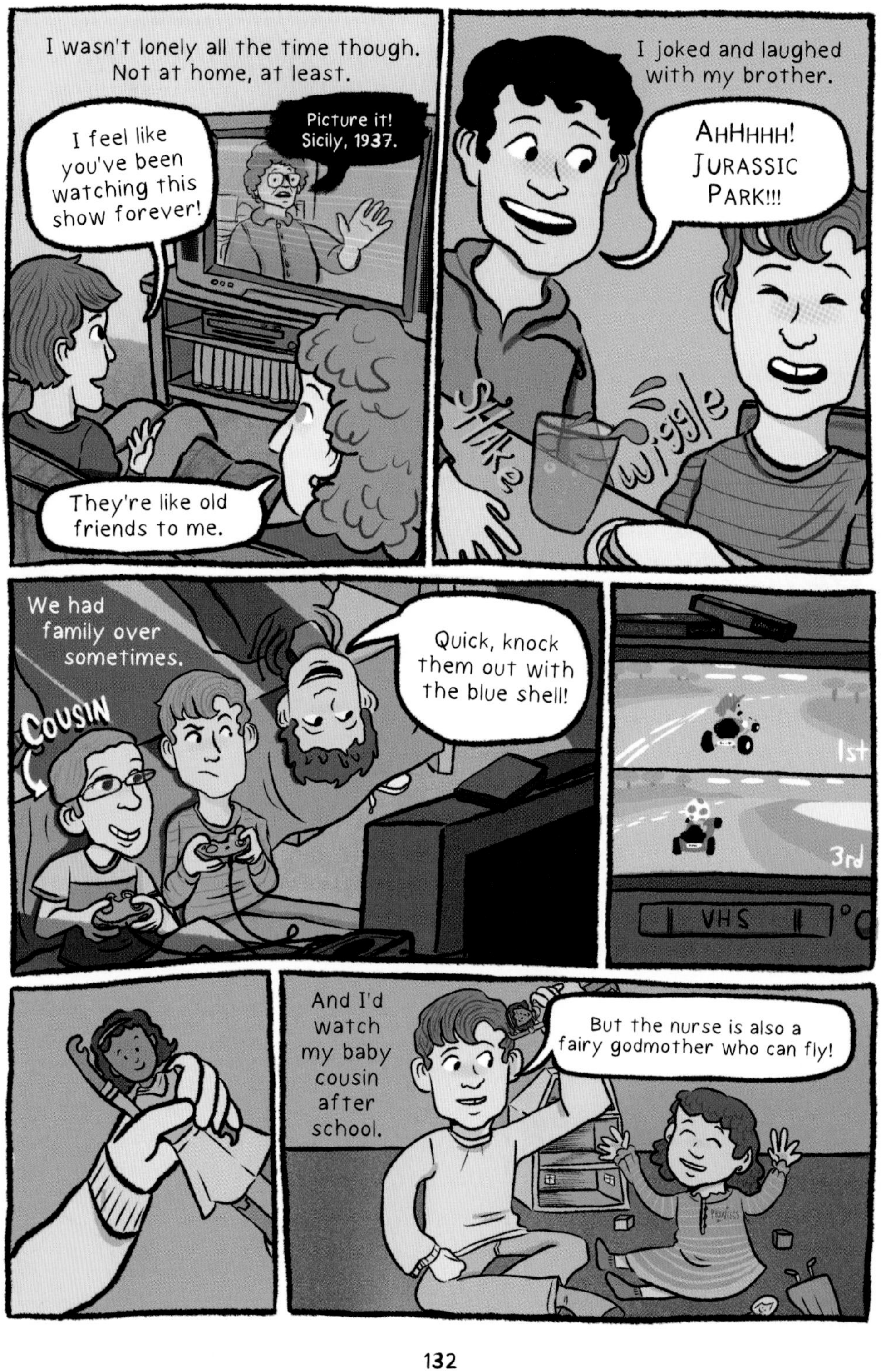

I wasn't lonely all the time though. Not at home, at least.
I feel like you've been watching this show forever!
Picture it! Sicily, 1937.
They're like old friends to me.
I joked and laughed with my brother.
AHHHHH! JURASSIC PARK!!!
SHAKE
WIGGLE
We had family over sometimes.
COUSIN
Quick, knock them out with the blue shell!
1st
3rd
VHS
And I'd watch my baby cousin after school.
But the nurse is also a fairy godmother who can fly!

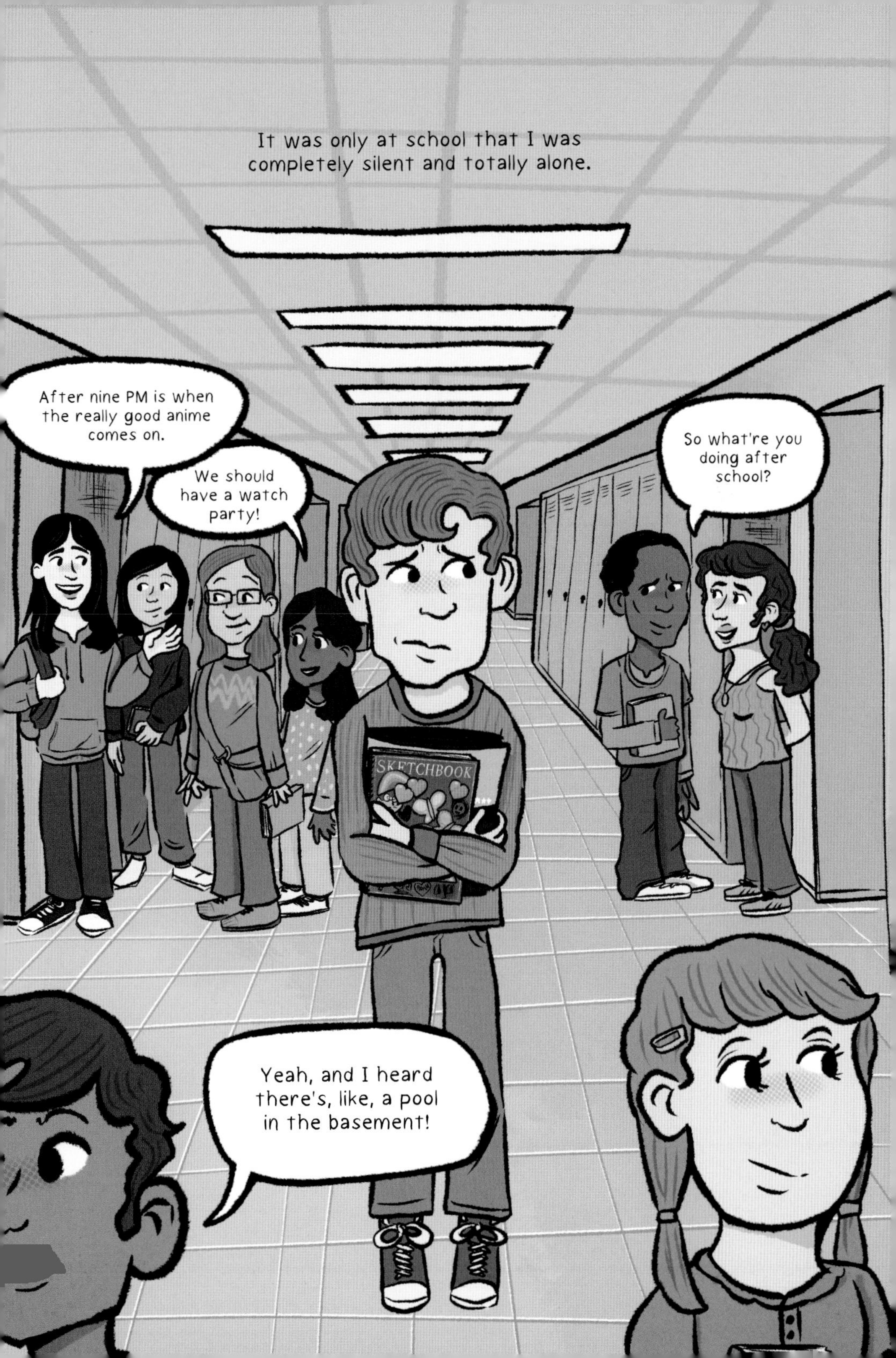
It was only at school that I was completely silent and totally alone.
After nine PM is when the really good anime comes on.
We should have a watch party!
So what're you doing after school?
SKETCHBOOK
Yeah, and I heard there's, like, a pool in the basement!

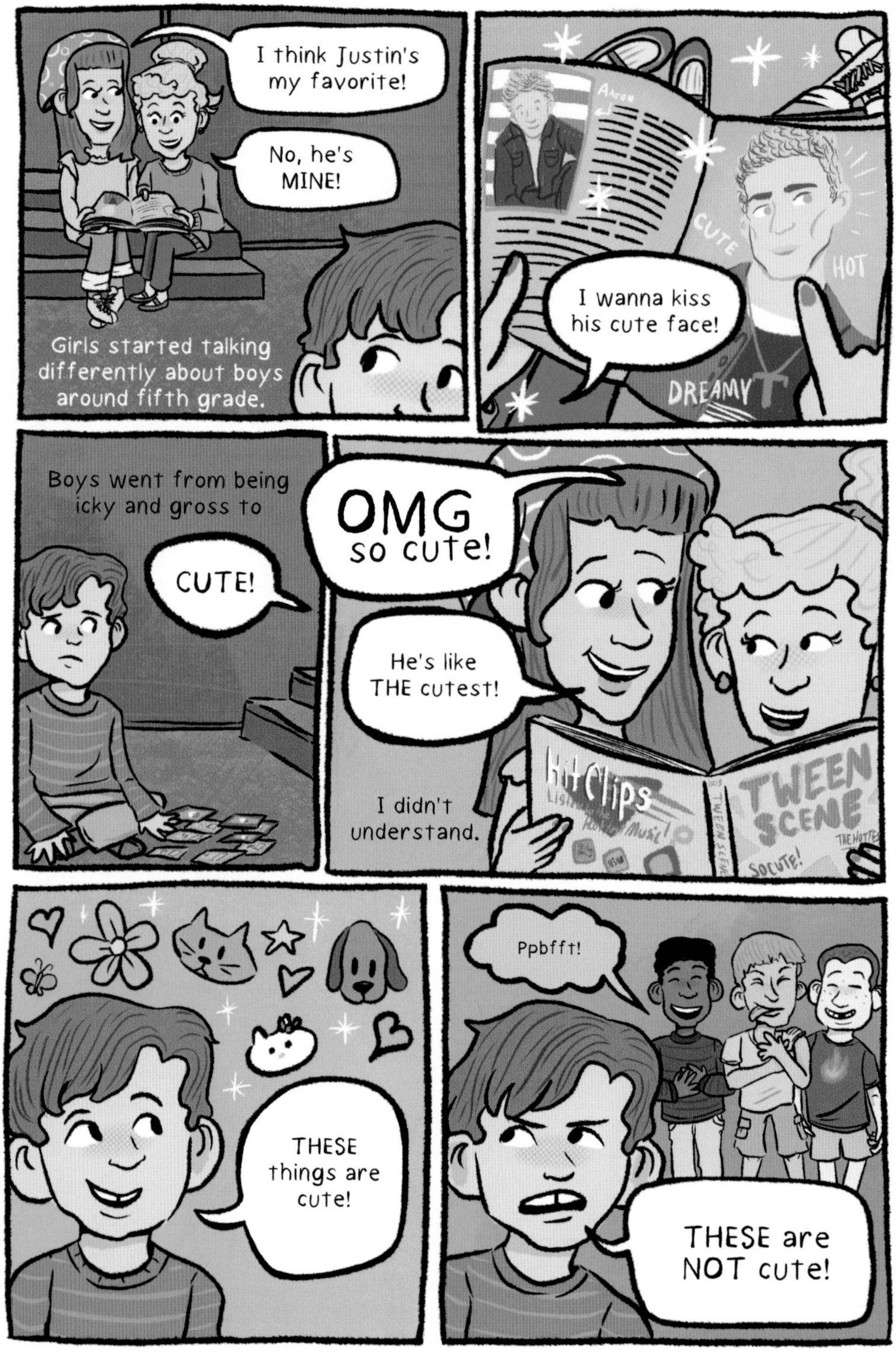
I think Justin's my favorite!
No, he's MINE!
Girls started talking differently about boys around fifth grade.
Aaron
CUTE
HOT
I wanna kiss his cute face!
DREAMY
Boys went from being icky and gross to
CUTE!
OMG so cute!
He's like THE cutest!
I didn't understand.
Hit Clips
TWEEN SCENE
SO CUTE!
THESE things are cute!
Ppbfft!
THESE are NOT cute!

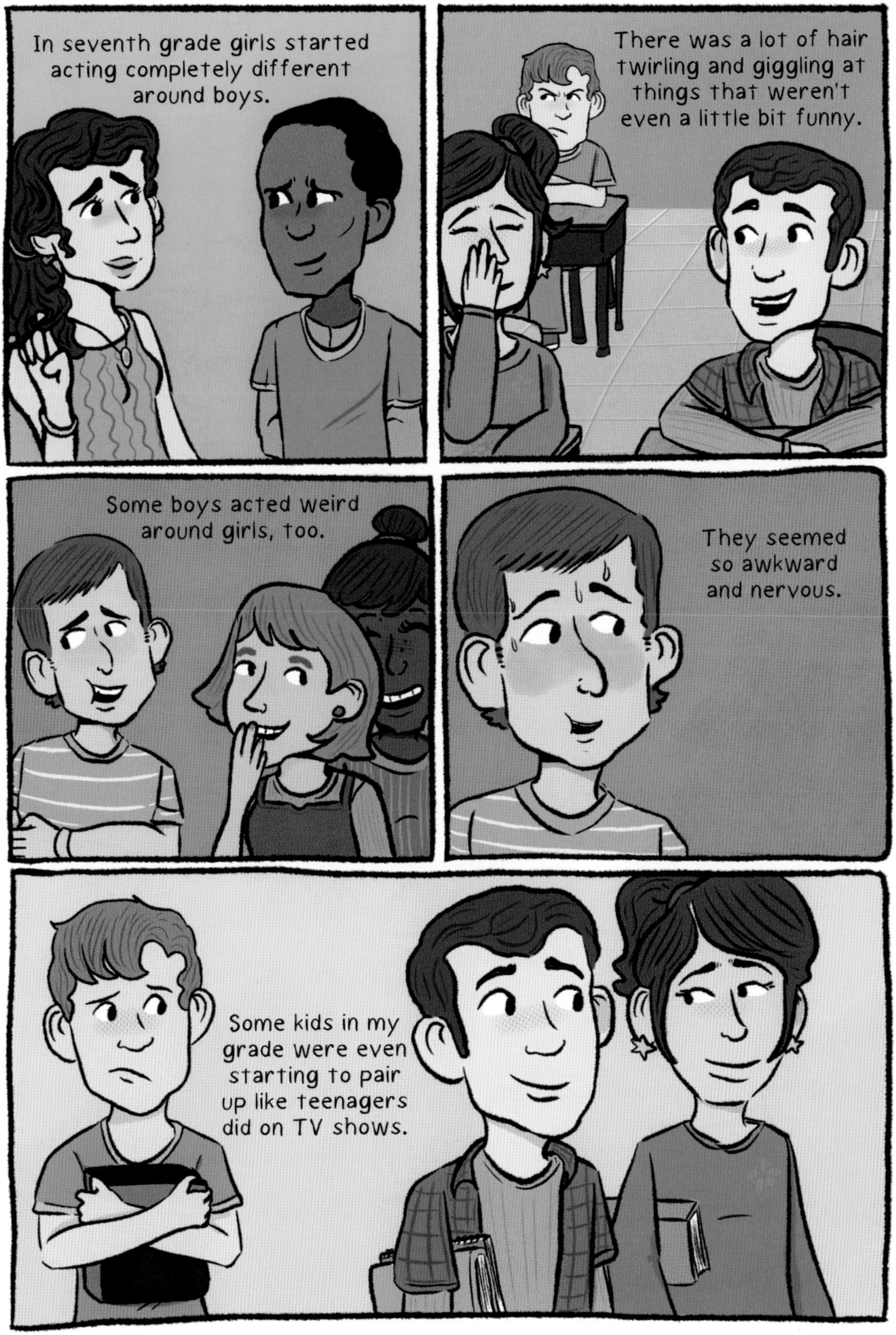
In seventh grade girls started acting completely different around boys.
There was a lot of hair twirling and giggling at things that weren't even a little bit funny.
Some boys acted weird around girls, too.
They seemed so awkward and nervous.
Some kids in my grade were even starting to pair up like teenagers did on TV shows.

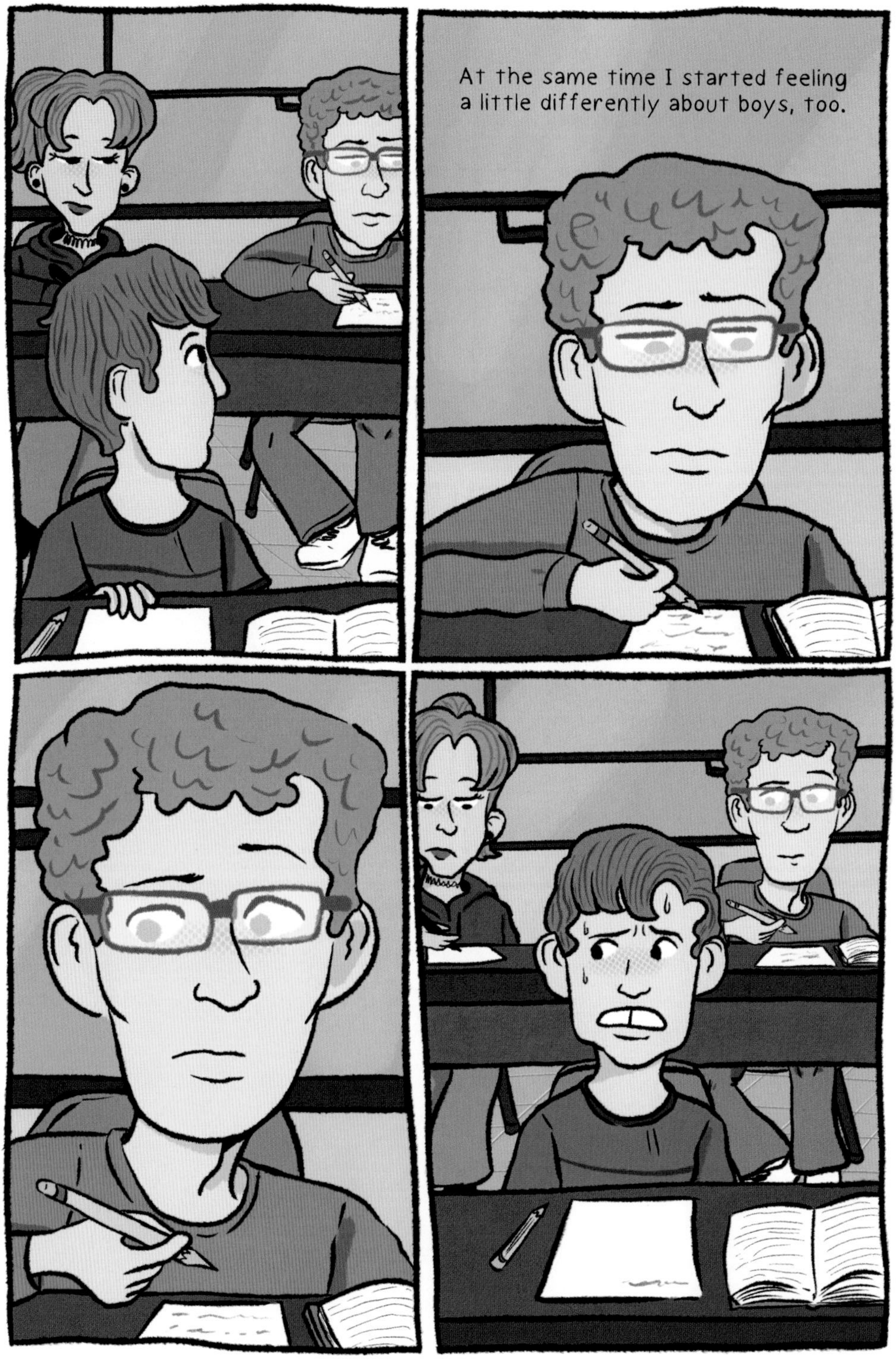
At the same time I started feeling a little differently about boys, too.

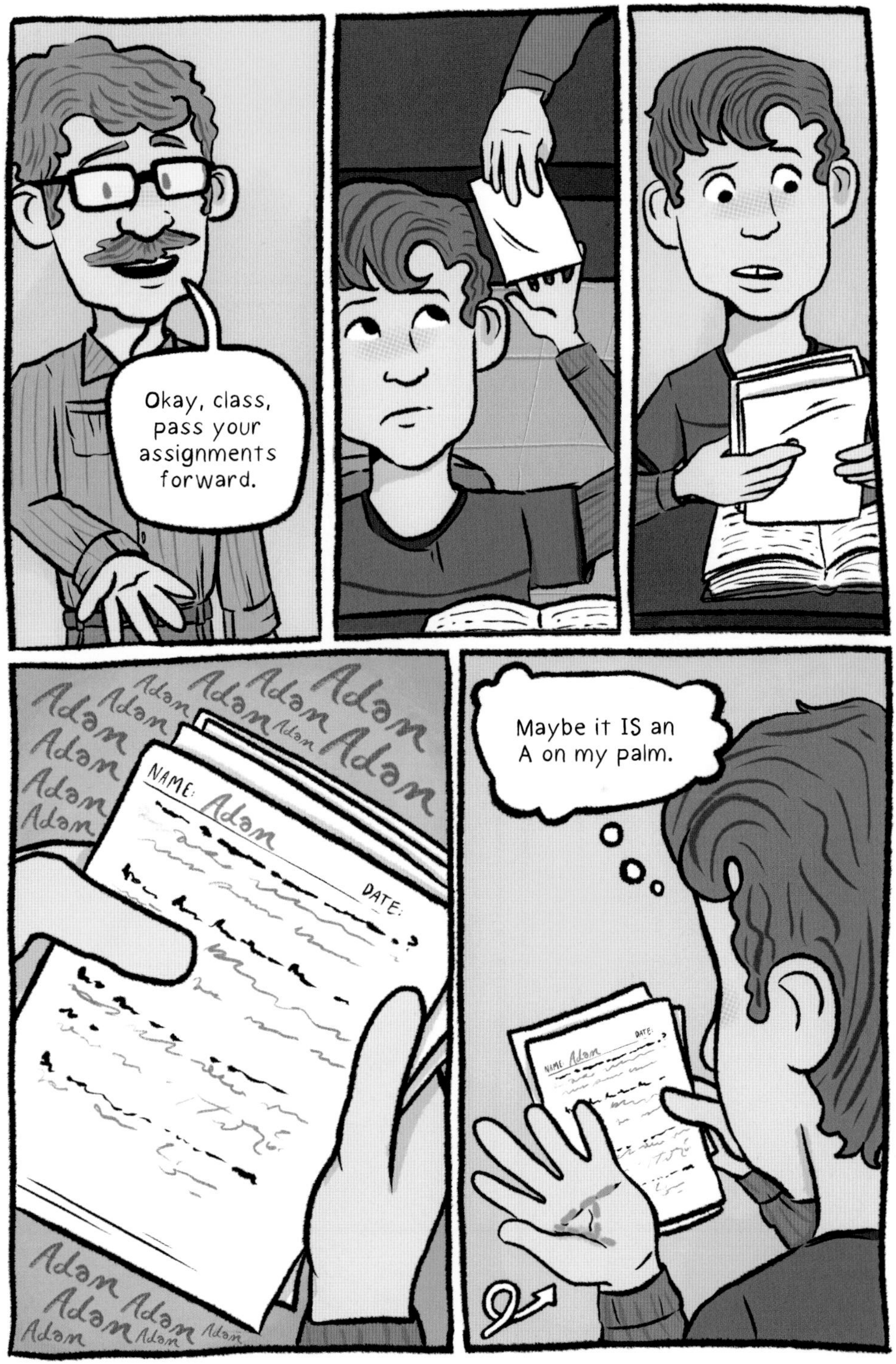

Okay, class, pass your assignments forward.
Adam
NAME: Adam
DATE:
Maybe it IS an A on my palm.

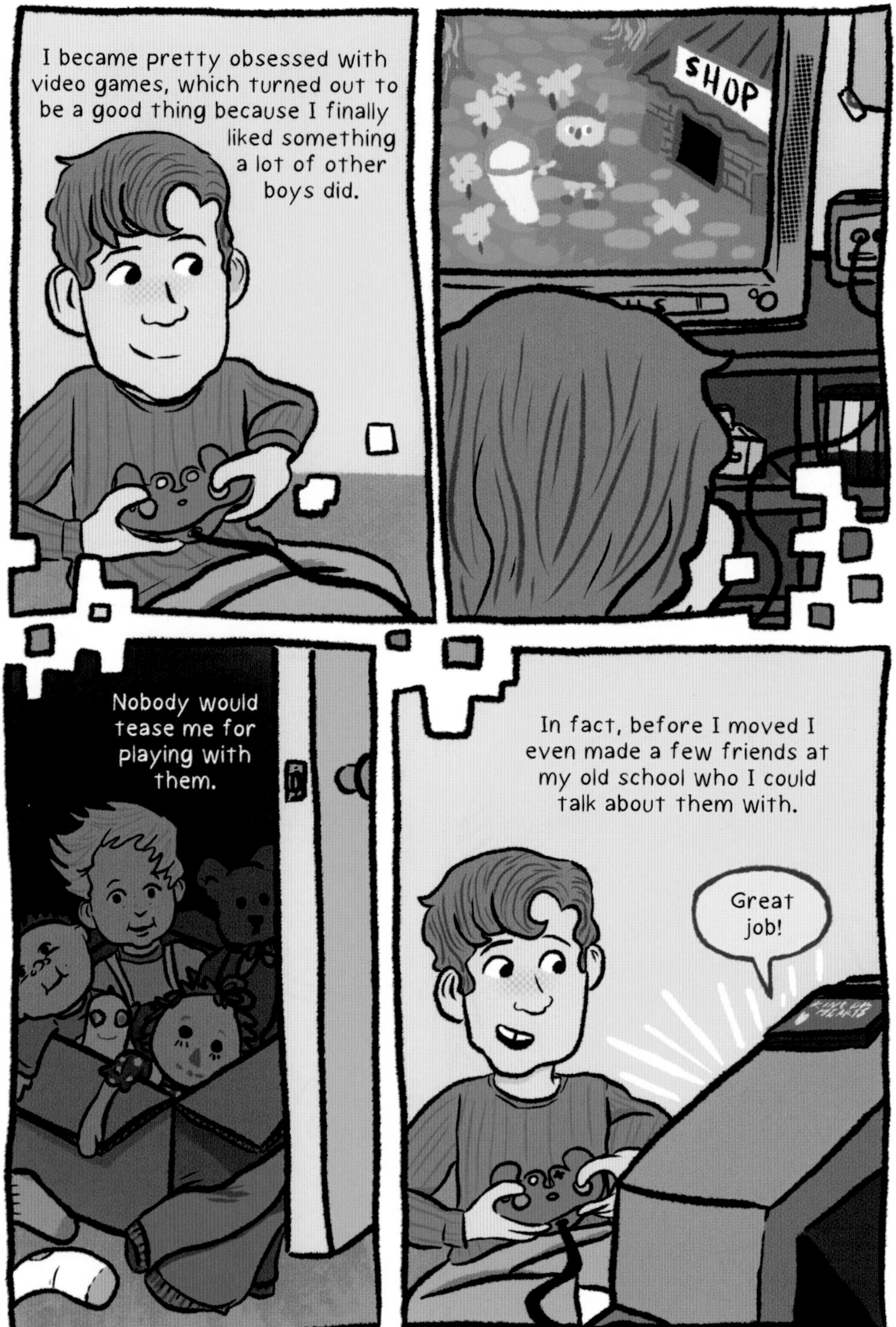
I became pretty obsessed with video games, which turned out to be a good thing because I finally liked something a lot of other boys did.
SHOP
Nobody would tease me for playing with them.
In fact, before I moved I even made a few friends at my old school who I could talk about them with.
Great job!

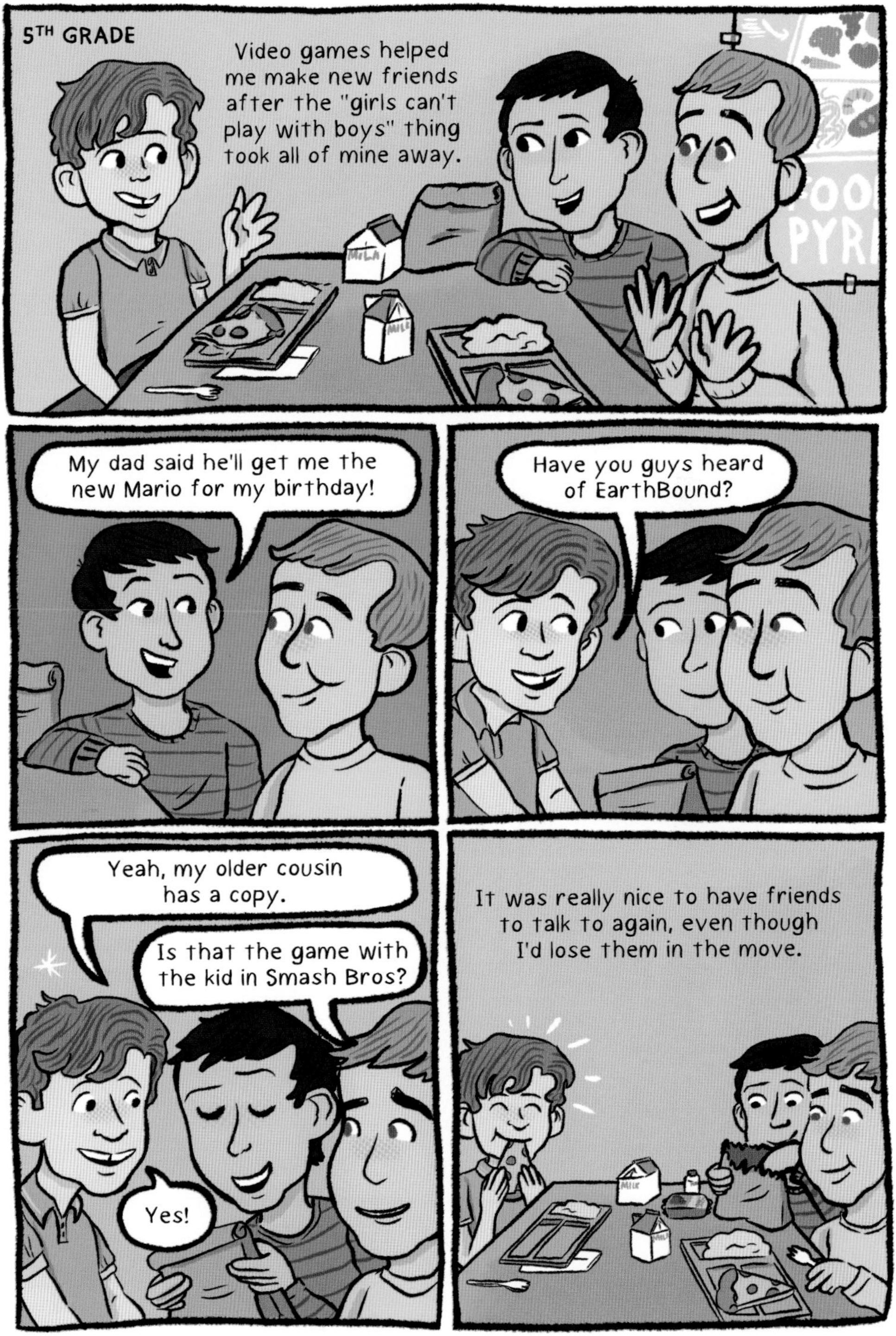
5TH GRADE
Video games helped me make new friends after the "girls can't play with boys" thing took all of mine away.
MILK
MILK
FOOD PYR
My dad said he'll get me the new Mario for my birthday!
Have you guys heard of EarthBound?
Yeah, my older cousin has a copy.
Is that the game with the kid in Smash Bros?
Yes!
It was really nice to have friends to talk to again, even though I'd lose them in the move.
MILK

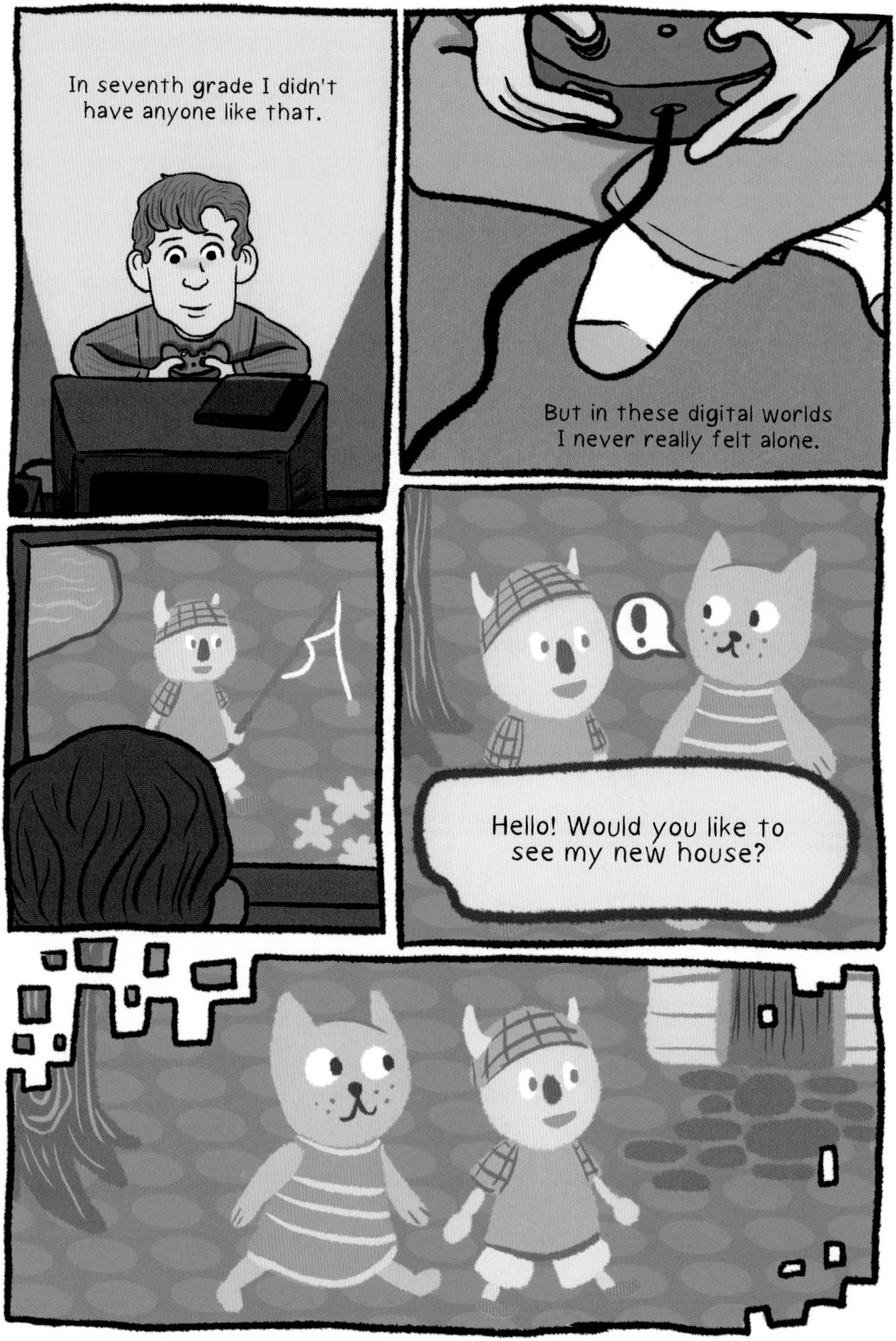
In seventh grade I didn't have anyone like that.
But in these digital worlds I never really felt alone.
!
Hello! Would you like to see my new house?

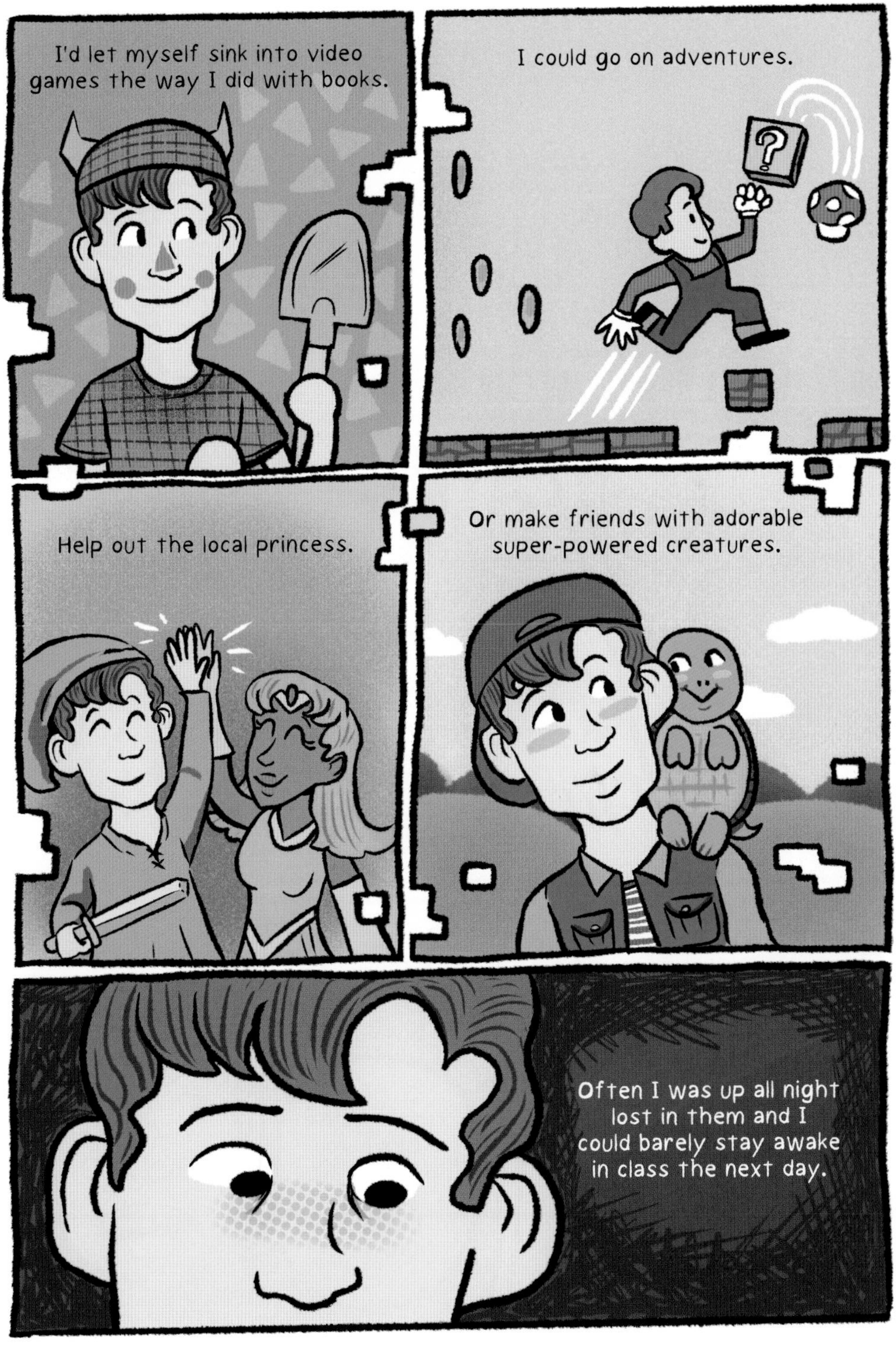
I'd let myself sink into video games the way I did with books.
I could go on adventures.
Help out the local princess.
Or make friends with adorable super-powered creatures.
Often I was up all night lost in them and I could barely stay awake in class the next day.

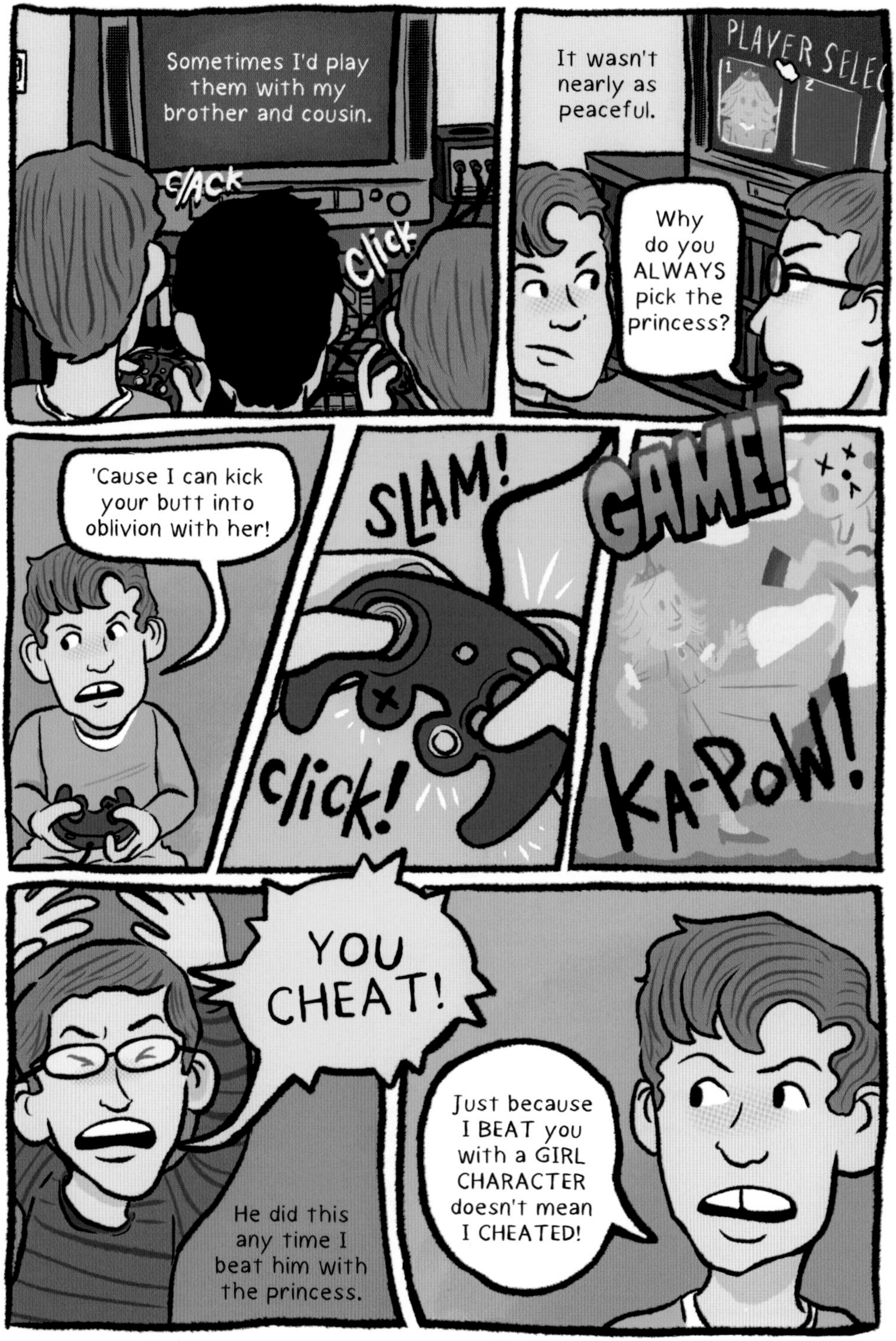
Sometimes I'd play them with my brother and cousin.
CLACK
Click
It wasn't nearly as peaceful.
PLAYER SELEC
Why do you ALWAYS pick the princess?
'Cause I can kick your butt into oblivion with her!
SLAM!
Click!
GAME!
KA-POW!
YOU CHEAT!
Just because I BEAT you with a GIRL CHARACTER doesn't mean I CHEATED!
He did this any time I beat him with the princess.

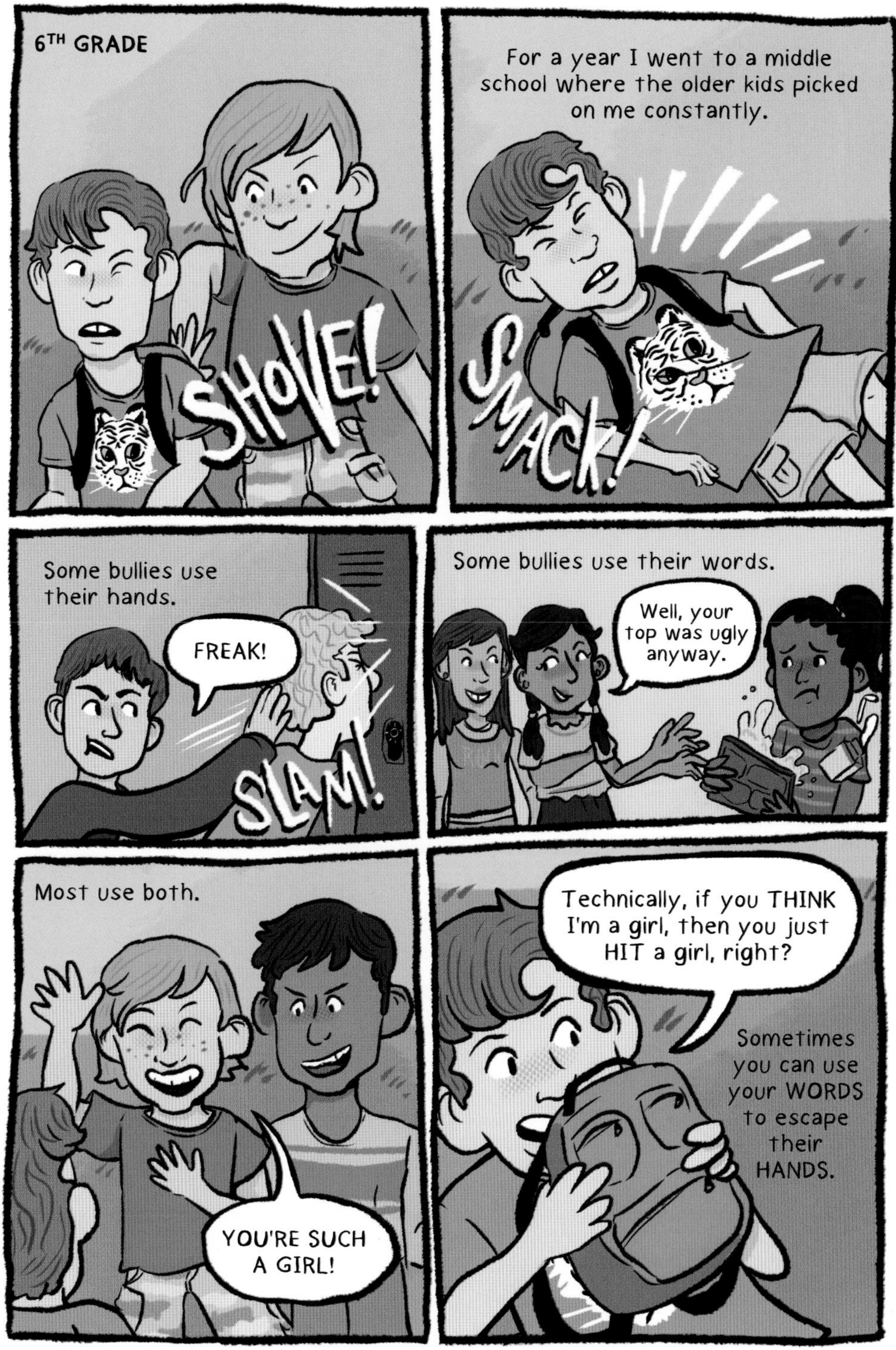
6TH GRADE
SHOVE!
For a year I went to a middle school where the older kids picked on me constantly.
SMACK!
Some bullies use their hands.
FREAK!
SLAM!
Some bullies use their words.
Well, your top was ugly anyway.
Most use both.
YOU'RE SUCH A GIRL!
Technically, if you THINK I'm a girl, then you just HIT a girl, right?
Sometimes you can use your WORDS to escape their HANDS.

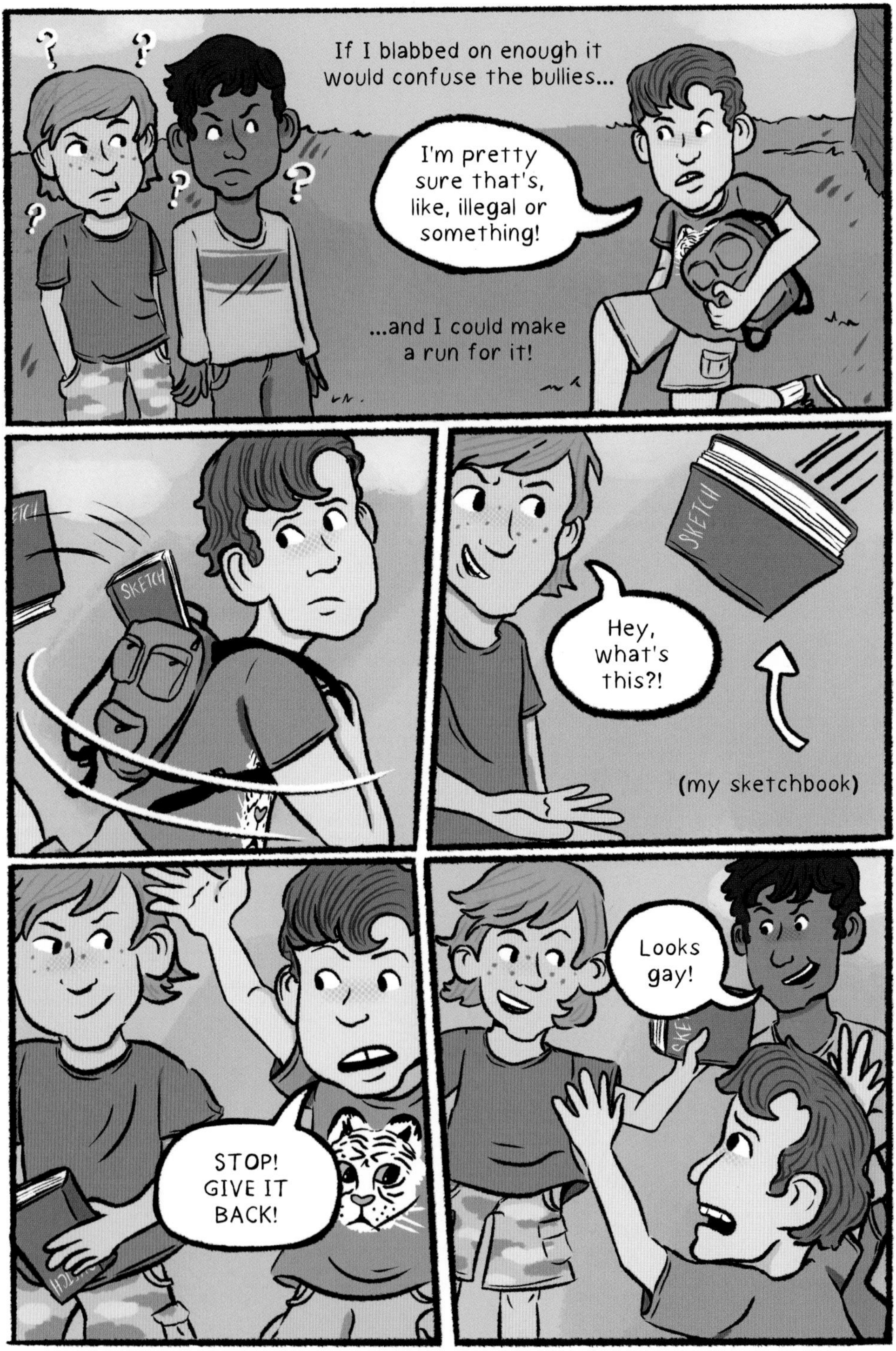
If I blabbed on enough it would confuse the bullies...
I'm pretty sure that's, like, illegal or something!
...and I could make a run for it!
SKETCH
SKETCH
Hey, what's this?!
(my sketchbook)
STOP! GIVE IT BACK!
Looks gay!

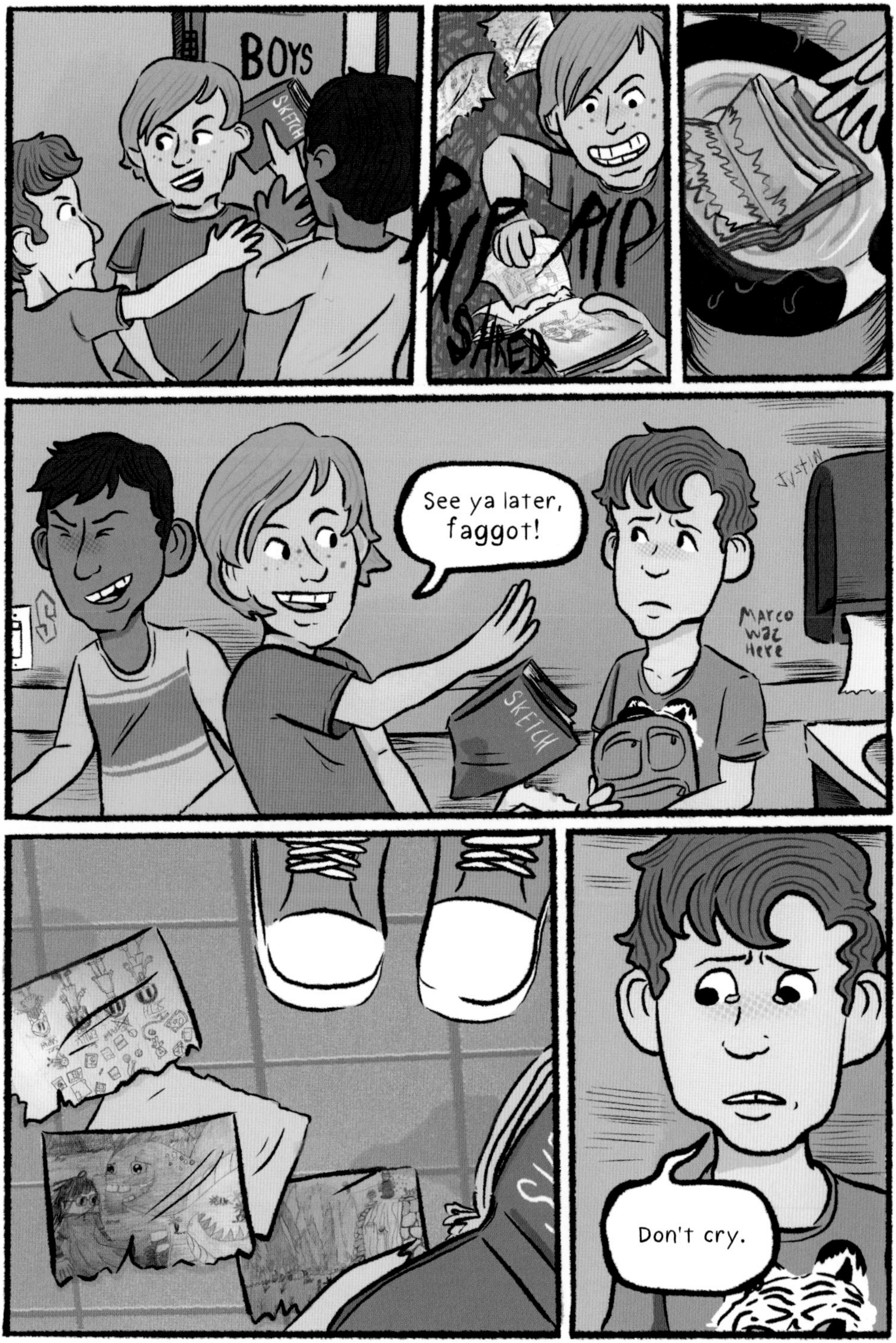
BOYS
SKETCH
RIP RIP
SHRED
See ya later, faggot!
JUSTIN
Marco waz Here
SKETCH
Don't cry.

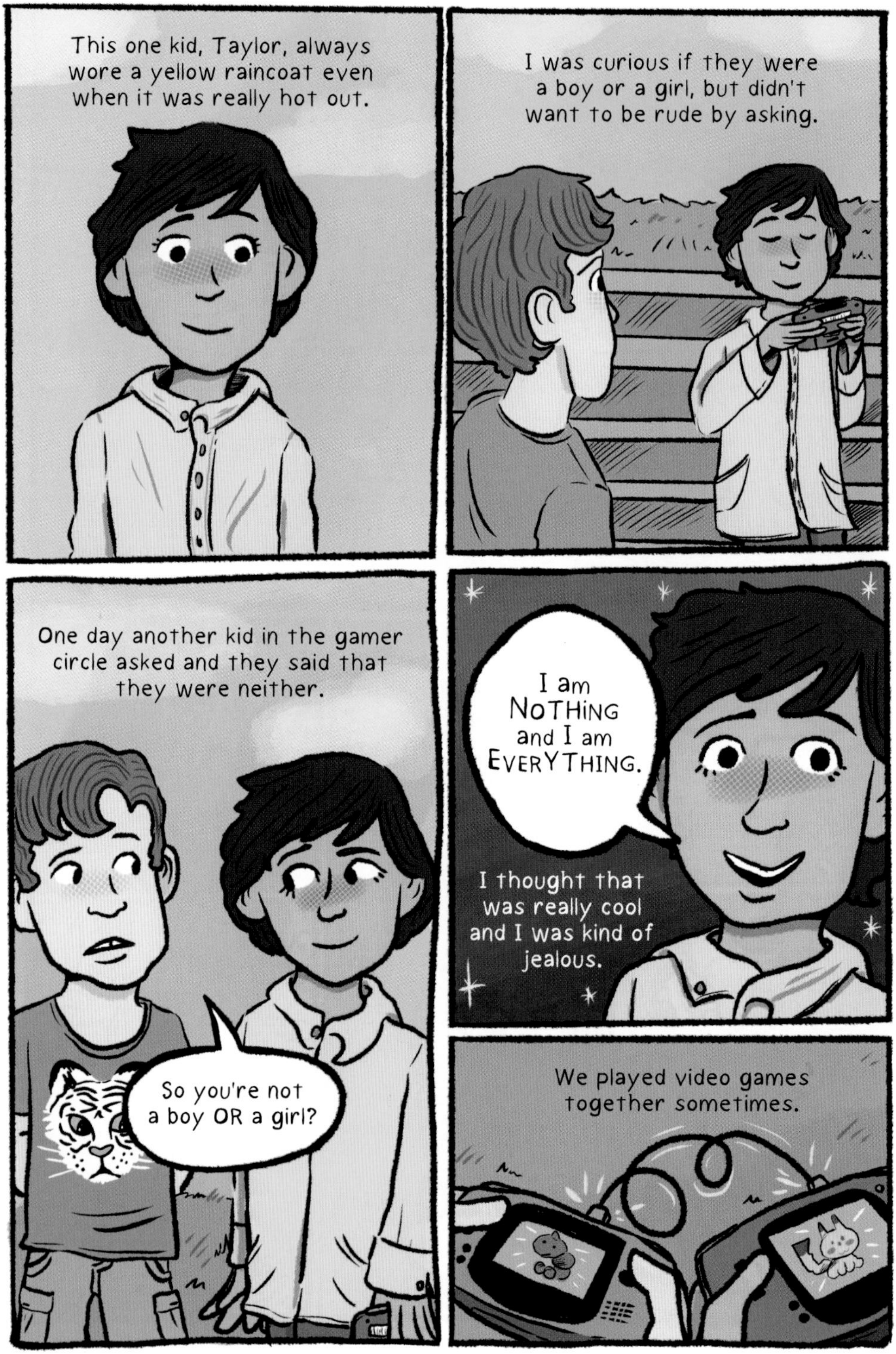
This one kid, Taylor, always wore a yellow raincoat even when it was really hot out.
I was curious if they were a boy or a girl, but didn't want to be rude by asking.
One day another kid in the gamer circle asked and they said that they were neither.
So you're not a boy OR a girl?
I am NOTHING and I am EVERYTHING.
I thought that was really cool and I was kind of jealous.
We played video games together sometimes.

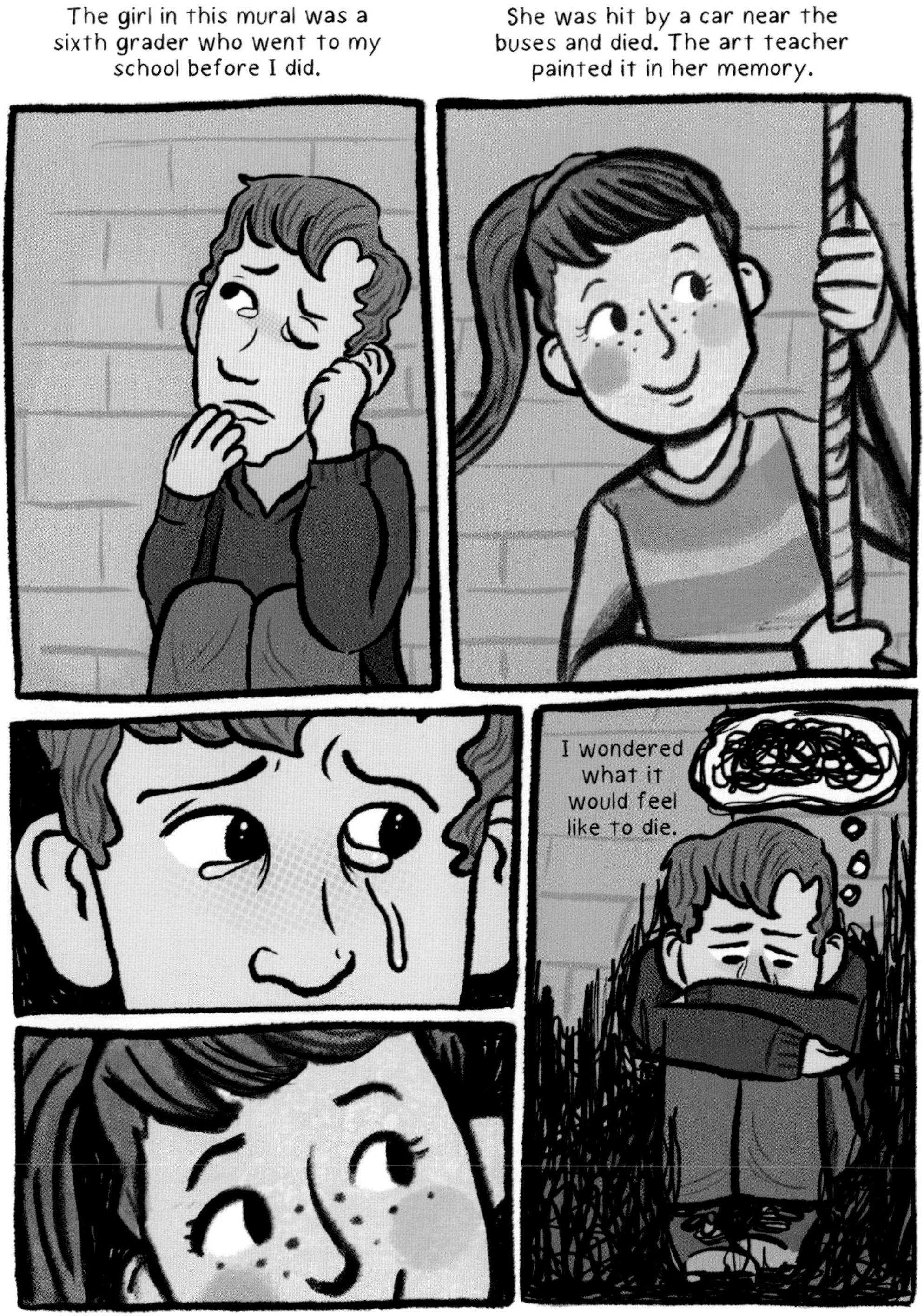
The girl in this mural was a sixth grader who went to my school before I did.
She was hit by a car near the buses and died. The art teacher painted it in her memory.
I wondered what it would feel like to die.

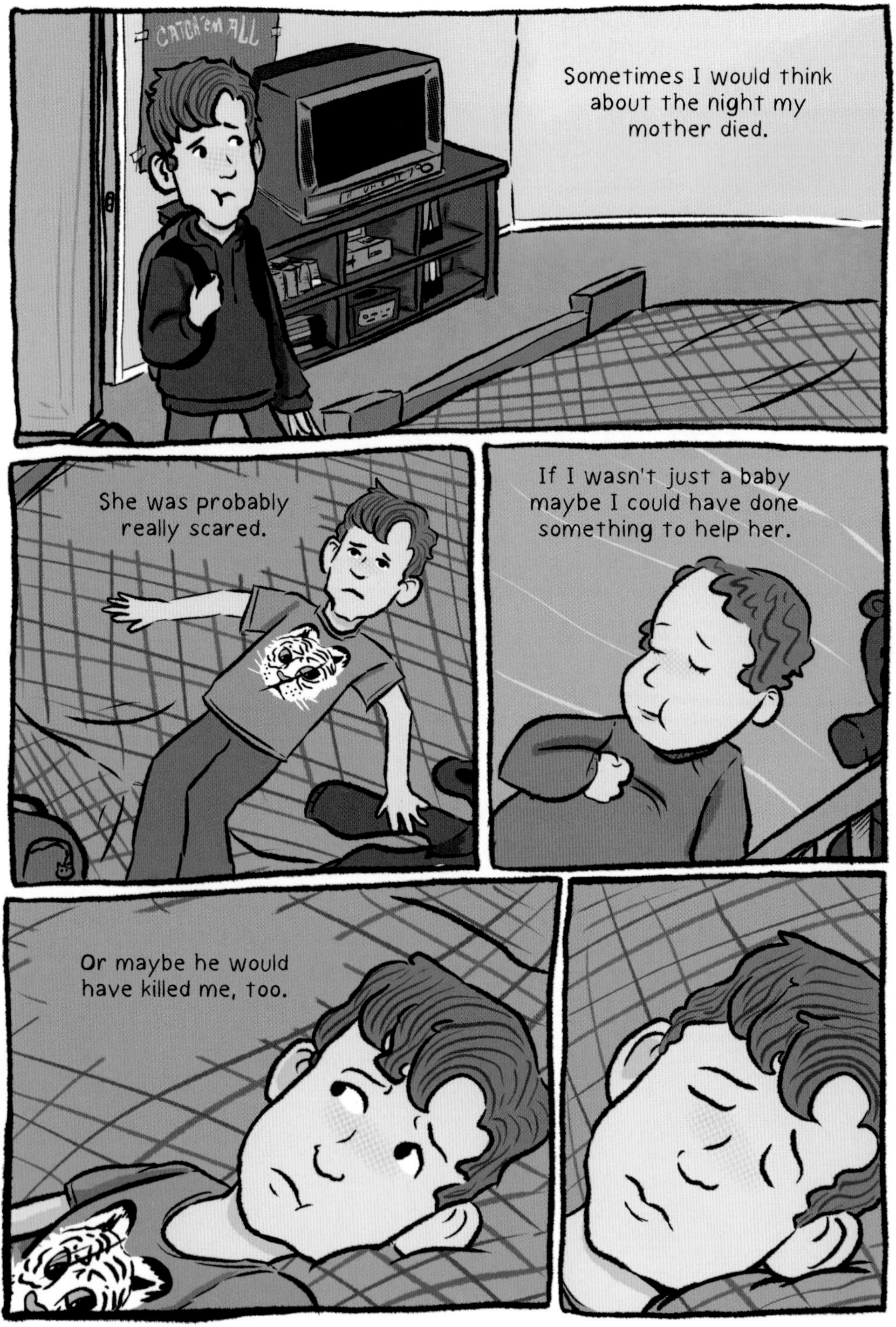
CATCH 'em ALL
Sometimes I would think about the night my mother died.
She was probably really scared.
If I wasn't just a baby maybe I could have done something to help her.
Or maybe he would have killed me, too.

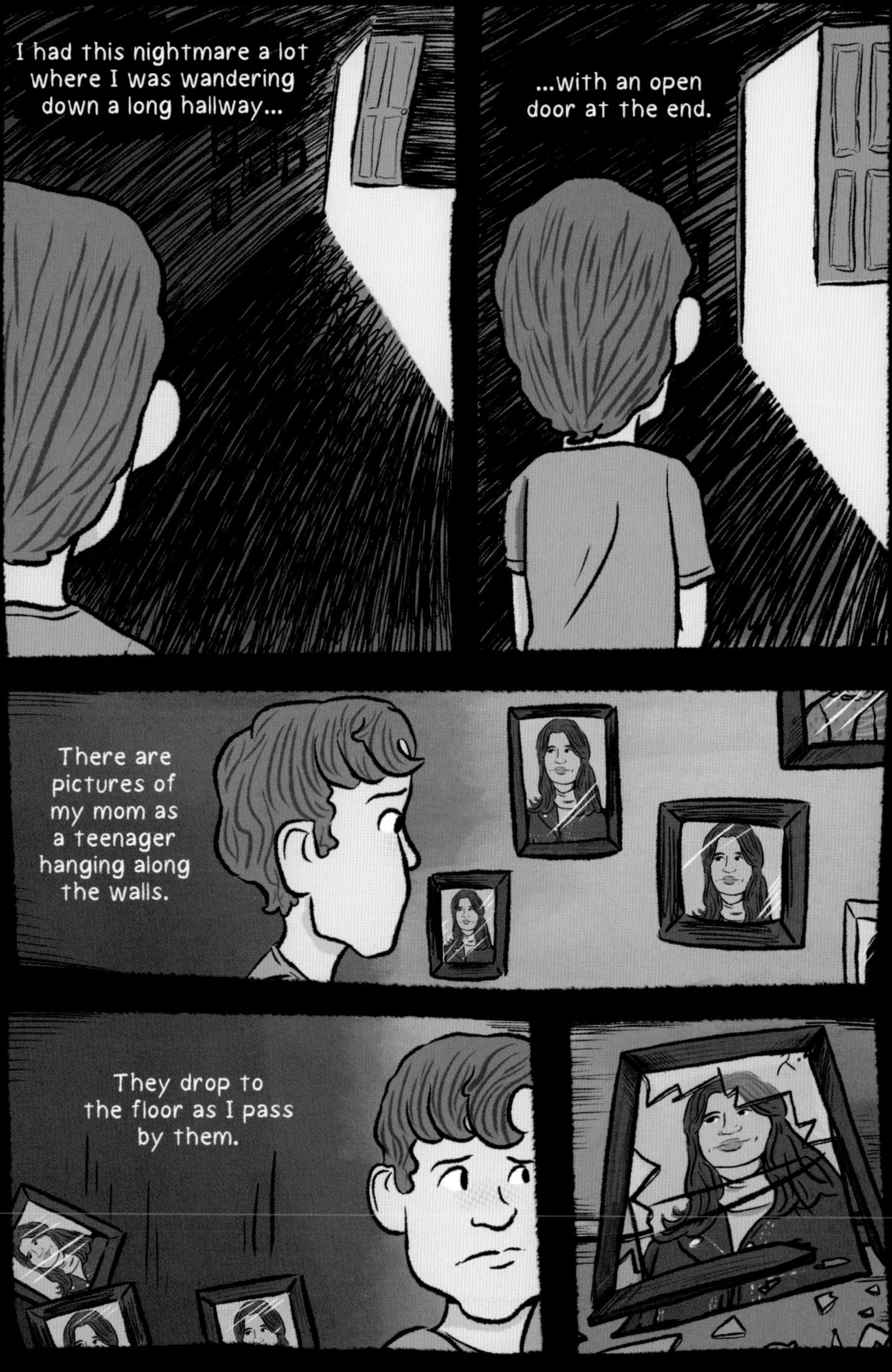
I had this nightmare a lot where I was wandering down a long hallway...
...with an open door at the end.
There are pictures of my mom as a teenager hanging along the walls.
They drop to the floor as I pass by them.

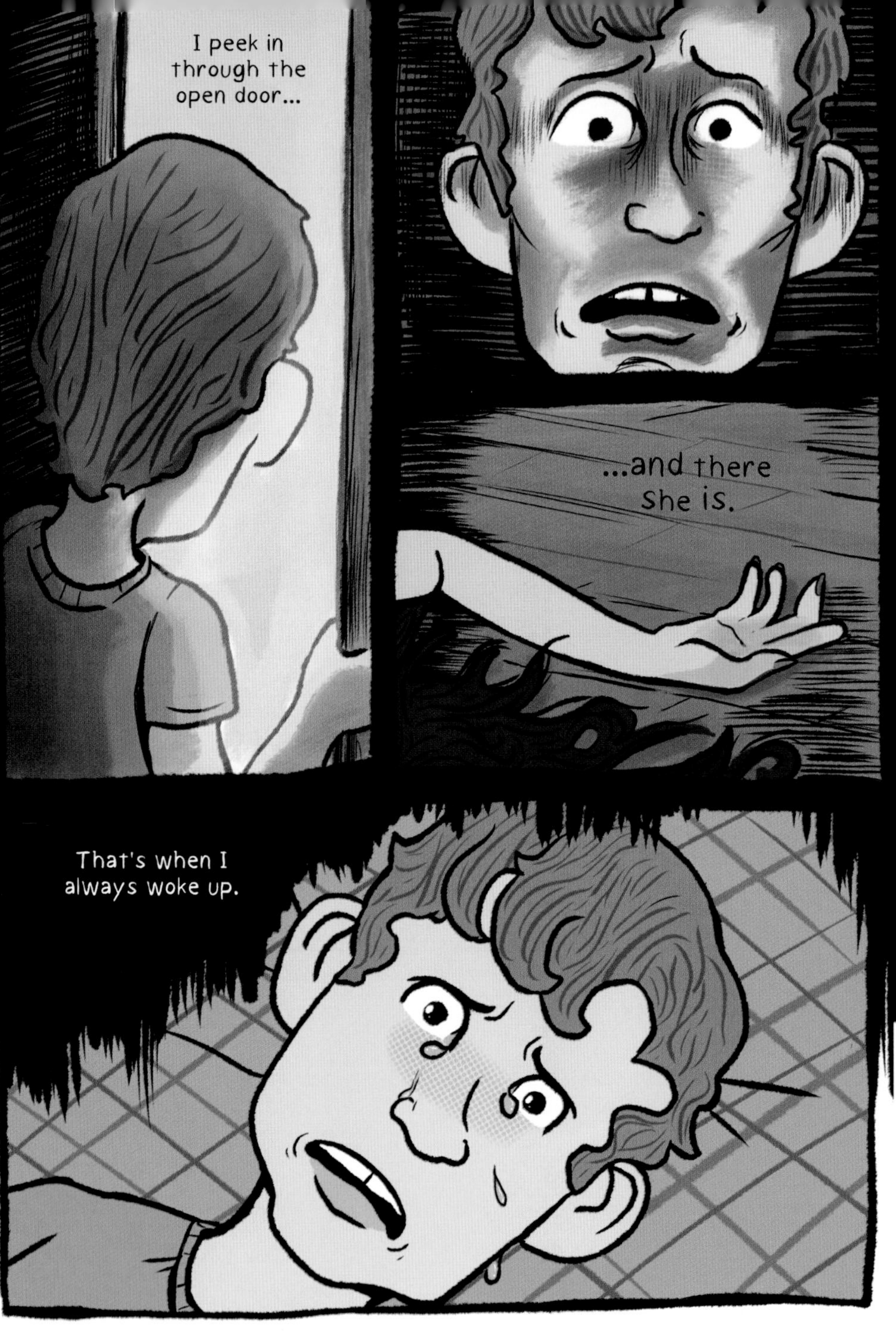
I peek in through the open door...
...and there she is.
That's when I always woke up.

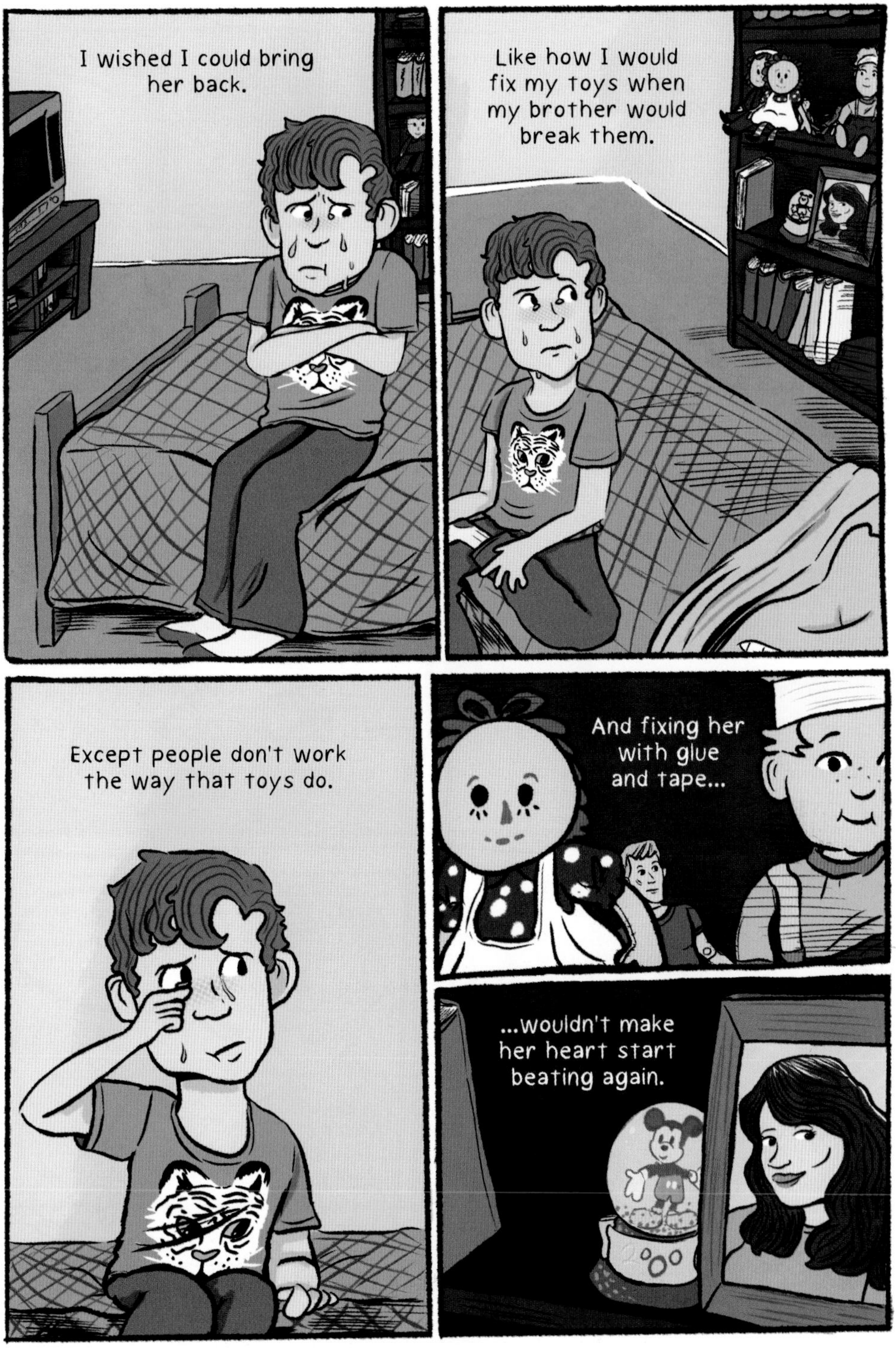
I wished I could bring her back.
Like how I would fix my toys when my brother would break them.
Except people don't work the way that toys do.
And fixing her with glue and tape...
...wouldn't make her heart start beating again.

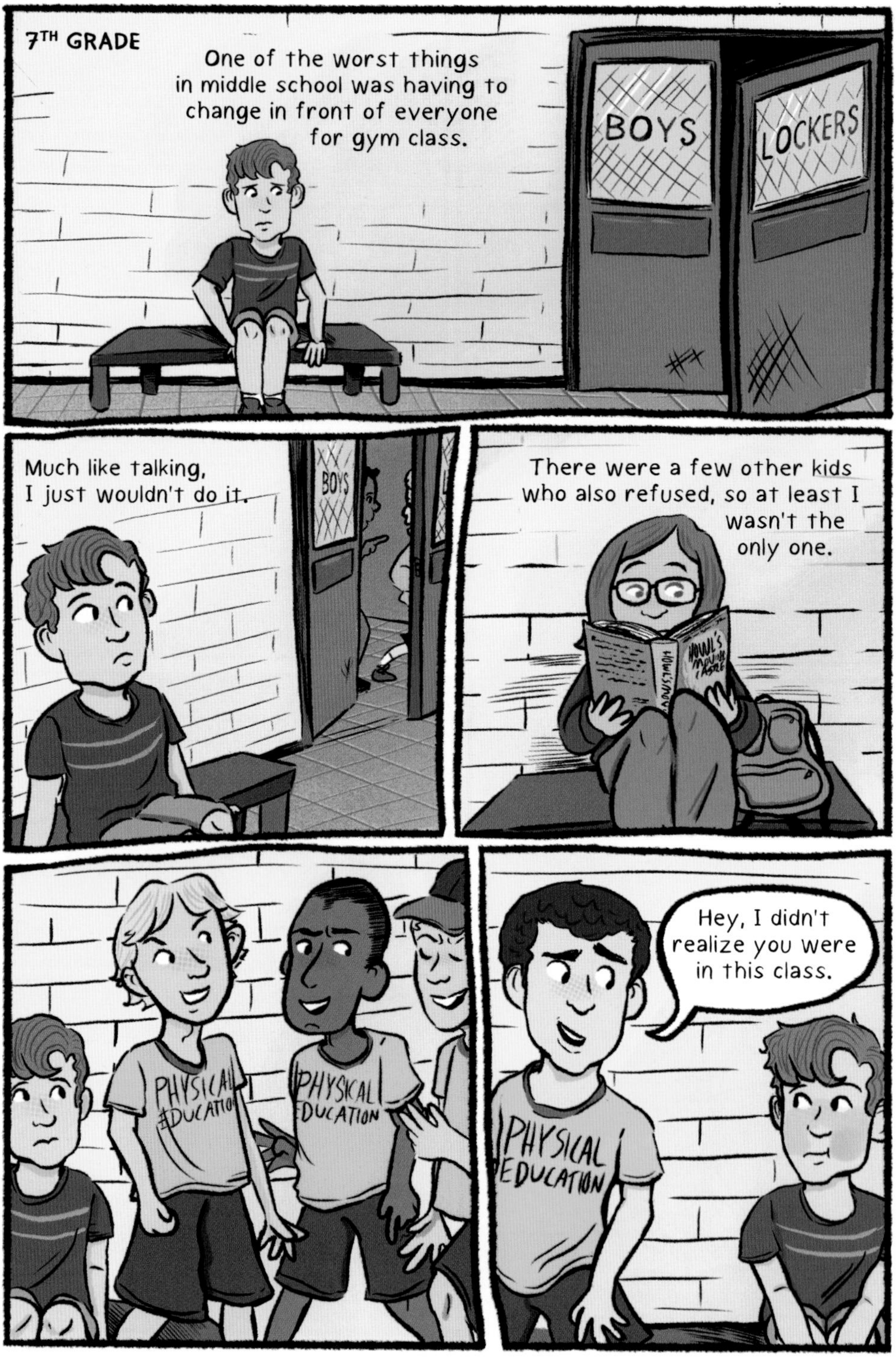
7TH GRADE
One of the worst things in middle school was having to change in front of everyone for gym class.
BOYS
LOCKERS
Much like talking, I just wouldn't do it.
BOYS
There were a few other kids who also refused, so at least I wasn't the only one.
PHYSICAL EDUCATION
PHYSICAL EDUCATION
PHYSICAL EDUCATION
Hey, I didn't realize you were in this class.

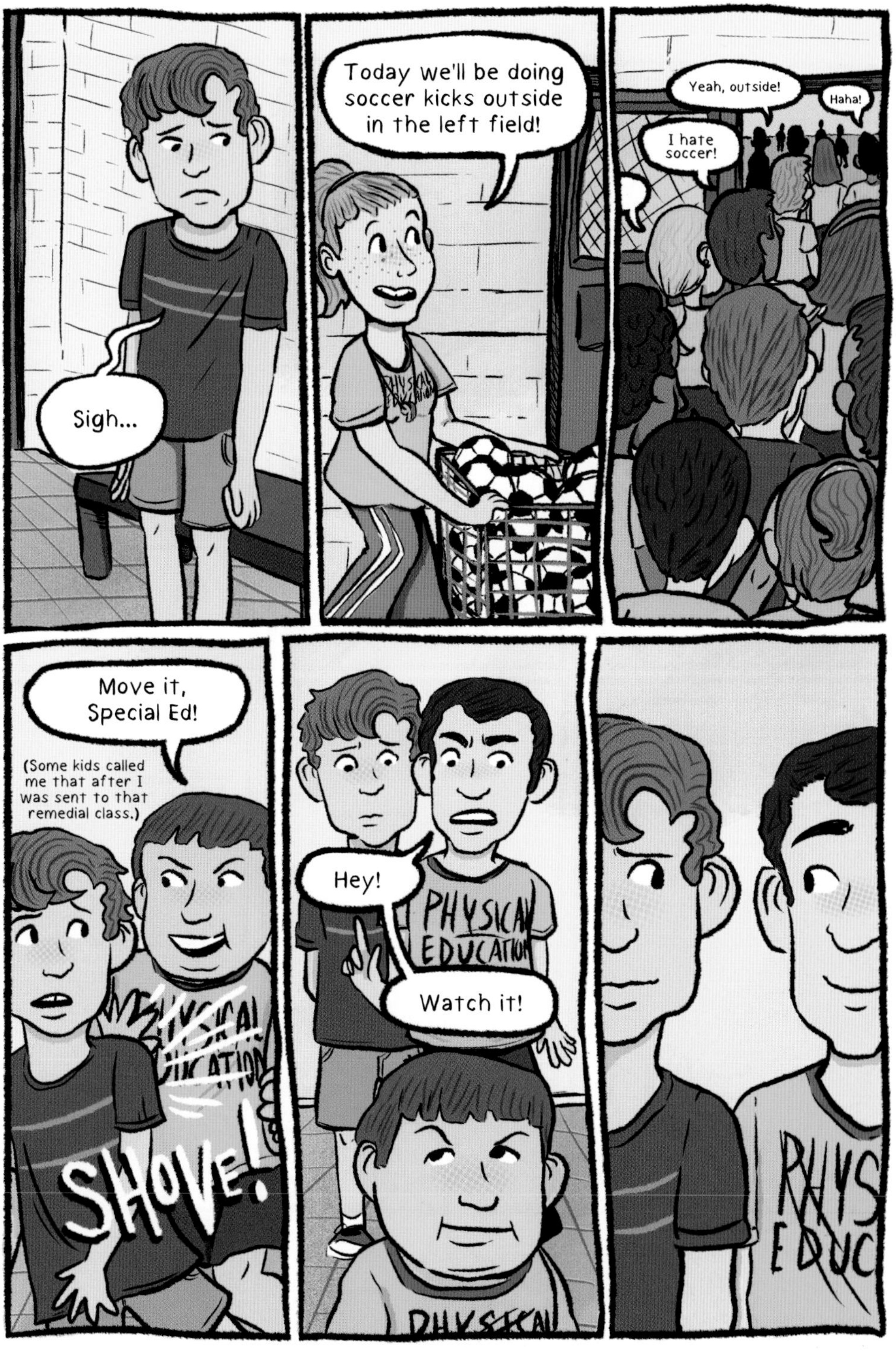
Sigh...
Today we'll be doing soccer kicks outside in the left field!
Yeah, outside!
Haha!
I hate soccer!
Move it, Special Ed!
(Some kids called me that after I was sent to that remedial class.)
SHOVE!
Hey!
Watch it!

I was never particularly good at any competitive sports.

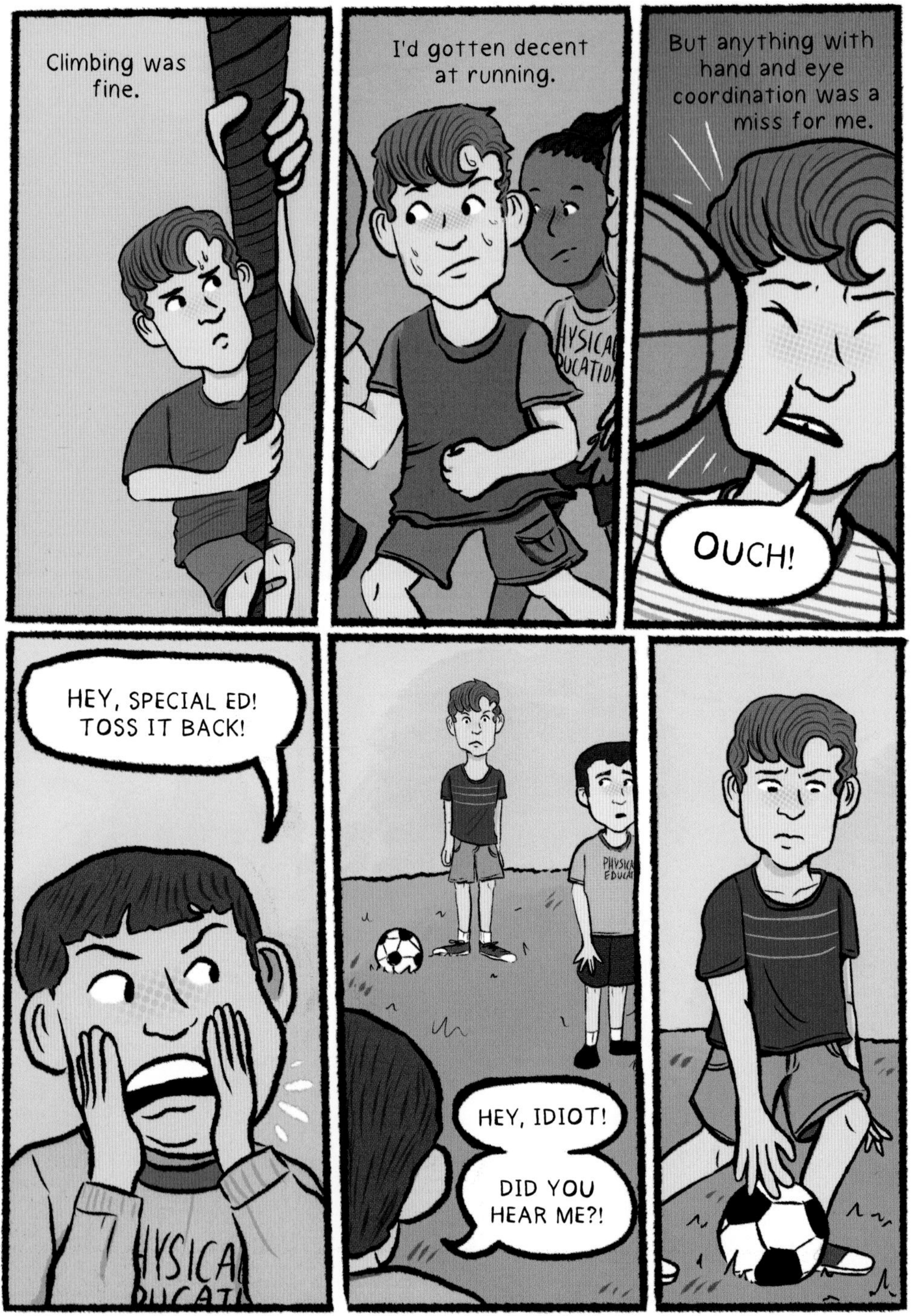
Climbing was fine.
I'd gotten decent at running.
But anything with hand and eye coordination was a miss for me.
OUCH!
HEY, SPECIAL ED! TOSS IT BACK!
HEY, IDIOT!
DID YOU HEAR ME?!

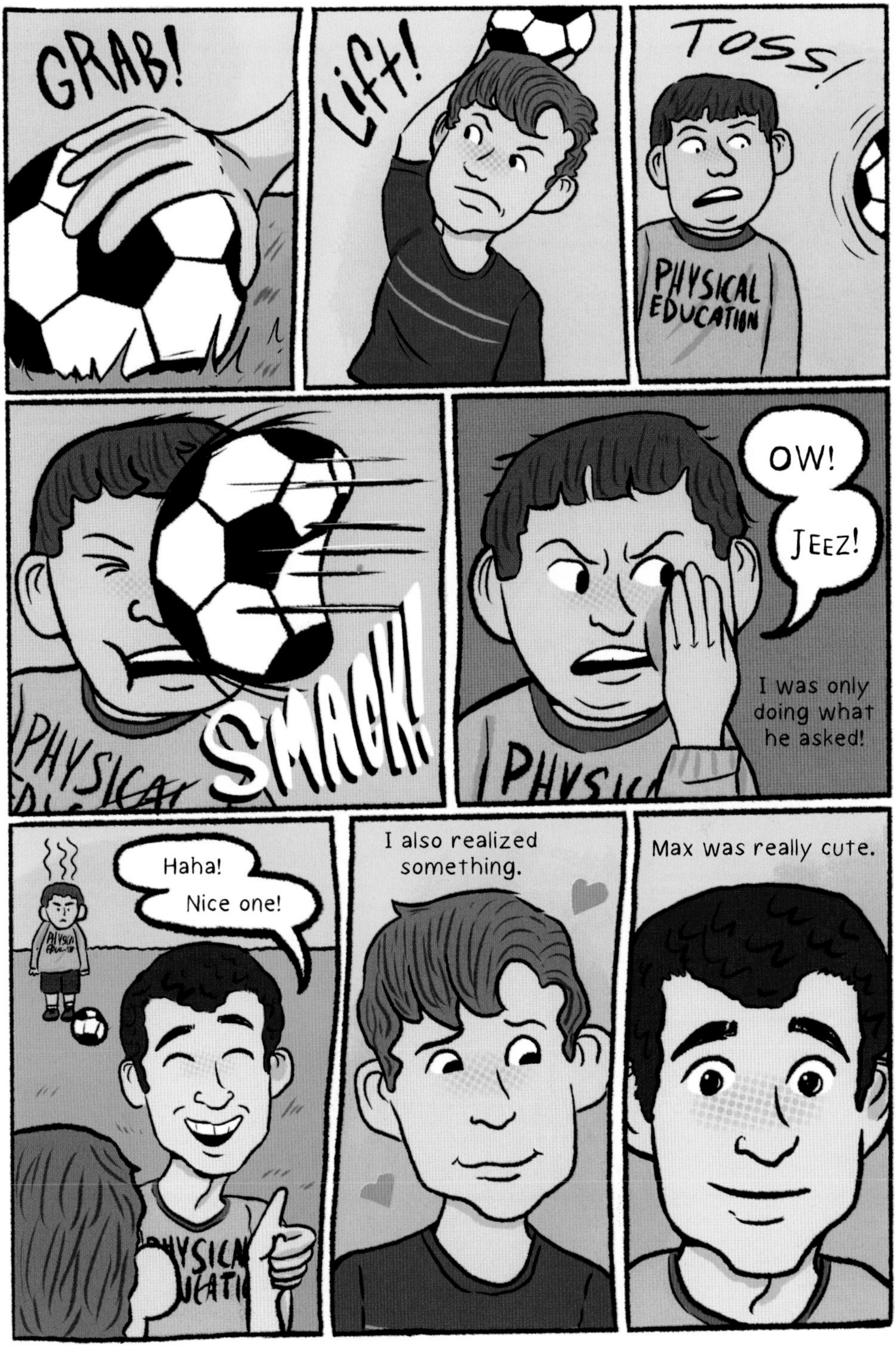
GRAB!
Lift!
TOSS!
SMACK!
OW!
JEEZ!
I was only doing what he asked!
Haha!
Nice one!
I also realized something.
Max was really cute.
PHYSICAL EDUCATION

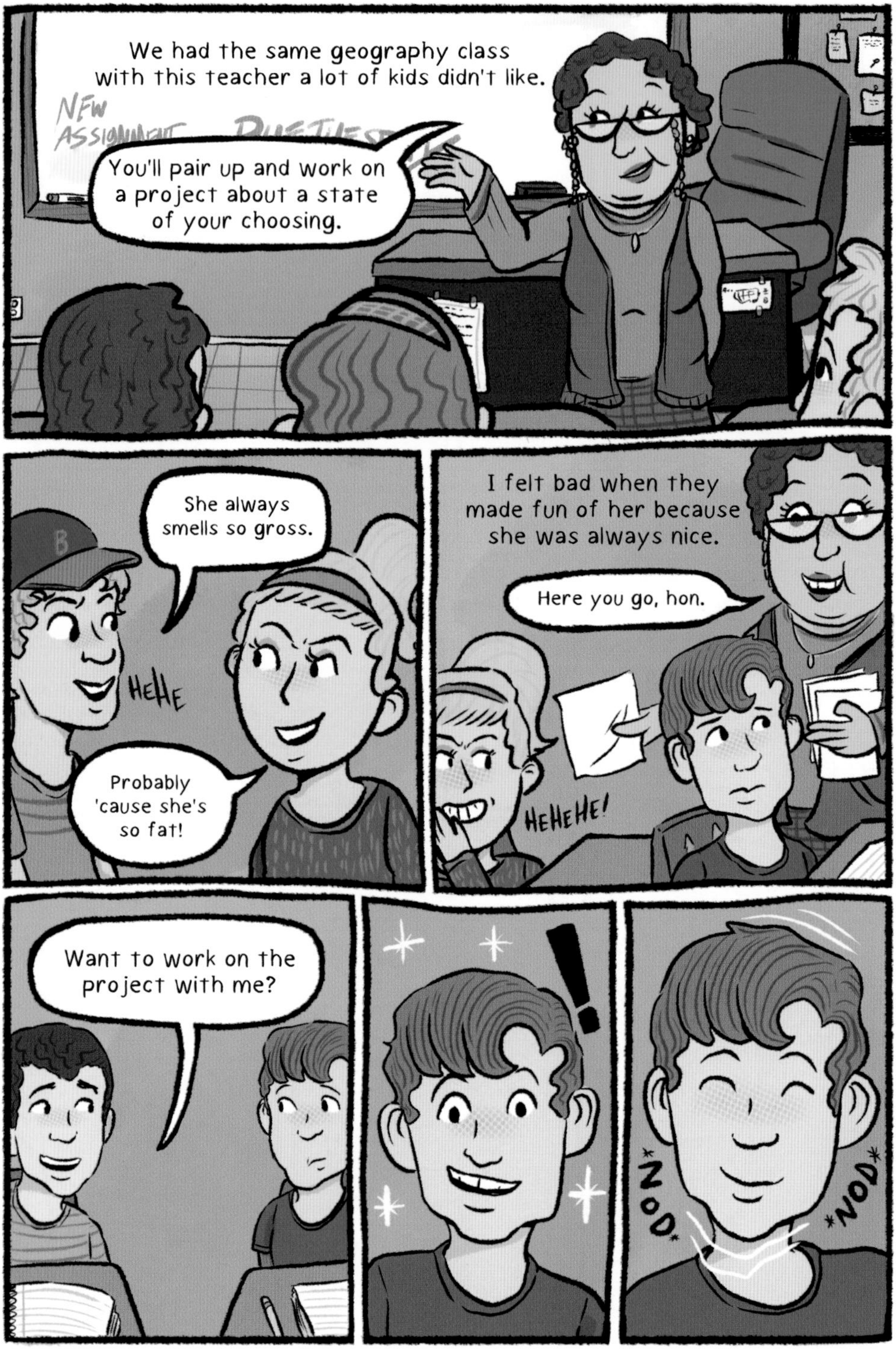
We had the same geography class with this teacher a lot of kids didn't like.
You'll pair up and work on a project about a state of your choosing.
She always smells so gross.
HEHE
Probably 'cause she's so fat!
I felt bad when they made fun of her because she was always nice.
Here you go, hon.
HEHEHE!
Want to work on the project with me?
!
NOD
NOD

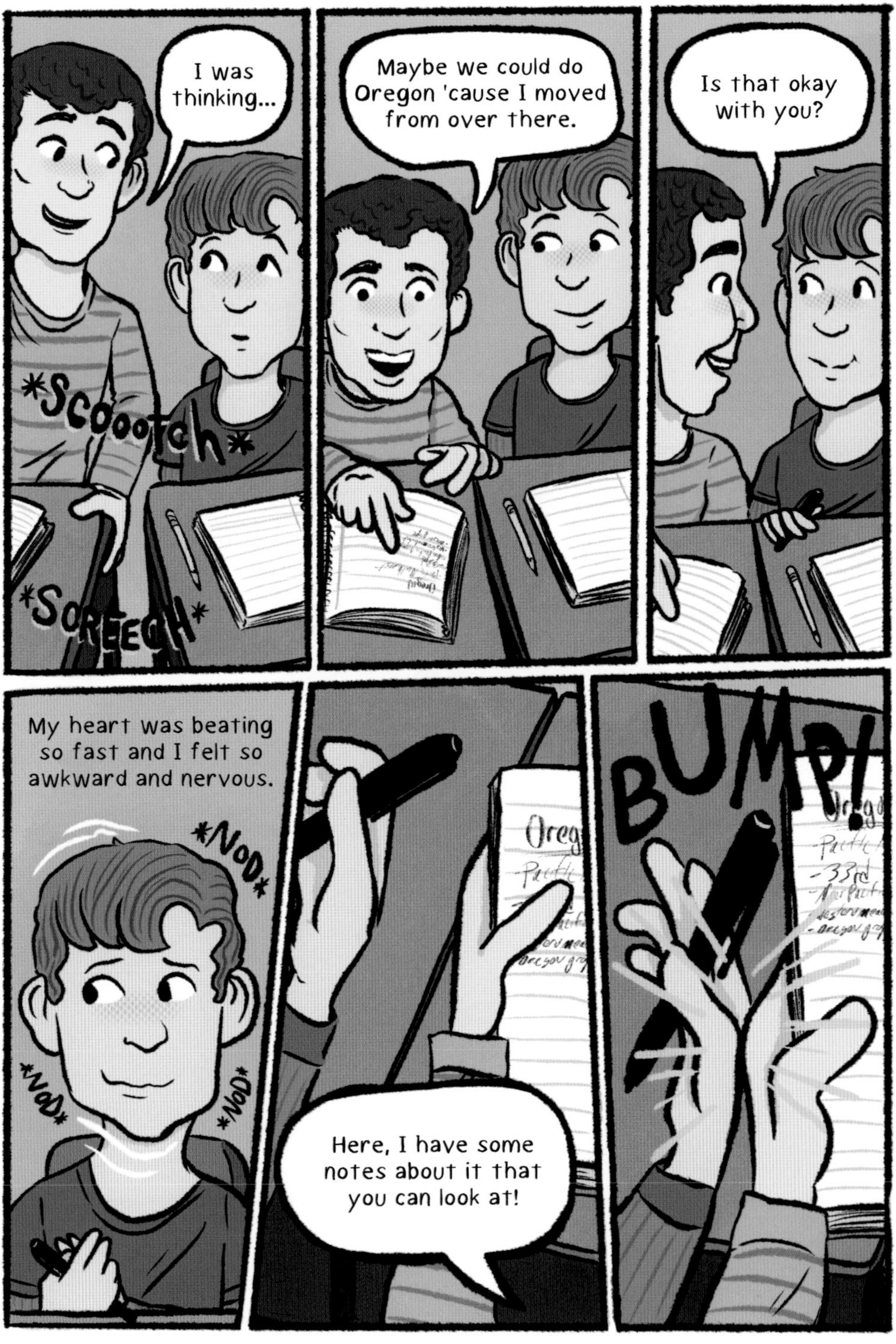
I was thinking...
SCOOOTCH
SCREECH
Maybe we could do Oregon 'cause I moved from over there.
Is that okay with you?
My heart was beating so fast and I felt so awkward and nervous.
NOD
NOD
NOD
Here, I have some notes about it that you can look at!
BUMP!

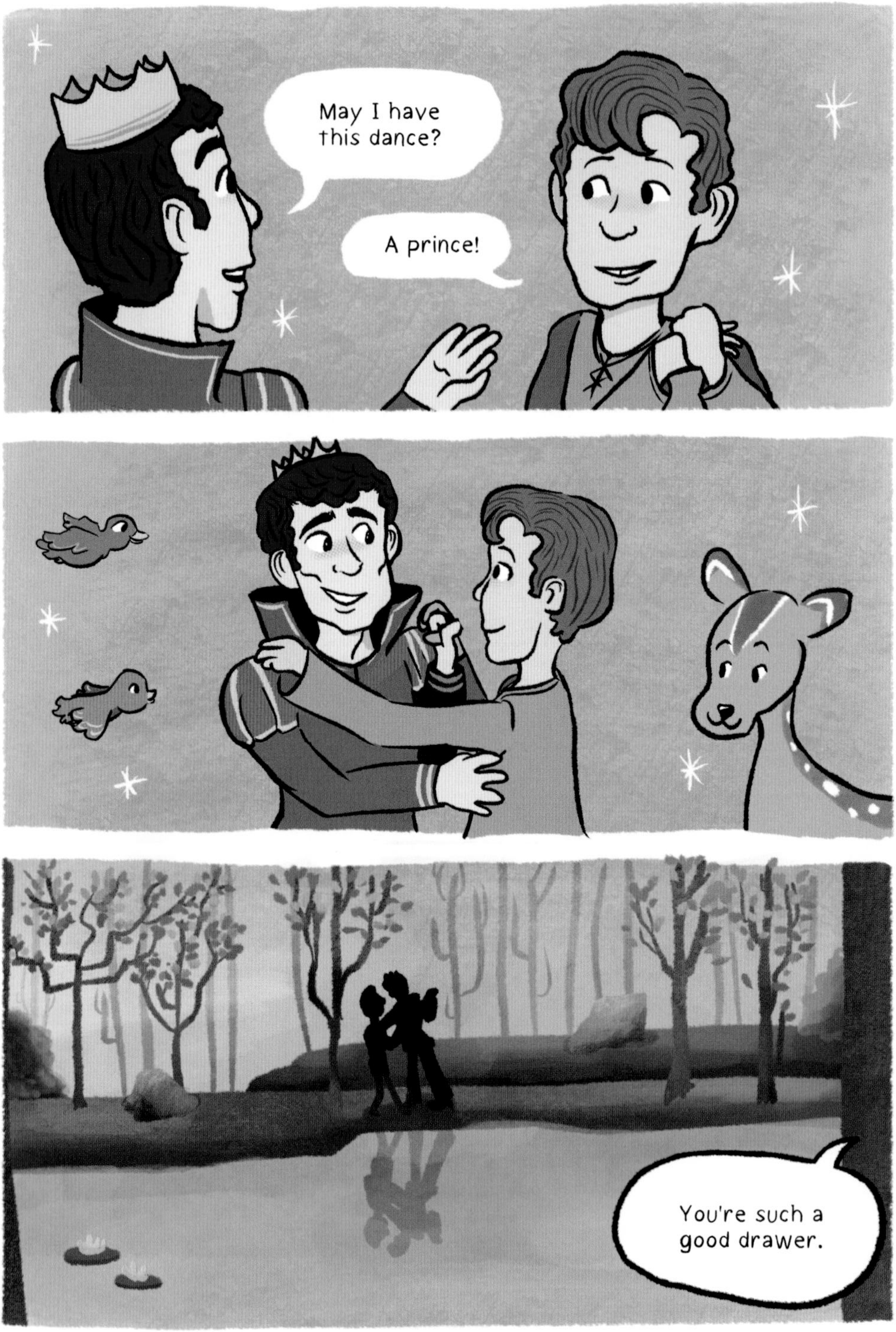
May I have this dance?
A prince!
You're such a good drawer.

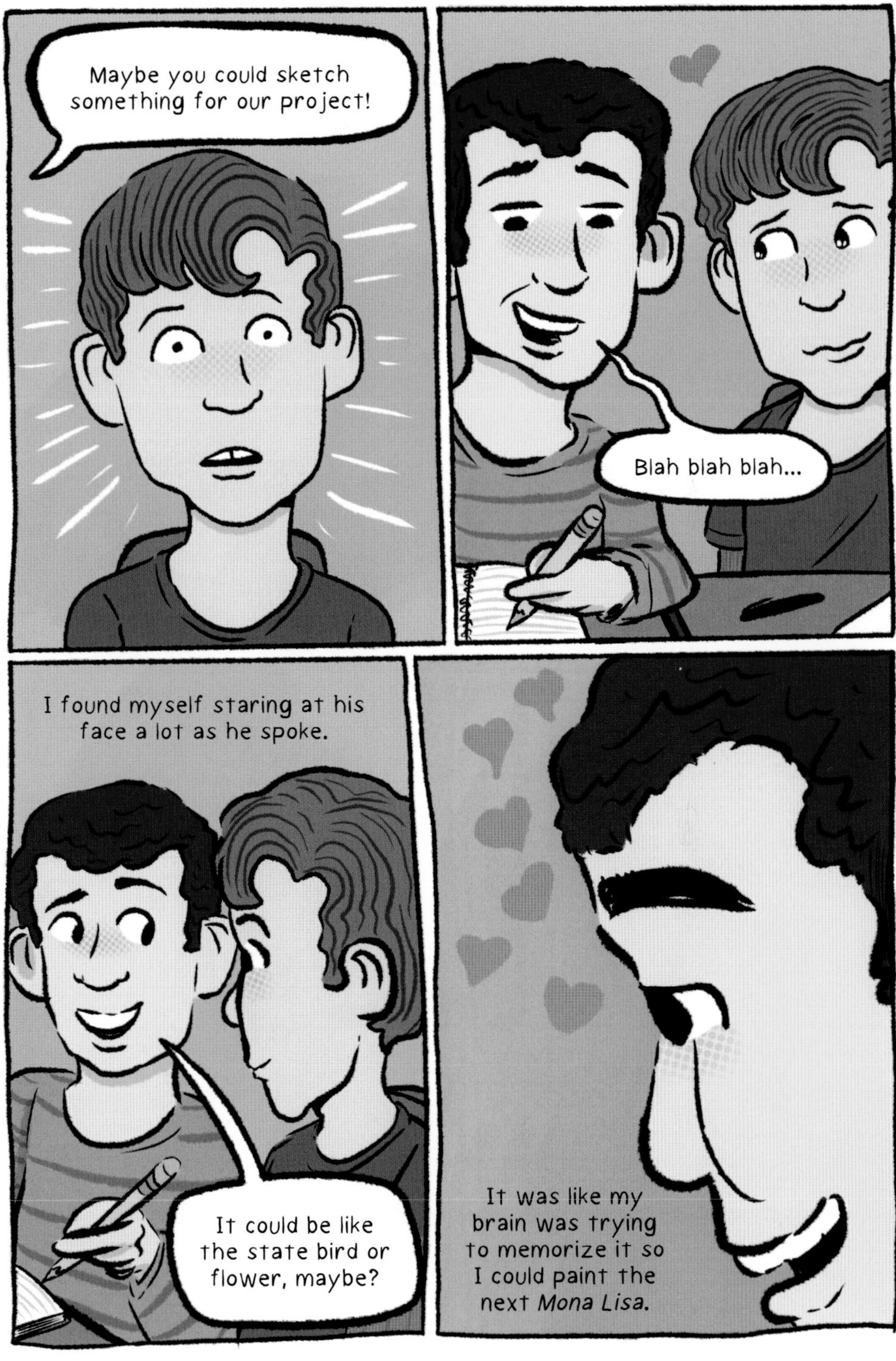
Maybe you could sketch something for our project!
Blah blah blah...
I found myself staring at his face a lot as he spoke.
It could be like the state bird or flower, maybe?
It was like my brain was trying to memorize it so I could paint the next *Mona Lisa*.

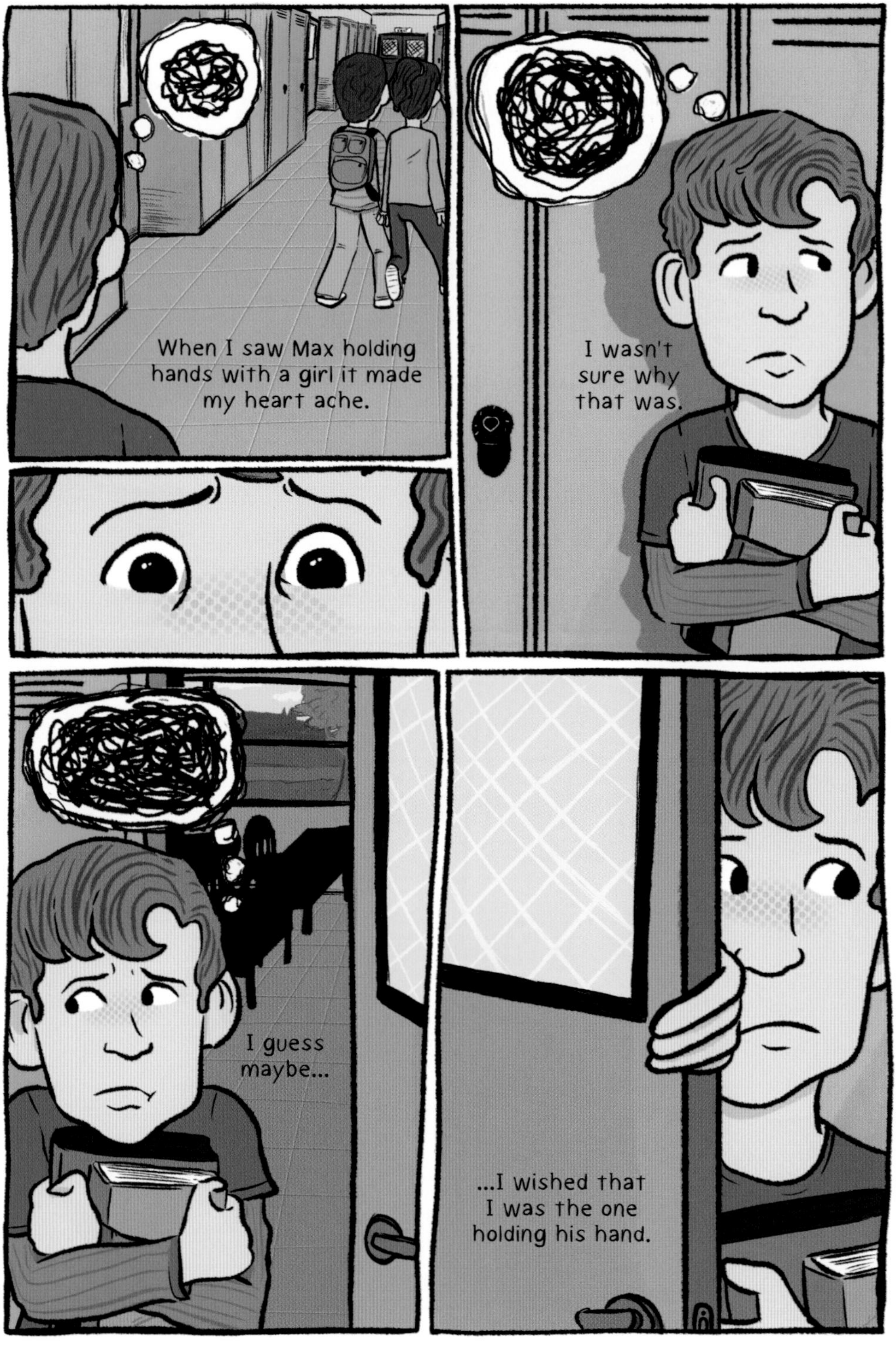
When I saw Max holding hands with a girl it made my heart ache.
I wasn't sure why that was.
I guess maybe...
...I wished that I was the one holding his hand.

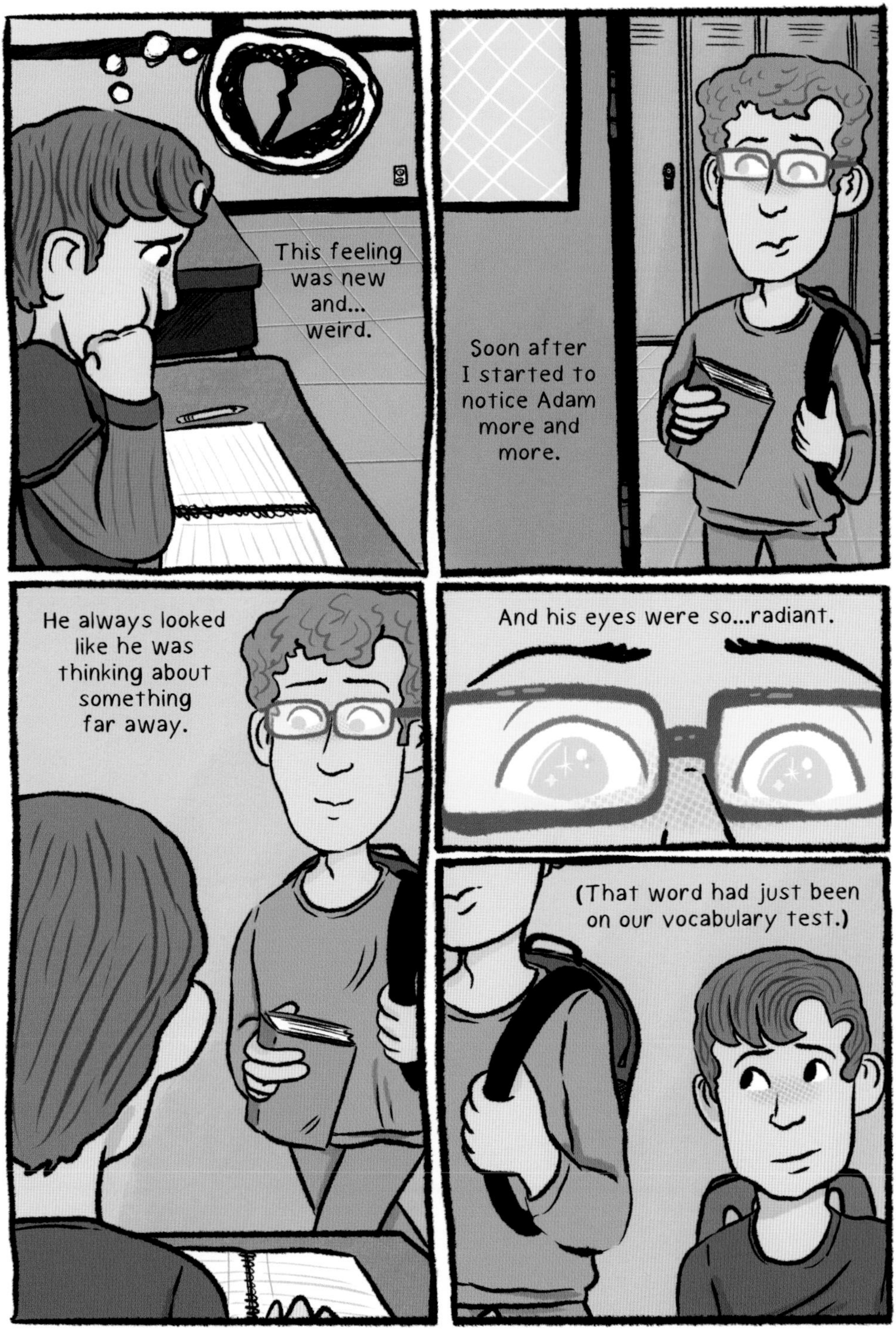

This feeling was new and... weird.
Soon after I started to notice Adam more and more.
He always looked like he was thinking about something far away.
And his eyes were so...radiant.
(That word had just been on our vocabulary test.)

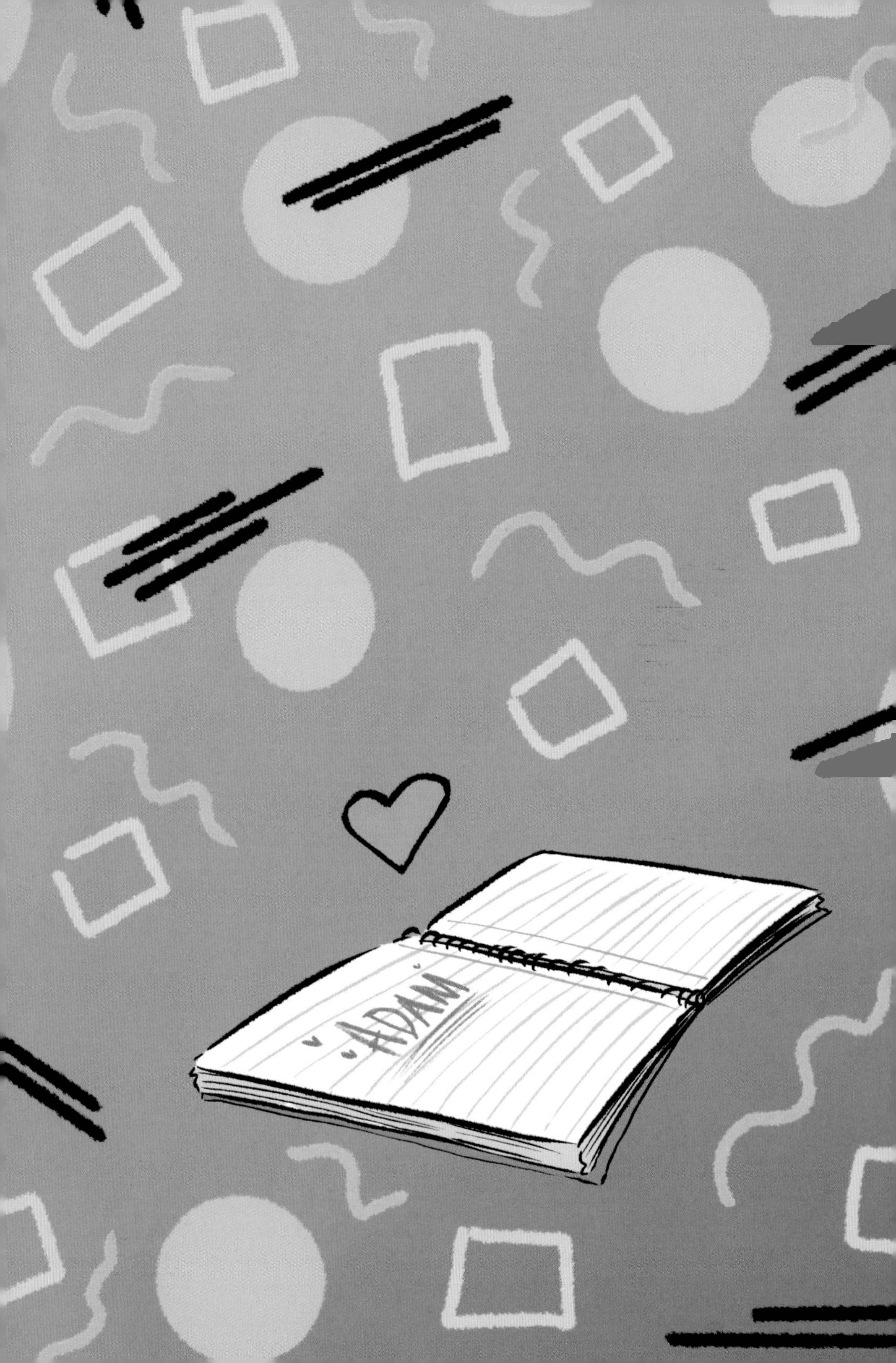
ADAM

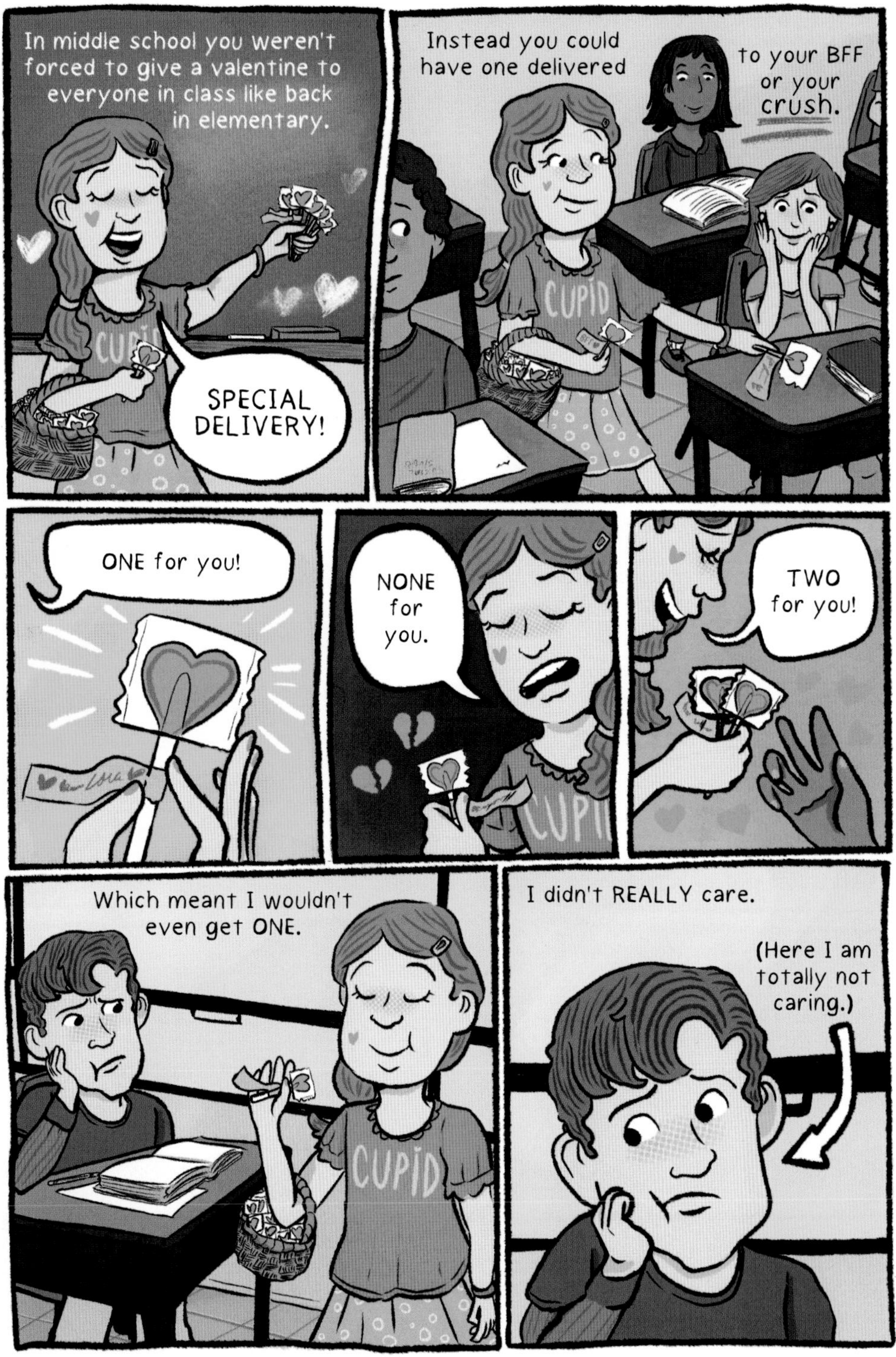
In middle school you weren't forced to give a valentine to everyone in class like back in elementary.
SPECIAL DELIVERY!
Instead you could have one delivered
to your BFF or your crush.
ONE for you!
NONE for you.
TWO for you!
Which meant I wouldn't even get ONE.
I didn't REALLY care.
(Here I am totally not caring.)

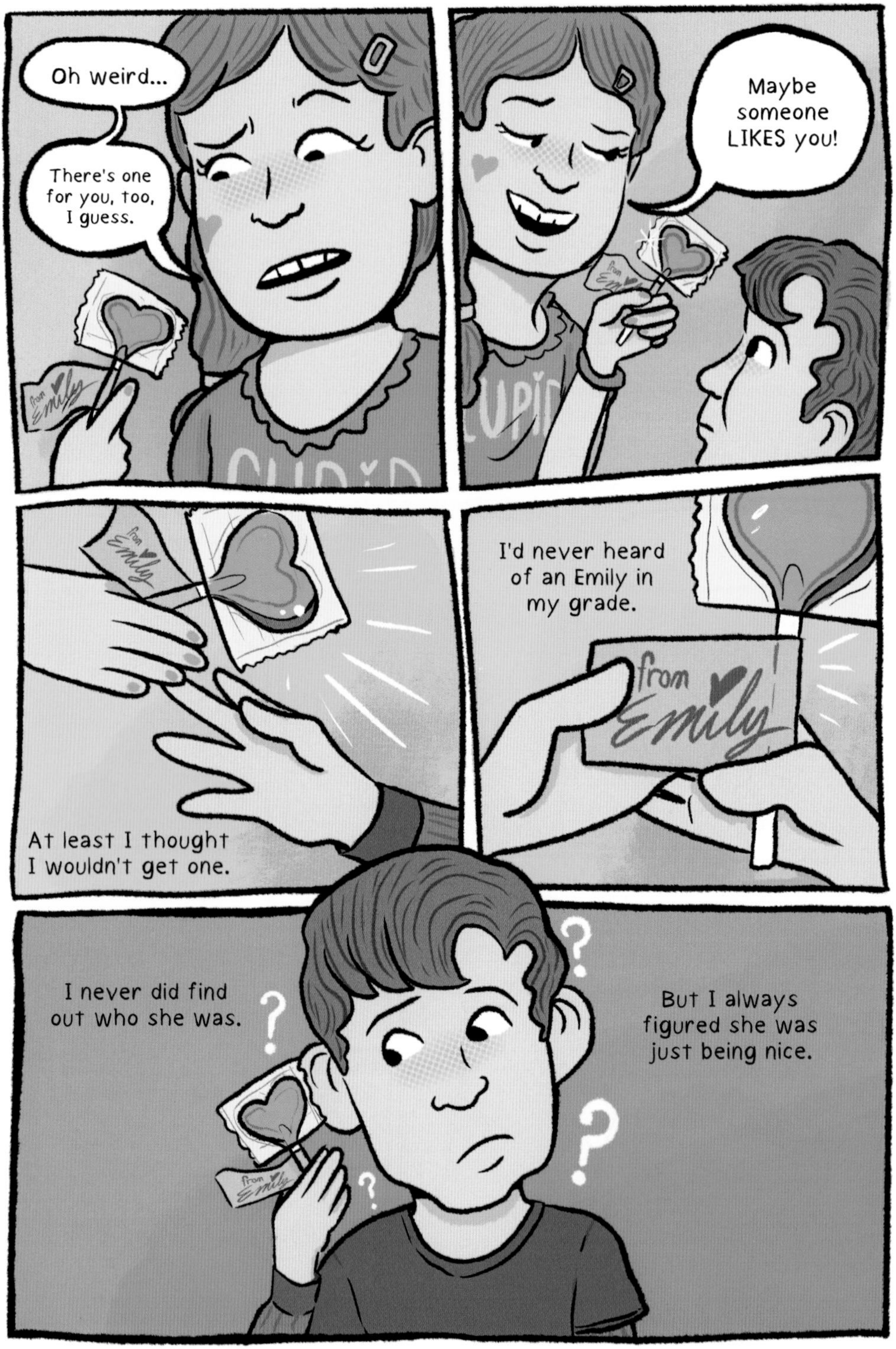
Oh weird...
There's one for you, too, I guess.
from Emily
Maybe someone LIKES you!
CUPID
from Emily
At least I thought I wouldn't get one.
I'd never heard of an Emily in my grade.
from Emily
I never did find out who she was.
But I always figured she was just being nice.
from Emily

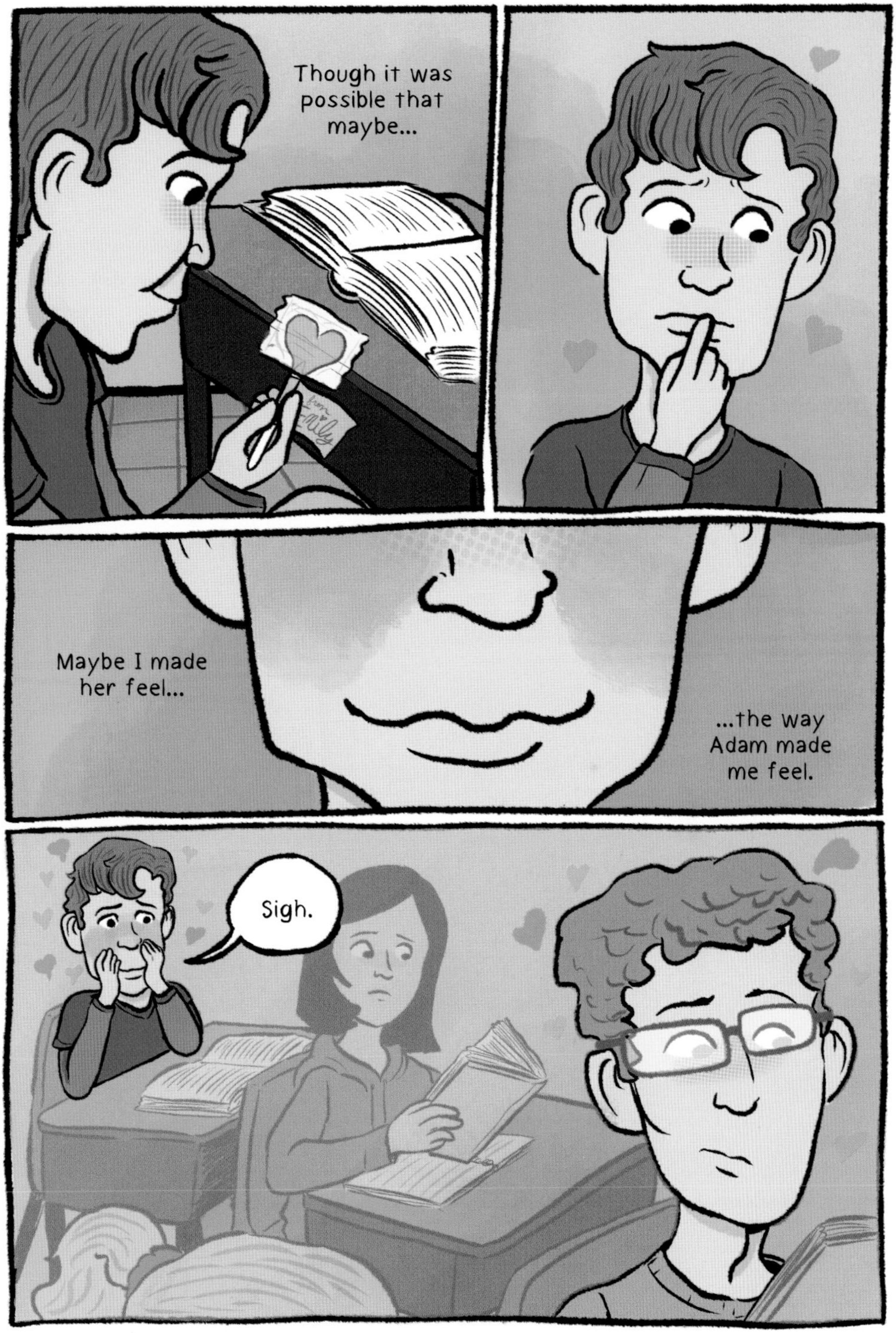
Though it was possible that maybe...
Maybe I made her feel...
...the way Adam made me feel.
Sigh.

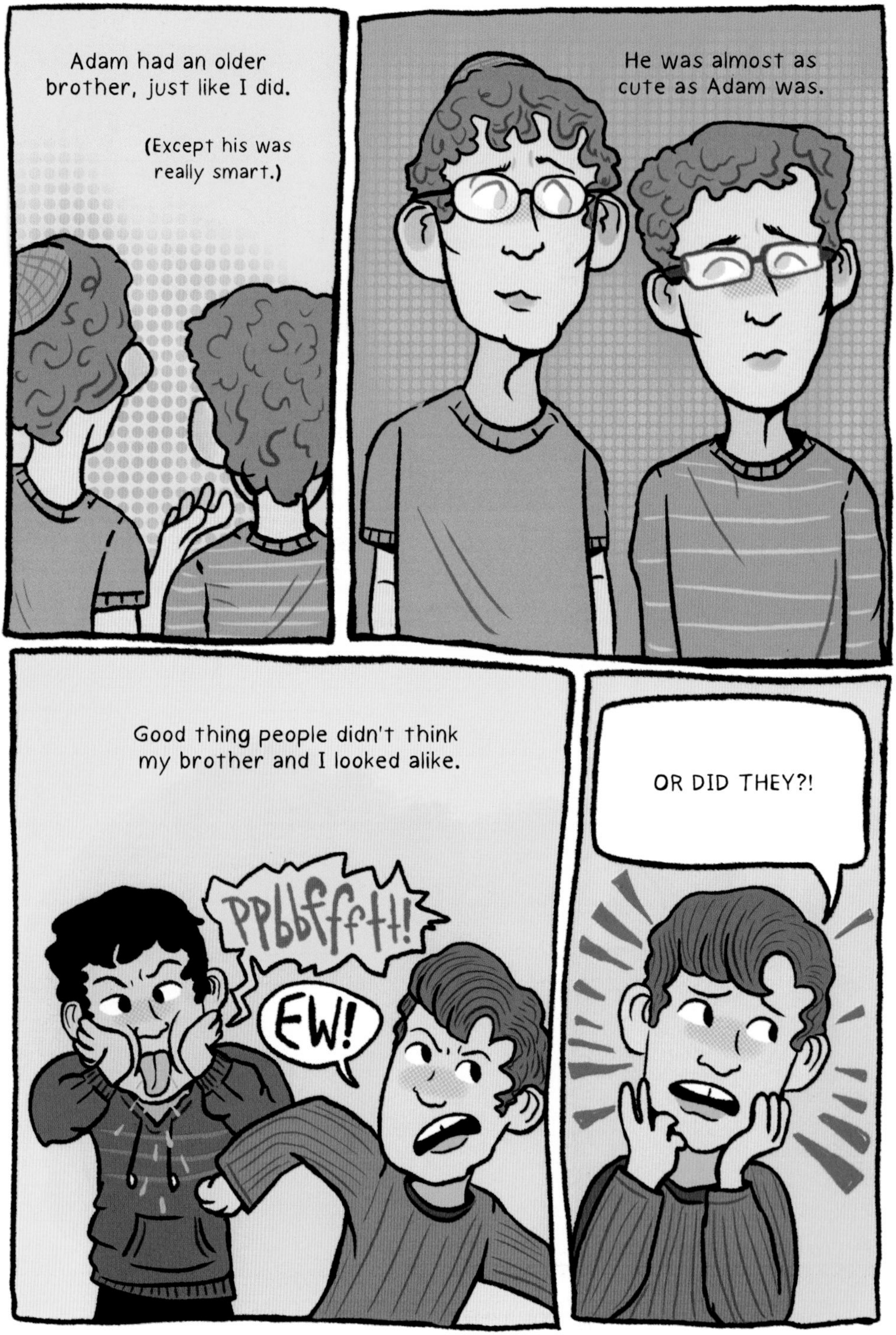
Adam had an older brother, just like I did.
(Except his was really smart.)
He was almost as cute as Adam was.
Good thing people didn't think my brother and I looked alike.
PPbbffftt!
EW!
OR DID THEY?!

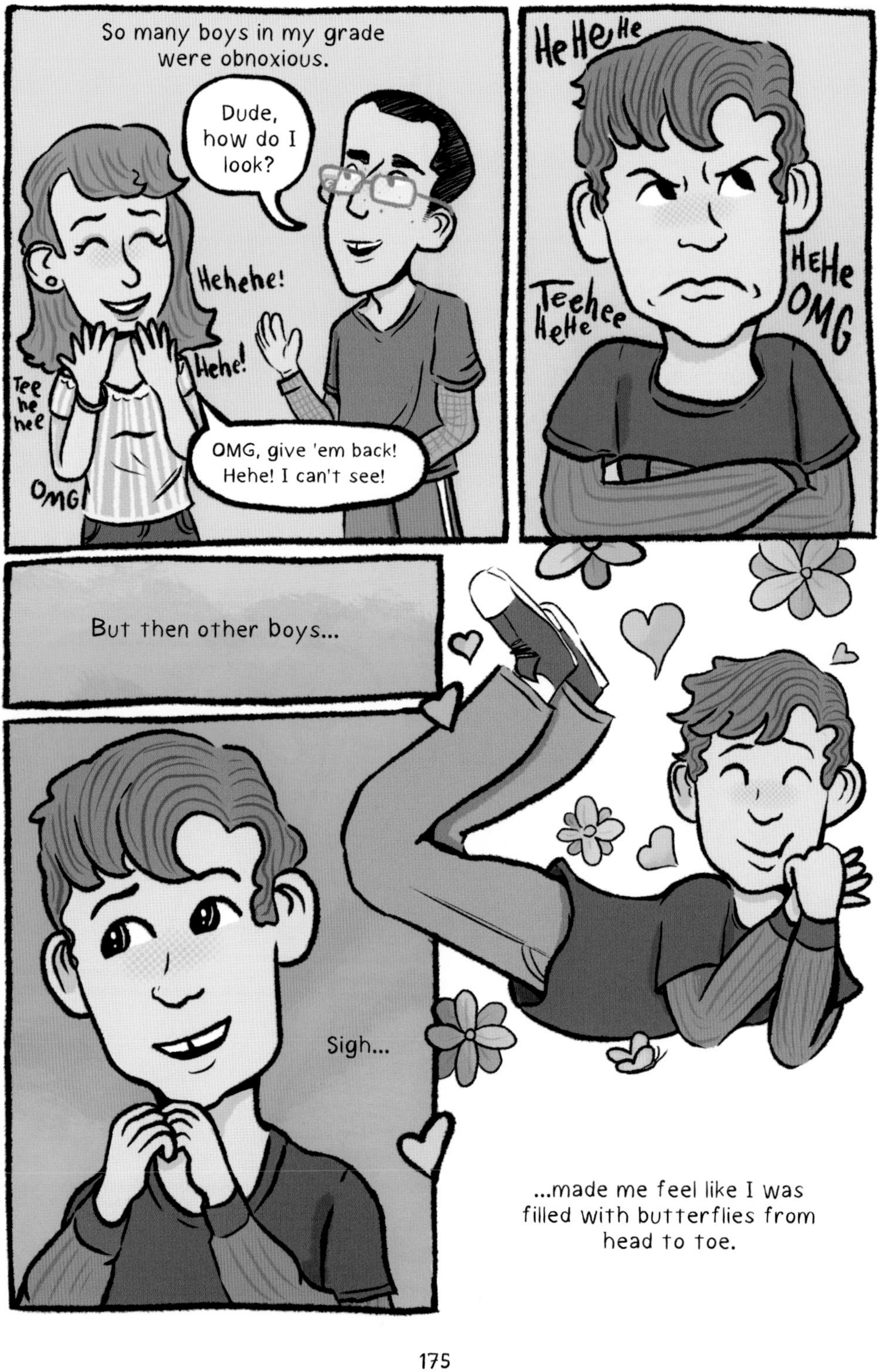
So many boys in my grade were obnoxious.
Dude, how do I look?
Hehehe!
Hehe!
Tee he hee
OMG!
OMG, give 'em back! Hehe! I can't see!
HeHeHe
Teehee HeHe
HeHe OMG
But then other boys...
Sigh...
...made me feel like I was filled with butterflies from head to toe.

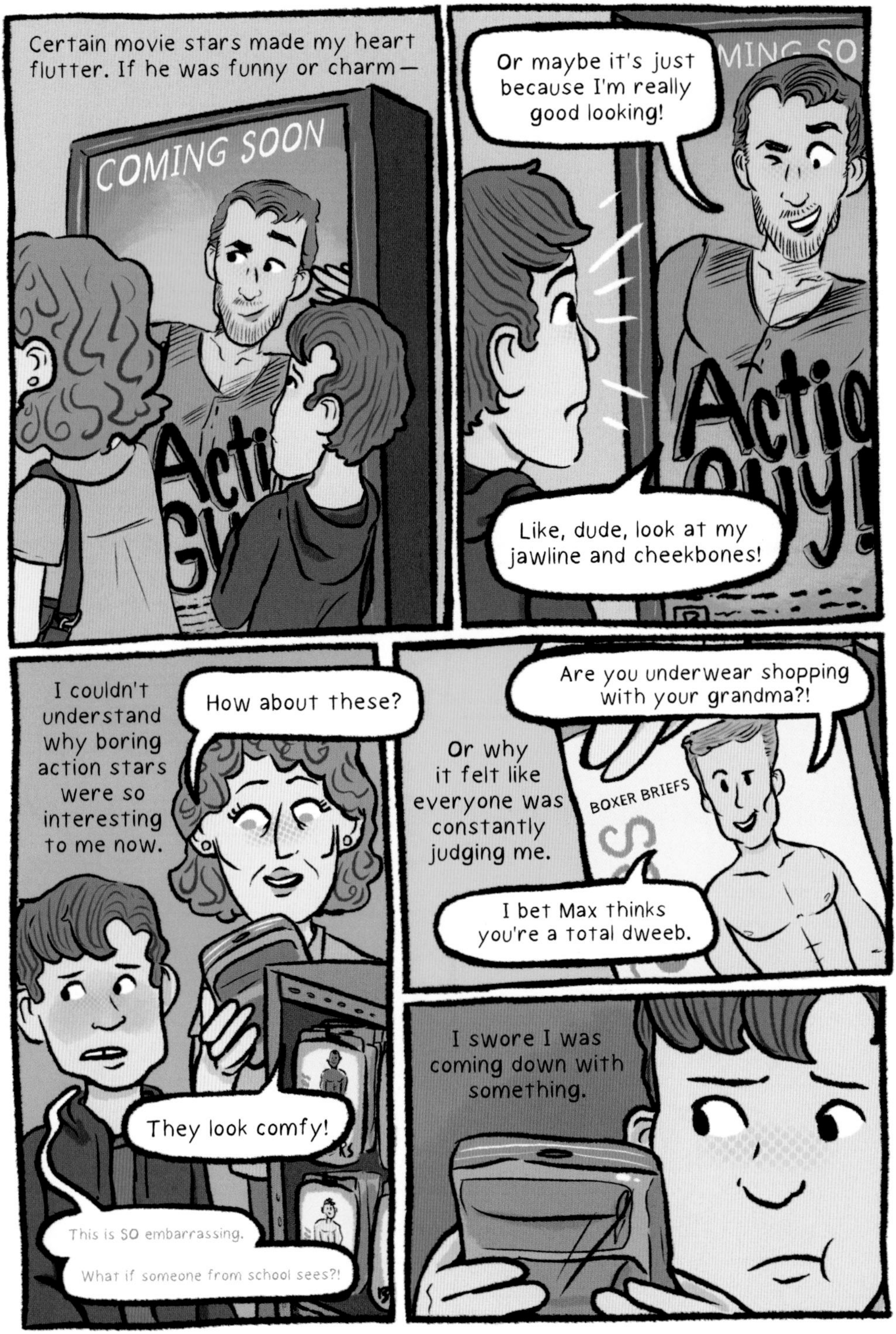
Certain movie stars made my heart flutter. If he was funny or charm—
COMING SOON
Or maybe it's just because I'm really good looking!
Like, dude, look at my jawline and cheekbones!
I couldn't understand why boring action stars were so interesting to me now.
How about these?
They look comfy!
This is SO embarrassing.
What if someone from school sees?!
Are you underwear shopping with your grandma?!
Or why it felt like everyone was constantly judging me.
BOXER BRIEFS
I bet Max thinks you're a total dweeb.
I swore I was coming down with something.

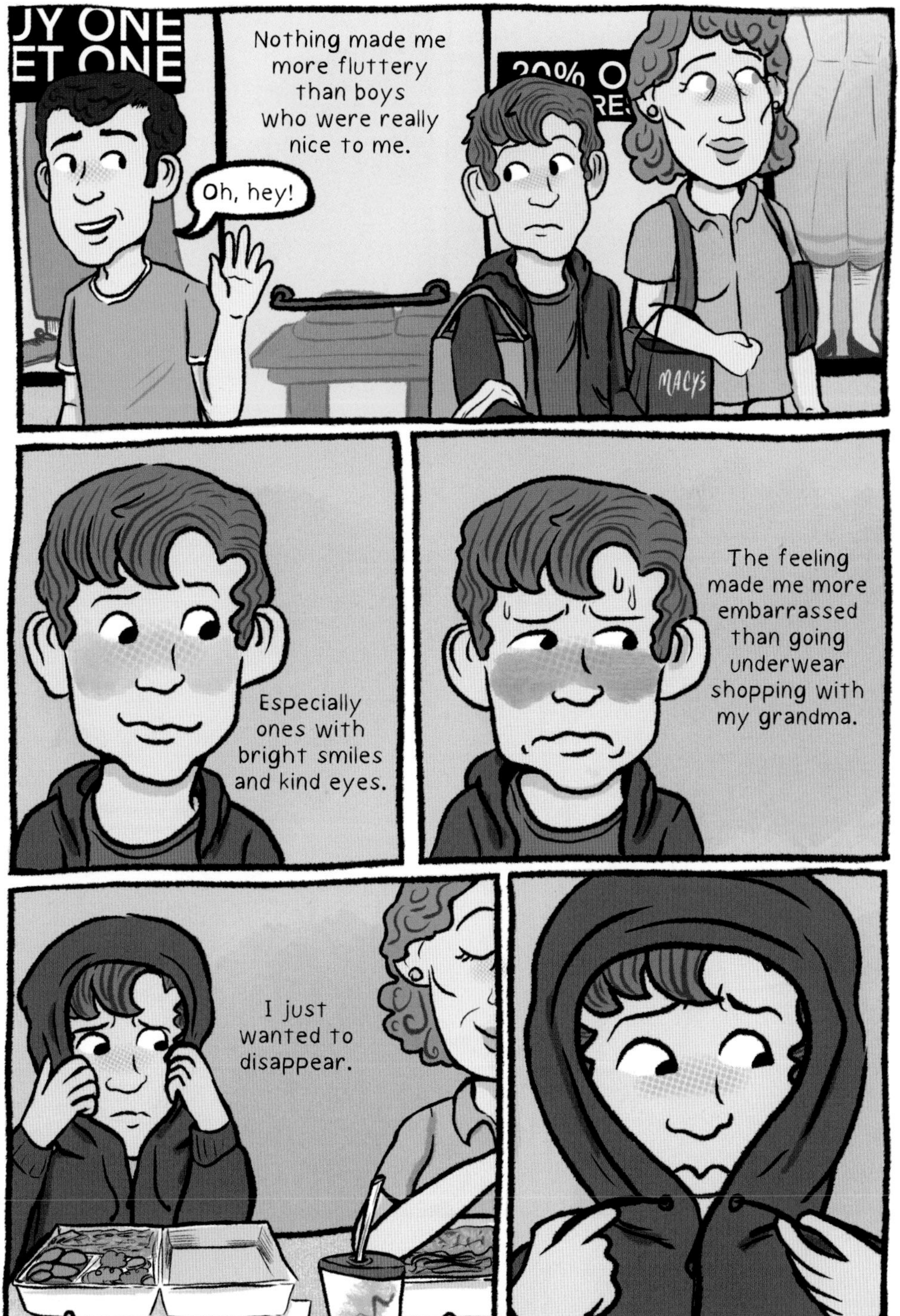
UY ONE
ET ONE
Nothing made me more fluttery than boys who were really nice to me.
Oh, hey!
MACY'S
Especially ones with bright smiles and kind eyes.
The feeling made me more embarrassed than going underwear shopping with my grandma.
I just wanted to disappear.

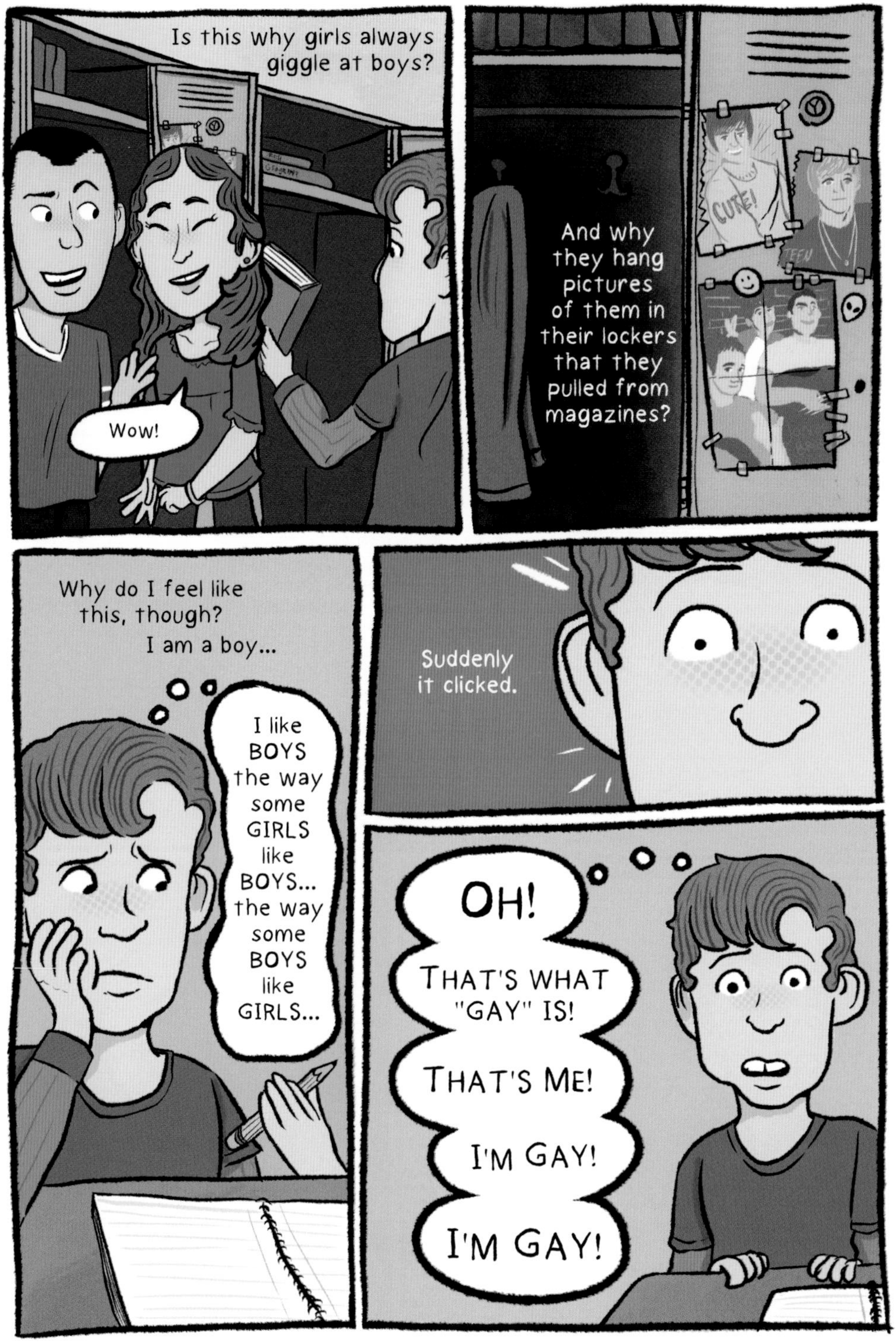
Is this why girls always giggle at boys?
Wow!
And why they hang pictures of them in their lockers that they pulled from magazines?
CUTE!
Why do I feel like this, though?
I am a boy...
I like BOYS the way some GIRLS like BOYS... the way some BOYS like GIRLS...
Suddenly it clicked.
OH!
THAT'S WHAT "GAY" IS!
THAT'S ME!
I'M GAY!
I'M GAY!

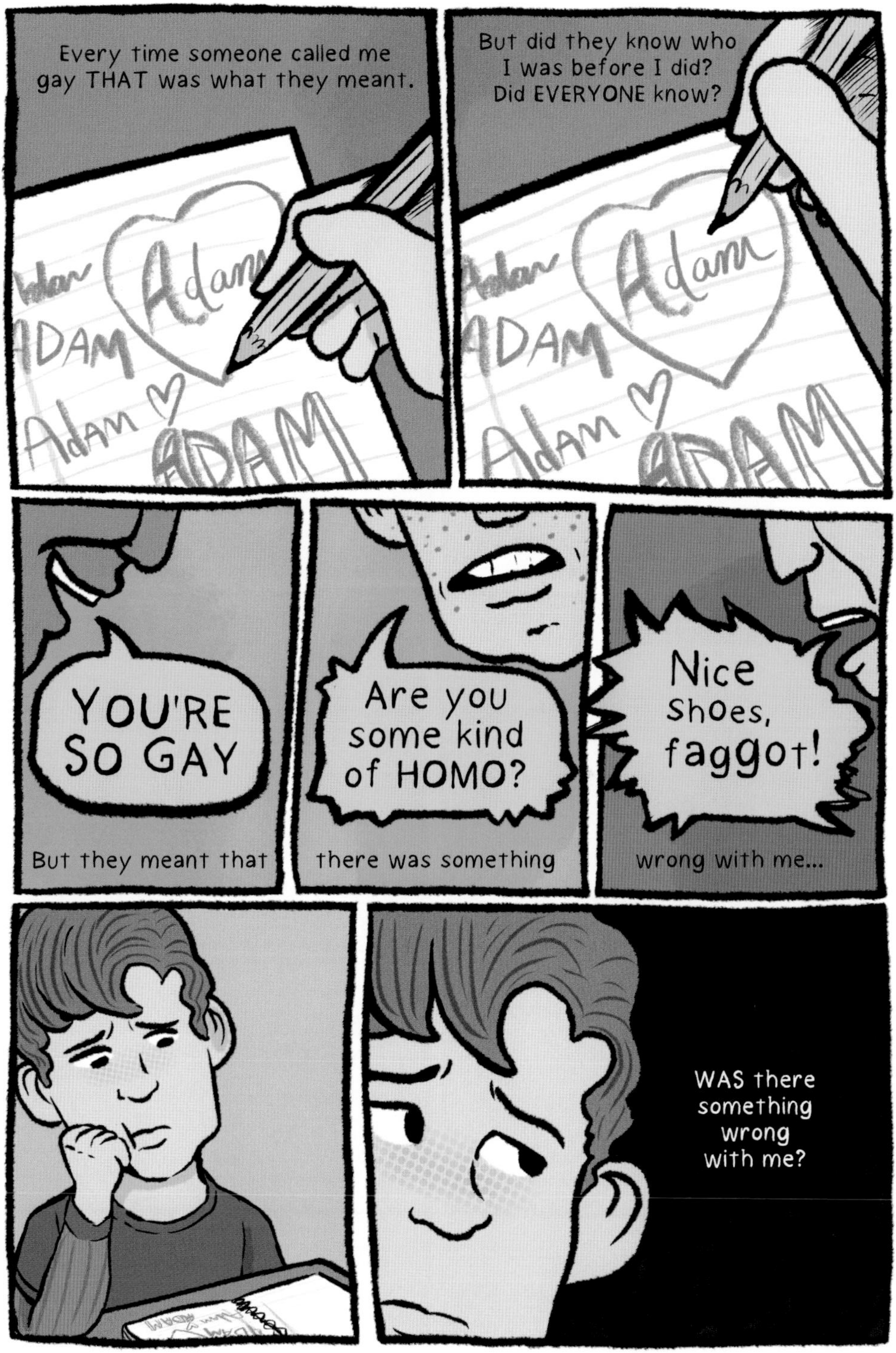
Every time someone called me gay THAT was what they meant.
Adam
ADAM
Adam
ADAM
But did they know who I was before I did? Did EVERYONE know?
Adam
ADAM
Adam
ADAM
YOU'RE SO GAY
But they meant that
Are you some kind of HOMO?
there was something
Nice shoes, faggot!
wrong with me...
WAS there something wrong with me?

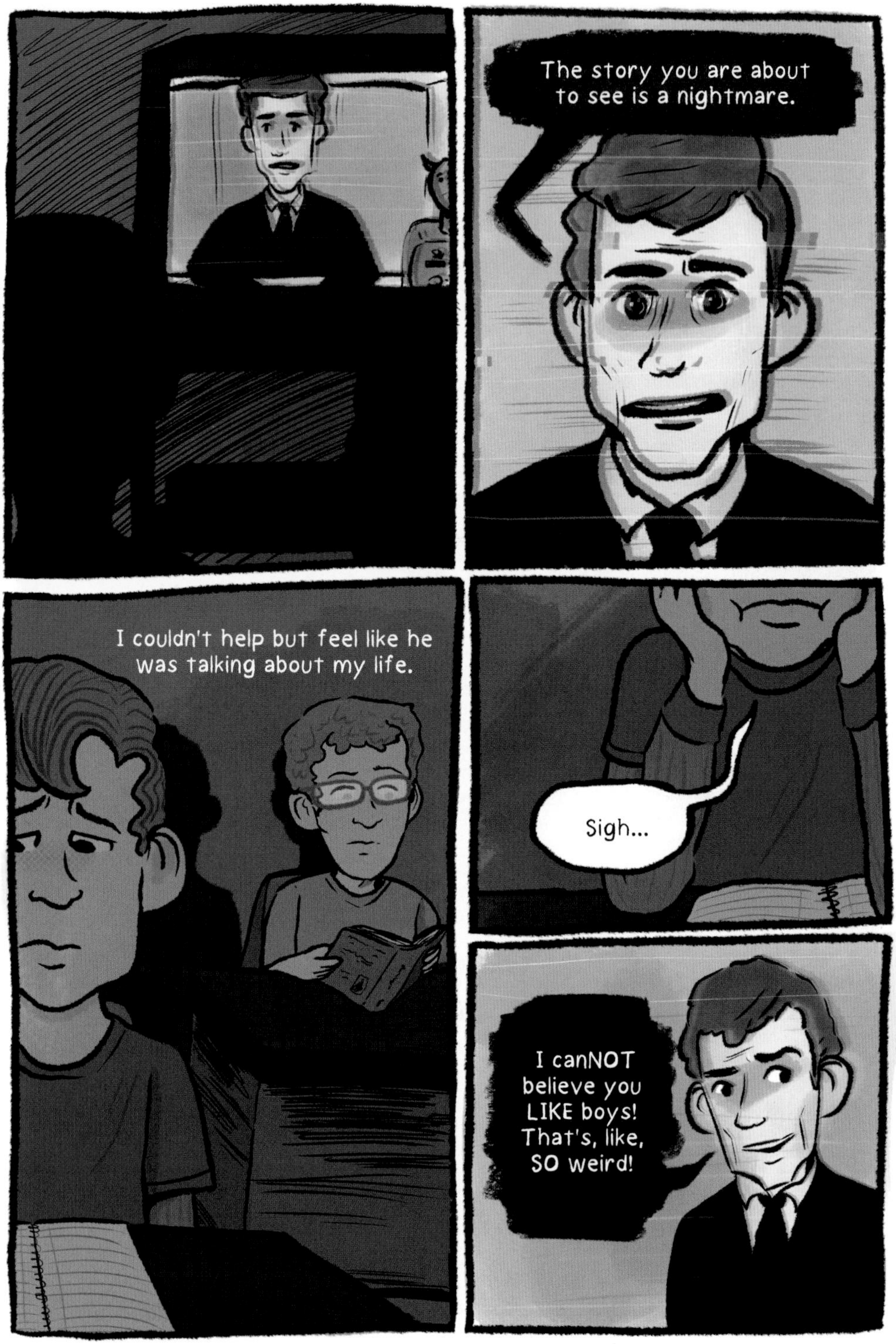
The story you are about to see is a nightmare.
I couldn't help but feel like he was talking about my life.
Sigh...
I canNOT believe you LIKE boys! That's, like, SO weird!

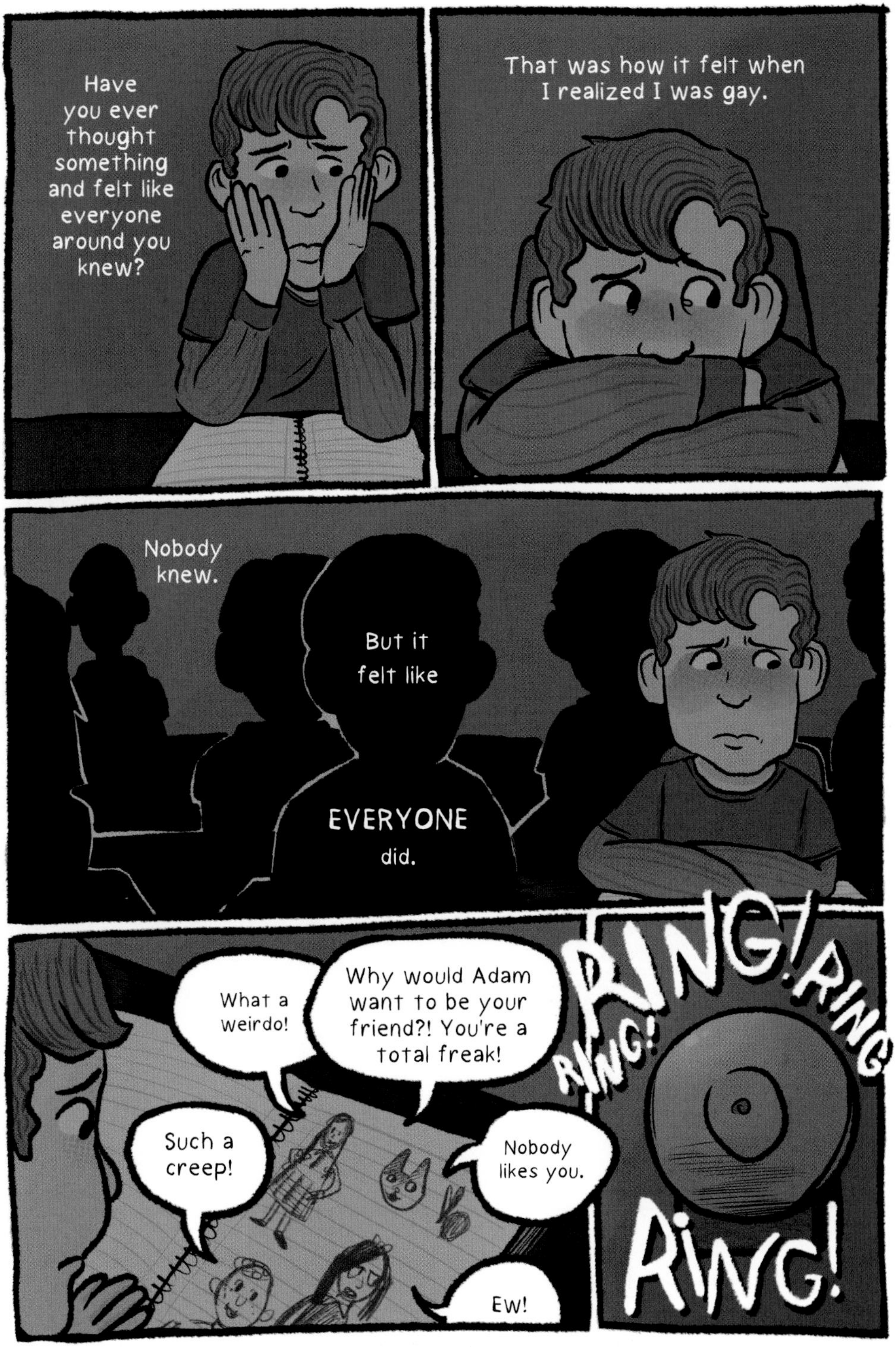
Have you ever thought something and felt like everyone around you knew?
That was how it felt when I realized I was gay.
Nobody knew.
But it felt like
EVERYONE did.
What a weirdo!
Why would Adam want to be your friend?! You're a total freak!
Such a creep!
Nobody likes you.
Ew!
RING! RING! RING! RING!

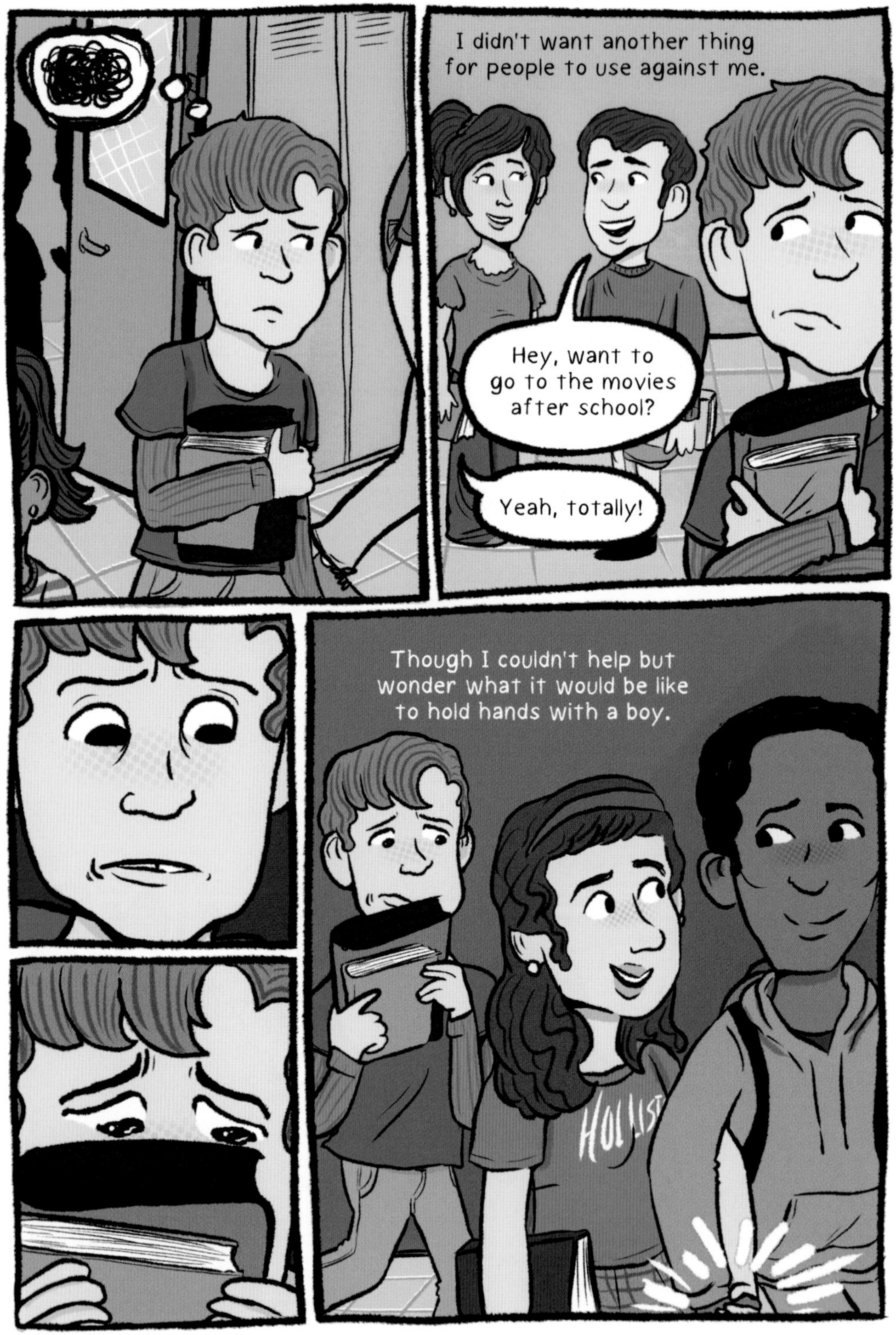
I didn't want another thing for people to use against me.
Hey, want to go to the movies after school?
Yeah, totally!
Though I couldn't help but wonder what it would be like to hold hands with a boy.

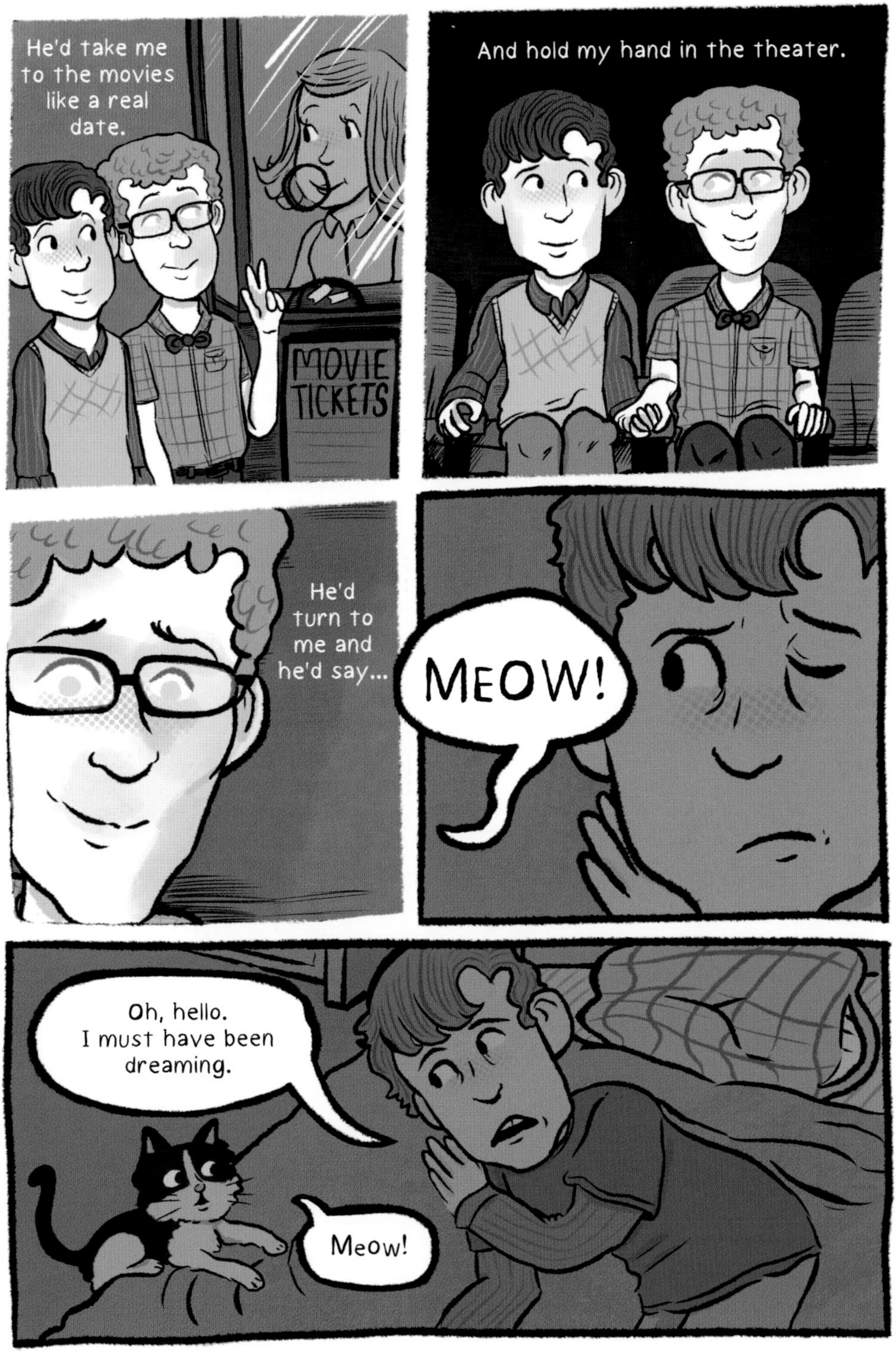
He'd take me to the movies like a real date.
MOVIE TICKETS
And hold my hand in the theater.
He'd turn to me and he'd say...
MEOW!
Oh, hello. I must have been dreaming.
Meow!

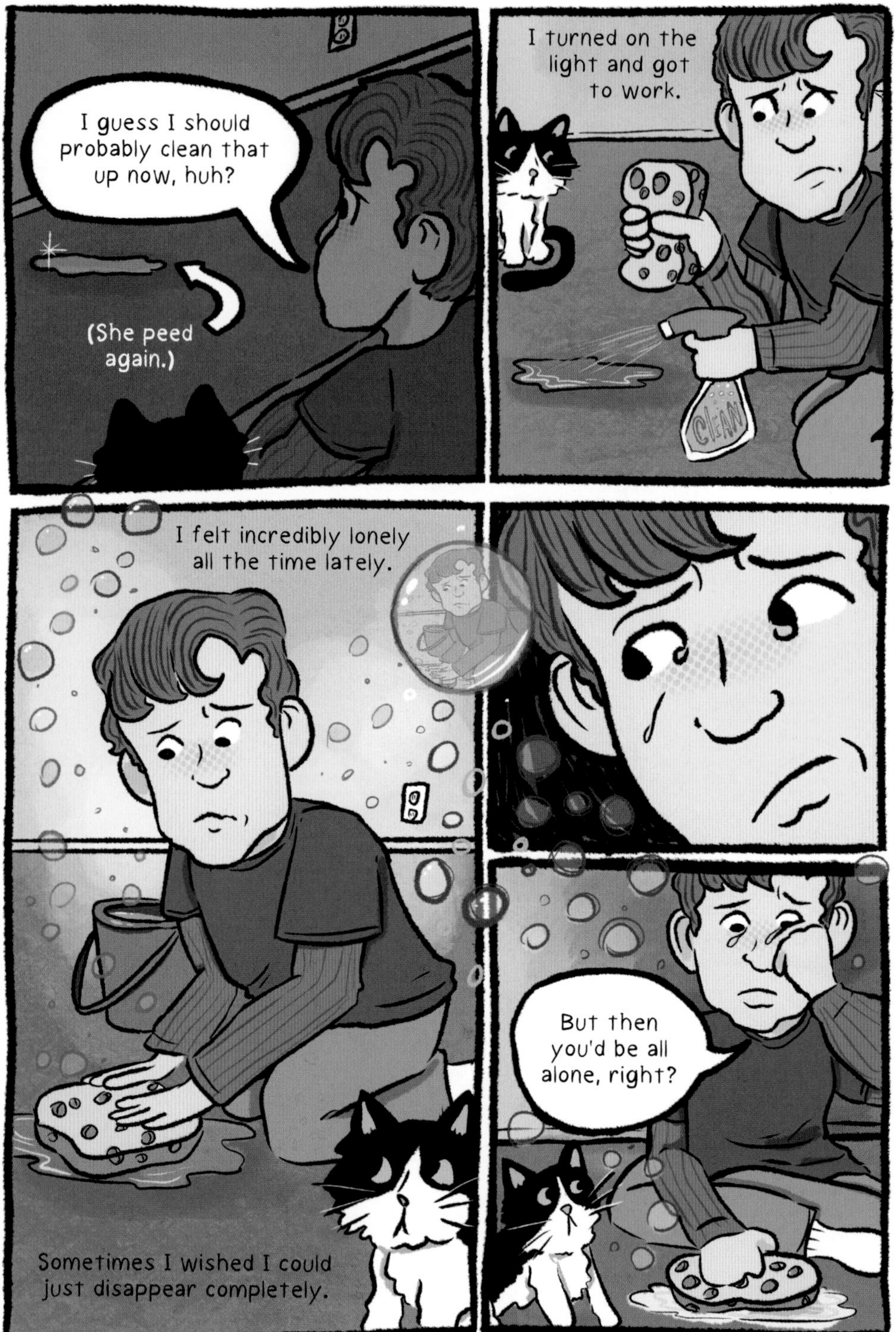
I guess I should probably clean that up now, huh?
(She peed again.)
I turned on the light and got to work.
CLEAN
I felt incredibly lonely all the time lately.
Sometimes I wished I could just disappear completely.
But then you'd be all alone, right?

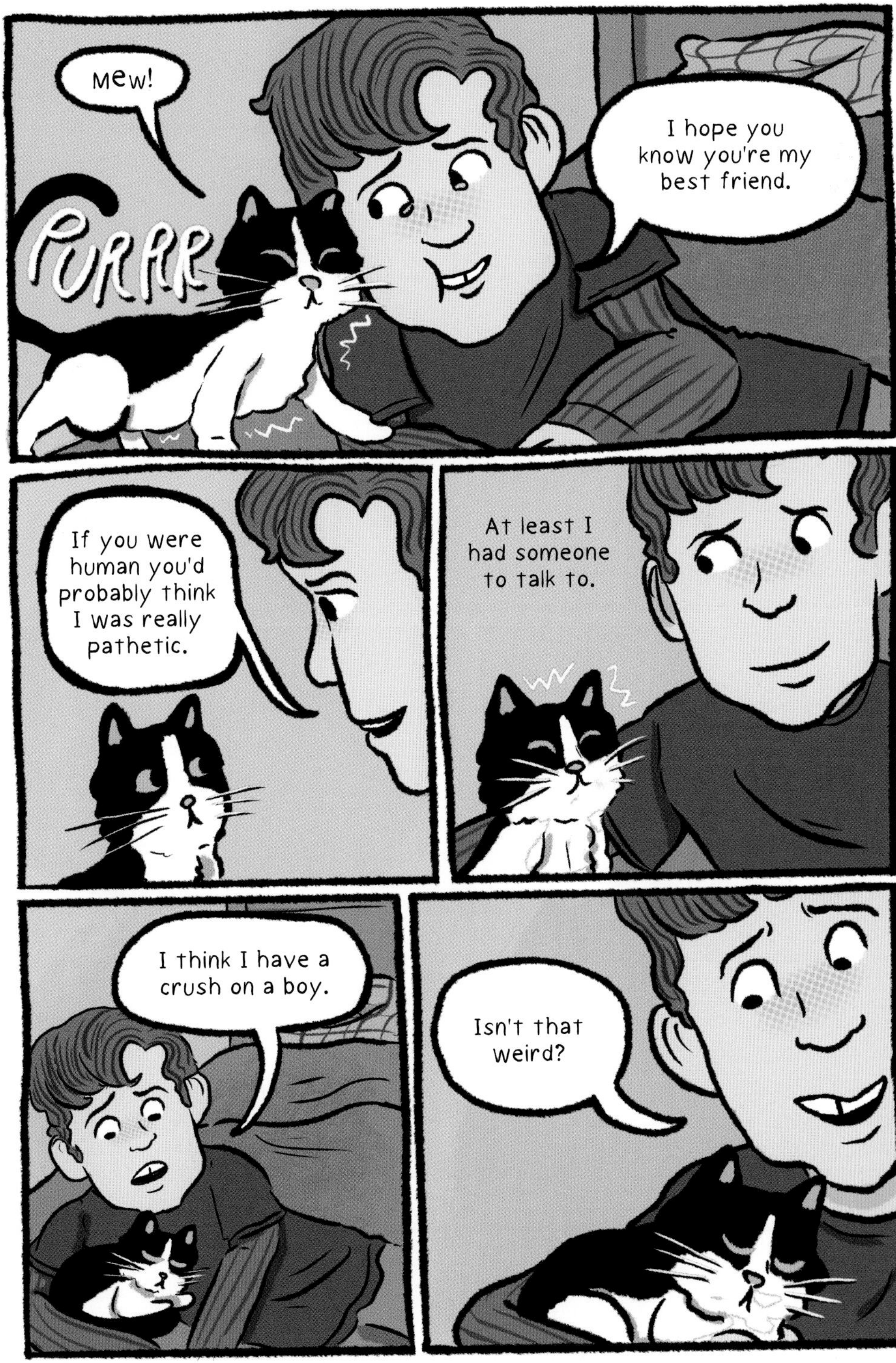
Mew!
PURRR
I hope you know you're my best friend.
If you were human you'd probably think I was really pathetic.
At least I had someone to talk to.
I think I have a crush on a boy.
Isn't that weird?

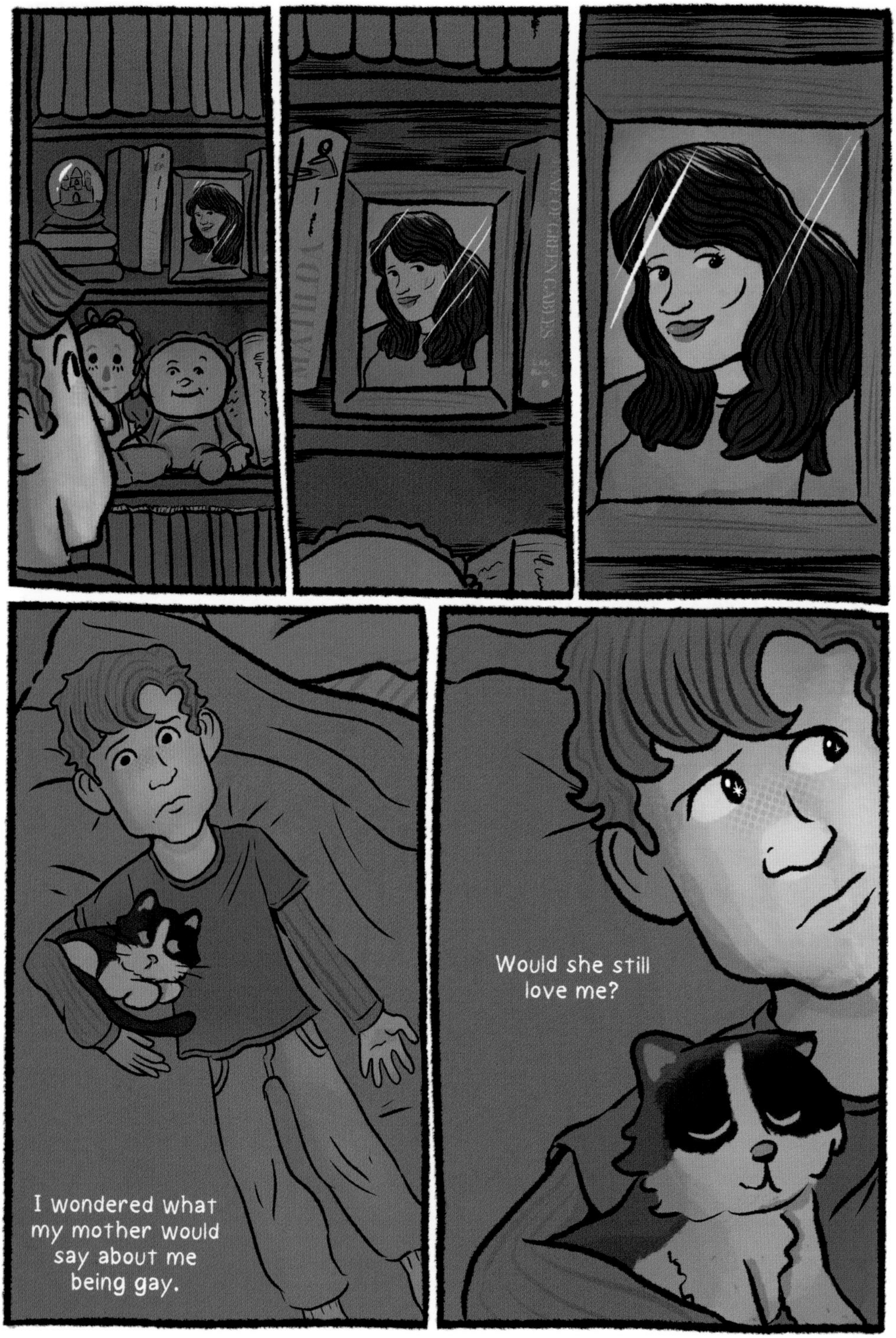
I wondered what
my mother would
say about me
being gay.
Would she still
love me?

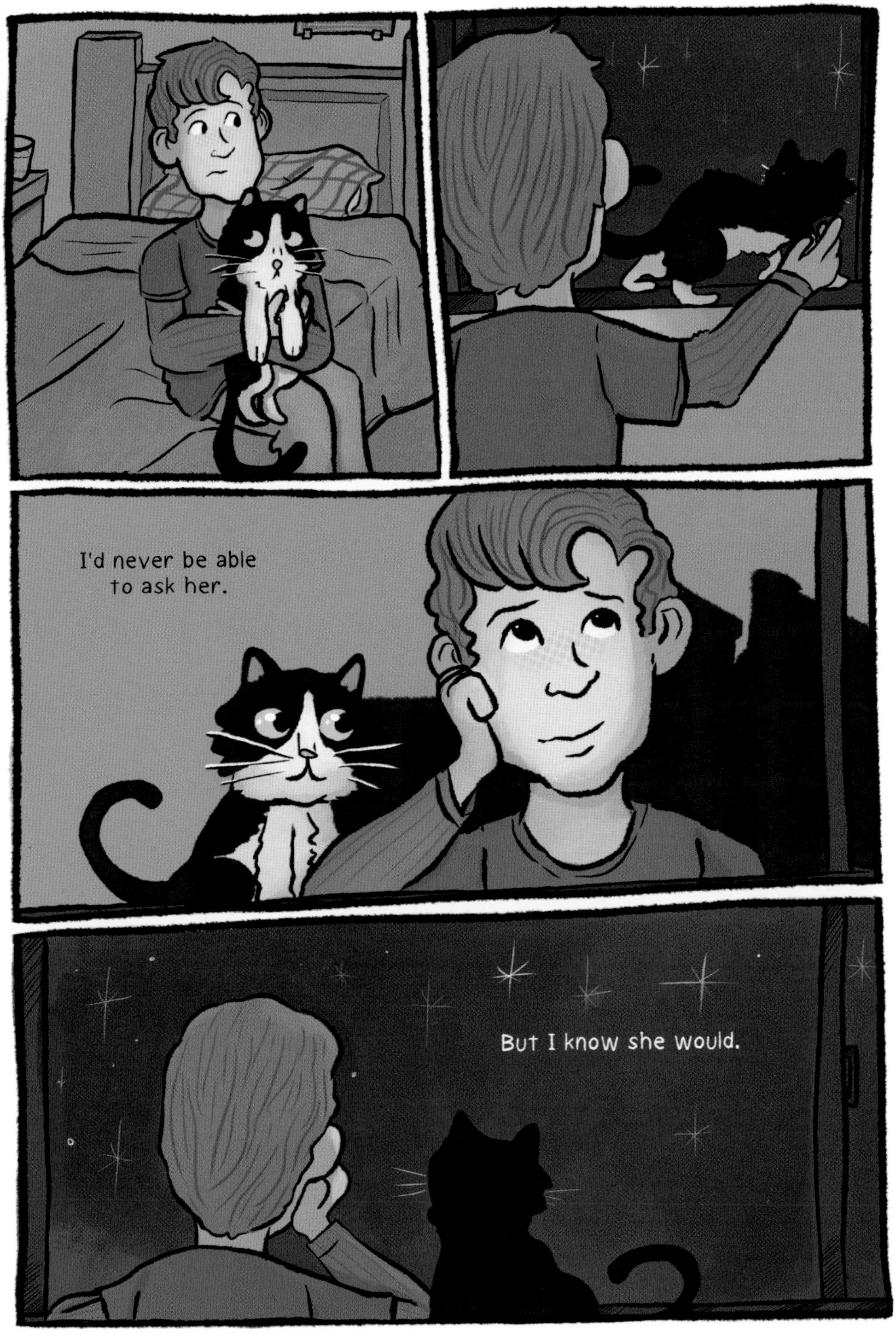
I'd never be able to ask her.
But I know she would.

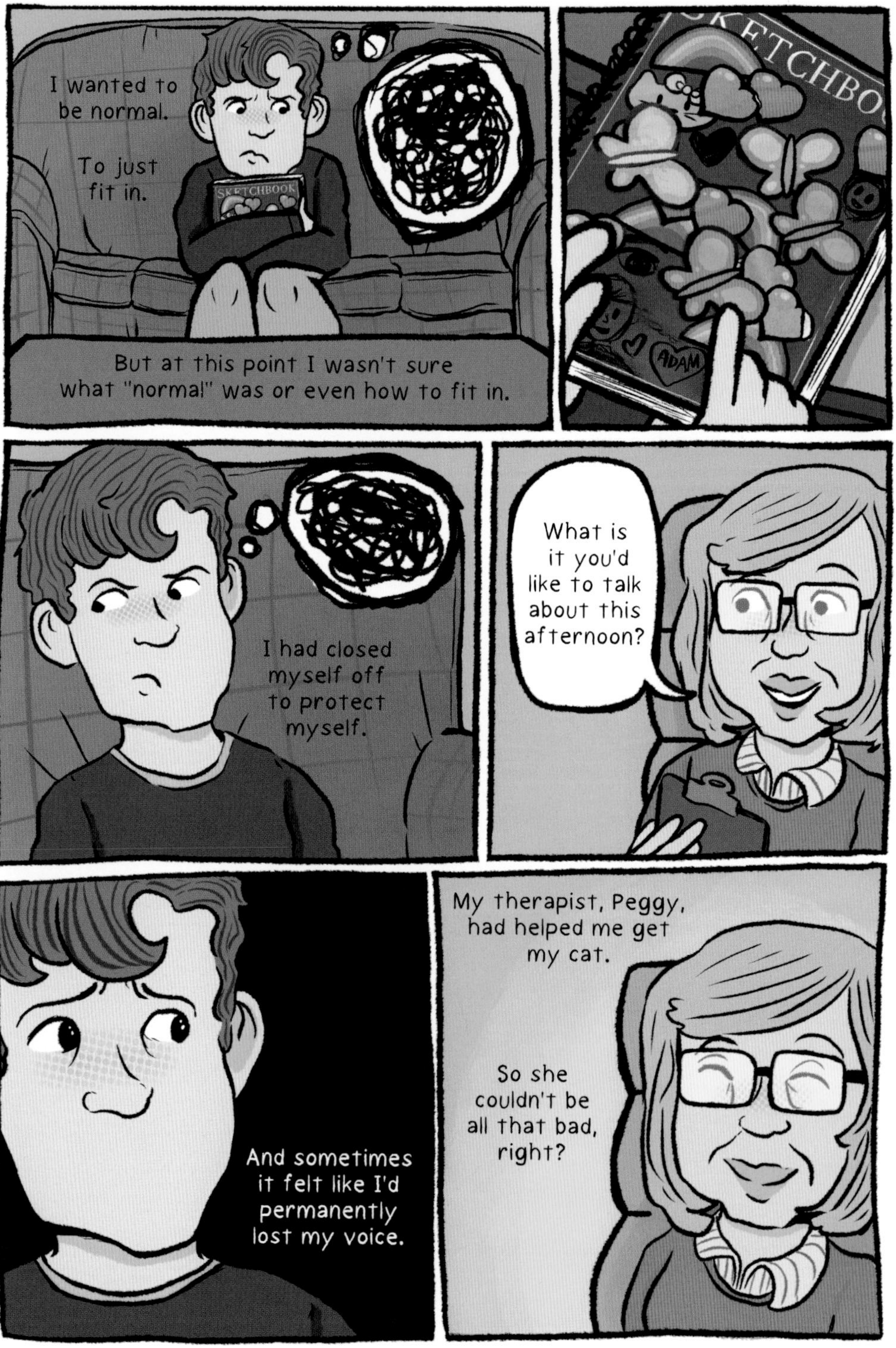
I wanted to be normal.
To just fit in.
SKETCHBOOK
But at this point I wasn't sure what "normal" was or even how to fit in.
SKETCHBO
ADAM
I had closed myself off to protect myself.
What is it you'd like to talk about this afternoon?
And sometimes it felt like I'd permanently lost my voice.
My therapist, Peggy, had helped me get my cat.
So she couldn't be all that bad, right?

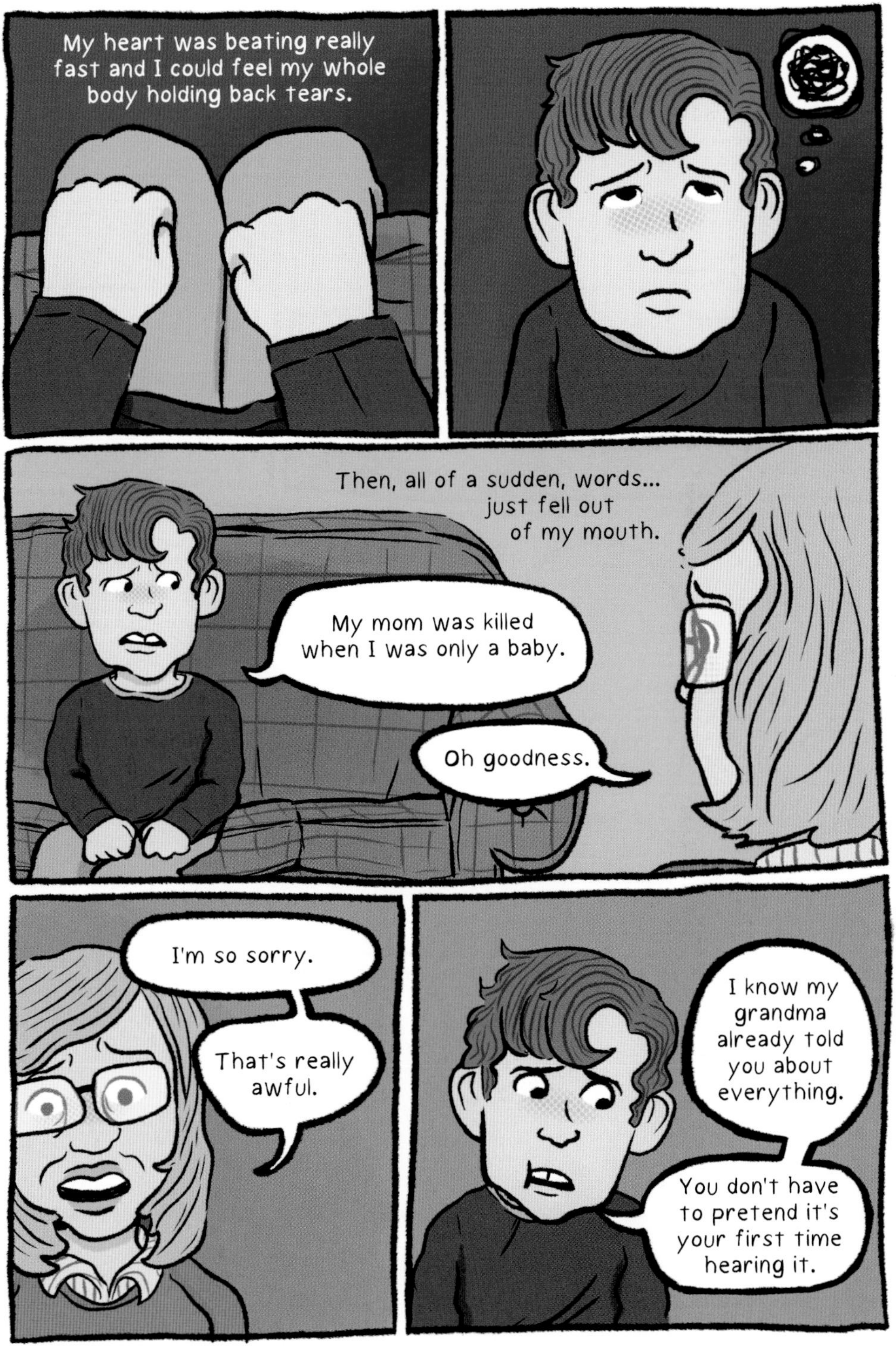
My heart was beating really fast and I could feel my whole body holding back tears.
Then, all of a sudden, words... just fell out of my mouth.
My mom was killed when I was only a baby.
Oh goodness.
I'm so sorry.
That's really awful.
I know my grandma already told you about everything.
You don't have to pretend it's your first time hearing it.

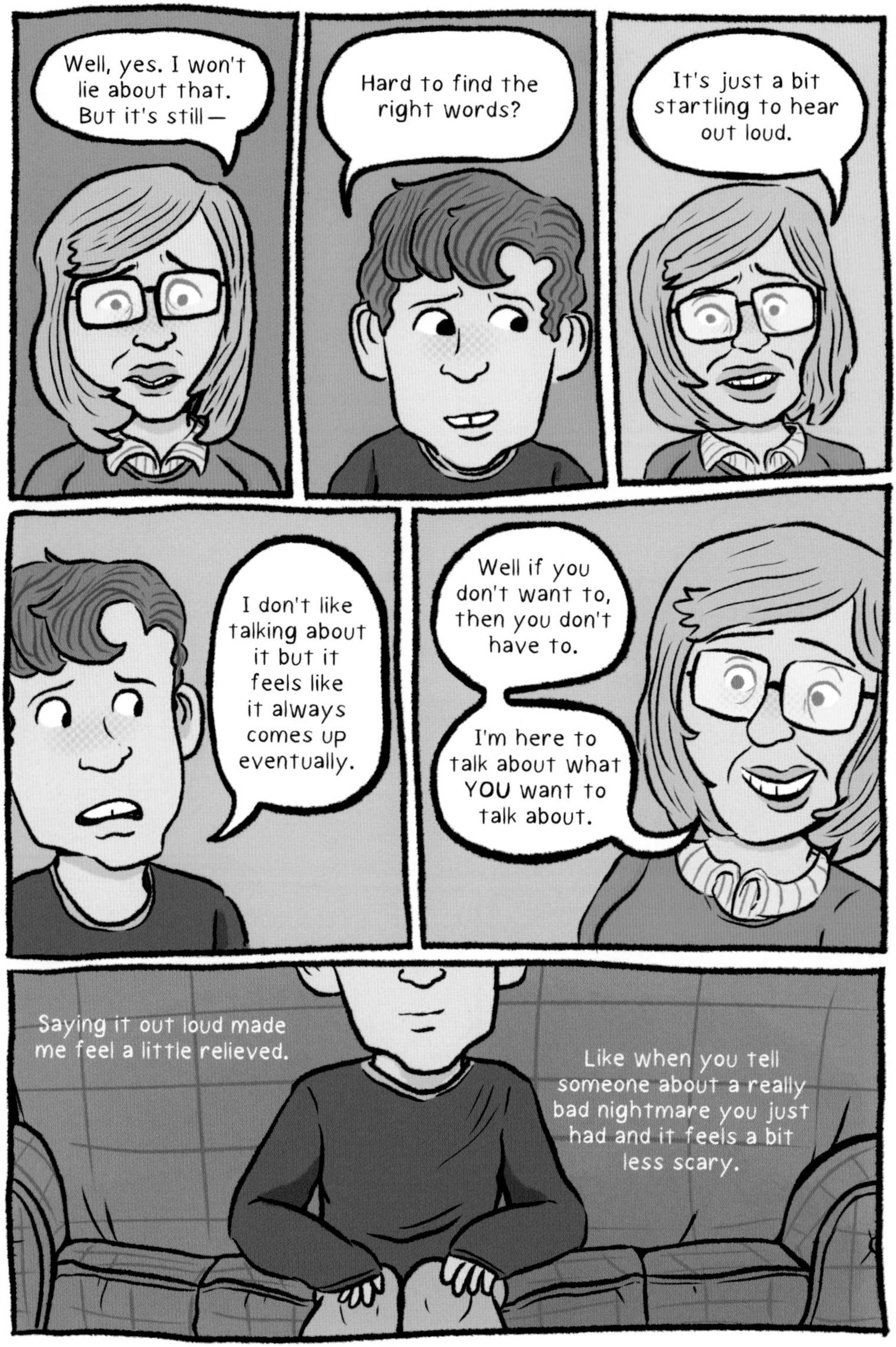
Well, yes. I won't lie about that. But it's still—
Hard to find the right words?
It's just a bit startling to hear out loud.
I don't like talking about it but it feels like it always comes up eventually.
Well if you don't want to, then you don't have to.
I'm here to talk about what YOU want to talk about.
Saying it out loud made me feel a little relieved.
Like when you tell someone about a really bad nightmare you just had and it feels a bit less scary.

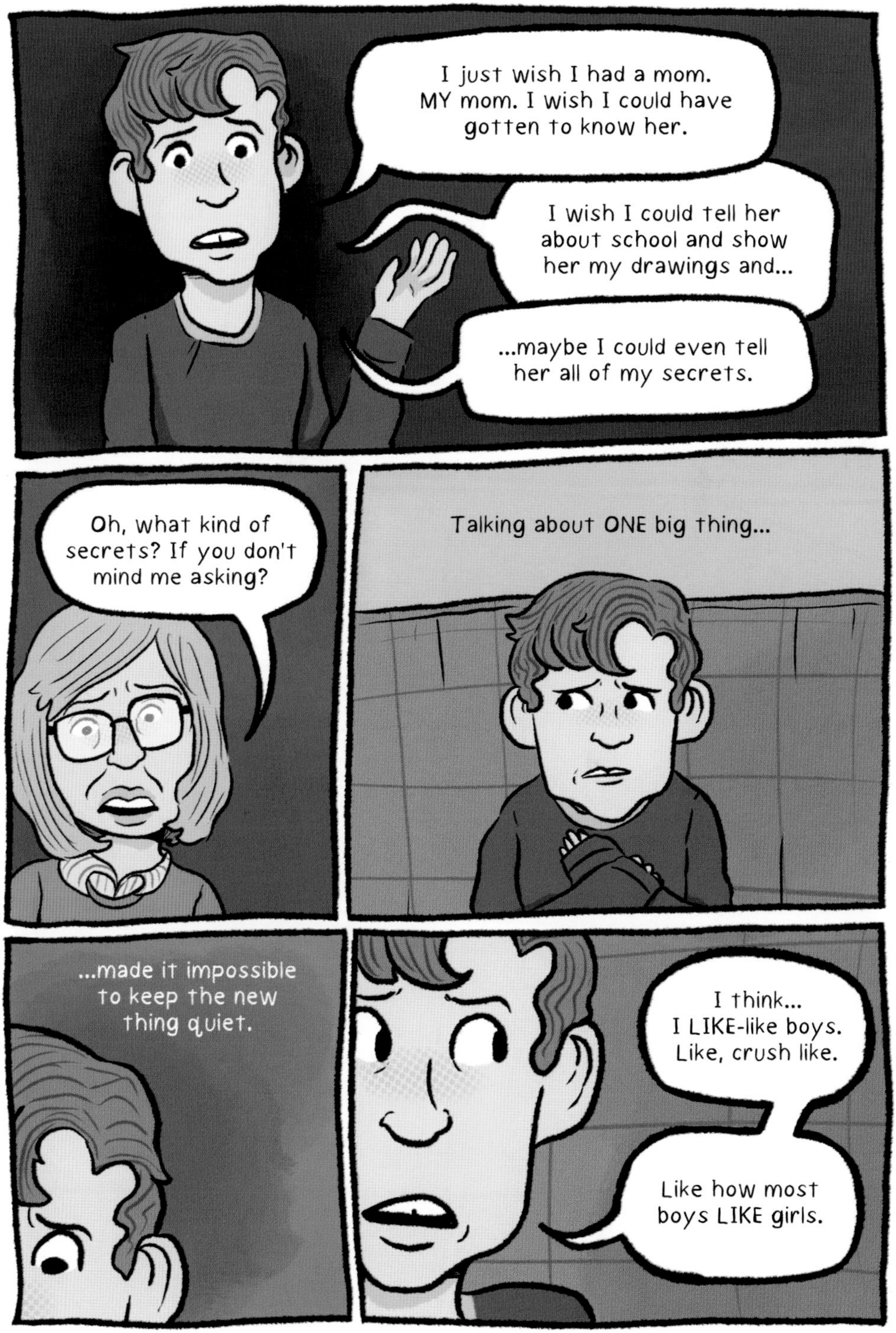
I just wish I had a mom. MY mom. I wish I could have gotten to know her.
I wish I could tell her about school and show her my drawings and...
...maybe I could even tell her all of my secrets.
Oh, what kind of secrets? If you don't mind me asking?
Talking about ONE big thing...
...made it impossible to keep the new thing quiet.
I think... I LIKE-like boys. Like, crush like.
Like how most boys LIKE girls.

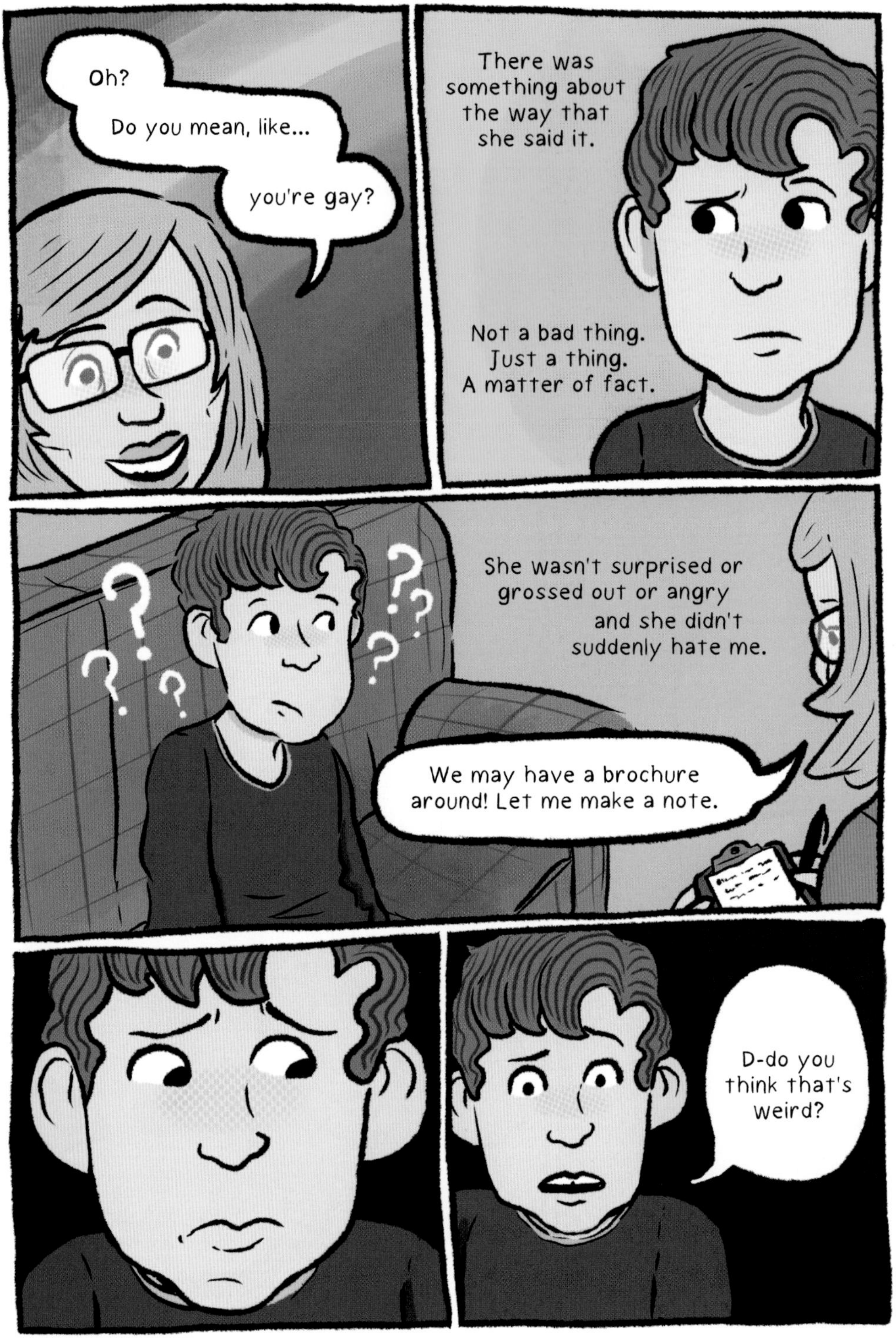
Oh?
Do you mean, like...
you're gay?
There was something about the way that she said it.
Not a bad thing. Just a thing. A matter of fact.
She wasn't surprised or grossed out or angry and she didn't suddenly hate me.
We may have a brochure around! Let me make a note.
D-do you think that's weird?

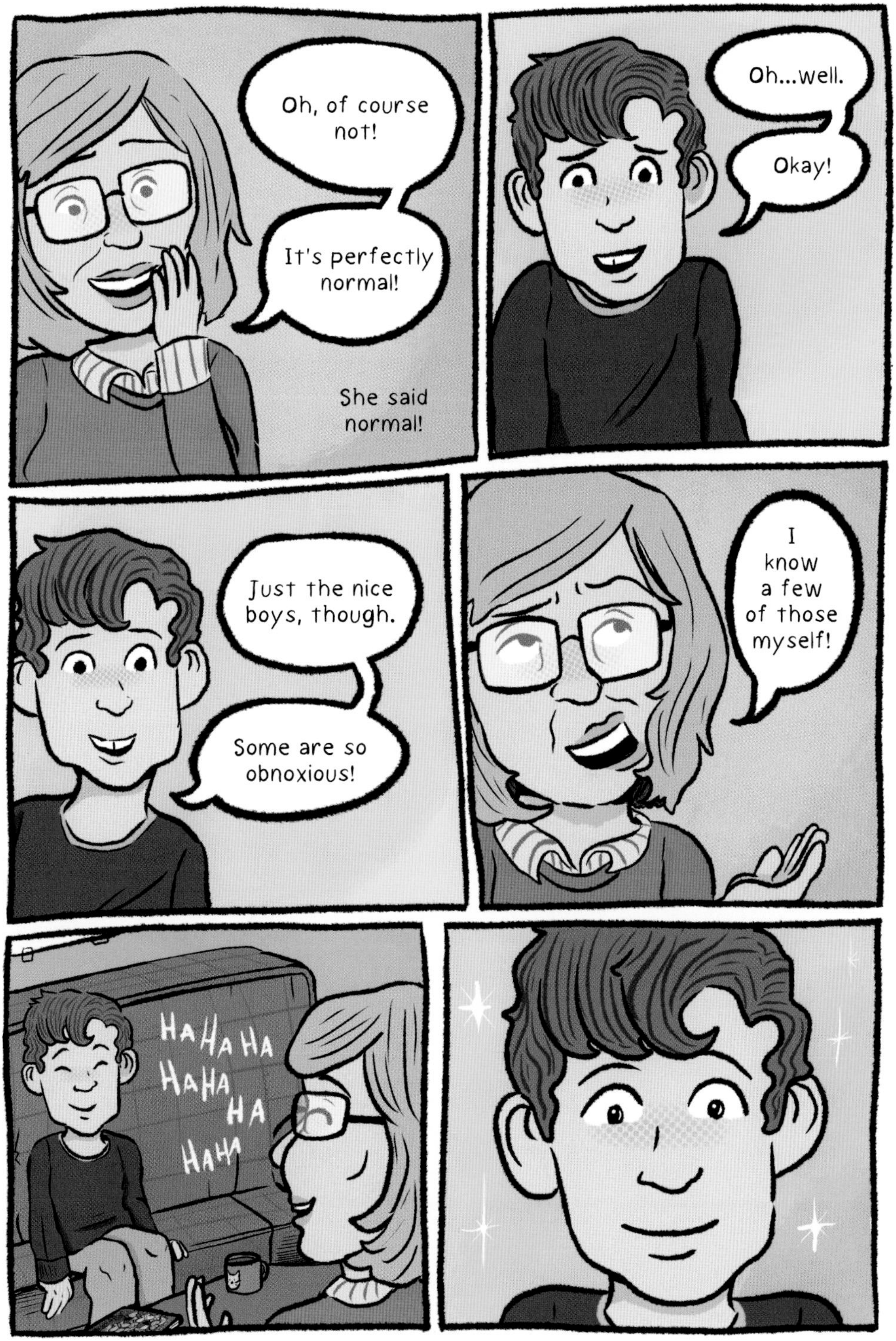
Oh, of course not!
It's perfectly normal!
She said normal!
Oh...well.
Okay!
Just the nice boys, though.
Some are so obnoxious!
I know a few of those myself!
HAHAHA HAHA HA HAHA

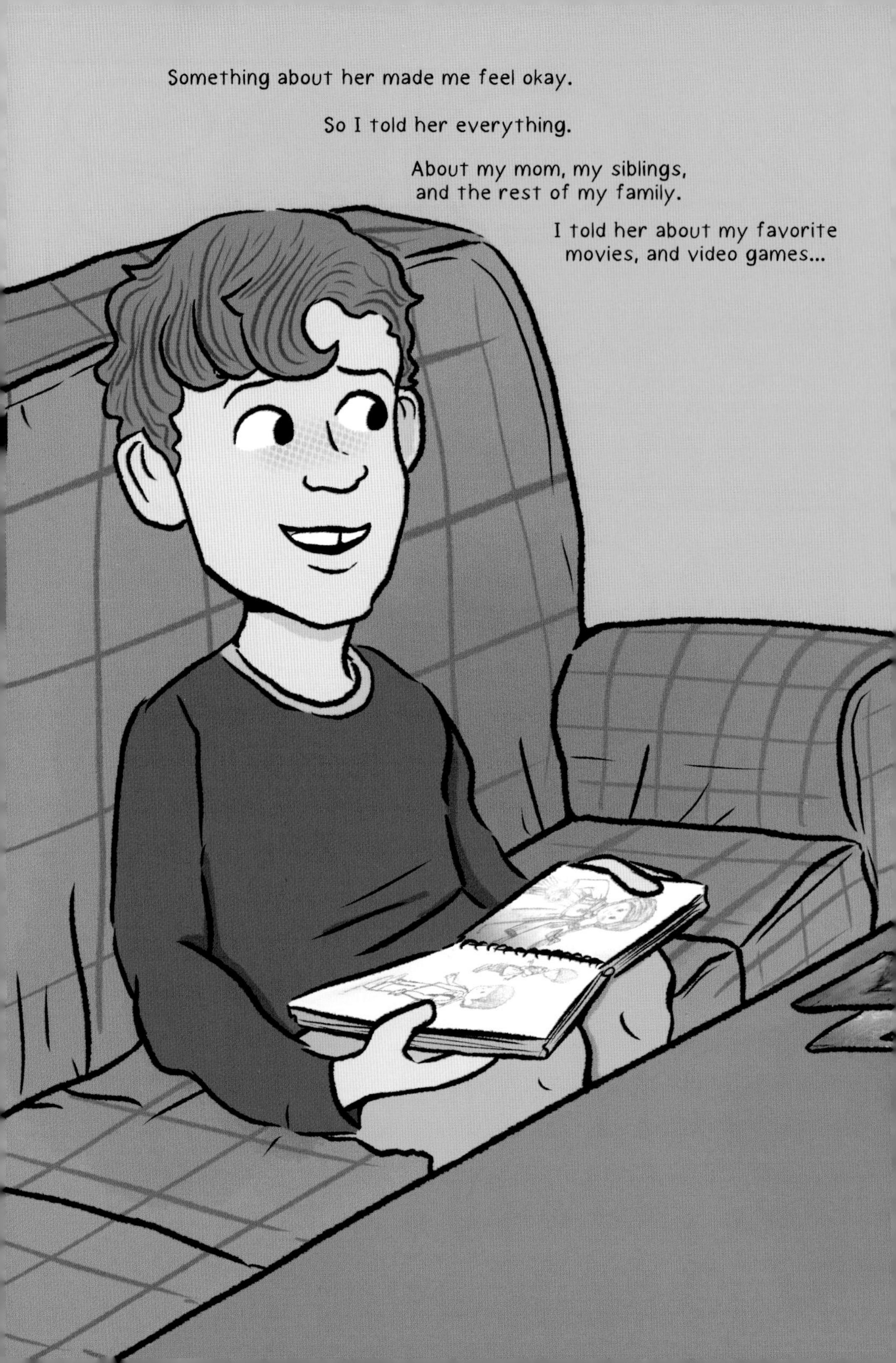
Something about her made me feel okay.
So I told her everything.
About my mom, my siblings, and the rest of my family.
I told her about my favorite movies, and video games...

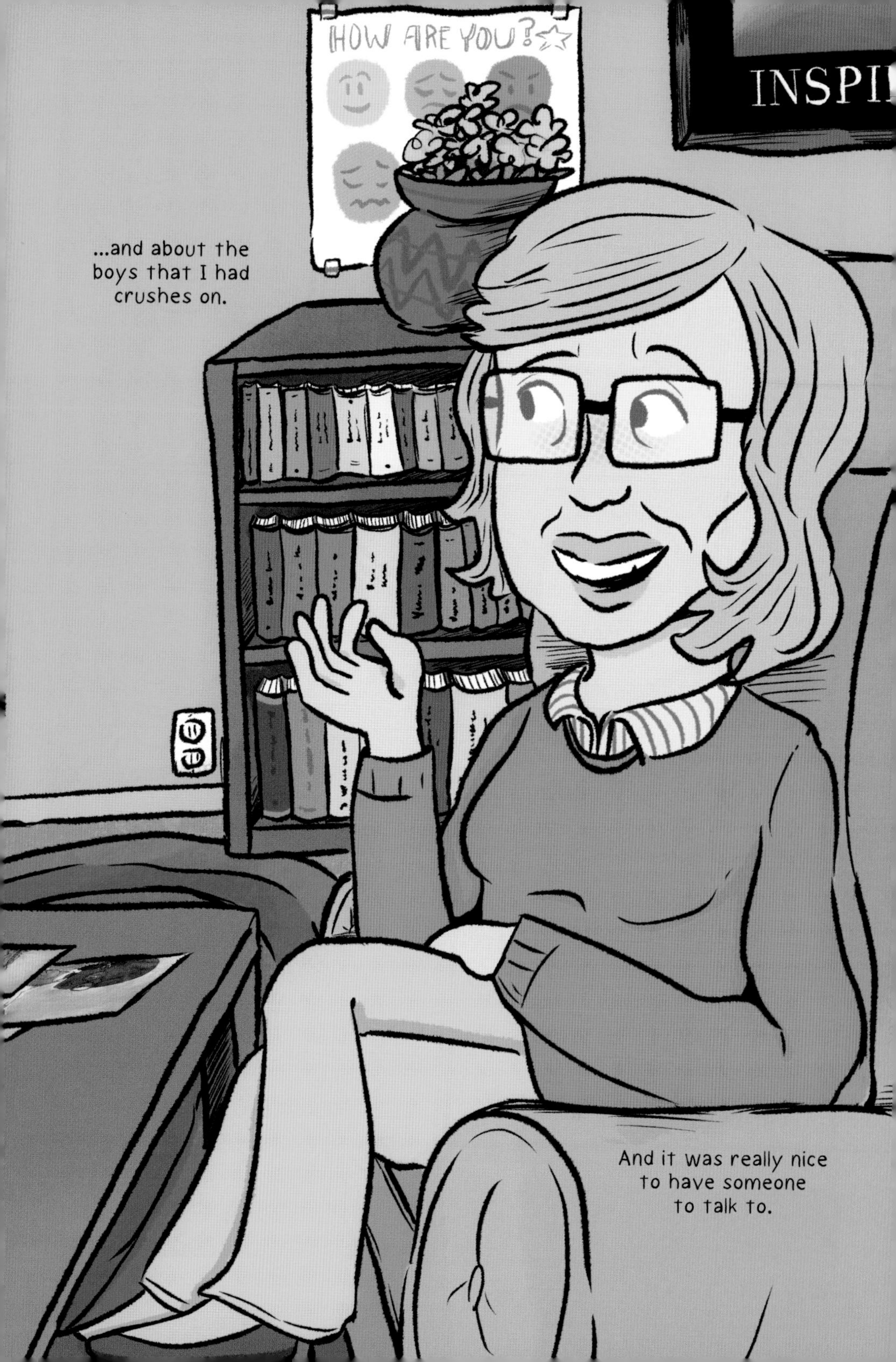
HOW ARE YOU?
INSPI
...and about the boys that I had crushes on.
And it was really nice to have someone to talk to.

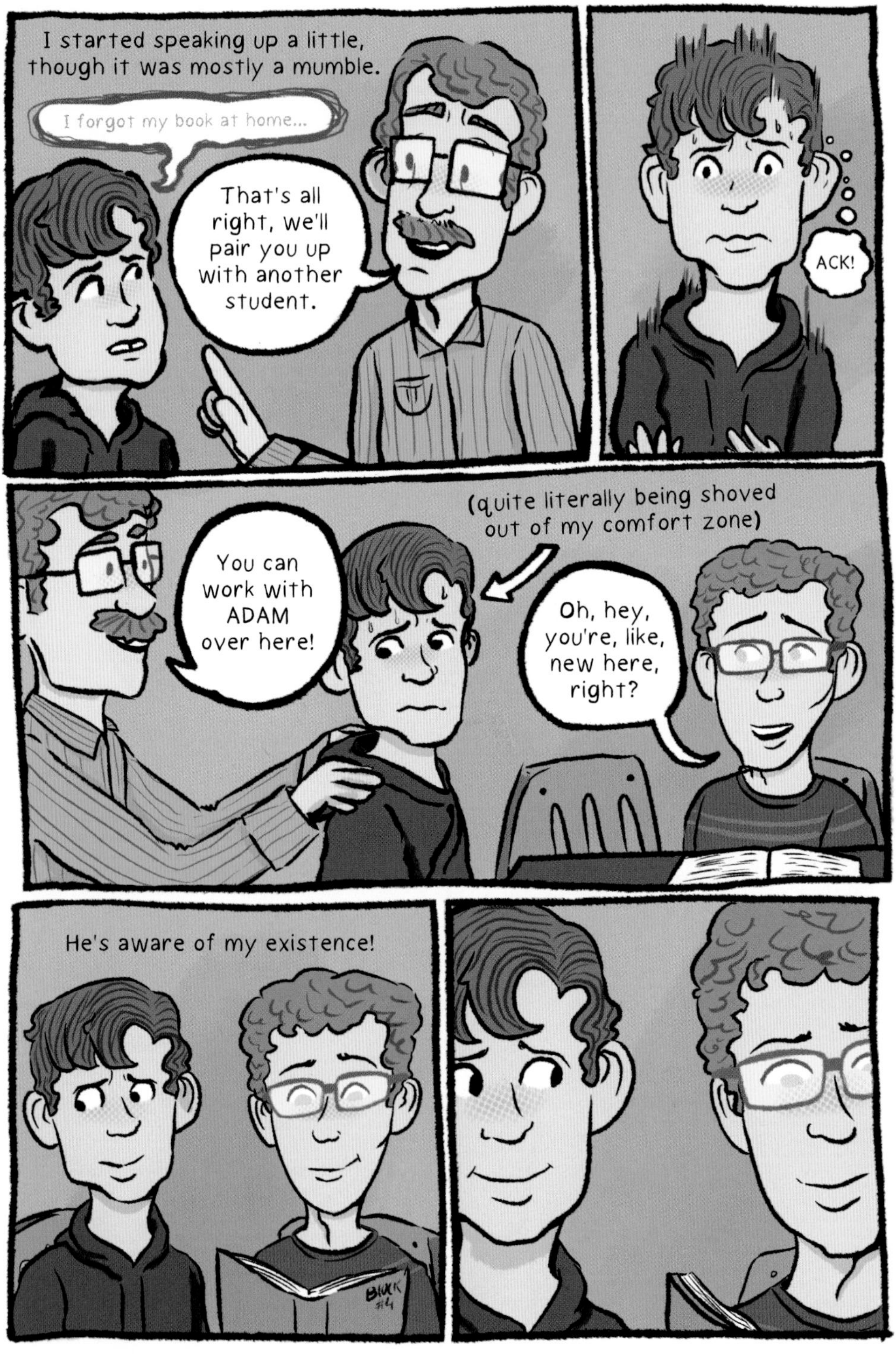
I started speaking up a little, though it was mostly a mumble.
I forgot my book at home...
That's all right, we'll pair you up with another student.
ACK!
You can work with ADAM over here!
(quite literally being shoved out of my comfort zone)
Oh, hey, you're, like, new here, right?
He's aware of my existence!

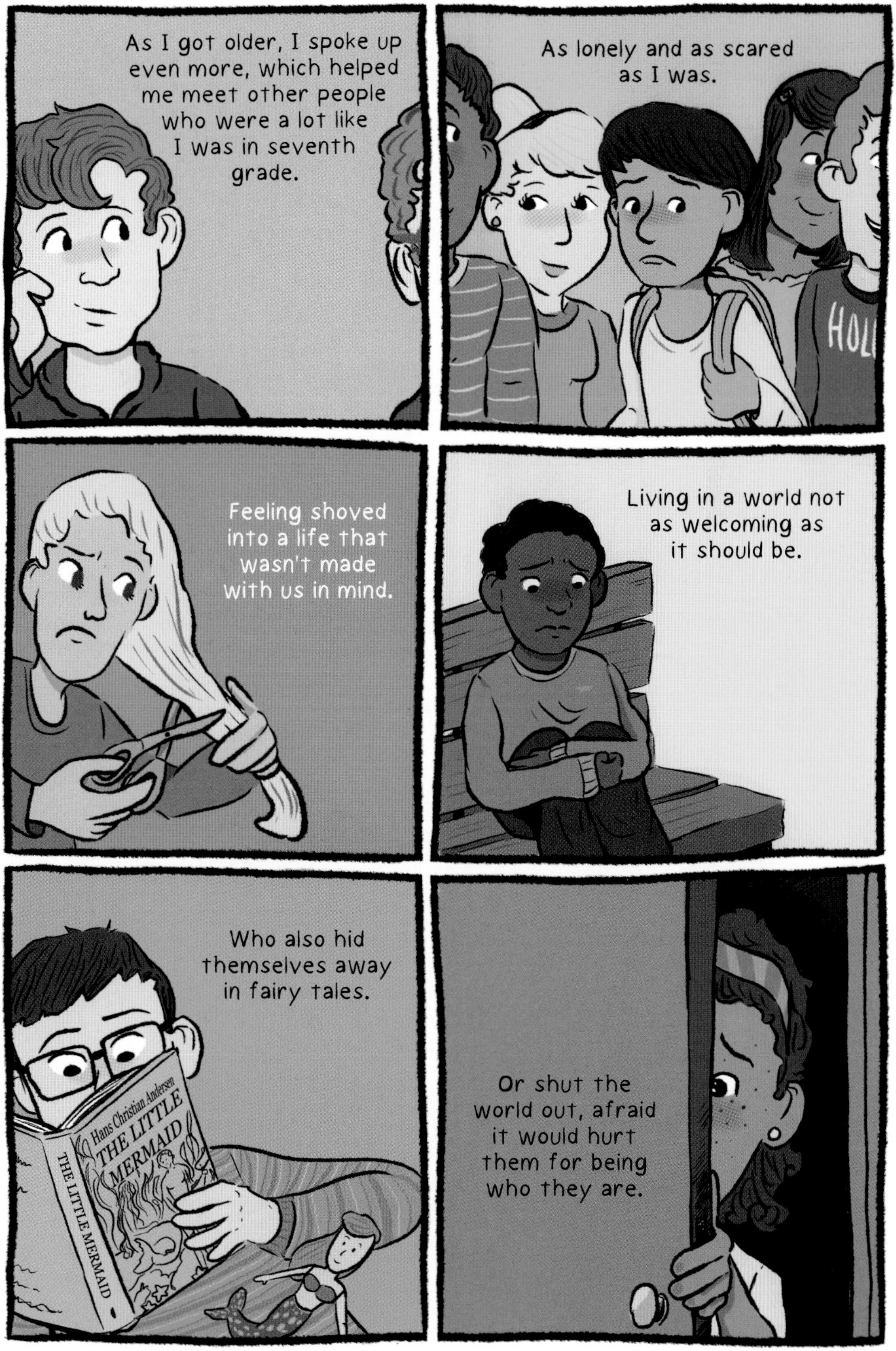
As I got older, I spoke up even more, which helped me meet other people who were a lot like I was in seventh grade.
As lonely and as scared as I was.
HOLL
Feeling shoved into a life that wasn't made with us in mind.
Living in a world not as welcoming as it should be.
Who also hid themselves away in fairy tales.
Hans Christian Andersen
THE LITTLE MERMAID
THE LITTLE MERMAID
Or shut the world out, afraid it would hurt them for being who they are.

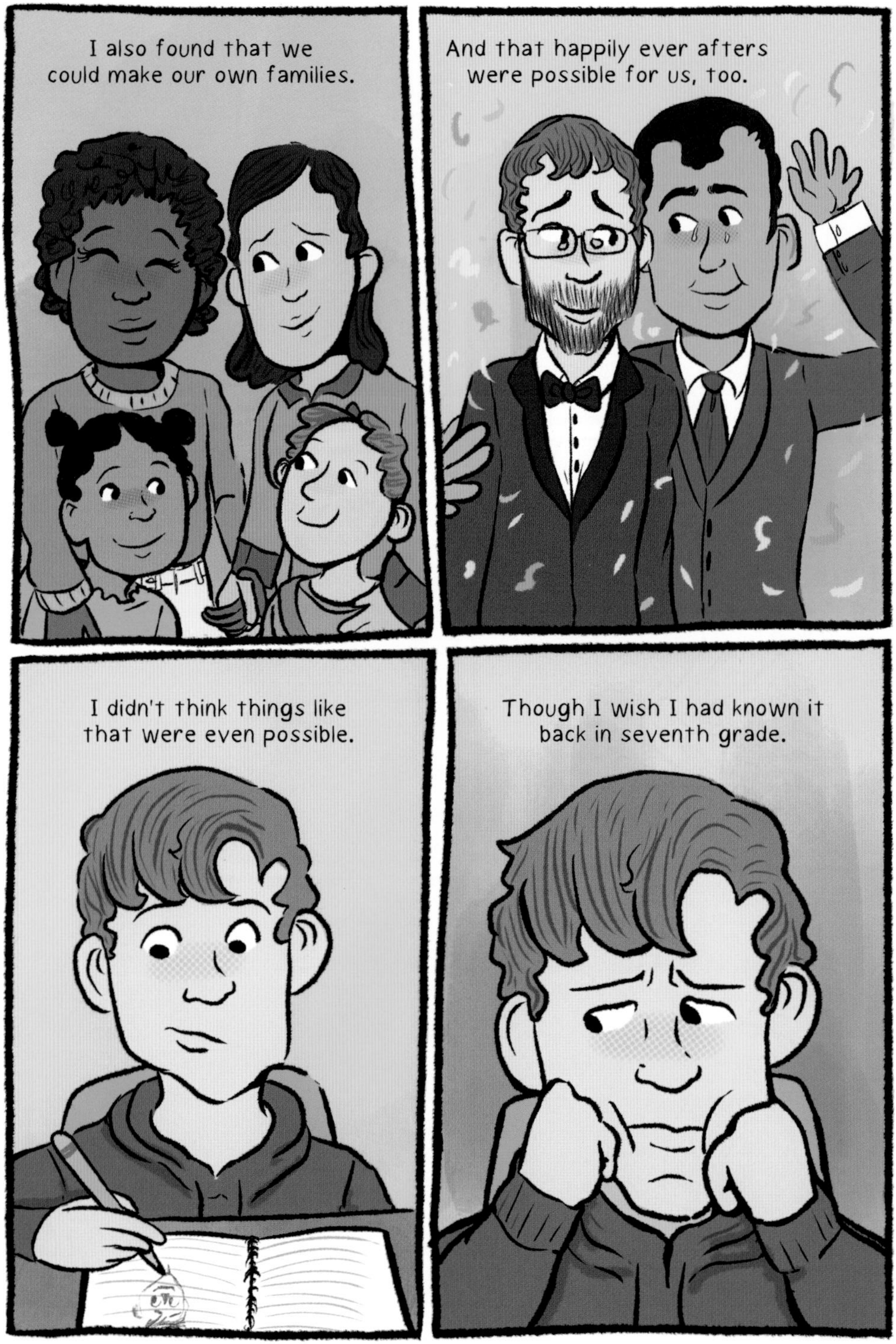
I also found that we could make our own families.
And that happily ever afters were possible for us, too.
I didn't think things like that were even possible.
Though I wish I had known it back in seventh grade.

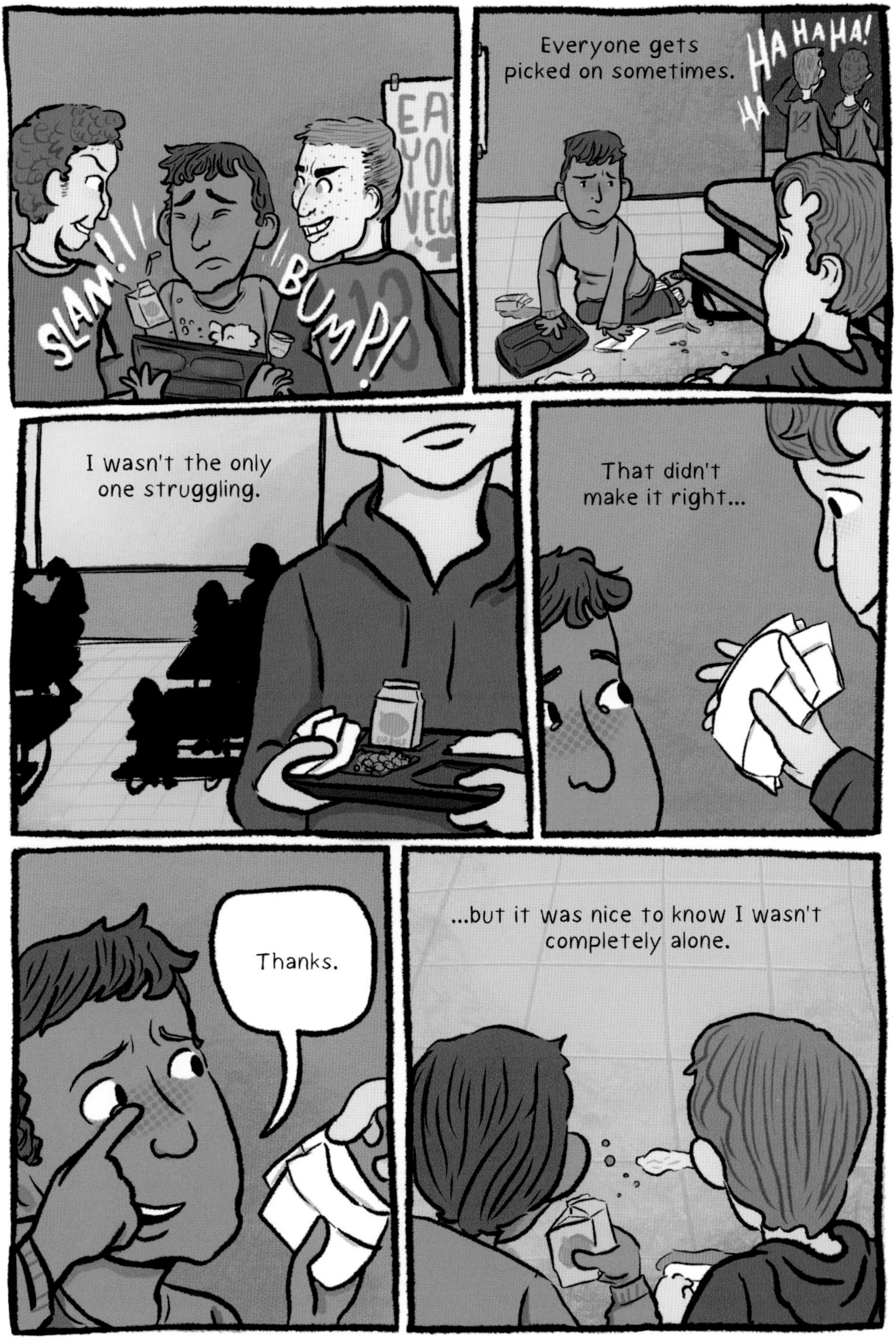
SLAM!
BUMP!
Everyone gets picked on sometimes.
HA HA HA! HA HA
I wasn't the only one struggling.
That didn't make it right...
Thanks.
...but it was nice to know I wasn't completely alone.

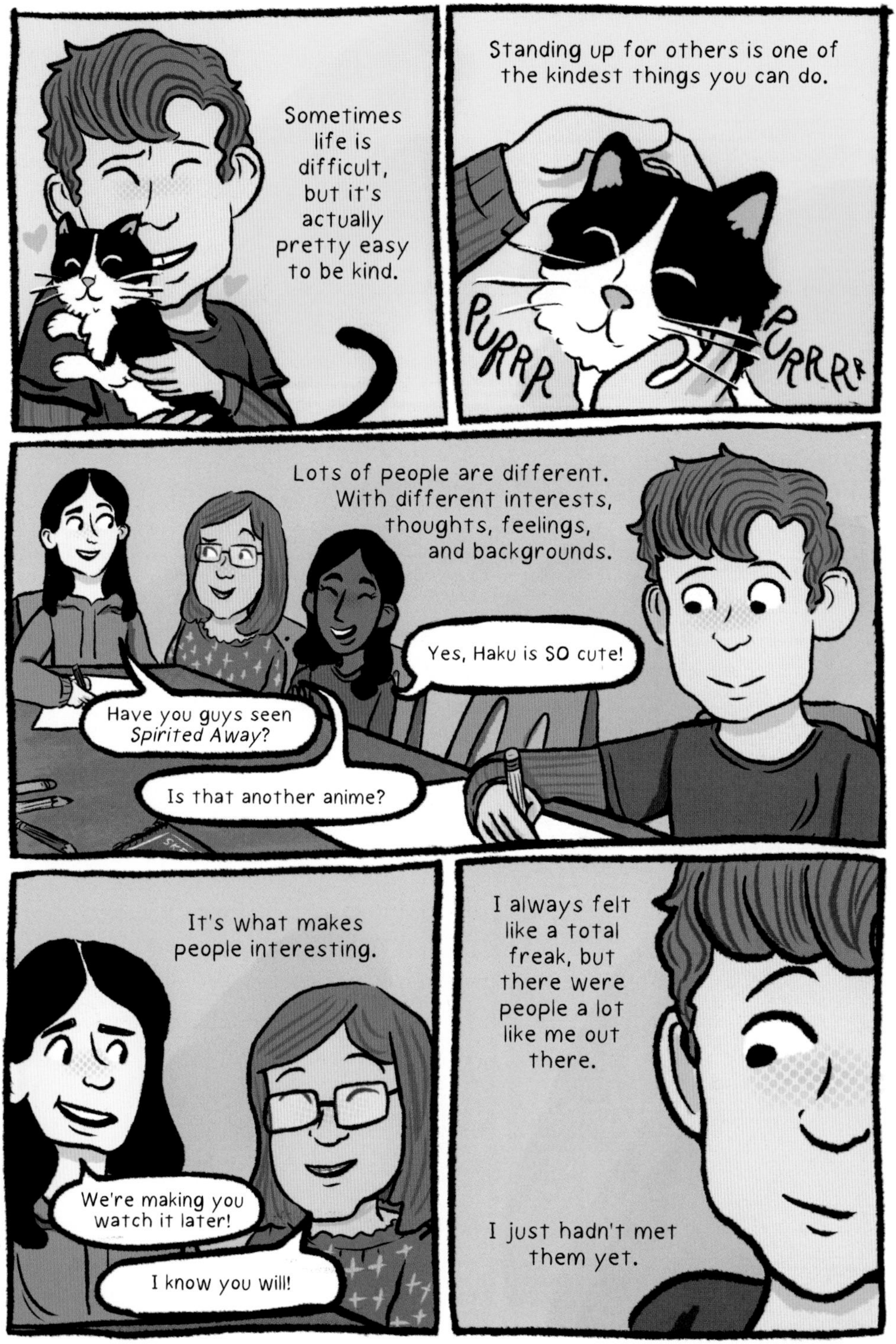
Sometimes life is difficult, but it's actually pretty easy to be kind.
Standing up for others is one of the kindest things you can do.
PURRR
PURRRR
Lots of people are different. With different interests, thoughts, feelings, and backgrounds.
Have you guys seen *Spirited Away*?
Yes, Haku is SO cute!
Is that another anime?
It's what makes people interesting.
We're making you watch it later!
I know you will!
I always felt like a total freak, but there were people a lot like me out there.
I just hadn't met them yet.

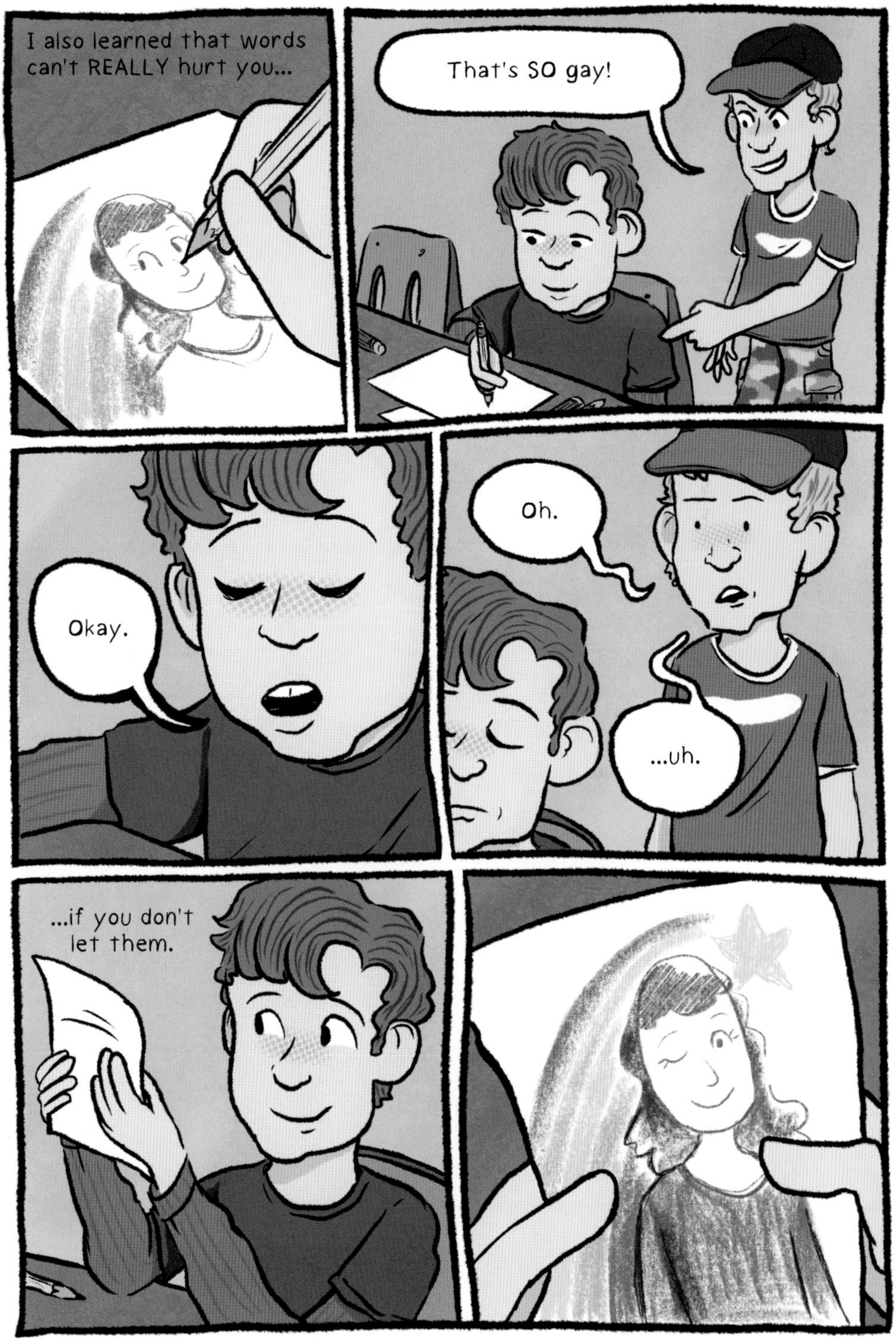
I also learned that words can't REALLY hurt you...
That's SO gay!
Okay.
Oh.
...uh.
...if you don't let them.

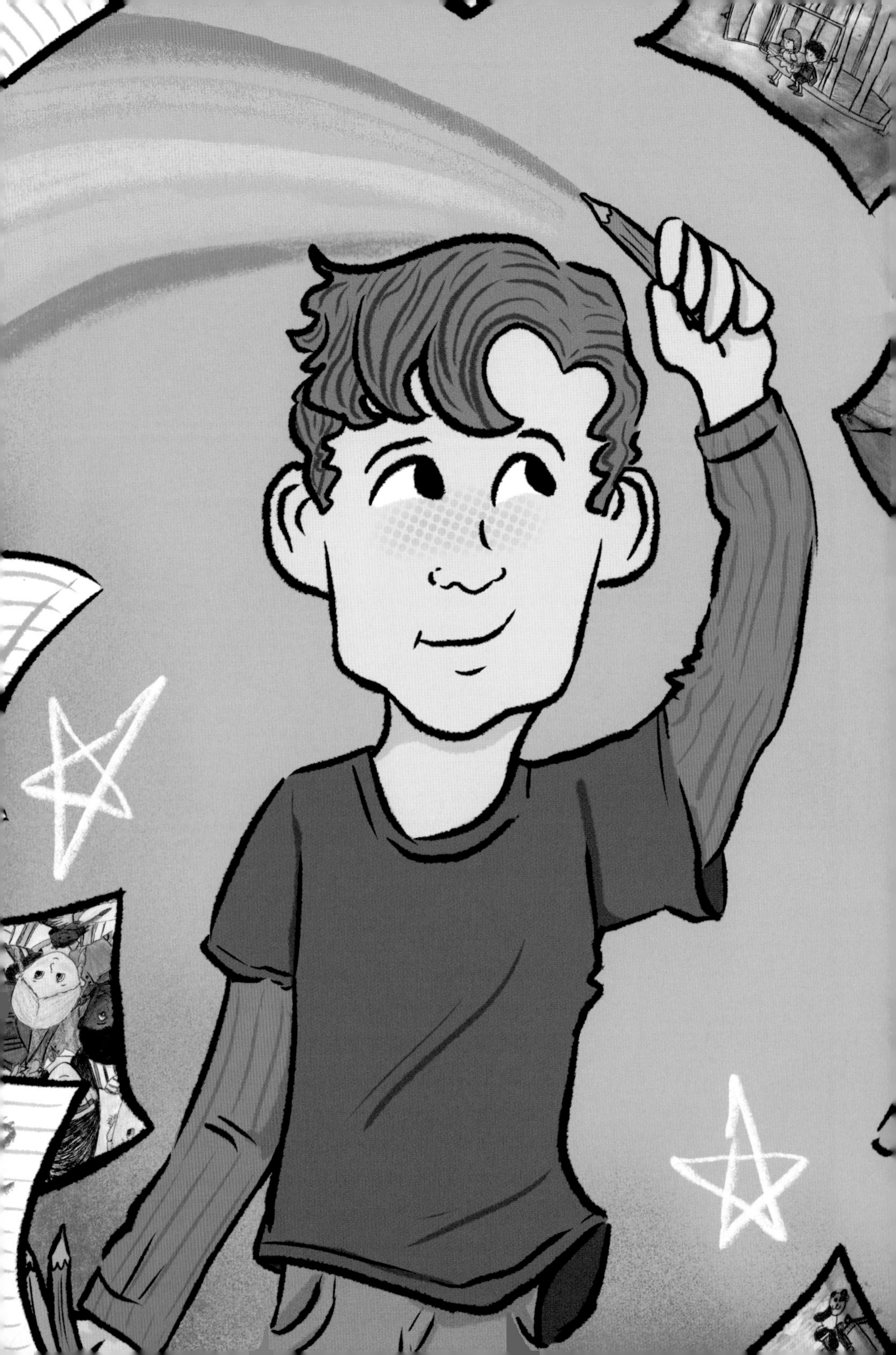

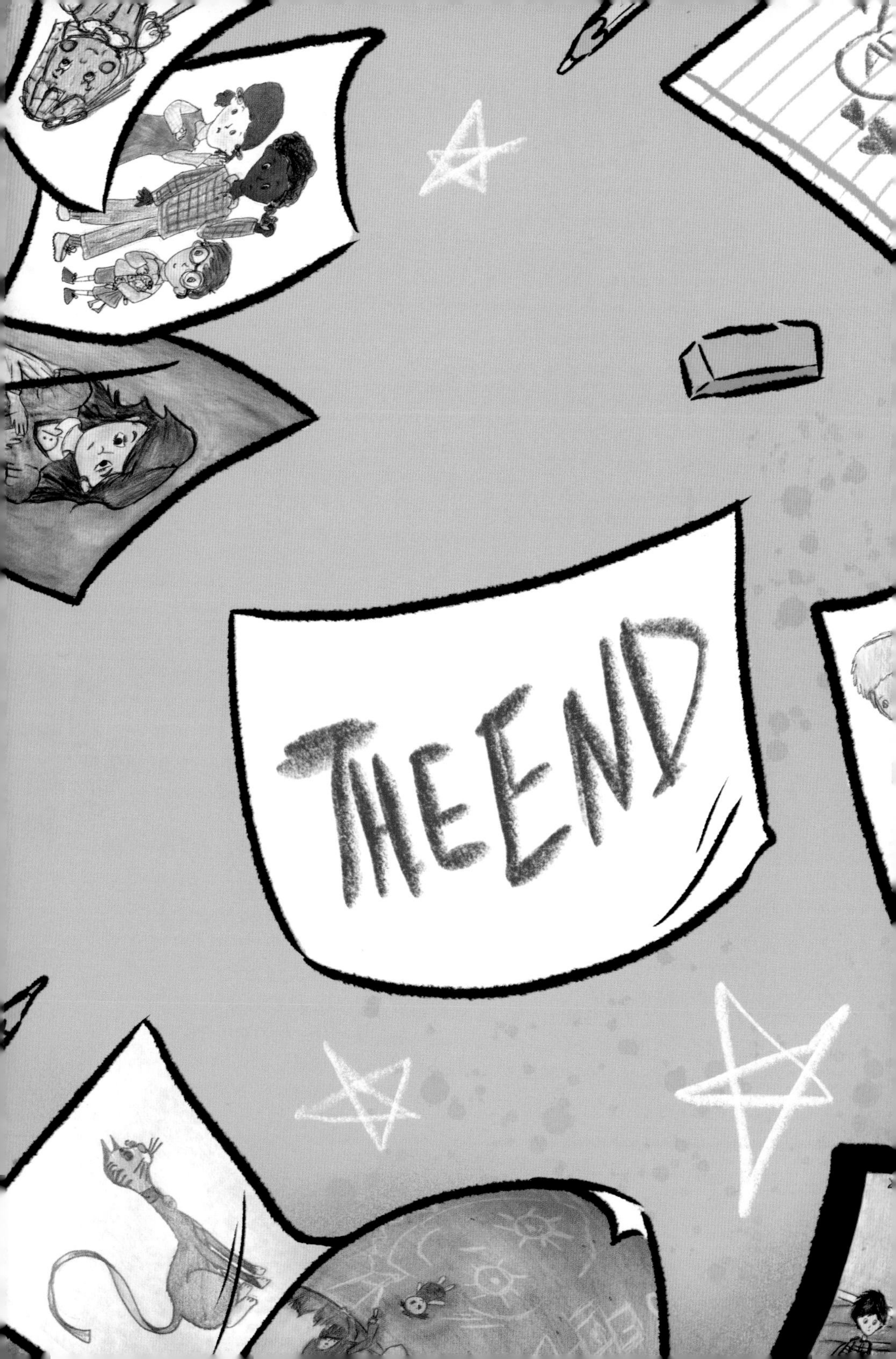
THE END

AUTHOR'S NOTE

I'd never planned on writing a memoir, because it's not the most enjoyable thing to write about a difficult time in your own life. How do you know where to start and where to end?

A person isn't just one story. We're hundreds of them all tied together. Months of boring days pass by, and then suddenly a week or even a single afternoon might stand out. Maybe it was incredibly romantic, or felt like the greatest adventure...or maybe something really awful happened. Those moments stick out like pages in a pop-up book, while the long, boring stretches in between fade into the background.

When we turn our lives into stories, some parts have to be skimmed over while we hyper-focus on the things we remember most. Kind of like how a bully might forget they said something cruel to you within an hour, yet you might hang onto it for a decade. While my story is true, it's hard to squish this period of my life into a contained narrative. Some things may have been rearranged for clarity or to make the story move faster, and some names have been changed to protect the privacy of those involved. The bullying I faced in sixth grade was significantly worse than it appears here, but if I focused on it too much, it could have been a whole story on its own. (The kids in middle school also used much harsher language than I've presented.)

In real life, my brother was alongside me more often than he appears in this book. As kids, the two of us were always referred to as "the boys" by our family, rather than by our individual names, and, as the youngest, I always felt second to him. For this story, though, I wanted to focus on my own perspective.

The style of this book was inspired by the colorful cartoons I watched growing up, which brought me comfort during days that were hard to get through. Crayon drawings, flashy toy commercials, funky arcade carpets, and orange VHS tapes decorated the little world I created around myself. That's what my childhood looked like, even when things were tough.

Talking about tragedy can be difficult, because the people you tell tend to focus only on the trauma. As a child, I desperately missed and wanted my mother, but also found it frustrating at times that I had been reduced to "the dead-mom kid." I felt perceived as the remnants of a tragedy, rather than as a person. Telling this story was difficult because I wanted to present the many issues I faced growing up, not just one defining tragedy. It's hard to cleanly balance a bunch of real-life issues when trying to build a single narrative. It would have been easier to make it just about my mother, or coming out, or bullying. But my life was all of those things, and if I told you every last thing that happened, it could have filled a thousand pages.

Eventually, I did speak and make friends, but it wasn't until I was well into high school. I learned later that I had C-PTSD, or complex post-traumatic stress disorder, not only because of the death of my mother, but because of the homophobic bullying I faced growing up. Many LGBTQ+ people I've befriended have found in their adulthood that they have, or had, a form of PTSD because they were bullied and internalized the hatred around them.

One night when I was a baby, my mother was murdered by my "father" while I slept in the room next door. I say "father" in quotation marks because real fathers should be loving and kind, and he was neither. My mother had experienced years of domestic abuse, and, one morning, it ended with my older sister finding her body. Our mother had been stabbed in the chest twenty-seven times. Writing it still sends a chill up my spine, and it's difficult for me to even fathom it happening, or imagine what my sister must have felt seeing our mother like that. I often think about how scared my mother must have felt. I was afraid to tell this story because it felt like I was reducing her to "the dead mom" when she was a real, complex person, just like any one of us, with her own hopes and dreams — things I would have liked her to tell me all about.

Instead, I learned about her from the stories my grandmother and aunt told me. I pieced together someone who acted a bit like Peppermint Patty. Someone who had learned to hide her insecurities. Someone who had nightmares. Someone who was filled with love and too forgiving. I may have never gotten to know her, but these stories assured me that she was a great mom.

RESOURCES

If you or someone you know needs help, please reach out to these resources. For domestic violence—related issues: TheHotline.org For LGBTQ-related issues: TheTrevorProject.org

Acknowledgments

Robyn Chapman, for all of your guidance and wisdom, along with the entire wonderful team at First Second.

Elizabeth Bennett, for seeing the potential in the project when it was still only doodles.

Everyone during my time at Simmons College, especially Megan Dowd Lambert, for pushing me in the right direction. Elaine, Caleb, Paige, SG, Shanna, Liv, Liz, Charlie, Flannery, and everyone else for being such a supportive and inspiring writing group. I loved being a part of it.

Kevin Savoie, for always cheering me on, and for putting up with all the toys and trinkets I added to his bookshelves.

My grandma, for her kindness, strength, and unconditional love.

My brother, my family, and friends.